ABORIGINAL PEOPLE

AND THEIR PLANTS

Wik woman gathering edible water lily flower stems and bulbs. The hollow stems could be used as straws to suck the cool water from the bottom of lagoons. *(Ursula H. McConnel, Archer River, northwestern Cape York Peninsula, northern Queensland, 1930s. South Australian Museum Archives.)*

ABORIGINAL PEOPLE

AND THEIR PLANTS

Philip A. Clarke

ROSENBERG

In memory of Allan, who loved plants

Acknowledgments

The following people provided helpful comments on various drafts of this book: Kim Akerman, Judith Clarke, Paul Monaghan, Daphne Nash, Peter Sutton and David Symon. Lynn Strefford provided research assistance, Ray Marchant produced the map, Lea Gardam assisted with sourcing archival material, and John Dallwitz and Ushma Scales of the Ara Irititja Project helped gain community approval for images. Many Aboriginal people have enthusiastically and openly discussed their use of plants with me. The South Australian Museum has provided many exciting opportunities to explore Aboriginal culture during over two decades of employment.

(*Front jacket:* Pitjantjatjara children, Andy Brown (left) and Tjunpatja Brown (right), collecting desert raisins (*kampurarpa*). These plants depend on frequent burning of the land and grow in sandy country. *(Norman B. Tindale, Musgrave Ranges, Central Australia, 1966. South Australian Museum Archives.)*

First published in Australia in 2007
by Rosenberg Publishing Pty Ltd
PO Box 6125, Dural Delivery Centre NSW 2158
Phone: 61 2 9654 1502 Fax: 61 2 9654 1338
Email: rosenbergpub@smartchat.net.au
Web: www.rosenbergpub.com.au

© Copyright Philip A. Clarke 2007

The National Library of Australia Cataloguing-in-Publication data

Clarke, Philip A.
Aboriginal people and their plants.

1st ed.
Bibliography.
Includes index.
ISBN 9781877058516.

1. Human-plant relationships - Australia. 2. Aboriginal Australians - Ethnobotany. 3. Aboriginal Australians - Medicine. 4. Aboriginal Australians - Food. 5. Aboriginal Australians - Social life and customs. I. Title.

333.9530899915

Printed in China by Everbest Printing Co Limited

Contents

Preface

Each human culture develops a set of relationships with the land it occupies. We can discover much about a people by looking closely at their association with plants, which are fundamental parts of the landscape that cultures occupy and transform. In Aboriginal Australia, the flora physically provides people with the means for making food, medicine, narcotics, stimulants, adornment, ceremonial objects, clothing, shelter and tools, and for creating artwork. Symbolically, plants feature heavily in Aboriginal myths and religious beliefs. In the early days of Western European expansion across the globe, the indigenous peoples the explorers encountered were defined according to their economic relationships with the environment. Cultural distinctions were made between those 'primitives' who derived all of their food from hunting and gathering wild sources, against those more 'civilised' groups who primarily relied upon nomadic pastoralism or horticulture.

Europeans have often in the past seen Australian hunter-gatherers as passively reacting to changes in their environment, rather than being able to initiate any of them actively.[1] Because of their apparent reliance upon 'stone age' technology, Aboriginal people were not credited with having had a major impact upon the development of the landscape.[2] Rather, they were seen as entirely opportunistic foragers. In 1879, James D. Woods, the editor of a book on Aboriginal people, summed them up as 'wandering savages, seldom staying long at one place, and dependent almost entirely upon the spoils of the chase or upon their success in fishing for subsistence'.[3] The Aboriginal use of a diverse flora was rarely considered.

Past scholars have attempted to rationalise the existence of hunter-gatherers on the basis of limits imposed by the environment they occupied. Commenting upon early European perceptions of 'Aboriginal man', scholars Colonel Harold F. White and Sir Cedric Stanton Hicks remarked in 1953 that, 'We could not see that he could never have established a culture because he could not have established an agriculture. There was no animal suitable for husbandry. He was doomed by natural events to be a hunting pedestrian nomad.'[4] In 1959, medical doctor and naturalist John B. Cleland stated that the 'environment kept the aboriginal inhabitant a nomad, seeking his food from God, like the ravens'.[5] Leading anthropologist Adolphus P. Elkin remarked in 1964 that the Australian 'food-gathering life is parasitical; the Aborigines are absolutely dependent on what nature produces without any practical assistance on their part'.[6] Such evaluations of food sources are highly subjective and unlikely to lead to in-depth investigations of Aboriginal plant uses.

From the late twentieth century, scholars have begun to question whether the activities of the world's hunter-gatherers really had only a minimal impact upon the environment.[7] In Australia, it was already known that Aboriginal people everywhere fired the landscape for short-term benefits. Scientists now considered the unintended long-term effects upon the environment of these practices over thousands of years. This shift in thinking came about through studies that provided deeper understanding of the interactions between hunter-gatherers and their environment. It became apparent globally that cultures of hunter-gatherers possessed complex relationships with the flora and fauna.

Since their ancestors came to Australia some 50,000 years ago, Aboriginal people have developed many unique ways of life and formed deep spiritual attachments to their country.[8] Although Europeans have often harshly judged Aboriginal cultures as 'primitive' because of the apparent simplicity of their hunting and gathering artefacts, a detailed examination of their socio-religious traditions and environmental knowledge provides compelling evidence against this. Today, it is recognised that there is great depth in the Aboriginal understanding of ecosystems in which they lived.

This book explores the links between Australian Aboriginal cultures and the flora. European readers will find extraordinary many of the Aboriginal uses of plants that are documented here. It is an ethnobotanical study, meaning that it is an investigation of specific groups of humans and their relationships with the plant world. As such, it draws heavily on the disciplines of social anthropology, botany, history, linguistics, cultural geography and ecology. The available sources of information on the Aboriginal uses of Australian plants are diverse, including European settlers, explorers, biologists, pharmacologists, nutritionists, herbalists, anthropologists, medical specialists, ethnologists, social historians, linguists, geographers and archaeologists, and Aboriginal people themselves. Ethnobotanists employ a large variety of techniques. Although united through the study of indigenous plant use, the peculiar interests of each category of recorder has led to specific strengths and weaknesses in the compilation of data. Many references to plant use are gleaned from brief sentences in otherwise unrelated texts.

The European documentation of the Australian flora begins with the expansion of world exploration in the seventeenth century, which intensified during the eighteenth and nineteenth centuries.[9] The early interest in plants was not just academic, but also driven by a desire to discover 'new' species that would have economic benefits to developing colonies. Plant hunters European botanists sent to the outer reaches of the empire worked closely with explorers and indigenous peoples. In Australia, their observations of Aboriginal hunting and gathering practices provided them with clues as they sought species that they thought might come to rival, in terms of their agricultural importance, maize, cultivated potato and commercial tobacco gained from colonies in the Americas.

In the twentieth century, interest in Aboriginal ethnobotany diversified.[10] Researchers who took a cultural approach investigated such topics as indigenous classification systems, the role of plants in economic life, and the symbolism of plants in religious beliefs and totemic systems. Amateur collectors of indigenous words and professional linguists found within Aboriginal languages a multitude of terms and concepts associated with the flora. Anthropologists began to focus upon cultures in their own right, with the ethnobotanists among them studying the complex ways, both physically and symbolically, in which people related to plants.

Medical researchers and scientists have had more practical concerns with ethnobotany. Scholars, such as health practitioners, pharmacologists and nutritionists, have studied Aboriginal plant use in their search for new medicines and foods for the wider community. Even when the plants concerned had limited potential for commercial development, knowledge of them has informed those trying to improve contemporary Aboriginal health conditions. Biologists have also taken ecological approaches when investigating the interactions between hunter-gatherers and the environment. The results of their researches are beginning to have greater impact within a wider domain. A deeper understanding of the Australian landscape, with its flora and fauna, developed as twentieth-

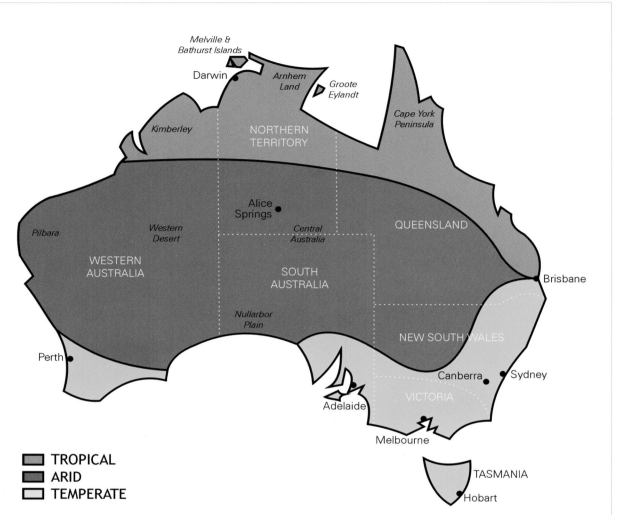

Australia today is geographically diverse, with three main climate regions. (*Map drawn from climate data obtained from the Bureau of Meteorology, Australian Government, 2005.*)

century scholars considered the Aboriginal role of vegetation burning in maintaining biodiversity.

To academic geographers, the cultural landscape is the product of a human culture modifying the land it occupies.[11] The landscape can be read as a type of 'text' that identifies its links to people, in the past and as it is today. As relationships between culture and environment are not always visually evident, cultural geographers search for the hidden 'authors' who may have helped to shape the land. Apart from its physical aspects, the cultural landscape is also an expression of how people engage with their world and it involves the ways people view their concepts and experiences of their surroundings.[12]

Cultural landscapes are not only the outcome of human activities, but are also the product of the perceptions of the people who live in them. Each human culture possesses its own set of relationships with the land and with the life forms that live upon it. As colonists, people take it upon themselves to forge new connections with the features of the land according to their own traditions: to give the land their own meanings and develop its physical form into something based in part upon models derived from previous homelands. Plants are a key part of the association between each culture and the space it occupies.

In Aboriginal Australia, the prospects for ethnobotanical research are vast. The Australian flora contains more than 20,000 terrestrial plant species,[13] many of which have been, and in some cases still are, economically and culturally significant to Aboriginal people. The Australian continent contains many different environments, which exist within climate regions ranging from the temperate south to desert interiors and to the tropical north. While the origins of ethnobotanical study are found within the European colonial past, its future in Australia lies in helping to gain deeper knowledge of Aboriginal relationships with the landscape.

My interest in Aboriginal ethnobotany began from an ecological perspective. In 1982, I arrived at the South Australian Museum as a recent biological science graduate and began working in the Aboriginal ethnographic collections. In my first task — sorting Aboriginal weapons in the basement — by chance I found there a large number of botanical specimens, samples of plants of economic importance to Aboriginal people. The collection included plants obtained by nineteenth-century missionaries in remote parts of Australia, some collected by museum researchers as scientific specimens, and others prepared as former gallery exhibits. These largely unsorted collections caught my attention and led to me conducting ethnobotanic research, aimed at creating regional lists of plant species that Aboriginal people utilised as foods and medicines, and as raw materials used in maintaining a hunter-gatherer lifestyle.

It soon became apparent from my reading of the available literature that plants, quite apart from their economic significance to the Aboriginal hunters and gatherers, had significant cultural roles. My studies evolved into a more detailed investigation of the broader set of relationships between people and environment. Working within the disciplines of social anthropology and cultural geography, I selected the cultures and landscape of southern South Australia for in-depth fieldwork.[14] Although initially examining plant use in the temperate areas of Australia, I have been able, during two decades of fieldwork with the Museum, to investigate also the ethnobotany of the arid and tropical regions of Australia. This experience provided insights into this fascinating topic from a number of perspectives.

This book begins by considering the role of plants within the Aboriginal cultural landscape. Part One commences with an investigation of indigenous cultural perspective on the flora, using scholarly tools chiefly derived from anthropology and linguistics. In Part Two I then discuss how traditional Aboriginal economies have impacted upon the Australian environment. With a joint cultural geographical and ecological focus, and by drawing heavily upon historical records, a model of pre-European Aboriginal interaction with the environment is constructed. I present an argument against the earlier model of Aboriginal foragers being passive managers of their resources and recognise that they actively manipulated their environment for particular intended outcomes.

Part Three delivers an overview of the technologies directly employed in Aboriginal plant use. Descriptions are given of how plants are involved in Aboriginal food and water procurement, artefact manufacture and the preparation of poisons, medicines, narcotics and stimulants. Although primarily focusing on physical characteristics, attention is also given to the cultural perceptions of plant properties. In demonstrating the wide range of Aboriginal uses of plants, this part chiefly draws upon material cultural studies, archaeology and pharmacology.

Part Four, the conclusion, brings together the preceding sections. A focus is upon the changing Aboriginal cultural landscape, in relation to the physical environment and to the many cultures within Aboriginal Australia. It is not possible to predict future trends in the study of Australian ethnobotany without considering the impact of change. This section also considers the possible application of Aboriginal botanical knowledge in a wider contemporary perspective.

References to 'European' explorers, colonists and settlers from the seventeenth to the nineteenth centuries concern people who would, in their own times, have considered themselves to be from smaller cultural groups based in the Northern Hemisphere, such as the Dutch, English, Irish, Welsh, Cornish, Scottish, Americans, Prussians and French. In the twentieth and twenty-first centuries, this term chiefly refers to 'White Australians', or in other words people of predominantly European extraction living in Australia who do not derive their identity from either indigenous or Asian Australians.

The historical sources quoted in this volume include phrases and descriptions of indigenous people that can cause offence if used without qualification in a contemporary context. Where possible, Aboriginal sources of the ethnobotanic data are acknowledged and standard word spellings employed when they occur. I use the term 'plants' for terrestrial species as well as seaweeds. Fungi are also included in this publication, although biologically speaking these organisms are not part of the plant kingdom. In the case of plant names, the main common forms, which often vary from state to state, are given. The names used by botanical specialists to identify specific species are listed in the technical names index. These scientific names are those recognised by the Australian National Herbarium when the book was written.[15] Over time, other names will undoubtedly supersede some of these, as botanists refine their notions of links between plant species — particularly with the accelerating use of DNA research.

In this book, 'wild plants' are defined as those that have not been deliberately grown by horticulturalists. This includes not only indigenous plants in the Australian flora, but also feral species introduced since European settlement began. The ethnobotany of the Torres Strait Islanders, who to varying degrees combine hunter-gatherer and horticulturalist lifestyles, are outside the scope of this book.[16] Many of the descriptions of Aboriginal plant uses in this volume will be brief, either because of the manner in which they were originally reported, or for the sake of brevity.

It is strongly recommended that untrained people do not experiment with any of the foods, medicines, poisons or narcotics discussed here. It is stressed that this publication is not intended for use as a survival guide. Notwithstanding, this book does indicate some developing areas worthy of future research and awaiting the application of ethnobotanical knowledge.

PART ONE
PLANTS AND THE CULTURAL LANDSCAPE

Chapter 1

Socialising Plants

In the pre-European period, Australian Aboriginal people did not see their land as a wilderness. They believed that their spiritual Ancestors had shaped the land during the Creation, while they established the sacred Law governing the manner in which people lived. In Aboriginal tradition, the people, animals and plants had a common origin. By honouring the deeds of their Ancestors, Aboriginal people maintained the order of the cosmos. In Aboriginal thought there could be no true distinction between culture and landscape. The British colonists who arrived in 1788 to settle permanently in New South Wales saw the land in vastly different ways. To them the Australian environment was wild and unkempt. They considered it something to conqueror and transform in the process of subordinating it to their purpose.[1] We will now explore the role of plants in the worldview of Australian Aboriginal cultures.

Dividing the World

All languages contain encoded information about how their speakers interact with their environment. While European scholars of the colonial period largely ignored the existence of complex class-ification systems in the cultures of hunters and gatherers they encountered, the modern field of anthropological linguistics uses the study of language as a tool for investigating how specific cultures order the universe.[2] In Australia, the study

of plant and animal classifications provides deep insights into Aboriginal views of their world.[3] At the time of first European settlement there were at least 200 distinct languages in Aboriginal Australia, and within them numerous speech varieties or dialects.[4] The ways in which languages reflect how people see their environment are far too diverse to receive full treatment here, although examples of language terms are given to show that there are many different ways of classifying the flora.

When I have made ethnobotanical inquiries about local plants, Aboriginal people have generally responded by talking about their uses, seasonal changes, physical appearances, and where in the landscape they are to be found. Australian hunter-gatherers possessed excellent powers of observation, as is shown by their historical involvement with explorers and police authorities as guides and 'trackers'.[5] This is reflected in their ability to notice detail. South Australian Museum director Edward C. Stirling remarked that when he was on the Horn Expedition to Central Australia in 1894, Aboriginal people at Finke River demonstrated their 'acuteness of observation which at once enabled them to distinguish animals or plants which very closely resembled one another. As Mr Schulze [a missionary] informs us they have separate names for twenty-two kinds of snakes, the distinction between some of which is a matter of difficulty even for a trained zoologist.'[6]

What people observe in the environment is as

much a product of the importance their culture places upon each type of object as it is an indication of the acuity of their vision. The importance of reading the country may lead to a proliferation of words in categories that are particularly important to the speakers. The vocabulary of the Inuit people from the Arctic Circle reflects a much greater interest in different types of snow than is the case in most Western European languages.[7] In a land dominated by snow, it is essential for the Inuit to have the means to communicate its physical properties and variations. In the case of Australian Aboriginal food, Protector of Aborigines George Augustus Robinson claimed in Tasmania that, 'Various are the fungus which the natives eat, and all are known to them by the different qualities which they possess, and all are known by different names.'[8] Many indigenous people know and use considerably more plant names than Europeans presently do in Australia. The number of terms that relate to the flora in each Aboriginal language is enormous.

Linguist David McKnight studied the systems of plant and animal classifications used by the Lardil of Mornington Island in the Gulf of Carpentaria. He remarked that, 'They often comment on the relationship between different species of plants … the Lardil single out the sort of characteristics (e.g., formation of bark, leaves, flowers, fruit, and habitat) that a botanist does. Hence, their botanical taxonomy is of the same intellectual order as our botanical scientific taxonomy.'[9] McKnight rightly recognised the great depth of biological-type knowledge held by Lardil people, but it does not follow that there exists a close match between indigenous and European classification systems, there or elsewhere. Ecologist Peter Latz warned that, 'Aboriginal taxonomy is not based on scientific floral characteristics, but is primarily concerned with the plant's useful features.'[10] Therefore, when studying indigenous classification of plants and animals it is necessary to consider how people interact with their environment.[11]

Aboriginal hunters and gatherers generally recognised two main classes of food: animal and vegetable. According to Gugadja man Wiminydji and Father Tony Peile, desert dwellers living

Woman and male child at a campfire. During the day, women and children generally gathered vegetable food and burrowing animals, while men hunted large game. *(George French Angas, watercolour, south of Lake Hawdon, southeastern South Australia, 1844. South Australian Museum Archives.)*

immediately south of the Kimberley in Western Australia define their 'bushtucker' as:

> *mangari, mayi* or *mirga* — these words refer to vegetable food, be it fruit, seeds, tubers or leaves of a shrub or tree. Even mushrooms and other edible Fungi are referred to as *mangari* (this is the more correct Gugadja word). Opposite to this word is *guga*, which refers, not only to meat, but also to any animal that may be killed for meat.[12]

Similarly, in other Western Desert languages spoken further south around the edge of the Great Victoria Desert, where I have done fieldwork, the plant and animal foods are categorised as *mai* and *kuka* respectively.[13] The Arrernte-speaking people of Central Australia divide their food a bit further at the primary level, having four main classes: *merne* is from plants and trees, *kere* is vertebrate meat, *tyape* invertebrate meat, and *ngkwarle* sweet food, such as honey and nectar.[14] There are related divisions in many other Aboriginal languages.[15]

Within Aboriginal Australia, the physical form of plants and their human uses are strong influences when classifying them. In the case of the Lardil, the major categories for plants are based on structural form — trees (*thungal*), bush (*wambal*), vine/creeper (*wurduwur*) and grass (*karnda*).[16] In the case of trees, these are further divided into fruit-bearing species (*diwal*) and mangroves (*murnda*). The Lardil people divide their whole territory into 'inside country' and 'outside country'.[17] The 'inside country' is comprised of grasslands, woodlands and scrublands, while the 'outside country' contains tidal flats, beaches and offshore reefs. Similarly, in their classification system the Lardil make a major distinction between sea and land-based organisms.[18] The basis for all these categories reflects their hunter-gatherer lifestyle.

In northeast Arnhem Land, the Yolngu people group plants into those with stems (*dharpa*) and those without (*mulmu*).[19] There are also other ways that the same people can classify plants, with the one chosen depending on the situation. The Yolngu people class themselves and most natural phenomena, such as plants and animals, into one of two categories, Dhuwa or Yirritja.[20] Known to anthropologists as moieties (= halves), these groupings are particularly relevant when organising marriages and ceremonies. The Yolngu use of such a system embraces the entire view of their universe.

In Aboriginal languages, as with English nomenclature, the different parts of useful plants often have separate names. Therefore, an ethnobotanist interested in a plant species may have to record a string of indigenous terms. In the Ngarinman language of the Victoria River area of the Northern Territory, the inland bloodwood tree is referred to as *narrka*, while its gummy kino that is used for antiseptic washes is *manyuwan*, and the tree's winged seeds that children use as 'helicopter' toys are *jirtpirtpi*.[21] Similarly, in the Pitjantjatjara

Black cypress pine is a source of wood for making spear shafts, and resin for adhesive and teething sticks. It is a fire sensitive plant that needs firebreak protection. (*Philip A. Clarke, Lower Murray, South Australia, 1988.*)

language of the Musgrave Ranges in Central Australia, the inland pigweed is known as *wakati*, the small capsule pods are called *ipi*, which also means 'breasts', and the cakes cooked from its seed in the hot sand are referred to as *nyuma*.[22] An example from the Nunggubuyu language of eastern Arnhem Land is the water lily, which bears many edible parts.[23] This plant has over a dozen terms associated with various plant structures and different growth stages. In some Aboriginal languages, plants have both secular and sacred names.[24] The vocabularies of Aboriginal languages are crucial repositories of ethnobotanical information. The loss of any language has serious implications for the continuity of knowledge about the cultural landscape.[25]

A family group, with adults wearing paperbark aprons. Aboriginal men would never leave their camp without weapons to protect themselves or to kill game opportunistically. *(A. Svenson, Adelaide River, northeast of Darwin in the Northern Territory, probably 1890s. South Australian Museum Archives.)*

While there are often specific Aboriginal language terms applied to categories of plants and animals that are equivalent to those biologists recognise as distinct species, there are other organisms of little or no direct interest to them that are referred to in broad terms. In the Nunggubuyu language of eastern Arnhem Land, linguist Jeffrey Heath recorded the term *madinjar*:

> which applies to a number of shrubs about one or two metres high, without economic value, with tiny or needle-like leaves, having sharp twigs capable of causing scratches or cuts, and having brightly coloured but small flowers (white, red, yellow, orange) in the dry season. This constellation of shared characteristics applies to three common species (*Acacia sublanata*, *Grevillea pungens*, and *Calytrix exstipulata* [turkey-bush]), and to a number of others (*Verticordia cunninghamii* [feather-plant], *Hibbertia lepidota*, *Dillenia* species, *Jacksonia thesioides* [jacksonia broombush], etc.). This term *madinjar* is thus easily extendable as a term for the scrubland which

Wik women gathering shore club rush corms from a swamp. Children were generally taken out with the women during the day. *(Ursula H. McConnel, northwestern Cape York Peninsula, northern Queensland, 1930s. South Australian Museum Archives.)*

includes most of these species.[26]

Even when a specific name exists, a plant may still be referred to as part of a group of 'rubbish' species. At Balgo in Western Australia, Peile remarked 'In my first botanical field-notes I have written *pukarra* as the term for *Calytrix microphylla* [turkey-bush, *Calytrix exstipulata*] … This term refers to a plant which is not used for anything or to a "bad" tree, as the Gugadja say in English. The correct term for this woody plant is *kuntilikuntila*.'[27]

In some Western Desert languages the word, *puta-puta*, is used like 'weed' in English — referring to a variety of plants not otherwise given a specific name, particularly tussocky sedges and grass.[28] In the Ramindjeri language of Encounter Bay in South Australia, the term *karte* was recorded to mean 'low thick scrub; everything useless'.[29] From my experience it is still a contemporary Aboriginal English term in the region that means 'rubbish'. In the perspective of local hunter-gatherers, some types of vegetation offered them very little in terms of food or medicine. When able to, Aboriginal hunter-gatherers would probably have actively modified dense stands of scrub dominated by 'useless' or 'rubbish' species by deliberately burning them.

In a few instances, Aboriginal classification of plants into types goes beyond the level of species recognised by botanists. In northeast Arnhem Land the members of the Rirratjingu clan of the Yolngu people recognise three distinct named forms within the one species of bush potato.[30] One has long thin tubers and is generally not disturbed, as it is found near a sacred site. The second is round, only found on a certain island and must be cooked before being eaten. The third is round and long, found on the mainland, and eaten either raw or cooked. Similarly, the Warnindilyakwa people on Groote Eylandt recognise two named forms of water-ribbon, one of which grows in swamps and billabongs and another that is found in creeks.[31] The Warlpiri people of the Tanami Desert have individual names for two different forms of the pencil yam (small yam).[32] It is a creeper that dies off a few months after rains, although the roots are available for eating most of the year, if one can find where it grows. One form of the yam has

narrower leaves than the other. To biologists, these observable variations would be seen as possibly due to specific responses to different physical environments, or being from genetically different populations, or maybe a mixture of both.

By looking at the use of some plant names we can gain an insight into Aboriginal understanding of their environment. In the Kilcoy district, northwest of Brisbane, Aboriginal people referred to the silky-oak tree as *duradi*, which is also the word used for eels.[33] According to local Aboriginal person Willie MacKenzie, this was because the fibre pattern of silky-oak wood with the bark removed looks like the flesh of an eel with its skin pulled off. The association between tree and fish went further as, when the silky-oak was flowering, the eels were at their fattest and considered best for eating.

Aboriginal people refer to their traditions of the Creation or 'Dreaming' period to explain close ecological alliances between particular plants and animals. Ngarrindjeri people from the Lower Murray of South Australia believe that lignum bushes and superb blue wrens have a special association, which is reflected in their shared name, *waatji*, which refers to 'whispering'.[34] In their Dreaming, the Wren Ancestor was found cheating during a flying competition and punished by never again being allowed to fly higher than the lignums, which are tangled bushes growing around swamp edges. From then on, wrens have lived among the 'whispering bushes', in constant fear of being caught by the descendants of other Ancestors, particularly eagles, hawks and owls.

A few plant names are based on their resemblance to other things. At Ooldea in western South Australia, the Aboriginal description for camel poison bush (or sandhill corkbark) was recorded as *guru mani*.[35] Western Desert people say that this means 'black eyes' and refers to small black knots which, exposed on the trunk when the branches drop off, look like eyes. Similarly, in the Western Desert languages, the Sturt desert pea is called *malukuru*, literally meaning 'kangaroo-eye' and a reference to black centres of the red flowers.[36] In my opinion, this plant is much better served by its indigenous name than by a relatively recent one that makes a superficial comparison to a European plant, while honouring the nineteenth-century British explorer, Captain Charles Sturt.[37]

Botanist/plant nurseryman Daniel Bunce provided another example of word association from the Gippsland area of Victoria. While travelling with local Aboriginal people in 1839, his guides gathered for him 'Some long tuberous roots, of a composite plant [yam-daisy], ... of which we partook. These plants produced a bunch of tubers like the fingers on the hand, from whence they were called *myrnong-myrnongatha*, being the native word for "hand".[38] The yam-daisy is a likely candidate for the many plants in the temperate zone that historical sources often recorded simply as 'edible root'. The tuber is recognised as one of the major food sources for Victorian Aboriginal people, who generally called it *myrnong* or by a variation of this word.[39]

Other phenomena were given names based upon their similarity to plants. In colonist James Dawson's dictionary of southwestern Victorian Aboriginal languages he records that speakers of

In Western Desert Aboriginal languages, the Sturt desert pea is known as 'kangaroo eyes' (*malukuru*), in reference to black patches in the centre of red flowers. *(Philip A. Clarke, Great Victoria Desert, Western Australia, 2006.)*

the Peek Whuurong ('kelp lip') dialect referred to the rays of light immediately after the sun has set as 'puungortuung munnanatt', meaning the 'rushes of the sun'.[40]

Botanical Placenames

Plant terminology is reflected in landscape iconography. In the 1980s when linguist Dorothy Tunbridge was surveying Aboriginal placenames in the Gammon Ranges National Park of the northern Flinders Ranges, she found that about 20% of the 200 recorded names referred to a plant term or a plant product.[41] Here, the majority of the species being referred to once had significance to the diet of the local Adnyamathanha people. Similarly, in a land claim by the Warumungu in the Northern Territory, 80 of the 680 placenames mentioned related to the vegetation.[42] Colonist James Dawson recorded indigenous placenames for western Victoria. Examples with a botanical reference are Buunong — 'ti-tree', the 'locality of Koort-koort-nong House'[43]; Kuutoit kill — 'wild parsley', 'Koroit township'[44]; Puuyuupkil — 'pig's face', 'Land at Port Fairy, celebrated for 'pig's face'[45]; and Paarang kuutcha — 'Name of an edible root found there', 'Tower Hill Island'.[46] There are many other examples recorded from southeastern Australia.[47]

The use of plant words in placenames does not appear to result from a random selection process. Tunbridge suggested that placenames encode

Wren in lignum. Some plants and animals have close mythological relationships. In Ngarrindjeri language of the Lower Murray, the wren and the lignum bush have the same name, *waatji*. The events of the Dreaming meant that wrens could never fly higher than the lignum. *(Philip A. Clarke, Narrung Peninsula, South Australia, 1990.)*

ecological history.[48] There is ethnographic and linguistic data to support this. In 1919, botanist John M. Black recorded a small vocabulary of Narangga words from Sarah Newchurch and Harry Richards at Yorke Peninsula in South Australia. This included the name for the country around the Point Pearce Mission Station, Burkiana, apparently so named from the high density of *burko* (oil-bush) that grew there.[49] The Western Australian Goldfields town, Kalgoorlie, possibly derives its name from *kalgula* (desert pear or desert banana).[50] Plant terms are also apparent in the placenames used by Iwaidja speakers in the area around Port Essington, north of Darwin.[51] There are instances when indigenous people use English placenames that owe their existence to hunter-gatherer land use patterns. On Cape Barren Island in Tasmania, Apple Orchard Point owes its name, not to European apples, but to kangaroo apples that the islanders gather there.[52] The use of plant-based names makes sense of the cultural landscape. Culture influences the things people see and recognise in the environment.

Plants as Personal Names

Aboriginal personal naming practices often seem complex to Europeans, with individuals usually having several names or titles, used in differing contexts throughout their life.[53] Colonist William Stanbridge claimed that central Victorian Aboriginal people generally had two personal names:

> one derived from birthplace, the other from some characteristic in later life; for example, a boy was born under a woorack (Banksia), he was therefore, named Yab-woorack, or leaf of the woorack; in after life, from the length of his legs, he was called Dittenaranarry.[54]

Among the Warlpiri people of the Tanami Desert in the Northern Territory, anthropologist Mervyn J. Meggitt claimed that, 'There are several terms of address that might be applied to a person in ritual and secular situations. They are in approximate order of frequency of usage: subsection terms, kinship terms, European names and Walbiri [Warlpiri] nicknames, matrimoiety and age-grade terms for men, and direction terms (north, south etc.) for men in small groups.'[55] Here, personal names reflect the various roles that Aboriginal people have in their society.

Aboriginal people were often given plant terms as personal names. In Tasmania, Bunce recorded the use of indigenous words for *Boronia*, 'a small heath-like plant, covered with pink, and sometimes faint-white blossoms during a greater part of the year. The aborigines ... were in the habit of naming their wives and daughters after it, from its rare beauty; in the same manner as we, their more cultivated brethren, have done with the rose and other favourite plants.'[56] Bunce did not give any actual names, although for the Tasmanians Robinson listed another plant-related personal name, Lone.ne.yac, for a man from the western coast that translated as 'a species of fern tree'.[57] In some Aboriginal cultures, people will take on the name of the plants or animals that are their totem.[58] Personal names could also be derived from dominant types of vegetation in the owner's clan land. In the Adelaide district of South Australia during the 1830s lived a Kaurna man known by Europeans as 'King John'. His Aboriginal name was Mullawirraburka, which was recorded to translate literally as 'dry-forest-old man'.[59] This name referred to an area of mallee vegetation typically found in his country, which is inland from Aldinga and south of the City of Adelaide.

The environment provided a means for defining groups of people, with Aboriginal clans and bands sometimes deriving their names from dominant plants growing in their country. For example, the name of an Eora clan along the south side of Sydney Harbour in New South Wales was Cadigal, which reportedly referred to the grasstree, *cadi* (or *gadi*).[60] For Aboriginal people living around Sydney this plant was a source of dry flower stems for making spear shafts, while the resin was used as artefact cement. Aboriginal naming systems were also flexible. For instance, South Australian missionary Samuel Klose claimed in the 1840s that, 'our Adelaide natives are called *Taralye Meyunna* by the other tribes. *Taralye* is any kind of split wood — as the Location [mission site] is now fenced in with wooden stakes — and when they are here in the city they camp there and so are called the stake-men. Formerly they were called *Wito Meyunna* = reed men.'[61] The Kaurna referred to the people living in the mountain ranges immediately north of Adelaide as the Wirameyu or 'peppermint box forest men'.[62]

People drew aspects of their own identity, and that of others, from the food they ate. In the southwest of Western Australia, the Nyungar people living along the coast at Albany were known as Mierngaanquaar, meaning 'pigface eaters'.[63] During his trip through southern South Australia in 1844, colonial artist George French Angas recorded the name of a Lower Murray Aboriginal person 'Chembillin', which was reputed to mean 'chewing the bulrush root', reference to a major food source in the region.[64] The distinctiveness of the food that Aboriginal foragers relied upon is reflected in some group names. The grass seed gathering people of the Western Desert were called Panara by their neighbours, based on the term *pana*, which is the oval wooden dish used in winnowing.[65]

In Aboriginal Australia, terms for plants, animals and other objects are often deliberately changed due to mourning practices.[66] It is widely believed that the mention of a recently deceased person's name would cause their spirit to appear and thereby cause havoc. This is demonstrated in an account by overlander James C. Hawker at Yodko (near Moorundie) on the Murray River in South Australia.[67] In his journal he recorded a conversation he had on the night on the 11 May 1844 with an Aboriginal man known as King Tenberry. When Hawker had used the word 'torpoul' for the teal duck he was corrected and told that the name was now 'touyoum'. This change had come about because 'torpoul' had also been the name of Tenberry's son, who had recently died. Hawker explained that, 'in this manner they are continually altering the names of plants, birds, animals &c. As almost every native is named after some of these.'

In relation to the name avoidance practices of the Maraura of the southern Darling River, the Reverend R.W. Holden stated 'the name for water was changed nine times in about five years on account of the death of eight men who bore the name of water'.[68] In 1989, when a book on the ethnobotany of Milingimbi in northeast Arnhem Land was being published, the local language name of a particular plant was omitted due to a recent death of a person with the same name.[69] After the period of mourning is over, the taboo words generally come back into use. This practice may have encouraged the accumulation of different language terms for plants over time.

Plants could also be used symbolically when talking about people. While travelling, Robinson noted that Tasmanian Aboriginal storytellers used leaves as an aid: 'They take the leaves off the large fern trees and strip off one side, and then compare the remaining leaves to natives walking, calling them by name … [and thus] described my journey and all the people'.[70] Totemic links between plants and people can be expressed in numerous ways. Robinson recorded a game in Tasmania where:

> The natives make small spears which they throw at and stick into the different trees. Those of Oyster Bay spear the stringy bark trees, peppermint trees, honeysuckle trees. The gum trees they claim as theirs and call them countrymen. The stringy bark trees the Brune [Bruny Island] call theirs, as being their countrymen, the peppermint the Cape Portland call theirs, and the Swanport claim the honeysuckle. Thus, if the natives of Oyster Bay spear the trees of another native they are much annoyed and go and pull them out.[71]

Through the Dreaming, people and plants have a common identity and are both linked to the landscape.

Plant Ownership

In many Aboriginal cultures, a clan or person would be considered the 'owner' of all the hunting and gathering resources of an estate.[72] It was protocol for the Lardil people of Mornington Island to ask the 'land owner' for permission to enter their territory to collect nuts from screw palms (pandanus) or cycads.[73] In southwestern Victoria, Dawson claimed that there were Aboriginal 'owners' of golden wattle trees, and 'each man has an exclusive right to a certain number of trees for the use of himself and family. As soon as the summer heat is over, notches are cut in the bark to allow the gum to exude. It is then gathered in large lumps, and stored for use.'[74] In this region wattle gum was a favoured food source and was also used medicinally and as an adhesive.

In some cases, landowners could give rights of access to other people for specified periods. In the case of Central Australian wild tobacco, Chief Protector and Chief Medical Inspector of Aborigines Herbert Basedow recorded that:

> The collecting grounds are as a rule owned by a circle of old men, each of whom clearly defines his boundaries by placing a number of stones upon the ground. A proprietor may give another person the necessary permission to gather leaves on his plot according to certain terms agreed upon. The owner usually takes a share of the leaves, and, in addition, levies other articles in exchange for what the collector has removed.[75]

Similarly, explorer George Grey recorded that in the southwest of Western Australia 'there are even some tracts of land which abound in [wattle] gum … which numerous families appear to have an acknowledged right to visit at the period of the year when this article is in season, although they are not allowed to come there at any other time'.[76]

In certain situations, the finders of plant foods were able to place a reserve on them for their own future exclusive use. Explorer Augustus C. Gregory stated that in the southwest of Western Australia, 'A native discovering a Zamia fruit unripe will put his mark upon it and no other native will touch this; the original finder of the fruit may rest perfectly certain that when it becomes ripe he has only to go and fetch it for himself'.[77] Ownership rights to a plant-based resource could also be conferred through the investment of labour. In the southwest of Western Australia, Aboriginal foragers deliberately killed grasstrees to encourage the growth of wood grubs, which were a favourite food.[78] Each tree was said to be the property of the man who had knocked the top off the tree. In another example of acquiring collecting rights, Ngarrindjeri people living in the Lower Murray of South Australia sought access to the large river red gums in the territory of their northern neighbours, the Peramangk in the southern Mount Lofty Ranges, in order to cut canoe bark.[79] Spear shafts, made from lengths of mallee that had grown in the whipstick form, were given in exchange for use of the river red gums, that were absent from the shallow soils and saline areas of the Lower Murray.

Family and Plants

At first glance, highly mobile Aboriginal lifestyles would appear to be un-nourishing to young children. But biologist/anthropologist Donald Thomson claimed that the Pintupi people of the Central Australia, who live in a harsh desert landscape, 'grow the fattest babies in the world'.[80] Anthropologist Isobel White also noted the plump appearance of Aboriginal children in the photographs taken by biologist W.B. (Baldwin) Spencer in the Northern Territory during the late nineteenth century. She remarked: 'Whereas very fat babies in Western society may grow into obese children and adults, there was no chance that this could happen in the traditional hunting and gathering life. It is even a wonder that the slim Aboriginal nursing mothers seen by Thomson and Spencer were able to grow such fat babies'.[81] White lamented the malnutrition that had spread among Aboriginal people since Europeans arrived. She added that, 'In the old hunting and gathering days weaning must have been an equally dangerous period because of the scarcity of suitable foods to supplement breast milk, but at least the babies approached this period with a reserve of fat. Moreover, breast-feeding usually continued to a much later age, providing a nutritional back-stop.'

As with human infants everywhere, there were physical limitations on what Aboriginal infants can eat before they are weaned. A special diet was prepared for babies, with foods that did not make the mouth sting. On Groote Eylandt, babies from six weeks of age onwards were given a mixture of honey and water.[82] When young enough to sit up, at about five or six months, babies were fed the cooked and hammered corms of the water-ribbon. The cooked roots were beaten with a stick to make them easier chewing for babies, as well as for elderly people without teeth. Until the children's teeth had grown, the main meats they ate on Groote Eylandt were cooked fish and crabs. Red meat was eaten after first being chewed by adults. After baking to remove the irritants and poisons that make them 'cheeky' (hot), the kernels of screw palm and the mature cycad nuts were also given to children.

In general, women within the foraging band were the main gatherers of food, particularly of plants and shellfish.[83] During the women's daily gathering trips, the children in their care assisted them. Prohibitions existed for children eating certain foods, which were generally thought to be a negative influence on the child's growth. After his Central Australian fieldwork, psychoanalyst Geza Roheim stated:

> The explanation offered as to why a certain plant or animal was taboo was always that some part of the child's anatomy would become like the article of food, or that ingestion of this food would interfere with some bodily function. Most often it was the genitalia or some secondary sexual characteristic which would be injured, or some sexual function which would be disturbed.[84]

During male initiations, the tradition in many Aboriginal cultures is that novices can only eat vegetable food.[85] In the case of pregnant Warlpiri women, the taboos generally involved not eating food derived from animals.[86] Elderly people tended to be subject to less prohibition, being able to consume most foods.[87]

Children learned to forage for food from an early age. In Tasmania and Victoria, an edible subterranean fungus known as 'native bread' or 'blackfellows bread' was highly sought after by Aboriginal gatherers, who looked for signs of it pushing up through the ground near rotting trees.[88] Colonist Robert Brough Smyth recorded that this fungus species was used in southern Australia to wean Aboriginal infants:

> And while very small — but yet able to move about only on hands and knees — it [the infant] has a little stick put into its hands, and, following the example of elder children, it digs for roots, for the larvae of ants, for such living things as it can find in decayed wood, and sometimes for the native bread ... where it is plentiful, and when the elder children are willing to help the little one. The infant soon learns to kill small lizards, and these, and the more easily procured kinds of food that the bush affords, serve to strengthen and fatten it.[89]

Young children were encouraged to eat the food they had collected. Explorer Major Thomas L. Mitchell remarked:

> There is a small cichoraceous [like the endive] plant named *Täo* by the natives, which grows with a yellow flower in the grassy places near the river [Darling], and on the root of this chiefly the children subsist. As soon almost as they can walk, a little wooden shovel is put into

their hands, and they learn thus early to pick about the ground for these roots and a few others, or dig out the larvae of ant-hills.[90]

The roots referred to by Mitchell were probably from the yam-daisy, which was a major food source in southeastern Australia.

Plants were used in specific ways for dealing with children. Anthropologist Ronald M. Berndt reported that Yaraldi people of the Lower Murray made teething-sticks from black cypress pine gum:

> This would be called *pitjingi*, deriving its name from the pine-gum used. A length of stick (about six inches [15 cm]) is procured, and the gum is made pliable by heating it over a fire. It is then moulded on to the stick at either end, or both. The *pitjingi* then resembles a dumbbell. The child sucks the gum which is believed by its mother to contain medicinal qualities, as well as being advantageous to a quick painless growth of the teeth.[91]

In Central Australia, children with severe teething problems were made to chew the scarlet bracket fungus, although it was known to be poisonous if swallowed.[92] Aboriginal people in the Cairns district of northern Queensland rubbed the milky sap of the white cheesewood onto the heads of babies in order 'to make hair curly'.[93] In the Victoria River area of the Northern Territory, Aboriginal carers place the heated pods of the yellow hakea on a child's navel to stop them bed wetting.[94]

Children make their own toys out of whatever is easily gained from their environment. Basedow recorded a number of Aboriginal children's games:

> On Bathurst Island a favourite amusement of the younger folk on a breezy day is to collect the light globular seed-heads of the 'spring rolling grass' ... that grow on every sandhill near the coast, and take them to the beach to release them on the hardened sand. Driven along by the wind, these seeds travel over the surface at no mean pace. Allowing them to gain a fair start, the children bolt after them, endeavouring to overtake them and pick them up from the ground while dashing past at full speed in 'cowboy' fashion.[95]

He also stated that on windy days in Central Australia, Aboriginal children used tussocks of roly-poly on clay pans in a similar way. In the Western Desert, Pitjantjatjara male youths would make their play spears out of thick stems chopped from bushes of the twiggy hemp.[96] Here, slabs of green gumtree bark were rolled along the ground as throwing targets.[97] In the north, catch-ball was played widely, with cycad and screw palm nuts as balls.[98]

Plant materials were used to make a large variety of ornaments and decorations. Those made by children were often ephemeral. When Aboriginal children have accompanied me on excursions into their country, I have noticed such activities as the picking of ruby saltbush berries in the Lower Murray to squeeze onto their faces to make them pink. Aboriginal girls in Central Australia would use eucalypt nuts to attach to the end of their hair strands for decoration.[99] In northern Queensland, Wik girls would place the blue flowers of water lilies behind their ears.[100] These flowers apparently made them appear more 'flash' for attracting boyfriends.

Body parts of people were sometimes compared to plants. For adolescent girls growing up in the Kimberley, it was a tradition that adults would hit them on their shoulder blades and say that this was to make them develop breasts like the fruit of kapok-bush.[101] In some Central Australian Aboriginal cultures, the pussytail plant is symbolic of the male sex, while the desert spurge represents the female sex.[102] Girls and boys tease each with these plants: girls grab the flowering heads (which look like penises) of the pussytail plant to pull them apart, while boys attack the desert spurge (which contains sap that looks like breast milk).

As children become adolescents, and finally young adults, they progressively take on greater responsibility in foraging food, while starting to participate more in ceremonial life. In former times, Aboriginal hunters and gatherers moved about their land as part of small bands, with mixed and changing membership.[103] The size and composition of the bands depended on the ability of the land within an area to support them economically. Aboriginal groups who camped together at the same hearth were generally comprised of a man, his wife or wives and young children.[104] Camps nearby might contain young unmarried men, while others had older relatives, such as parents of the main adults. An individual often had clan links to particular sites or estates that did not match the area their band generally hunted and gathered in. Groups became larger during ceremonies and trade meetings.

Aboriginal men and women have different, but complementary, relationships to plants. This pattern was set by the Dreaming Ancestors and is enshrined in Aboriginal mythology. German missionary Christian G. Teichelmann described the Skyworld beliefs of the Kaurna people of the Adelaide Plains, where 'The Pleiades are girls gathering roots and other vegetables; the Orion are boys, and are hunting'.[105] This tradition reflects the gender division of labour with Aboriginal hunting and gathering practices. Although the whole community shares plant use knowledge, women tend to know more about the gathering of plant foods, while men have greater interest in the plant species eaten by the animals they hunt.[106] Plants were also involved in 'love magic'. In the Bloomfield River area of northern Queensland, rainforest people considered that the strong aroma from bruised roots of the veiny pittosporum would cause sexual excitement in women, and men left the material near their shelters for this purpose.[107]

The role of individuals in Aboriginal religious life is determined by their descent, sex, age and possession of ritual knowledge.[108] Older people in Aboriginal society are often believed to have immense spiritual power, which gives them considerable authority over younger people. The elders are regarded as being repositories of knowledge concerning the landscape, including its Dreaming sites and physical resources. The memory of elderly members of the band was crucial for their survival at times of hardship. During severe droughts, Pitjantjatjara people of the Musgrave Ranges in Central Australia would make their 'hard time' food from the seed of heliotropes, which grow around waterholes.[109] Normally this plant, known as *mamukata* (literally 'evil spirit's head'), was ignored as a food source. The seed capsules have irritant hairs that cause much discomfort if inhaled, with women needing to position their heads upwind when winnowing. Such knowledge of where and how to access emergency foods helped Aboriginal bands to weather the bad times.

Ngaatjatjarra girl biting lerp sugar from mulga. Lerps are small sapsucker bugs that produce a sweet white protective covering on the leaves upon which they live. Plants that host insects that produce sweet exudations are referred to in Aboriginal English as 'sugarleaf'. *(Norman B. Tindale, Lightning Rocks, Western Australia, 1957. South Australian Museum Archives.)*

Ruby saltbush has numerous small edible fruit, which Aboriginal children used to paint their faces for play. *(Philip A. Clarke, Cordillo Downs, Central Australia, 1986.)*

Plants are conspicuous and fundamental parts of the environment utilised by Australian hunter-gatherers. The economic importance of particular

Golden wattle gum was highly prized as a food source, so much so that Aboriginal families in western Victoria had ownership over particular trees. *(Philip A. Clarke, Mount Barker, South Australia, 1986.)*

species was such that rules existed to govern access to them. Plants had symbolic value too, with many of their names having been adopted for people and places. The set of relationships each person has with plants depends on their status in the community. While Europeans have traditions of studying plants in isolation from other elements of the natural world, through the academic discipline of botany, Aboriginal interests in the flora were much broader, with less distinction made between human culture and nature.

Chapter 2

Plants of the Dreaming

The 'Dreaming' is an Aboriginal English term used to embrace indigenous religious beliefs about the Creation and the laying down of Aboriginal Law.[1] Aboriginal people believe that the cosmos exists because of the actions of their spiritual Ancestors. At the close of the Creation period, Ancestors were transformed into landforms, heavenly constellations, humans, animals and plants. Therefore, in Aboriginal thought, people and plants have the same origin. Knowledge of indigenous plant uses is essential for appreciating and gaining some understanding of Aboriginal mythology. This is because in Aboriginal tradition plants have symbolic significances and form integral parts of the cultural landscape.

Sacred Plants

There are many Aboriginal beliefs about Dreaming Ancestors who became plants. The Gunwinggu people of western Arnhem Land believe that Namalbi and Ngalmadbi husband and wife Dreaming Ancestors were transformed into screw palms at the end of the Creation.[2] Across Aboriginal Australia there are plants, whether single or in clusters, that are seen as sacred memorials. To the Adnyamathanha people of the northern Flinders Ranges in South Australia, a number of large and isolated wild orange trees represent their Iga Ancestors who spread out across the landscape in the Dreaming period.[3] Their 'droppings' are said to have become other wild orange trees. Apart from the *iga* trees providing good shade, they are also a source of excellent fruit, which Aboriginal foragers dried and stored for later use.

Dreaming events lead Aboriginal people to recognise the existence of strong bonds between people and plants. Geographer Elspeth Young demonstrated this in Central Australia, relating that, 'when discussing the activities of ancestral "bush plums" with an elderly Anmatyerre woman on Ti Tree station in Australia's Northern Territory in 1984 I was firmly told that the informant's grandfather, camping at the spring at Aliyawe, was himself a "bush plum".[4] In the Western Desert, Aboriginal people believe that large inland bloodwood trees with large woody lumps on the trunk represent their Dreaming Ancestors.[5] Aboriginal links to their land and the plants growing on it extends far beyond just the economic interests of hunter-gatherers.

The Aboriginal landscape is considered full with sacred plant manifestations. Even when plants do not represent the actual Ancestors, they may

Wangkangurru woman Linda Crombie collected the sporocarps (spore cases) from the nardoo water fern (*ngardu*). Dreaming accounts explain the importance of this food source. *(Philip A. Clarke, Pandi Pandi, near Birdsville, Central Australia, 1986.)*

be seen as having been involved with Dreaming activities in the Creation. At Mount Purvis in Central Australia, it is an Aboriginal tradition that a meteoric crater there resulted from a blast created when an elderly woman Ancestor passed wind after eating too much pigface fruit.[6] A case that I encountered in the Western Desert during fieldwork in 2002 involved a belief that Kuniya the Python Ancestor spat out native pear (bush cabbage) bushes that now grow in profusion around the base of a certain rock outcrop. These plants apparently do not occur anywhere else in the surrounding region. The Dreaming Ancestors left evidence of their actions everywhere. In eastern New South Wales, woody outgrowths that occur on lower parts of tree trunks were said to have been the seats of the male supreme Dreaming Ancestor Daramulun, who lived in trees.[7]

In Aboriginal Australia, parts of plants have ritual uses as tools when dealing with powerful Dreaming forces. Along the Murray River of southern Australia, red ochred male initiates maintained their spiritual charge by avoiding direct contact with water, and were only permitted to drink through a straw made from a segment of the common reed growing in profusion around the edges of the lagoons.[8] The Meru and Ngarrindjeri people believed that if this practice were not upheld during the several weeks of the initiation period, then the Dreaming powers of their whole society would be dissipated.

Linguist Luise Hercus provided another example of the involvement of plants in the Dreaming when she recorded in Nukunu language the Urumbula song-line, a saga based on a large tree. The track starts at Port Augusta in South Australia, heading north and eventually going all the way through Central Australia to the Gulf of Carpentaria in western Queensland. In her recorded version obtained from the Nukunu people in the southern Flinders Ranges:

> The main feature was a huge tree, so high that it was like a great ceremonial pole which in turn represented the Milky Way. This giant tree was located close to the present-day Port Augusta Hospital. According to the oldest singers of the Urumbula this tree was destroyed long before their time, in the very early days of European settlement.[9]

Many of the large arid zone trees that appear in Aboriginal mythology are centuries old and have gained the status of major Dreaming features in the landscape.[10] Aboriginal people see plants as sacred signatures in their country that, along with topographic features such as hills, creeks and waterholes, came into existence through the actions of Dreaming Ancestors.

Through the Dreaming, some plants are of totemic significance to certain Aboriginal clans. In Central Australia, anthropologist Theodor G. H. Strehlow claimed that:

> Every plant and animal of any economic value whatever forms a separate totem. Accordingly, if the myths gathered in the Northern Aranda [Arrernte] area are treated collectively, a full and very detailed account will be found of all the occupations which are still being practised in Central Australia. In his myths we see the native at his daily task of hunting, fishing, gathering vegetable food, cooking, and fashioning his implements.[11]

Many Aboriginal groups performed 'increase' rituals and held ceremonies that they believed would continue the cycle of renewing the species of their country.[12] Medical doctor George Horne and former outback policeman George (Paddy) Aiston described the yalka sedge in the northeast of South Australia as 'A small yam called *yaua* [that] comes up after the rain and is much prized by the natives, who scatter magic stones (*yelka*) to make it grow. It is from 1 to 1.5 cm. across and, I am told, has a nutty taste.'[13]

Aboriginal hunter-gatherers believed that they had the responsibility of maintaining the fertility of their country. At a site called Kurumi in the desert of central Western Australia, Aboriginal custodians ritually 'sowed' the edible seeds of bulli bulli bushes on the surface of a claypan.[14] Songs and other rituals helped hasten the production of favoured foods. On Yorke Peninsula in South Australia, the Narangga people had a song to ripen the quandongs (wild peaches). Translated it meant 'Wild peaches hanging in the trees, the sun will burn you (to the colour of fire), we will gather you (for food).'[15]

Ritual Use of Trees
Aboriginal rituals were involved in modifying trees. Large tree trunks form suitable surfaces

Aboriginal artists painted images of Dreaming Ancestors and spirit beings onto tree trunks and rock surfaces. To Aboriginal people, their country was not a wilderness, but rather a creation of their Ancestors. *(W. Holtze, Daly Waters, Northern Territory, about 1910. South Australian Museum Archives.)*

for engraving and painting, in ways similar to decorations applied to rock walls and wooden artefacts. Kimberley Aboriginal people carved figures of snakes, crocodiles and turtles into the trunks of large boab trees around campsites.[16] Over the years, figures would be re-engraved and repainted. Colonists found similar drawings on trees at an Aboriginal camp on the Darwin River in the Northern Territory.[17] Eucalypt trees growing around 'bora' ceremonial grounds in eastern New South Wales had totemic designs carved deeply into their trunks.[18] In the southeast districts of New South Wales, Aboriginal men organising revenge

expeditions would mark particular trees.[19] In the southern Gulf of Carpentaria region, explorer Friedrich W.L. (Ludwig) Leichhardt found that, 'A native had carved a representation of the foot of an emu in the bark of a gum tree; and he had performed it with all the exactness of a good observer'.[20] Leichhardt did not record anything else about the carving, although it possibly had some commemorative or ceremonial function.

In some regions, images of people were carved onto special tree trunks for sorcery purposes.[21] The Madi Madi people of western Victoria believed that by putting personal objects stolen from an intended victim into a hole carved into a quandong tree, the owner would waste away.[22] Tasmanians treated specific trees as 'sacred' to particular individuals, and it was regarded a calamity if they were damaged or destroyed.[23] In the southwest of Western Australia, Aboriginal clans recognised certain trees as landmarks to identify their ownership of land.[24] Here, notches in trees also signified that there were graves nearby.[25]

The Adnyamathanha people of the northern Flinders Ranges believe that two eucalypt trees growing at a certain waterhole are associated with the weather. Tunbridge recorded that, 'In very hot weather, people would go to these trees and hit them with a stone or a stick or some such thing, in order to bring about a change in the weather. The trunks appear to bear the record of many years of having been hit'.[26] Striking the trees was thought to bring on a cool change, which was then usually followed by a dust storm. Such trees are seen as harbouring powerful forces, derived from the Dreaming itself.

Aboriginal mourning practices resulted in the killing of trees in the Goulburn River area of eastern New South Wales. During the mid-nineteenth century, naturalist Wilhelm Blandowski was passing through and found many dead trees in a forest.[27] Upon inquiring about this among local Aboriginal people he learned that it was the indirect result of a fight between the Goulburn and Murray 'tribes' that had led to many deaths. Blandowski noted that each of the dead trees represented a deceased member of the local clan. This association of trees with people came about

'Mulga Seed; Warndipiri near Papunya.' A Warlpiri painting of a Dreaming showing women grinding wattle seed to make damper. Although labour-intensive, the use of seed to make food became important when other sources were scarce. *(Peggy Nampitjinpa Brown, acrylic on canvas, Yuendumu, Central Australia, 1987. © Licensed by VISCOPY, Australia, 2006.)*

through a male initiation ritual. As a youth, each man knocked out two of his front teeth on his upper jaw. The loose teeth were presented to his mother who:

> having selected a young gum tree, inserts the teeth in the bark, in the fork of two of the topmost branches. This tree is made known only to certain persons of the tribe, and is strictly kept from the knowledge of the youth himself. In case the person to whom the tree is thus dedicated dies, the foot of it is stripped of its bark, and it is killed by the application of fire; thus becoming a monument of the deceased. Hence, we need no longer be surprised at so frequently finding groups of dead trees in healthy and verdant forests, and surrounded by luxuriant vegetation.[28]

The distinctiveness of such memorials would probably have vanished once Aboriginal fire management practices in the area had ceased through European settlement, leading to more devastating forest fires.

Plants as Spirit Homes

In Aboriginal tradition, certain plant formations are associated with spirits and are therefore dangerous places. Leichhardt recorded that Aboriginal people in eastern Australia referred to thicket areas where the bastard box grew as 'Devil-devil land', as they believed that an evil spirit created them.[29] On one occasion in 1844, when trying to pass through a river system covered in a mass of bastard box saplings, Leichhardt's Aboriginal guide, Charley, exclaimed that he 'never saw such a rum river'.[30] To Aboriginal people, such rampant plant growth is suggestive of poor management by 'land owners', who have failed to maintain the land through ritual and by their burning practices. The general movement of Aboriginal people into settlements over the last hundred years has created, in many Aboriginal eyes, a dangerous situation through the lack of regularly firing the more distant parts of the country. It is thought that spirits accumulate in overgrown vegetation.

Aboriginal people believe that spirits lurking in unkempt areas may be cause sickness among them. In northeast Arnhem Land, Yolngu people will say that they get sick because there are 'too many "devil devils" out there in the swamps and the scrub'.[31] There are also plants considered too dangerous for humans to eat, regardless of how they are prepared. In the Cobourg Peninsula area of the Northern Territory, Aboriginal people do not eat the cabbage of the Wendland palm, although they believe devils and ghosts do so.[32] The same plant food is eaten by Aboriginal people elsewhere.[33] Spirit beings can also use plants in their dealings with humans. At Elliot in the Northern Territory, Aboriginal people believe that evil spirits feed the toxic caustic-vine to human babies in order to kill them.[34]

In the Top End, Aboriginal people maintain that the sound of the wind passing through the beach sheoak, also known as the 'whistling tree', will 'sing people to sleep'.[35] During my fieldwork in southern South Australia during the 1980s, it was noted that Ngarrindjeri people believed that one group of drooping sheoaks, which had branches that rustled or 'spoke' in the wind, was

The banyan fig tree has bark that was a source of string fibre, as well as sap used as paint fixative. According to Aboriginal tradition, the numerous folds in the trunk harbour spirits. *(Norman B. Tindale, Atherton Tableland, northern Queensland, 1972. South Australian Museum Archives.)*

the home of malevolent spirits. Similarly, in other parts of Australia trees with crossed branches that rubbed together and made noises in the wind are sometimes regarded as sorcery or spirit being places.[36] The Potaruwutji people of the southeast of South Australia believed that sacred trees were imbued with spirits that 'talked' when the branches chafe together or when the tree ignites as the result of friction during a storm.[37] Among the Bibbulmun in southern Western Australia, passing travellers threw rushes around the bases of certain trees to appease *djanga* spirit beings living there.[38] Here, the spirits of dead people were said to reside in the 'tree of souls', a Christmas bush, before departing to the land of the dead.[39]

Enormous trees, known to attract lightning strikes, were regarded as spiritually dangerous, possibly through the rationalisation that they reached up into the Skyworld.[40] During Aboriginal inquests in southeastern New South Wales, 'wizards' climbed large trees to bring back the spirits of the recently deceased, in order to determine blame for the death.[41] In a manner similar to Odin of pre-Christian northern European mythology, a healer in the lower southeast of South Australia had reportedly gained knowledge through crossing into the heavens by climbing a tree.[42] In northern Australia, Aboriginal people often associate stands of the banyan fig with Dreaming sites and sacred places.[43] In the Top End, it is an Aboriginal tradition that Ancestors brought banyans there

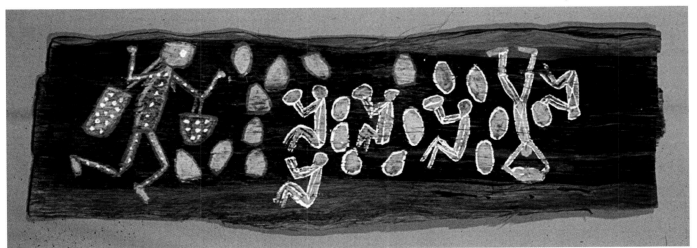

'The woman, Adurimya, with baskets of water lily bulbs and her children. A Dream story.' Water lilies have edible leaf stems, seeds and tubers. *(Unknown artist, ochre on bark, collected by Charles P. Mountford, Oenpelli, western Arnhem Land, 1949. South Australian Museum Aboriginal Artefact Collection.)*

from somewhere to the northwest.[44] In the Arnhem escarpment country, Aboriginal people refer to large bushes of a particular species as 'devil-devil trees', due to their spirit associations.[45]

Plant Dreamings

The flora is featured in much of Aboriginal mythology, not just as part of the general environment but also as major Dreamings. In the Western Desert art movement of acrylic painting on canvas and art board, which developed from traditional art forms in the 1960s, the painted Dreamings have included Small Yam, Big Yam, Bush Potato, Desert Banana, Bush Tomato, Wild Orange, Sugarleaf and Bush Cabbage.[46] Many Dreaming narratives can only be fully appreciated by taking into account the economic importance of the plants involved.

Nardoo and Grass Seed Dreaming

Anthropologist and explorer Alfred W. Howitt recorded the Ngardu-etya and Anti-etya Dreaming of the Yandruwandha people at Cooper Creek in Central Australia during the nineteenth century.[47] Based in a desert landscape, it describes the creation of grindstones and the use of nardoo (*ngardu*) fern sporocarps (spore cases) and grass seed.

Briefly, two closely related Mura-mura (Dreaming Ancestors) lived in the Skyworld at Kadri-pairiwilpa, a riverbed in the heavens recognised by Europeans as the Milky Way. Both Mura-mura were male: one a nardoo-gatherer was known as Ngardu-etya, the other the hunter called Anti-etya. After returning to camp one evening, Anti-etya started grinding his nardoo, while Ngardu-etya prepared the meat he had caught. When Ngardu-etya noticed that his relative had eaten some of the nardoo meal without sharing it, he chastised him. Anti-etya denied that he had eaten the meal. Ngardu-etya then thrust a hand down the Anti-etya's throat and pulled up a lump of nardoo from his stomach. In revenge, Ngardu-etya ate the retrieved meal, the rest of the ground nardoo, as well as all the food he was cooking.

The next morning, Ngardu-etya wondered how to stop his relative from cheating him. He lagged behind during their search for food, and then secretly returned to camp. Ngardu-etya made a group of huts and spread his footsteps around to give the impression that a large number of people were staying there. He then started to grind grass seed, but the stone broke. Ngardu-etya got another, but this also broke. He then made a large grinding slab from his own shoulder blade and cut off the tip of his tongue to make the smaller upper stone to grind with. As the seed was ground, it was dropped into a wooden bowl hidden in a hole under the stones.

Anti-etya returned to camp that night and could not find Ngardu-etya or any food. He was frightened, thinking that the people whose footsteps were everywhere had killed his relative. By the following morning, Ngardu-etya had baked a large number of cakes from the seed and sporocarps he had ground the day before. He threw them towards the hut where Anti-etya was sleeping, making a path back to his own shelter. Anti-etya awoke to the smell of freshly baked cake and followed them to Ngardu-etya, who was sitting on top of the grindstones. Anti-etya did not at first recognise his relative, but when he did he rushed to embrace him. After sinking into the ground, the Ancestors rose and Anti-etya stayed at Kadri-pairi in the Skyworld and Ngardu-etya went to live at Innamincka on the banks of Cooper Creek.

The use of grindstone technology to gain sustenance from nardoo and grass seed was fundamental to the Aboriginal economy in the arid region, when Europeans first arrived.[48] Both the plants and the material culture that Aboriginal hunter-gatherers routinely use are believed by them to have been created through the actions of their Ancestors in the Dreaming period.

Cheeky Yams

Paintings of yams depicted in human form are a prominent feature in the rock art of the pre-estuarine period (over 7000 years ago) in Arnhem Land of the Northern Territory.[49] There are many different types of edible yam across northern Australia. The tubers of the long yam were widely used, and taste like cultivated potato after preparation.[50] Like many yams, they are 'cheeky', meaning in northern varieties of Aboriginal English that they taste hot and may be poisonous to eat if the toxins are not first removed.[51] They and other poisonous yams are generally rendered safe by a drawn out process of cutting the tubers, soaking them in water, and then baking them.

Although yams are seasonally used as food and medicine in the tropics, they also have major symbolic value in ceremony.[52] Ethnobotanists would not consider some yam species as major foods at all, if the plants were only being assessed on the merits of their physical properties and the duration of dietary use. The foods of the Tiwi on Melville and Bathurst Islands, off the Northern Territory coast, provide an illustration of this. The Kurlama initiation ceremonies they hold are centred on the increase of a bitter tasting tuber — the Kurlama yam or air potato.[53] The Kurlama is held around February, towards the end of the wet season, when the yams are ready for harvesting, and runs for over three days and nights.[54]

The Tiwi men collect the Kurlama yams for the ceremony, placating the spirits in the roots by calling to them before digging and by taking much care in keeping the roots undamaged when the yams are removed from the ground. Should the root spirits become frightened, it is thought that everyone in the community is likely to get Kurlama sickness. During Charles P. Mountford's anthropological fieldwork in 1954, the Tiwi people told him of an incident when a Kurlama yam was once accidentally broken. He recorded that, 'Instantly, he [the digger] was on his feet, and, with the broken yam in his palm, dodged in and out among the trees, to escape the spirit of sickness released by the angry yam'.[55]

On the first night of Kurlama ceremony, the Tiwi eat another 'cheeky yam' species, the sweet snakeskin lily, after it is cooked from sunrise to sunset in hot coals.[56] The Kurlama yams are cooked on the third day of the ceremony, and are ritually rubbed on the joints of the body to impart strength before they are eaten. At other times, the flesh of the Kurlama yam is used medicinally, by being rubbed directly onto sore limbs and aching joints to reduce swelling.[57] The Tiwi consider that, at certain growth stages during the rainy season, particular yam species are harmful to people.[58] In the case of small new yams, it is pregnant women who are most at risk.

Fire and the Religious Landscape

In Aboriginal tradition, the spirits of the deceased continue to hunt and gather, both on earth and in the Skyworld. Anthropologist and linguist John Bradley recorded amongst the Yanyuwa people of the southern Gulf of Carpentaria that, 'up until quite recently, country that was burnt was left for several days so the spirits of the deceased could hunt first'.[59] The Yanyuwa consider country that had not burned in recent years, and which was overgrown with tangly vine thickets, to be 'shut up' by spirits of the deceased angered by their living descendants failing to keep up the firing regime. Bradley explained that the Yanyuwa have a tradition that when the spirits of those who have recently died are approaching the 'Land of the Dead', crows armed with digging-sticks attack them. The crows are said to be angry with all people, who have routinely chased them away when scavenging at camps. The spirits are rescued by hawks and falcons armed with fighting-sticks. These raptors are 'followers of the fires', and by helping out the spirits of the deceased, the birds are repaying their debt to people who burn the land and thus provide them with a means to hunt game.

An Aboriginal vision of the Skyworld above in the heavens reflects the use of fire by spirits. A nineteenth-century European colonist, Charles White, claimed that, 'In parts of Queensland and South Australia the natives believed the "Milky Way" to be a sort of celestial place for disembodied spirits. They said it was the smoke proceeding from celestial grass which had been set on fire by their departed women, a signal intended to guide the ghosts of the deceased to the eternal camp fires of the tribe'.[60] Similarly, Warnindilyakwa people living on Groote Eylandt in the Gulf of Carpentaria consider that the ancestral fishermen, known as the Burum-burum-runja, are the three stars in the belt of Orion, with the flames and smoke of their fires being adjacent parts of the Milky Way.[61]

The flames of large fires were also seen in the Skyworld. In the Clarence River area of northeastern New South Wales, the Ancestor Karambal stole another man's wife, and was then chased up into the canopy of a tall tree.[62] His

'Dreaming Ancestors and their food yams.' In tropical Australia, yams have a major symbolic role in many religious ceremonies. *(Unknown artist, ochre on bark, collected by Charles P. Mountford, Oenpelli, western Arnhem Land, 1949. South Australian Museum Aboriginal Artefact Collection.)*

pursuer gathered wood and made a fire at the base of the tree. The fierce flames carried Karambal up into the Skyworld, where he is seen as Aldebaran (Alpha Tauri), which is the brightest star in the constellation Taurus. Aboriginal people remarked that in the night sky Karambal retains the colour of the fire.

Fire is widely used in many Aboriginal ceremonies and rituals.[63] Firebrands were considered part of the sorcery kit for 'medicine men'. In the Brisbane area of southeast Queensland, Howitt recorded that:

> The Turrbal believed that a falling star was a *Kundri* (medicine man) flying through the air and dropping his fire-stick to kill some one, and was sure if a sick man was in the camp he would die. Mr. Petrie [an ethnographer] relates that once he was in a camp when a woman was sick and a meteorite was seen. Her friends at once began to mourn and cut themselves for her.[64]

Tasmanian Aboriginal people would thrust a burning stick into the air in the direction to which they wanted the wind to start blowing.[65] In Central Australia, Aboriginal people believed that they could drive away clouds after too much rain by burning kerosene-bush to create smoke.[66] In 1986, while on a fieldtrip to the Sturt Stony Desert, west of Innamincka, I watched Wangkangurru man Jimmy Harris perform a similar ritual, when he lit up a pile of dried branches leaning against a coolibah tree that made smoke intended to stop a downpour of rain.

Fire plays a prominent role in ceremonies. There are 'fire' ceremonies that take place in Central Australia, held by groups such as the Warlpiri and the Arrernte.[67] Here, anthropologist Howard Morphy explained:

> The ritual is one in which past grievances are brought out into the open and resolved dramatically yet cathartically with the burning brands. ... Indeed, fire is itself a powerful component of the aesthetics of ritual. It heats and it purifies through burning, it provides the light at night for ritual performance and is integral to the aesthetics of viewing. Fire gains symbolic power from the devastation that it can cause, and its potential danger. It is an ideal symbolic medium for expressing anger and resolving conflict through catharsis.[68]

There are rules for the participants' use of fire in the ceremony, to ensure that no one is hurt.

At night, Aboriginal campfires were a comfort against the perceived threat of darkness and spirits, as well as providing warmth. During the day, smoke was employed to drive away malignant spirits. A hunter will smoke himself before leaving camp to ensure that lingering spirits do not follow him, as they will frighten away the intended game.[69] Smoke is also believed to conceal the human soul. In the Top End of the Northern Territory and in the Wik area of Cape York Peninsula, the leaves of

'Bushfire Dreaming.' A Luritja painting featuring the impact upon the land of Lungkarda (Bluetongue Lizard Ancestor), whose breath fanned fires that burnt off the desert grass. Aboriginal 'fire-stick farming' practices modified the vegetation into a mosaic, as shown in this painting. *(Johnny Warangkula Tjupurrula, acrylic on hardboard, Papunya, Central Australia, c.1976. © Estate of the artist licensed by Aboriginal Artists Agency 2006.)*

the northern ironwood are burned when 'smoking' houses during the final stages of Aboriginal funeral ceremonies, which clears the area of spirits.[70] Firewood was the subject of prohibitions. The Ngarrindjeri people of the Lower Murray in South Australia believed that if their boys cooked food with *palyi* (possibly white box) or *panpandi* (native cherry) wood, then all the Murray cod fish would forsake the lakeshores.[71] In Aboriginal tradition, plants have varying properties that may impact upon their ritual use.

There are many Aboriginal Dreaming accounts that explain the Ancestor's discovery of fire making practices and the subsequent spread of the technology among people and as wild fires at the end of Creation.[72] Some of these myths have inspired European writers who have published Australian legends.[73] A common theme is that there is one among the Ancestors who knows how to make fire, but who selfishly keeps it secret from all others. Eventually, this knowledge of fire is discovered and stolen, and in this manner becomes widely available to all. Another perceived result was that fire had escaped and is now present as bushfires, such as those uncontrolled fires resulting from lightning strikes. The mythology also explains how fire 'got into plants', so humans could release it when needed.

German missionary Heinrich A.E. Meyer obtained the following fire myth account from Ramindjeri people living at Encounter Bay in South Australia during the 1840s.[74] Here, whales are connected with the origin of fire. During the Creation period, all the Ramindjeri Ancestors gathered to dance at a place known as Moota-paringa (Spring Mount), on the Hindmarsh River. They did not have a fire, so they had to dance all day to keep warm, which tired them. Sweat from their bodies dripped down to become large ponds, and hills and valleys formed as the ground buckled under their stamping feet.

Eventually, the Ancestors, who were cold and tired, sent for Kondoli, who was a large and powerful man known to possess fire. He came, but kept his fire hidden. This made the other Ancestors angry, leading to Riballi the Brown Skylark throwing a spear at Kondoli, which struck him in the neck. The resulting commotion forced the transformation of the Ancestors into different animals, such as fish and birds. Kondoli himself rushed into the sea to become a whale and ever after blew 'steam' out of his 'wound' — the spout. Riballi took Kondoli's fire and placed it in a grasstree, where it can be removed by using the dried flower stems as a fire drill. Examples of similar Fire Dreaming accounts from other parts of Australia are the Crocodile and Rainbird from Katherine in the Northern Territory, the Raven and Firetail Bird in western Victoria, and the Water Rat and Hawk in northwest Victoria.[75] Fire Dreamings are a major theme in twentieth century Aboriginal art, particularly for the desert region.[76]

Plants have primary roles in some Dreaming accounts of the Creation, and are part of the background for many others. Explanations of how people first learned to use grindstones and fire, which are technologies that involve plants, are enshrined in Aboriginal mythology. Through ceremony, senior Aboriginal custodians believed that they had an active role in the production of plants and in maintaining their cultural landscape. In Aboriginal culture, the ritual powers of plants draw not only on their pharmacological properties, but also upon the Dreaming essences that they contain.

Aboriginal mythology explains how Dreaming Ancestors placed the fire making property into the dry flower spikes of the grasstree. When fresh, the flowers provide nectar for drinking. *(Philip A. Clarke, Flinders Ranges, South Australia, 1984.)*

PART TWO
CULTURAL IMPACT ON PLANTS

Chapter 3
Leaving a Mark

Given the initial apprehension of both Europeans and indigenous people over meeting face to face, it is not surprising to find that much of what early explorers recorded about the Aboriginal inhabitants of Australia was based on inspections of abandoned campsites and marks made on trees and the ground. Europeans also observed Aboriginal hunter-gatherers setting the bush on fire and noted how parts of the landscape had the appearance of having been regularly burnt. Most signs of Aboriginal occupation left behind were ephemeral and would have largely disappeared once European settlement had brought an end to hunting and gathering in each area. The newly created European-style landscapes, comprising what we call 'settled Australia', absorbed many elements of the indigenous cultural landscapes it overlayed. In determining the likely impacts of Aboriginal hunters and gatherers upon the Australian landscape, consideration must be given to the accumulative effects of their foraging activities over the millennia.

Tree Climbers

Early European visitors to Australia were in awe of the apparent abilities of Aboriginal tree climbers. Dutch captain Abel Tasman was in command of the *Heemskerck* and *Zeehaen* and trying to find a route from Batavia to Chile when he reached Van Diemen's Land (later changed to Tasmania) on 24 November 1642. He noted that a landing party had:

Seen two trees about two or two and a half fathom [3.7 to 5.5 m] in thickness, measuring from sixty to sixty-five feet [18.3 to 19.8 m] from the ground to the lowermost branches, which trees bore notches made with flint implements, the bark having been removed for the purpose. These notches, forming a kind of steps to enable persons to get up the trees and rob the birds' nests in their tops, were fully five feet [1.5 m] apart, so that our men concluded that the natives here must be of very tall stature, or must be in the possession of some sort of artifice for getting up the said trees.[1]

Not having seen any Aboriginal people, let alone observed the manner in which they climbed trees, Tasman had to speculate on both the physical size of Tasmanians and on their climbing aids, based upon his reading of the marks on tree trunks. Much later, Europeans discovered that Tasmanians, who were of normal human stature, employed a rope and a sharp stone when tree climbing.[2]

When the first European settlers started expanding into the inland forests along the eastern coast of Australia, they often found trees with chopping marks on the trunks. In eastern New South Wales, Aboriginal climbers were seen using stone hatchets when scaling trees.[3] In 1817, John Oxley's expedition to the west of the Blue Mountains in New South Wales actively looked for fresh 'marks usually made by the natives in ascending the trees', deducing from this whether or not Aboriginal people had been recently hunting in each area through which they were passing.[4] Oxley noted:

Trees associated with ceremonial or 'bora' grounds in eastern New South Wales were permanently scarred with engraved totemic designs. *(Henry Barnes, eastern New South Wales, about 1900. South Australian Museum Archives.)*

> We have for several days past seen no signs of any natives being recently in this part of the country; the marks on the trees, which were the only marks we saw, being several months old, and never seen except in the vicinity of water. Marks of the natives' tomahawks were to us certain signs of approaching water.[5]

The assumption was that Aboriginal hunting and gathering activities were highly dependent upon the availability of water.

On a trip from Sydney to Moreton Bay in 1827, Allan Cunningham, who was one of Sir Joseph Banks' plant hunters, observed chopping marks in the trees.[6] They were made by Aboriginal foragers who appeared to have possessed steel axes, that might have been obtained through trade commencing with Europeans. At the Severn River in northeast New South Wales, he noted:

> The marks of natives wandering in quest of food were noticed on the timber through which the travellers passed on this day. There were steps on the tree trunks, evidently cut to aid the blacks in climbing, although the bush furnished few opossum and apparently the natives had been seeking larvae or pupae, upon which they must have chiefly lived. These were most often found in the knot at the upper limbs of a straight-growing box.[7]

The major food sources located in trees included marsupials, birds and their eggs, bee honey, wood-boring insects, leaf lerp, galls, nectar flowers, fruit and seeds.

The Aboriginal hunters and gatherers of the inland forests and woodlands were notable for their ability to scale trees. The coastal people around Sydney referred in their own language to inland groups as 'climbers of trees'.[8] According to Howitt, the tree climbing people living in the dense forests of southern New South Wales were known by other Aboriginal groups as 'waddy-men', because they 'get their living by climbing trees for game'.[9] The 'waddy', or throwing club, would have been frequently used in the woods for hunting birds, possums and koalas. In the eastern colonies, European settlers contrasted the tree climbing 'mountaineers' among the Aboriginal people they met with those who had a coastal technology.[10]

The ability to climb trees without lower branches would have extended the impact zone of Aboriginal hunting and gathering upwards from the ground. The rarity of forest mammals, such as koalas, in the earliest years of British settlement is testimony to the effectiveness of Aboriginal hunting.[11] Europeans considered particular Aboriginal men to be champion climbers. During the late nineteenth century in the Mannum district of the Murray River in South Australia, an Aboriginal climber known as 'King Jerry' was often paid by European settlers to climb tall trees to collect parrots and cockatoos, which were probably used as pets.[12] It has been suggested that Aboriginal practices of climbing trees and collecting fruit probably once helped keep down the numbers of the parasitic mistletoes infesting western myall trees in South Australia.[13] Other tree species suffered directly through Aboriginal gathering activities. The east coast Aboriginal practice of removing the edible growth centre from the

The crowns of many palms, such as the cabbage palm, are edible. Harvesting these growth centres kills the plant. *(Philip A. Clarke, southeastern Queensland, 2004.)*

crown of cabbage palms caused the death of the tree.[14]

The tools used for climbing could also be used in food collecting. In the southwest of Western Australia, Aboriginal tree climbers used both a knife and an axe.[15] In northern Queensland, stone axes were used to chop steps into trees for the purpose of collecting bee honey, which was a favourite food.[16] Here, climbers also used a climbing device, a knotted loop of lawyer-cane that was looped around the trunk. In the tropics, older trees of allosyncarpia, Darwin stringybark and northern woollybutt often have hollows eaten out by termites, which carry bee nests known in Aboriginal English as 'sugar-bag'.[17] On Melville and Bathurst Islands in the Northern Territory, Tiwi hunters climbed trees with a large girth by using ladders.[18] These were constructed from long cut saplings, the tops of which were placed in the tree crotch where the limb meets the trunk, with the bases firmly positioned on the ground.

The regularity of Aboriginal movement patterns was reflected in the vegetation. The Aboriginal act of breaking down wooden branches to make shelters left many coppiced trees around favoured campsites. British settler Tom P. Bellchambers noted in the 1920s that at a former Aboriginal campsite along the Murray River in South Australia:

> There appears a clump of box gum [black box] whose tops, from frequent cutting by the blacks, have grown thick and bushy. Several wurlies [shelters], built with these boughs, cluster around an old midden.[19]

Many of these regular campsites would have been apparent to early observers, whether occupied or not. Upon arriving at a new camping place,

Aboriginal hunters cut footholds into the trunk of this river red gum to make it easier to climb when catching possums. *(Herbert M. Hale, Mannum, Murray River, South Australia, 1927. South Australian Museum Archives.)*

Aboriginal forager ascending a tree trunk with the aid of a knotted loop of lawyer-cane and a hatchet to collect fruit and seed from the canopy. For hunters and gatherers of the rainforest, no tree is too tall for climbing. *(Photographer unknown, Atherton Tableland, Queensland, about 1890. South Australian Museum Archives.)*

Aboriginal band members would set about removing the bushes and grasses from the vicinity of their camps.[20] Trees that provide shade or have boughs useful for storing items by hanging them were left standing, being in any case too difficult to remove. By opening up the surrounds, the campers would be safer from wildfires and suffer less from insects and pests such as spiders, centipedes, scorpions and snakes.

Campfires also left their marks on trees, creating hollows at the bases of large eucalypts. Ecologist Stephen J. Paine remarked: 'The process began by using large trunks as reflectors for campfires. The fire naturally ate into the green bole, and the more the site was revisited, the larger the fire-excavated cavity. ... The larger cavities could even shelter Aborigines.'[21] Campers would generally leave their fires burning when moving on. The burning of trees made hollows that Aboriginal hunters could, at each visit, search for arboreal animals. In the case of possums, when the animal retreated deeply into the tree, it was either chopped out or forced into the open with smoke.[22]

Diggings

Early European explorers frequently encountered the signs of Aboriginal digging activities as they travelled beyond the frontier of settlement. On 5 July 1789, Captain John Hunter and his party were exploring along a river near Port Jackson in New

South Wales. He remarked that:

> The natives here, appear to live chiefly on the roots which they dig from the ground; for these low banks appear to have been ploughed up ... We put on shore, and examined the places which had been dug, and found the wild yam in considerable quantities, but in general very small, not larger than a [English] walnut; they appear to be in the greatest plenty on the banks of the river; a little way back they are scarce.[23]

From its description, this yam may have been from the marsh club rush, which grows on river flats and was widely used as food in southeastern Australia.[24] Such plant sources in the wetlands would have been relatively easy to dig during winter.

Plant corms and tubers were not the only food source that Aboriginal foragers gained from the earth. In the arid zone across South Australia, Western Australia and the Northern Territory, Aboriginal people prized the 'native truffle' fungus, which grew along the edges of the sand dunes.[25] It was so nutritiously rich that it often became fly blown when exposed. Donald Thomson described how Pintupi women around Lake Hazlett in the Western Desert located truffles.[26] From July to September they were found in large numbers by looking for cracks in the firmer sand.

Diggings around trees also produced insect food. In 1827, Cunningham was on one of his plant collecting expeditions inland from Sydney when he noted finding trees under which Aboriginal foragers had recently dug to obtain insect larvae from the roots.[27] Other holes were made in the ground when hunting such things as burrow-living reptiles and mammals, as well as for the gathering of honey ants.[28] On a daily basis, women were usually the main diggers — it being their job to gather ground-based foods, such as roots and small burrowing game. Across Australia, the digging-stick was as much a symbol of womanhood as the spear was representative of men.[29] It should be noted that this was not an absolute rule — men did dig when necessary and in some areas women used small spears. Most of these casual diggings would have soon disappeared through the action of weather and bush regeneration.

Aboriginal earthworks involved in building fish traps, digging soakages and excavating rock from quarries were generally large and long-lasting landscape features.[30] In a few areas, the practice of Aboriginal women constantly digging up plant roots also produced landforms that persisted. At Sunbury on the northern side of Melbourne in Victoria, the first European settlers found numerous earth mounds that had been created by the 'accidental gardening' of Aboriginal gatherers who were digging up yam-daisy tubers.[31] The origin of these large piles of soil quickly became obscured as Europeans began to transform the landscape, with the yam-daisy being replaced with introduced forage plants.

Observations of Aboriginal large scale root harvesting were not just restricted to southeastern Australia. In May 1839, the colonist and explorer George Grey, who later became Governor of South Australia, of New Zealand, and then of the Cape Colony of South Africa, was travelling down the coast of Western Australia by land after being shipwrecked near the mouth of the Murchison River. Near Geraldton, he came across extensive diggings by Aboriginal foragers looking for warran yams. When his party reached Hutt River he reported:

> for three and a half consecutive miles [5.6 km] we traversed a fertile piece of land, literally perforated with the holes the natives had made to dig this root; indeed we could with difficulty walk across it on that account, whilst this tract extended east and west as far as we could see. ... more had here been done to secure a provision from the ground by hard manual labour than I could have believed it in the power of uncivilised man to accomplish.[32]

Grey's observations appear to suggest that these Aboriginal people had agricultural practices, although it is not clear whether their enhancement of the soil to promote further plant growth was being done consciously.

European explorers noted other areas of Western Australia that bore the effects of Aboriginal gathering activities. In 1876, explorer Ernest Giles was in upper reaches of the Gascoyne River when he 'noticed large areas of ground on the river flats, which had not only been dug, but re-dug, by the natives, and it seems probable that a great portion of their food consists of roots and vegetables'.[33] In the Kimberley, anthropologist Ian M. Crawford more recently described Aboriginal women drawing heavily on their previous experiences when collecting plant foods, having clear ideas about what they were likely to find at any particular spot according to season.[34] The regular use of reliable food sources demonstrates that Aboriginal foragers worked to a plan, rather than waiting to see what each season brought them, and suggests that gathering was focused on particular areas.

Sedge tubers were a major source of food for many desert people. Being underground protects roots from some of the short-term effects of drought. When the Horn Expedition reached the Macdonnell Ranges in 1894, Stirling recorded the use of yalka (onion-grass):

> In almost every camp we saw large quantities of the tunicated tubers of this plant, which are generally called 'Erriakura' or 'Irriakura' by the Arunta [= Arrernte] natives. In some parts however the term 'Yelka,' 'Yelki' or 'Yilka' is used, and this is the name by which it is generally known amongst the whites. ... These little tubers which sometimes are aggregated into masses, nearly as large as the fist, are dug up by the women with yam-sticks, and are either eaten raw or very slightly roasted by shaking them in a wooden vessel with a few live embers. ... 'Erriakura' must possess good nutritive qualities, as in many camps it appeared to be the only food that was being used.[35]

The sedge mentioned above is the same food that Wangkangurru woman, Linda Crombie, collected for me during a fieldtrip in 1987 to the eastern edge of the Simpson Desert. Here, a few minutes digging in loose sand in a dry riverbed produced several handfuls of tubers. Herbert Basedow stated that 'When a tribe has been camped for a while near a favourable collecting ground [of yelka], many acres of soil are turned over, giving one quite the impression of a cultivated field'.[36] Ecologist Peter Latz said that 'The women sometimes dig a trench at the edge of a patch and then, working in a line, turn over the ground, picking out the bulbs as they go'.[37]

The Aboriginal harvesting of plant roots had long-term impacts upon the environment. The yearly digging of soil and the redistribution of small edible tubers, whether deliberately or by accident, probably acted to maintain an abundance of plant foods favoured by Aboriginal people.[38] Tindale described a ritual of replanting tubers he observed in 1927 at Flinders Island in northern Queensland:

> Women dig for the yams with digging sticks following them to a depth of up to 3 feet (nearly 1 m), repeating a formula that is supposed to make the yam large and shapely. Having recovered their prize, the women's attitudes change. They now scold the stem that has guided them to the tuber, even beat and bruise it and throw it back in the hole. Then they are rude to it to the extent that they urinate and on occasion defecate on it, at the same time telling it to go back and do better since its yam was poor. Finally, they may push some of the earth back into the hole.[39]

Aboriginal replanting practices were also observed in the southwest of Western Australia and have been noted in other regions too.[40] For some plant species, the damage of roots through digging is known to encourage bud development at the top, bringing on the production of more plants.[41] Actions by Aboriginal gatherers which inadvertently helped or promoted the developments of new plant growth have been described as a form of 'incipient' or 'proto agriculture'.[42]

Aboriginal gathering practices that targeted insects that infest plants may have been beneficial to the health of the whole vegetation.[43] Aboriginal foraging of grubs found in tree trunks and roots would have kept their numbers down. The grub-like larvae of insect woodborers are known in Australian English as 'witchetty grubs', probably derived from words, *wityu* (grub hook) and *varti* (grub), from the Adnyamathanha language of the Flinders Ranges in South Australia.[44] Basedow claimed that the witchetty grub is 'regarded as a very tasty dish. The flavour of the cooked witchedy [witchetty] is like that of scrambled egg, slightly sweetened'.[45] It has been observed in parts of the desert that, since Aboriginal gathering practices have ceased, the ravages of root grubs upon the vegetation have gone on unchecked.[46] Similarly, Aboriginal harvesting of plant galls and sugar lerps probably controlled the abundance of the insects involved.

Aboriginal cooking activities, when concentrated at the same site for decades, have created landscape features known as middens.[47] Depending on the area and the food sources utilised, many of these are made up of ash, bone, shell and decaying

The yam-daisy produces numerous finger-like tubers. It was widespread across southeastern Australia prior to the introduction of European livestock and the 'improvement' of pastures. *(Philip A. Clarke, Bridgewater, Mount Lofty Ranges, South Australia, 1984.)*

plant material. While passing through the Lower Murray of South Australia in 1844, George French Angas found the fibrous parts of bulrush roots, in the shape of pellets, discarded in heaps surrounding Aboriginal campsites.[48] Bulrush roots were steamed between heated stones beneath ovens or in cooking fires resembling kilns, and were often eaten with mussels.[49] Over time, large middens became key places for campsites in areas subject to flooding. For the Riverine district of western New South Wales, colonist Peter Beveridge noted 'As a general rule the aborigines do not erect their *loondthals* (huts) on these cooking mounds; an exception to this exists, however, on the extensive reedy plains of the lower rivers, which are annually inundated, remaining so for at least five months in the year.'[50]

The middens at favoured camps, over time, became topographical features that European settlers recognised as having been made by Aboriginal people. In northern parts of the Adelaide Plains it was reported in a local newspaper in 1908 that:

> evidence of the fact that the natives used to congregate there has been found on many occasions by the turning over of small hillocks on the slopes near the creek,

which have been built up by generations in the process of baking the game and fish on which the blacks used to live. The remains of numerous Aboriginal ovens have been unearthed, and the soil, which was little else but decomposed vegetable matter and ashes, has been spread over many of the gardens as manure. One of the last of these mounds has only recently been reduced to the level of the surrounding land on Douglas Park, the farm of Mr W. J. McNicol, and the material carted away consisted of ashes and rotten vegetable substances, which had been piled up little by little probably for a century.[51]

In the same region in 1926, it was reported in the newspaper that human skeletons were often found buried in the middens: 'Mr Brooks added that many scientific men had visited the district to inspect these relics of former days, and their opinion, he believed, was that the mounds served as tribal ovens until a death occurred in the tribe, when the body was buried and a fresh site found for the camp kitchen.'[52] Whether or not ancient human remains were found, European settlers used the rich earth taken from midden mounds to improve the soil in their gardens. Shell from middens could also be burnt to make lime for painting houses.

The shell mounds of coastal Cape York Peninsula were the product of the build up of Aboriginal cooking fire remains at major seasonal campsites.[53] As middens, these places have the nutrients and drainage conditions to favour the growth of tropical vine forests. Aboriginal actions when harvesting plants would have helped disperse seeds, so it is not surprising that plant resources growing on the shell mounds tend to be Aboriginal foods, medicines and the raw materials used in artefact making and for the construction of shelters.

It was noted in the late nineteenth century at Swan Hill in northern Victoria that large bushes of dillon (nitre-bush) often grew around Aboriginal camps, possibly due to their seeds having been thrown away or by having passed through the consumer.[54] Aboriginal foragers ate the dillon fruit, which look like European grapes and tastes salty, raw — stone included.[55] For the Nawu Banggarla people at Port Lincoln in South Australia, it was a highly desirable food source when in season.[56] Here, Dresden seedsman J.F. Carl Wilhelmi stated that 'In December and January the bushes are so

Yalka (yelka or onion-grass) corms were a reliable source of food over much of Central Australia. Aboriginal 'increase' ceremonies were aimed at assuring their abundance. *(Philip A. Clarke, Seven Mile Creek, northeast of Lake Eyre, Central Australia, 1987.)*

The yalka corms, which have a nutty taste and texture, are either eaten raw or slightly roasted, by shaking them in a wooden vessel with a few live embers. *(Philip A. Clarke, Seven Mile Creek, northeast of Lake Eyre, Central Australia, 1987.)*

Aboriginal people ate the stoned fruit of the dillon (or nitre-bush) whole. The bushes were often found growing around swamps and Aboriginal campsites. *(Philip A. Clarke, Narrung Peninsula, South Australia, 1988.)*

Wangkangurru woman Linda Crombie digging yalka from the edge of a creek bed. The corms are found by tracing the dead stalks into the sand. *(Philip A. Clarke, Seven Mile Creek, northeast of Lake Eyre, Central Australia, 1987.)*

full of fruit that the natives lie down on their backs under them, strip off the fruit with both hands, and do not rise until the whole bush has been cleared of it's [sic] load'.[57] The dillon bushes prefer growing in disturbed situations, as demonstrated more recently by this plant spreading along stock routes in overgrazed areas of the southern arid zone.[58] This plant therefore has an association with humans. It is also likely that Aboriginal foragers dispersed edible species of solanums, such as the desert raisin, across the land.[59] Aboriginal hunter-gatherers have helped spread plant species around, by creating suitable environments and simply by discarding the parts they have used.

Pathways

Aboriginal cultural landscapes were criss-crossed with pathways.[60] European explorers found indigenous tracks in places were they appeared to connect camping places with major hunting and gathering resource areas. Some paths led to frequently used plant foods. At Goulburn Island off the coast of Arnhem Land, Cunningham recorded on 28 March 1818 that 'Tracing a beaten path made by the natives, I observed the roots of *Tacca pinnatifida* [Polynesian arrowroot], a plant abundant in low shaded situations had been taken up in quantities, which tempted me to conclude they are eaten by these Australians'.[61] The discovery of pathways by early European explorers gave them clues to how hunters and gatherers used the land.

During the overland expedition (1844-45), from Derby in Queensland to Port Essington in the Northern Territory, Ludwig Leichhardt frequently came across Aboriginal 'foot-paths' which led to river and swamp crossings, and linked together places associated with activities such as water collecting, camping, fishing, hunting emus and gathering roots, gum and fruits.[62] He was travelling up the Burdekin River in northern Queensland when:

> Among the patches of brush which are particularly found at the junction of the larger creeks with the river, we observed a large fig-tree [cluster fig?], from fifty to sixty feet [15 to 18 m] high, with a rich shady foliage; and covered with bunches of fruit. The figs were of the size of a small apple, of an agreeable flavour when ripe, but were full of small flies and ants. These trees were numerous,

and their situation was readily detected by the paths of the natives leading to them: a proof that the fruit forms one of their favourite articles of food.[63]

These trees would also have been good hunting spots for birds, such as pigeons. Such places would also have provided shade, shelter from rain, fibre for string, as well as being good campsites with water close to the surface.

Aboriginal tracks were actively maintained, with travellers regularly adding stones and branches to a cairn marking a path.[64] In 1839, north of Perth in Western Australia, Grey found distinct pathways connecting swamps where bulrush roots were obtained.[65] After seeing 'native villages' nearby with permanent-looking huts plastered with clay and covered with turf clods, he concluded that 'these superior huts, well marked roads, deeply sunk wells and extensive warran grounds, all spoke of a large and comparatively speaking resident population'.[66] Grey's description does not fit well with later European views of passive 'primitive' Australian hunter-gatherers and their supposed random movements across the country.

During their movement across the land, Aboriginal bands frequently burnt areas crossed by their pathways.[67] During his searches for Tasmanian Aboriginal people between 1830 and 1834, Robinson frequently took advantage of travelling along Aboriginal 'roads' through the dense forest, which had been maintained with the help of fire.[68] For Europeans, the direction of pathways indicated the type of hunting and gathering favoured by Aboriginal inhabitants. South Australian Museum researchers Herbert M. Hale and Norman B. Tindale found during their expedition in 1927 to Princess Charlotte Bay in northern Queensland that the Mutumui people were specialists in coastal technology, only occasionally visiting the inland sandstone country to gather honey and to hunt possums and rock wallabies. It was noted that their 'native tracks or pads extend everywhere along the coast, turning inland only when necessary to avoid rocky cliffs. ... Their water supplies are obtained chiefly in little soaks along the beaches'.[69]

In Aboriginal tradition, the Dreaming Ancestors left signs of their tracks across the land in the form of such topographic features as creeks, hills, boulders and pockets of vegetation. Aboriginal people considered that, through the Creation, the actions of the Ancestors also influenced the direction of human pathways. There are traditions that certain places must be generally avoided and skirted around. At various times during my Western Desert fieldwork I have accompanied senior Aboriginal custodians on visits to sacred sites. At such places they have guided me along ritualised approaches, which determine the direction of access to sites. The tracks of people and their Ancestors ultimately converge. Tasmanian Aboriginal people perceived that their established foot tracks continued into the Skyworld, where there was 'white streak' in the Milky Way going 'all along down to the sea'.[70]

The indigenous system of pathways was a key component of the land that Europeans absorbed when settling Australia. Since many of the tracks connected major topographical features, such as mountain passes and water sources, they provided colonists with a framework for their own intended land uses. Many Aboriginal pathways were taken over by Europeans, eventually to be made into roads that are today part of the national highway system.[71]

Explorers Observing Fires

Across Australia, the first European settlements tended to occur in country that had been opened up and maintained by Aboriginal fire-makers.[72] The intense fire regimes in these areas suggested to the colonists that there were more hunter-gatherers living there, possibly because of reliable water supplies. The regular firing of the landscape therefore reflected better qualities in the landscape.

Aboriginal tracks connected camping sites with places where food and water were often obtained. The palm leaf container is being used to carry a baby. *(Norman B. Tindale, Princess Charlotte Bay, northern Queensland, 1927. South Australian Museum Archives.)*

Spinifex grass fire under a ghost gum. Fires could occur at most times of the seasonal cycle in desert country dominated by spinifex grass. *(Norman B. Tindale, Officer Creek, Musgrave Ranges, Central Australia, 1957. South Australian Museum Archives.)*

In order to imagine the pre-European Australian landscape, as it was when Aboriginal custodians solely managed the environment, we must largely restrict ourselves to historical accounts from early explorers.

In 1642, Abel Tasman considered that the clouds of dense smoke his party saw in Van Diemen's Land (Tasmania) were from the fires of the 'giants' they believed occupied the island.[73] Similarly, British explorer James Cook stated while in Australian waters on his 1768–71 trip that he 'saw upon all the Adjacent Lands and Islands a great number of smokes — a certain sign that they are inhabited — and we have daily seen smokes on every part of the Coast we have lately been upon'.[74] These 'smokes' would not have been produced by small campfires, but were the product of deliberately lit bushfires. The first wave of European explorers rarely got close enough to observe directly the people who created the fires. Therefore, it is unlikely that this frequent burning was simply an indigenous reaction to the trespass of strangers.

The early European perception of the link between the Aboriginal inhabitants and fire was strong. In March 1802, circumnavigator Matthew Flinders was able to deduce that Kangaroo Island in South Australia was uninhabited, because of the thick impenetrable forest growing there and the lack of evidence for regular burning.[75] To Flinders, this contrasted with the open park-like vegetation he found on the Fleurieu Peninsula, eight kilometres away. Flinders reasoned that he had located the mainland when 'The fires [of people] bespoke this to be part of the continent'.[76] Before landing on uncharted coasts, mariners looked for smoke indicating human occupation.

European explorers and the first settlers understood that Aboriginal people started many fires intentionally, with predetermined outcomes. The early botanical collector and explorer

George Caley recognised that Aboriginal hunters frequently used fire to assist them. In a letter to Banks in 1802, Caley described the marsupials he encountered. One was the 'betony' (bettong) and he noted, 'It does not dwell in rocky ground but in (almost) impenetrable thickets and is only caught by the natives when they set these places on fire'.[77] In February 1804, Caley had first hand experience on the use of fire for hunting in inland New South Wales. There he came across an Aboriginal 'walbunga' or kangaroo drive in progress. It was a case of hunters 'catching kangaroos by setting the place on fire and by placing themselves in the direction the animal is forced to pass and by throwing spears at it as it passes along'.[78]

The explorer and navigator Phillip Parker King recorded the use of fire for catching large numbers of marsupials at a single event in December 1817. When his expedition sailed past Cape Howe (Howe Hill) in eastern Victoria, they 'observed large fires burning on the hills, made by the natives for the dual purposes of burning off the dry grass and of hunting the kangaroos, which are thus forced to fly from the woods, and thereby fall an easy prey to their pursuers'.[79] Such observations suggest that Aboriginal hunters were able to predict and control the course of the fires they started.

The records of plant collector Allan Cunningham indicate that Aboriginal people were responsible for the creation of at least some forms of vegetation. While passing through the Lachlan River area of New South Wales on 4 August 1817 as part of John Oxley's inland expedition he noted:

> Some patches of land that had been formerly fired by the natives producing some good tufts of grass induced us to turn out of our course in the scrub and halt upon it. This [surrounding] scrub continues for some miles with all the sterility imaginable, hence we are extremely fortunate in having an opportunity of turning out of it to a spot where our horses would find good grass, and where we found some water in two native wells.[80]

Local Aboriginal groups were often invisible to European explorers and the first settlers, although on some occasions the signs of old fires provided indirect evidence of indigenous seasonal use of the region. In 1828, Cunningham noted in the Bremer River district near Brisbane that 'No natives were met with in this stage, although patches of the forest grasses had been very lately fired and the recent traces of these people were noticed on the trunks of the trees, from which they had torn off the outer paper-like bark to roof their huts'.[81]

The first-hand observations of the explorers give us some indication of the frequency of burning in Australian landscapes caused by Aboriginal land use practices. Early records confirm a pattern of high fire use, to the extent that explorers could use it to monitor Aboriginal movements in the district. During John Oxley's expedition into the interior of New South Wales, Cunningham noted at Peel Range on 5 June 1817 that 'The country at the verge of the horizon southerly is in flames, being fired by the natives'.[82] Again, on 3 May 1818, when in Van Diemen Gulf of northern Australia as a part of Phillip Parker King's expedition, he noted that 'The western horizon was much gloomed by extensive bodies of thick smoke of natives, who appear to be burning off the bush and grass of the country in that direction'.[83] Fires were also noticeable on 8 May 1818, when the expedition party had travelled further east to the coast of the Kakadu region. Here, Cunningham noted, 'The fires of the natives continue to be numerous in various directions; these conflagrations extend over immense tracts of flat country, at intervals bursting into large flames as the wind rises, and continuing until a heavy shower extinguishes them'.[84]

It appeared that all Australian Aboriginal groups set fire to their country, regardless of the climate. In August 1872, the inland explorer Ernest Giles was travelling along a tributary of the Finke River in the Central Australian deserts when he 'saw great volumes of smoke from burning grass and triodia [spinifex] rising in all directions. The natives find it easier to catch game when the ground is bare, or covered only with a short vegetation, than when it is clothed with thick coarse grasses or pungent shrubs'.[85] In October 1872, when his expedition was near the Ehrenberg Ranges, he claimed, 'the natives were about, burning, burning, ever burning; one would think they were of the fabled salamander race, and lived on fire instead of water. The fires were starting up here and there around us in fresh and narrowing circles.'[86] Similarly, in March 1889, William H. Tietkens, who had accompanied Giles on several of his expeditions, was exploring west of Alice Springs and remarked 'the country had been burnt for a considerable distance by the blacks.'[87]

Giles claimed that the desert dwellers were deliberately burning their hunting and gathering estates. According to him:

> The few natives inhabitants of these [desert] regions occasionally burn every portion of their territories, and on a favourably windy day a spinifex fire might run on for scores of miles. We occasionally cross such desolated spaces, where every species of vegetation has been by flames devoured. Devoured they are, but not demolished, as out of the roots and ashes of their former natures, phoenix-like, they rise again.[88]

With these remarks comes an acknowledgment that Australian landscapes were adapted to fire. In spite of the explorers observing Aboriginal uses of fire, the settlers did not take up their vegetation firing practices. As each wave of European settlement reached regional Australia, the indigenous fire regime generally ended fairly abruptly, triggering relatively quick changes in the vegetation. Archaeologist Rhys Jones provided an example from European colonist Louise Meredith who, when writing in Tasmania during the 1840s, was able to contrast the 'open parkland' of decades before with the thick bush that had developed

since, and which fostered the outbreak of terrible fires.[89] The Europeans coming to Australia had different ways of living on the land, which did not include deliberately and constantly firing parts of the vegetation. At a time when burning property, such as haystacks and barns, was a hanging offence in England, the settlers tried to suppress the fire regime in Australia whenever possible.

Over the millennia, the ancestors of contemporary Aboriginal people shaped the Australian landscape, using such simple looking tools as digging-sticks, stone axes and fire-sticks. Many of their marks upon the landscape, such as chopped trees and holes dug for yams, were ephemeral. However, the early European observations demonstrate that the totality of hunting and gathering activities had long-lasting impacts upon the environment. In particular, Aboriginal firing practices altered the structure of the Australian vegetation. When Europeans arrived, they found much of the land was relatively open, with pathways connecting major topographical features. Without the Aboriginal management of the environment over the previous tens of thousands of years, the European settlers would have found a continent with far less country that was already suitable for agriculture. The Aboriginal creators of the Australian landscape had left their mark.

Chapter 4

A Seasonal Life

Nowhere in pre-European Australia were there any truly sedentary Aboriginal people living. The constantly moving lifestyle of hunter-gatherers had considerable advantages over more sedentary ways of living on a drought-prone continent with marked seasonal weather. The uncertainty of Australian weather patterns, which are influenced by the El Niño Southern Oscillation (ENSO), did

Canoe made from river red gum bark and pushed along with a punting pole. Watercraft was essential for travelling through the backwaters of the river system during flood time. *(Daniel H. Cudmore, Avoca Station, Darling River, New South Wales, 1904. South Australian Museum Archives.)*

Wild cherry fruits were highly valued foods during the summer months, when Aboriginal people camped near the coast. In Aboriginal English, the fruits were also known as 'dolls-eyes'. *(Philip A. Clarke, Kingston, southeastern South Australia, 1987.)*

not favour foragers staying in one place for long. Aboriginal hunter-gatherers developed ways of living that coped with the seasonal variations of their plant and animal foods. Historian Geoffrey Blainey referred to the reasoning behind the nomadic Australian existence as 'the logic of unending travel'.[1]

Land and Climate

A broad sweep from south to north across the Australian continent passes through temperate, desert and tropical climate zones. Although the division of Australia into just three zones does not do justice to the immense cultural and environmental diversity found within, it does serve the purpose of looking at the distinctive features of Aboriginal relationships with plants across Australia.

Temperate South

Since the arrival in Australia of the ancestors of modern Aboriginal people, some 50,000 years ago, the temperate zone has expanded and contracted due to changes in world climate.[2] From the beginning of the geological period known as the Pleistocene, about two million years ago, 'ice ages' have come and gone. During the 'interglacials', which were brief warm and wet periods of several thousand years duration, the forested areas in southern Australia were extensive.[3] In contrast, at the last glacial maximum, around 18,000 years ago, Australia was quite arid. With the expansion of the deserts, the temperate zone was pushed further south. Due to low sea levels, it extended to the edge of the southern continental shelf, covering coastal lands now largely under the sea. From about 10,000 years ago, the commencement of the Holocene period has led to generally higher temperatures and a rise in sea levels, which eventually separated Tasmania from mainland Victoria and northern Australia from New Guinea.[4] The current Australian coastlines were established by around 7000 years ago.

Today, the temperate zone covers both the southwestern and southeastern parts of the continent, including Tasmania. It is dominated by numerous mountain ranges, such as Stirling Range in the southwest of Western Australia, the Mount Lofty Ranges in South Australia, the Grampians in western Victoria. The southeastern seaboard, commencing in eastern Victoria and extending north through New South Wales and Queensland, is comparatively humid due to the presence of the Great Dividing Range. Tasmania is a mountainous island, with central inland plains. The vegetation of the temperate zone is variable — ranging from closed forest, open woodland and low growing mallee, to wetland vegetation and coastal scrub.[5]

Due to a present rainfall in excess of 300 millimetres per year, the temperate zone has many watercourses and lakes. To the west of

Winter shelters in southern Australia were often substantial structures, made from wood, earth and foliage. *(George French Angas, watercolour, Portland, western Victoria, 1844. South Australian Museum Archives.)*

the Great Dividing Ranges, the Murray–Darling River system drains 910,000 square kilometres and at this size is comparable with the Danube of Europe and the Indus of the Pakistan, although it pushes far less water into the sea. In the south, the Australian and Tasmanian coastlines front onto the Southern Ocean, where the anticyclonic weather belt generates rainfall during the colder months. The temperate rainfall calendar varies from mostly winter rains around the capital cities of Perth and Adelaide, to more uniform rain throughout the year around Hobart, Melbourne, Canberra and Sydney, to the mainly summer rains at Brisbane.[6] Temperate Australian summers are noted for the hot dry winds that blow in from the interior, which have in recent decades caused devastating bushfires.

With reliable water supplies, Aboriginal population levels in the south were very high in comparison to arid parts of Australia. In favoured areas, hunter-gatherers were able to live within relatively small territories, where they developed distinctive cultures and invested much labour on maintaining resources such as fish traps and weirs.[7]

Central Deserts

On world scale, Australia is a dry continent, with 80% of the land having a rainfall less than 600 millimetres per year and 50%, the arid zone, having less than 300 millimetres. The extent of Australia's inland deserts has varied considerably since the first Aboriginal ancestors arrived. During the Pleistocene 'interglacials' the arid zone was confined to the centre of the continent.[8] For the last few thousand years, until the present, Australia has been in an arid phase. Today, the Western and Central Deserts combine to cover

Dry season camp, with shelters made from loose slabs of paperbark placed over a wooden frame, with the occupants sleeping on the ground. *(W. Holtze, Daly Waters, Northern Territory, about 1910. South Australian Museum Archives.)*

Wik woman gathering edible water lily flower stems and bulbs. The hollow stems could also be used as straws to suck the cool water from the bottom of lagoons. *(Ursula H. McConnel, Archer River, northwestern Cape York Peninsula, northern Queensland, 1930s. South Australian Museum Archives.)*

two thirds of the Australian continent. In Western Australia the vast desert region spills over into the Indian Ocean, but is elsewhere largely contained by coastal belts of higher rainfall and forest.

The arid zone in Central Australia is divided into low lying areas by a number of east–west running mountain ridges, such as the Warburton, Musgrave and the Macdonnell Ranges.[9] The Lake Eyre Basin on the southern side has no outlet to the sea and is a land surface mostly below sea level. The watercourses in Central Australia flow mainly from the northern side of the ranges, passing through deep gorges and finally disappearing into sandy flats on the southern side. For most of the time, the permanent surface water in Central Australia is confined to isolated waterholes, with the downstream parts of desert creeks flowing only after infrequent heavy rainfalls. In the southern lowland areas, springs and soaks are the main water sources.

Because of the impact of the El Niño Southern Oscillation upon Australia's climate, rainfall in the arid zone is particularly uncertain.[10] Aboriginal hunter-gatherers living here were highly nomadic, with some desert groups ranging over considerable areas. The rains that penetrate into the desert from the coasts can come from either the northern summer

Wik woman gathering edible water lily bulbs, which were a reliable food source when other types were scarce. To preserve them, the bulbs were sun-dried, coated with ochre and stored on paperbark sheets in a dry place. *(Ursula H. McConnel, Archer River, northwestern Cape York Peninsula, northern Queensland, 1930s. South Australian Museum Archives.)*

monsoon or the southern winter anticyclonic storms. The arid zone often has little or no rain for years, and then extensive flooding when the drought cycle breaks. The desert flora is diverse and forms desert woodlands, shrublands, savannah, hummock grasslands and succulent steppe.[11]

Moreton Bay fig. Australian fig species are found in their greatest variety in the northern rainforests. Aboriginal toolmakers collected string fibre from the bark of many fig tree species. *(Philip A. Clarke, southeastern Queensland, 2004.)*

Desert cassia (limestone senna) leaves are used for making a medicinal wash, while the flowers from the bush are employed as ceremonial decorations. *(Philip A. Clarke, Flinders Ranges, South Australia, 1983.)*

Tropical North

Northern Australia, situated above the Tropic of Capricorn, has a climate under the influence of the northwest monsoons. There were several long periods since the human occupation of Australia began some 50,000 years ago when the island of New Guinea was connected to northern Australia, creating a much larger landmass.[12] At these times of lower sea levels, the Asian landmass was also much larger. The land now submerged under the Arafura Sea probably had a monsoonal climate similar to eastern Indonesia today. The present northern Australian coastline and associated estuarine environments are about 7000 years old.

The Australian tropics are immensely varied geographically. Starting in the west, the Kimberley is a large mountainous area adjacent to the sea and provides a rainfall barrier to the inland deserts to the south. East of the Kimberley is the Top End of Australia, with two prominent features being the Kakadu floodplains and the Arnhem Land escarpment. Further east is the Gulf of Carpentaria, which separates Arnhem Land from Cape York Peninsula. While the western side of the Cape has a climate similar to that of Arnhem Land, the eastern side has a weather pattern strongly influenced by the Pacific Ocean and the proximity of the Great Dividing Ranges. Off the northern coasts there are several major island groups that are large enough to support Aboriginal populations using ocean-going watercraft.

The tropical hunting and gathering areas are diverse, ranging from the sea, tidal inlets, mangroves, sandy shores, dune thickets and inland waters, to grasslands, shrublands, woodlands and pockets of dense rainforest.[13] In contrast to desert dwellers, who travel light, northern Aboriginal people had a relatively large set of tools, such as different types of clubs and spears, to help them hunt and gather the wide variety of animals and plants. Due to the high plant diversity, and to a smaller resident population of Europeans in comparison to the temperate zone in the south, a greater proportion of the flora used by Aboriginal hunters and gatherers presently has no common Australian English name.

Much of the tropical zone receives well in

Tropical shelters, made from foliage woven into a wooden frame, provided protection from insects and heavy rain. *(Archibald Meston, Mulgrave River, northern Queensland, 1905. South Australian Museum Archives.)*

excess of 600 millimetres of rainfall per year. As the monsoon moves in, the north experiences 'the wet', with the showers and thunderstorms generally lasting from October to April. Rainfall varies from year to year, with occasional tropical cyclones bringing abundant rainfall to coastal regions and sometimes further inland towards the deserts. After the monsoon season comes 'the dry', with more mild and drier conditions prevailing from about May to September. Its marked seasonality makes the Australian tropics distinctive from the tropical areas closer to the equator, such as the western Indonesian Archipelago and parts of Papua New Guinea, where the climate is more constant.

Population Densities

Coming from a cool temperate land, the British first chose southern Australia to settle, as this was a landscape with a climate most like that of England, albeit with a reversed calendar and many strange plants and animals. In the temperate south, settlers proceeded to transform Australia into something more like Europe by vegetation clearance, draining swamps, damming rivers and by the deliberate and accidental introduction of various exotic plants and animals. In arid and tropical Australia, intensive European settlement has been impeded by geographical factors, such as harsh seasons and remoteness from temperate Australia. Development therefore commenced later and at a slower pace in central and northern regions, driven by the need for transcontinental communication systems, and aided by pastoral and mining pursuits. British agriculture was unprepared for the dry country. As put by a nineteenth-century explorer, John Forrest, in the Australian arid zone, 'square miles represent less than acres to graziers and sheep farmers in England'.[14] European perceptions of the physical environment in Australia, based on agricultural potential and similarity to former homelands, differed greatly from early Aboriginal views.

From 1788, starting from Sydney, British settlers spread out across the Australian continent through the southern inland river systems and along the coasts. The impact of European colonisation upon Aboriginal people was immense. Due to the relatively early date of Aboriginal dispossession of their lands in the south, followed by rapid depopulation, the records for temperate hunting and gathering cultures are incomplete.[15] In areas of Australia where European settlement was intense, it resulted in a collapse of the Aboriginal population through conflict, disease and land alienation.[16] Shortly after the British settled in New South Wales, they introduced diseases, such as smallpox and influenza, which spread quickly beyond the frontier and caused many Aboriginal deaths.[17]

The numbers of hunter-gatherers living on the land when Europeans first arrived can only be guessed at. In the thousands of years of occupation prior to this, there would also have been major fluctuations in Aboriginal population levels, in response to climate changes and to technological and cultural developments.[18] Even without considering the population crash, resulting from British colonisation, the nature of dealing with a highly mobile people makes estimating their numbers and distribution extremely complicated. From historical and archaeological evidence we can surmise that, in contrast to the large inland deserts, the coastal and adjacent riverine areas would have had the greatest number and diversity of people living there, due to higher and more dependable rainfall.

Speculations of Aboriginal population density range from about a square kilometre per person in resource rich areas, such as in western Victoria and Arnhem Land, to over 30 square kilometres per person in parts of the Western Desert.[19] The population levels in the northern coastal areas were probably closely comparable to those of the most densely populated parts of the temperate south.[20] Due to the manner in which Europeans settled Australia, there will probably never be a widely accepted estimate of the indigenous population level and density for 1788, when British colonisation commenced.

Aboriginal Calendars

Culture shapes the ways people divide the year and how they relate to seasonal changes within the landscape. The British colonists, and their descendants, staunchly retained a European calendar, even though the seasons of summer, autumn, winter and spring are ill defined for much of Australia. In contrast, the annual cycles formerly recognised by Aboriginal hunters and gatherers varied widely across the continent, ranging between four and nine distinct seasons.[21]

Understanding the local calendar informed people of the sequences of available resources and their distribution. This situation is summed up by colonist Robert Brough Smyth, who claimed in 1878 that Aboriginal foraging bands, 'were always mindful of the seasons in selecting the localities in which to spend their time, taking into account not only the natural features of the ground, but the facilities for obtaining food'.[22] Similarly, linguist John Rudder more recently stated that for the Yolngu of northeast Arnhem Land, 'hunting and gathering was not a process of searching for what they could find, but rather of choosing to go to particular places at particular times, to gather at its best what was known to be there'.[23] This situation was not unique to Australia, but existed with hunter-gatherers in other parts of the world too.[24] The Aboriginal 'walkabout' had an underlying pattern.

For societies that do not possess systems for counting the days of the year, having calendars that are cued to short-term changes observed in the heavens and in the landscape makes good sense. In Aboriginal Australia, the movements of stars and animals, weather changes and the flowering of certain plants together indicate the onset of each season.[25] In Tasmania, Aboriginal Protector George A. Robinson claimed that:

The Aborigines have considerable knowledge of the signs of the weather ... Indeed they have numerous signs by which they judge and I have seldom found them to err. Thus they are enabled to know when to build their huts, to go to the coast for fish, travel &c. They also judge by the stars and have names by which they distinguish them.[26]

For hunter-gatherers, certain plants were like a 'bush calendar', being crucial for keeping track of where they were in the seasonal cycle. Robinson stated that, 'The natives calculate the times of the seasons by various methods. Hence I enquired of the TYREELLORE woman when the time was for the mutton birds to come in and they shewed me the lightwood tree that was near them and said that when that tree was in blossom the mutton birds would be in.'[27]

At Marion Bay on Yorke Peninsula in South Australia, the prolific flowering of 'tea-trees' was a sign to the Narangga people that the mullet fish were soon to come in large numbers.[28] Here, it was claimed that initiation ceremonies were held at this time to take advantage of a seasonally abundant food source, required to support a large number of visitors. Little is known about Aboriginal calendars from the temperate zone, although it is claimed that the Riverina people in western New South Wales recognised four seasons, while the Nyungar people in the southwest of Western Australia had six.[29]

Aboriginal calendars in the deserts are more generalised than elsewhere, due to uncertain rainfall.[30] The northwest monsoonal rains begin to reach the Centre in December, there being a lag of several weeks from the northern coastal seasons as the winds change to the south.[31] The clouds are largely emptied of water by the time they reach inland Australia, producing irregular rainfall, both in quantity and distribution. Desert people recognise from three to five main variable seasons of the year.[32] They were always scanning the horizon looking for clouds, and travelled large distances to take advantage of areas that had, by chance, received reasonable rainfalls.[33] During the worst droughts, it was imperative that they knew which of the rockholes, wells and soakages were still likely to contain some water when all the other sources had failed and which of the neighbours'

land still might have some food and water. It was Aboriginal tradition that certain individuals were 'rain-makers', having the ritual power to alter the weather and bring rains to their country.[34]

In spite of an uncertain climate, desert plants still have optimum periods of use, depending on the recent rainfall and fire history. When the leaves of the roly-poly, which is a prickly annual that forms a rounded bush, turn yellow it is a sign that the edible small white cossid moth grub living inside the top ends of the root is ready for gathering.[35] Similarly, when the leaves of the desert poplar become yellow, Aboriginal foragers would push these small trees over to expose roots where beetle larvae can be collected for eating.[36]

Most of what we know about Australian Aboriginal calendars comes from studies of communities in the tropics, where there is a monsoonal weather pattern.[37] The recorded seasonal calendars of northern people charter their movements and lifestyles. Depending on the region, from five to nine seasons were recognised, each of them associated with particular camping and foraging areas. In the Brisbane area of south-east Queensland, Aboriginal man Willie Mac-Kenzie explained that the flowering of waterlilies signalled that river mussels were at their best for eating, while the ripening of the wild passionfruit meant that carpet snakes were fat and therefore able to be hunted.[38] Similarly, the Kuku Yalanji people of Mossman Gorge in northern Queensland know that when the black bean is ready for eating, it is time to catch jungle fowls.[39]

To the Lardil people of Mornington Island in the Gulf of Carpentaria, the screw palm was a calendar tree.[40] When the nuts ripen red and fall, this is a sign that the *dulnhu* fish will soon appear. For Aboriginal people of Dampierland in northern Western Australia, the screw palm is also a seasonal indicator, with the ripening of the fruits heralding the arrival of the 'straight down' rains and 'cold time'.[41] In northeast Arnhem Land, the flowering of the monkey-bush in the forests indicates that it is time to collect tern eggs, which are laid on offshore islands.[42] This plant has yellow flowers that look like an ornamental hibiscus,

Anangu Pitjantjatjara plant foods collected by Dr Charles Duguid, who instigated the establishment of the Ernabella Mission at Pukatja in 1937. *(Charles Duguid ethnographic collection, Musgrave Ranges, Central Australia, 1930s. South Australian Museum Aboriginal Artefact Collection.)*

In the summer months, eucalypt leaves are the source of sweet white cases produced by lerp insects. As a source of sugar, these can be removed by pulling the leaves through the teeth. *(Philip A. Clarke, Adelaide Plains, South Australia, 1986.)*

being similar in shape and colour to egg yolk. Plant changes helped hunter-gatherers position themselves in the landscape to take maximum advantage of seasonal resources.

Water-ribbons (centre) and bulrushes (rear right) are reliable sources of edible tubers, particularly important when other more favoured foods are seasonally scarce. *(Philip A. Clarke, Lake Condah, western Victoria, 1988.)*

Mobility

Aboriginal people moved across the landscape in accordance with their reading of the seasonal changes occurring in their country. Aboriginal campsites tended to be in places where there was protection from weather and insect attacks. Most had access to water and food supplies, an abundance of firewood, and were more easily defended from surprise raids by marauders.[43] Camps could not be situated too close to favoured hunting places and water sources or game might be driven off making the hunt more difficult. By regularly moving their camps throughout their foraging territory, Aboriginal foragers maximised their opportunities and avoided having to increase their labour when relying on declining food sources. In general, they would stay longer within an area if there were a large amount and variety of food available.[44]

As dictated by their mobile lifestyle, Aboriginal eating arrangements were flexible. Medical officer and Protector of Aborigines Walter E. Roth stated: 'Food may be prepared, cooked, and eaten wherever it is caught out in the open, though it is usually brought back to camp where, about sundown, the main meal is eaten'.[45] In central Arnhem Land, archaeologist Betty Meehan described 'dinnertime camps' (*rrauwa djigudaridja* in Gidjingarli language) as 'small camp sites used during the middle of the day while people are engaged in hunting trips away from their home base. At these sites they cook and eat food that has been procured up to that time'.[46] In Aboriginal Australia, men and women generally foraged separately.[47]

In the temperate zone, with its relatively high rainfall, hunter-gatherers had seasonal population movements to avoid inclement weather and local food shortages. In eastern New South Wales, Aboriginal groups appeared to have made their summer camps near the ocean, then moved inland during the colder months.[48] The Kaurna people of the Adelaide region in South Australia spent summer in the vicinity of the coastal dunes, moved inland across the plains in autumn when Parna the Autumn Star appears, then spent winter in the more densely wooded foothills of the Mount Lofty Ranges.[49] Tangani people in the Coorong area of South Australia lived near the ocean in summer, where they fished, gathered fruit and collected shellfish.[50] At the onset of winter, they moved inland to build more substantial shelters in camps along the mainland side of the Coorong Lagoon, where they had plenty of firewood and were less exposed to weather. There were similar movement patterns recorded for the coastal regions of Tasmania, Victoria and the southwest of Western Australia.[51]

Aboriginal bands in the temperate zone generally travelled more during the summer months than in winter.[52] Adelaide missionary Christian G. Teichelmann stated that when the Kaurna people were on the move, 'The women and children generally arrive first at the place intended for an encampment, which is always a spot where they have been living the past year; here they fetch branches, fuel and water, and build a hut'.[53] Actual campsites were changed frequently, even when the distance between them was relatively small. It was reported that Aboriginal Tasmanians rarely camped at exactly the same place for two nights running.[54]

In Central Australia, desert dwellers ventured away from permanent sources of water whenever the irregular precipitation allowed them to.[55] In the Macdonnell Ranges of Central Australia,

Desert people had several distinct forms of shelter, which were built according to the season. This example has windbreak extensions to deflect cold winds. *(Charles Duguid, Pukatja, Central Australia, 1960s. South Australian Museum Archives.)*

missionary Carl Strehlow described the 'wanderlust' of the local Arrernte people to visit distant relatives, which came about after a season of good rains had made travelling in large numbers much easier.[56] The Pitjantjatjara of the Musgrave Ranges referred to times immediately after heavy showers had fallen over much of the desert as 'anywhere is a camp'.[57] As stated by patrol officer Gordon Sweeney, for the Warlpiri living in the Tanami Desert, 'native foods can only be harvested where native water supplies will allow the native to "work" the area'.[58] These desert dwellers came together in large groups during favourable seasons, particularly in autumn and early winter.[59]

The size and composition of Aboriginal camping groups varied seasonally, according to the capacity of the land to support people. This oscillation in numbers was markedly apparent in the arid zone. As the seasons became harsher, Aboriginal people dispersed into smaller groups, often comprised only of a man, his wives, their children, and perhaps some aged relatives. By adjusting the size of their foraging groups and frequently moving camp, Aboriginal people minimised their impact upon the local environment and conserved resources. Their movements also avoided the build up of camp refuse. Cleland stated that desert people were constantly moving in a circuit around their hunting and gathering territories, although 'Deviations may occur from a more or less regular routine when conditions, such as thunderstorms, produce a crop of yams in one place or some particular food is expected to be available in another'.[60]

Even in the deserts, with their uncertain rainfall, camping took place according to predictable patterns. Horne and Aiston described the best location for campsites in the Lake Eyre region of Central Australia:

> Of course the proximity to water is always a requisite and usually it is a soak, which has been sunk under the dream-conveyed advice of a moora [Mura-mura — Dreaming Ancestor]. On the whole the camps are surprisingly clean, except for the dogs. When it gets too bad, their idea of sanitation is certainly primitive — simply to move. Everything not in immediate use is left. *Nardoo* and *munyeroo* stones [plant food grindstones] lie just where they were, *kirra* [boomerang] and *murrawirrie* [fighting

stave] are thrown on the top of the *poonga* [hut]. If the owners leave them, no one else will ever interfere. Their cupboards consist of scratched holes in the sand.[61]

Heavier items were usually left behind when Aboriginal people changed camps. On the move, Western Desert men would generally carry one or two spears and a spearthrower, while the women took with them some wooden bowls and a digging-stick.[62]

An incentive for desert dwellers to visit distant places with less certain water supplies was the opportunity to forage for foods that were out of their range when conditions became drier. Moving away from the main waterholes for a while allowed the food sources in the surrounding areas to recover. During severe droughts, most Aboriginal movements within a large region tended to converge on the most reliable waters. At such times, the lack of food became severe, with people having to rely on 'hard time' sources. The perpetual fear that desert dwellers had of an impending drought and of extreme food shortages were a driving force for them to move into European settlements being established in the Outback from the late nineteenth century.[63]

As with the Bedouin of Northern Africa,[64] the demographic, political and cultural features of the Australian desert dwellers enabled them to live in harsh arid environments. The 'Spinifex people', who live in the southern deserts from Kalgoorlie in Western Australia to Yalata in South Australia, form a highly mobile group with far reaching social and cultural links.[65] The Western Desert kinship system tends to be inclusive, in contrast to that of Aboriginal peoples based in more fertile areas, who actively defend their territories. The long and interlocking Dreaming tracks of the Western and Central Deserts form an extensive web of connections that can be utilised in times of need. Spinifex is a large tussocky grass and a major plant feature of the arid zone. Sweeney claimed that, 'The tribal groups who held the spinifex desert areas had to hold larger areas and hunt in smaller numbers than the natives in the mulga and creek areas'.[66] In making a living in an uncertain landscape, desert dwelling foraging bands were forced to travel hundreds of kilometres through the course of their seasonal cycle, in contrast to coastal people who moved far less.

In the tropical coastal regions, Aboriginal people generally moved between camps at distinct 'dry season' and 'wet season' locations. The modes of living at each place could be dramatically different. In the north, biologist/anthropologist Donald Thomson remarked:

> Within the bounds even of a single clan territory a people may spend several months of the year as nomadic hunters, in pursuit of bush game, wild honey and small mammals, and exploiting the resources of vegetable foods of which a great number are known. A few months later the same people may be found established on the sea coast in camps that have all the appearance of permanence or at least semi-permanence, having apparently abandoned their nomadic habits.[67]

By constantly moving according to their reading of seasonal indicators, Aboriginal foragers in the tropics maximised the availability of their resources while minimising the labour required for making a living. As with other climate zones, vegetation around favoured camping sites was able to regenerate between periods of occupation.

European explorers noted that the type of Aboriginal shelter used in the far north varied considerably according to the season. On 14 July 1845, Ludwig Leichhardt's overland expedition, crossing from the eastern central coast of Australia to Port Essington, was in the southern Gulf of Carpentaria region when it came across a deserted camp. Here, Leichhardt:

> observed a hedge of dry branches, and, parallel to it, and probably to the leeward, was a row of fire places. It seemed that the natives sat and lay between the fires and the row of branches. There were, besides, three huts of the form of a bee-hive, closely thatched with straw and tea-tree bark. Their only opening was so small, that a man could scarcely creep through it; they were four or five feet [1.2 or 1.5 m] high, and from eight to ten feet [2.4 to 3 m] in diameter. One of the huts was storied, like those I noticed on the banks of the Lynd. It would appear that the natives make use of these tents during the wet and cold season, but encamp in the open air in fine weather.[68]

Aboriginal builders located and constructed their shelters in response to the seasons. Along the northern coastal regions, enclosed domed shelters were made to keep mosquitoes out and to shed rain.[69] As with people living in the temperate and desert regions, in the tropics people generally left behind the tools peculiar to each environmental zone when moving on. When the Warnindilyakwa changed camp on Groote Eylandt in the southern Gulf of Carpentaria, the mortar and pestle stones were buried at the old site, where they could be located during the next visit.[70]

In deciding when to move, Aboriginal hunter-gatherers were influenced by a number of factors: exploiting favoured seasonal resources; avoiding undue exposure to weather in extreme seasons; aiming to minimise the amount of exertion; surviving food and water shortages; and reducing their impact upon the landscape by not depleting resources and allowing them to be replenished. To meet their long-term requirements for survival, the resources they foraged needed to be present in certain configurations, as the lack of any key component would work against the presence of others. Aboriginal foragers moved with confidence across the landscape due to their possession of detailed knowledge of the variations in their plant and animal resources, according to habitat and season. In general, Aboriginal bands moved smaller distances through the course of the year in resource-rich temperate and tropical areas, than did those living in deserts.

Raft made from buoyant paperbark and screw palm stems. Such watercraft are made, as needed, when ferrying people and their gear across rivers swollen with monsoonal floodwaters. (*B.S. Coaldrake, Drysdale River, northern Western Australia, 1954. South Australian Museum*

Chapter 5

Fire-stick Ecology

Due to the nature of the continent's climate and topography, natural fires have had a major role with shaping plant and animal communities in Australia.[1] Since their ancestors arrived many thousands of years ago, Aboriginal hunter-gatherers have further burnt the vegetation — a process that sculpted the landscape. A close association has developed between Aboriginal people and fire. Historian Geoffrey Blainey remarked that, 'Fire dominated the life of the aboriginals to an even greater degree than the motor-engine dominates western nations today'.[2] Contemporary Aboriginal people recognise the importance of fire in their culture with their saying, 'fire-stick way', used when referring to their 'old' traditions — from a time when they lived as hunter-gatherers.[3]

Cultural Fires

To varying degrees, fire is important to all the peoples of the world. It was probably one of the first technologies developed by the antecedents of modern humans.[4] In Aboriginal Australia, fire was central to the hunting and gathering lifestyle and key to many social and cultural activities. Today, for many remote communities fire still plays a significant role in their culture. The fire hearth is not just a means for keeping warm and cooking food — it is symbolic of the Aboriginal family unit.[5]

Making Fire

Across Aboriginal Australia, fire was made by one of three main methods: by firesaw, fire drill or percussion.[6] Materials such as powdered sun-dried kangaroo dung, bark, northern sandalwood scrapings and dry grass were used as tinder and for this purpose often kept dry in fur wrappings and carried. Dried fungus was also widely used as tinder.[7] The 'kerosene-grasses' are considered to be good for starting fires.[8] In northern Australia there are a number of tree species, collectively called 'kerosene-woods', that could be used to start a fire even in the wet season.[9]

Firesaws are hand-sized slivers of hardwood that produce fire when vigorously sawn across a dry log as a base, which has a split in it packed with tinder. When there was a shortage of suitable wood, artefacts were sometimes used as base material. The fronts of Central Australian softwood shields made from beantree (grey corkwood) wood were often used with a firesaw.[10] There are many such shields in museum collections that bear the marks of fire making. Sometimes the edge of a spearthrower was employed as a firesaw. Fire drills were comprised of two sticks, with one of them held to the ground by the foot, while in a socket at the end of this stick another was vertically twirled.[11] Dried grasstree flower stems were also utilised in this manner. The use of percussion methods to make fire, by striking flint together with iron pyrites, or 'ironstone', was recorded for

Ngarrindjeri man using dried flower stems from the grasstree as a fire drill. The piles of green leaves served to protect the maker, as well as to guard the flame from wind. *(Unknown photographer, Lower Murray, South Australia, about 1900. South Australian Museum Archives.)*

southern Australia.[12]

In campfires, particularly during the night, Aboriginal people prefer slow burning types of dense wood that give out plenty of heat.[13] Fire can be started at most times of the year, although in

the past it was often easier to carry it from camp to camp, especially during cold and wet weather.[14] By lighting fires in the vegetation as they walked, the firebrands could be replenished. In the Top End of the Northern Territory, Aboriginal travellers used old flower cones of the swamp banksia for setting alight as firebrands.[15] When lit at one end, the cone takes as long as two hours to burn through to the other end. Southern Aboriginal travellers carried fire, between camping places, inside bracket fungus.[16] During particularly cold and wet seasons, when lighting fires was difficult, it could be obtained through trade.[17]

Fire Use
Campfires help to drive away vermin, such as snakes, spiders, scorpions, centipedes, mosquitoes and leaches. In the Top End, smoke from burning leaves of the turkey-bush repels insects, particularly mosquitoes, sandflies and march flies.[18] In the Kimberley, the bunch spear grass is similarly employed.[19] Fire is used for hardening wood and melting resins in the manufacture of artefacts.[20] People carry firebrands to keep themselves warm when walking and for setting alight pockets of scrub along the way.[21] Campsites are prepared by burning the surrounding vegetation, which is necessary around waterholes when brush and thorns have accumulated since the last visit.[22]

For healing, fire is utilised for stemming the flow of blood, while ashes are used for cleaning newborn babies.[23] In the past, smoke was employed therapeutically to make babies and young children 'stronger' and to treat the sick, including those suffering from madness.[24] Children who are overexcited and silly are held over fires to quieten them.[25] In southern Australia it was a mourning tradition that adult female relatives of the recently deceased would singe off their hair with a firebrand.[26] During ceremonial performances held at night, firelight is used to illuminate the dancers.[27] In some Aboriginal communities, fire was used either to cremate the dead or to dry the corpses before the final stages of burial.[28]

Poisonous smoke from certain plants was used to kill or drive out animals that lived in burrows and tree hollows. John Harris Browne, who had been the medical officer on Captain Charles Sturt's expedition to Central Australia during 1844-45, provided one of the most detailed accounts of the Aboriginal smoking technique. In the southern Flinders Ranges the leaves and stems of the

scented mat rush were used to suffocate bettongs (rat kangaroos) in their burrows.[29] First, all of the exit holes of the burrows were closed off. The exceptions were the hole for the smoking material and the exit hole on the opposite side of the burrow complex, that was simply blocked with a digging-stick or grass so that it could be quickly opened up to see if the smoke had penetrated all the way through. The fire hole was placed on the windward side and the smoke fanned in with either an owl's wing or a bettong skin sewn onto a forked stick. This smoking process took about fifteen or twenty minutes. The precise location of the dying animals was determined by crouching on the ground and listening for their movements and coughing, with spots marked for digging up later. Browne claimed that he once saw eleven bettongs removed from one burrow complex in this manner.

The appearance of smoke plumes in the distance conveyed information, both intended and inadvertent. At Cobourg Peninsula in the Northern Territory, Aboriginal people burn the beach spinifex grass to produce thick black smoke.[30] Under prior arrangement, this signals a person's position or indicates that they are ready to be picked up by boat. In earlier times, the sight of smoke on the horizon resulting from the activities of kin was reassurance that all was well. Smoke from the wrong direction was a warning of suspected trespassers. Anthropologist Robert Tonkinson explained that the Mardudjara people of the western Gibson Desert in Western Australia felt secure 'in knowing both what can be seen and what lies beyond, and in the certainty that other groups, of kin and friends, are out there, perhaps visibly manifested by their hunting or campfire smokes, which can often be seen from distances of up to 50 miles [80 km]'.[31]

Desert people develop keen eyes for detecting faint atmospheric phenomena at great distances. This was demonstrated to me in early 2006, during fieldwork in the Great Victoria Desert of central Western Australia, when I was amazed by the ability of 'Spinifex people' to detect faint dust plumes coming from vehicles being driven on roads that were over the edge of the horizon. In earlier times, desert people would have been able to use thin wisps of smoke as a form of 'bush telegraph', as evidence to determine where neighbouring groups were camping.

Managing Country

Ever since the ancestors of modern Aboriginal people arrived in Australia during the late Pleistocene, cultural fires have been part of the set of dynamic relationships that have shaped the animal and plant communities that live here. Other factors in driving shifts in the environment during this period would have included changes in climate, technology, human population density and distribution, as well as the arrival of exotic organisms. It was the opinion of colonist and scholar Edward M. Curr that the impact upon the landscape of Aboriginal-made fires was considerable. Concerning the Australian hunter-gatherer, Curr claimed in his reminiscences that:

> Living principally on wild roots and animals, he tilled his land and cultivated his pastures with fire, and we shall not, perhaps, be far from the truth if we conclude that almost every part of New Holland [Australia] was swept over by a fierce fire, on an average, once in every five years. That such constant and extensive conflagrations could have occurred without something more than temporary consequences seems impossible, and I am disposed to attribute to them many important features of Nature here ... it may perhaps be doubted whether any section of the human race has exercised a greater influence on the physical condition of any large portion of the globe than the wandering savages of Australia.[32]

In Australia, Curr attributed the generally poor soils and the thin covering of vegetation to the frequent Aboriginal use of fire. Rhys Jones coined the phrase, 'fire-stick farming', to describe Aboriginal burning practices and to emphasise their use in actively managing the environment.[33] There is growing acceptance by many biologists and ecologists of the view that the controlled use of fire is not all that ecologically destructive, and that it could potentially help maintain biodiversity in many present day Australian plant and animal communities.[34]

In 1907, John B. Cleland remarked that the high degree of fire adaptation with the Australian vegetation may have been due to human causes and that this suggested a considerable antiquity for the ancestors of modern Aboriginal people arriving on the continent.[35] Academics have more recently speculated, based on a wide range of evidence, that these people arrived in Australia between 46,000 and 50,000 years ago, bringing with them both fire-making technology and burning practices.[36] Even if they did not originally use extensive bush firing techniques, then their own expansion across Australia from the north may have led them to develop seasonal burning strategies as a hunting and gathering strategy and as a means for creating more useful areas in the landscape.

Blainey suggested that the introduction of Aboriginal fire practices to Australia would have resulted in massive deforestation, followed by the silting up of many waterholes.[37] These wet places, he argued, were previously refuges that would have offered protection from wild fires for large marsupial herbivores, like Diprotodon, Zygomaturus and Procoptodon. After siltation, Blainey reasoned that the animals would have been left exposed, leading to their extinction. Palaeontologist Tim Flannery put forward another theory, arguing that Aboriginal burning practices may have developed further within Australia as a response to the extinction of large browsing animals, through over hunting, and the grasslands left to grow unchecked.[38]

Evidence for changes in vegetation due to an increase in fires comes from an unlikely source — the study of jungle fowl mounds on Melville Island in northern Australia.[39] Jungle fowls do not nest in eucalypt forests, although ancient mounds are found in areas now dominated by this type of vegetation, which loves fire. Charcoal dated from these mounds has shown a general reduction in monsoon forest cover on the island over the last few thousand years, which is possibly due to Aboriginal controlled use of fire. Across Australia, it is possible that Aboriginal burning practices became more intensive since the beginning of the Holocene period — that is during the last 10,000 years.

When Europeans first arrived in Australia, the vegetation was being deliberately and systematically burned to maintain the 'integrity of the land' in the form of a patchwork of vegetation

Fire drill, made by Warumungu man Dick Kubatji, who acted as a guide, interpreter and go-between for explorer David Lindsay during expeditions to Central and northern Australia. *(David Lindsay ethnographic collection, Central Australia, 1880s. South Australian Museum Aboriginal Artefact Collection.)*

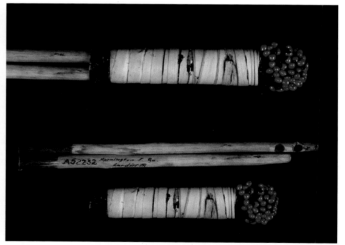

In the tropics, fire drills have a protective case to keep the ends of the sticks dry. The case is made from orchid fibre and beeswax, decorated with gidgee gidgee (jequirity) seeds. *(Norman B. Tindale ethnographic collection, Mornington Island, Gulf of Carpentaria, Queensland, 1963. South Australian Museum Aboriginal Artefact Collection.)*

Woody bracket fungus was used to carry fire between camps in southern Australia. *(Philip A. Clarke, Bridgewater, Mount Lofty Ranges, South Australia, 1985.)*

types and firebreaks that reduced the risk of high intensity fires over large areas.[40] Today, northern and Central Australian Aboriginal people will sometimes remark that the more remote parts of their country have become 'rubbish' and therefore require a 'clean up' — that is, a fire to remove dead wood and aged grass to help revive the country.[41] By burning away old and rampant growth, the growth of favoured food and resource plants was promoted, as well as providing fresh new growth fodder for game animals such as kangaroos and wallabies. In the words of Mak Mak woman April Blight from the Wagait area southwest of Darwin, 'One of the reasons for burning is saving country. If we don't burn our country every year, we are not looking after our country.'[42]

There were spiritual elements to the Aboriginal care of the environment using fire. Land that has not been burnt for many years is not only difficult to travel through, but is seen to harbour bad spirits. Such areas are also likely to be devastated when they eventually do burn, as the build up of fuel in the form of dry plant litter creates a high intensity fire. Aboriginal hunters and gatherers possessed intimate knowledge of the succession of plant species that grow after a fire, as well as responses from the fauna. The Aboriginal-controlled fire regime was maintained to keep the landscape in a productive and safe form.

There are a number of studies that consider the timing and seasonality of Aboriginal burning practices.[43] At the time of first European settlement, Aboriginal people generally burned widely throughout the year, with fires started in seasons for which natural fires, such as from lightning strikes, were rare or unknown.[44] Many of the earliest historical sources, as discussed in Chapter 3, have stated that Aboriginal-lit fires would be started even under the hottest, driest and windiest conditions, as at the end of summer. This would not have been a serious threat to humans in a landscape that contained a reduced fuel load through the action of early season fires, which had also maintained a mosaic of succession vegetation and firebreaks. Other sources cited earlier have suggested that fires were started in all but the wettest times of the year.

Aboriginal fire-starters worked to predetermined pattern, using knowledge of wind changes to help direct the blaze. This control over the course of fires was employed to stop sacred areas being burnt and also to protect particular food sources from being destroyed. Although the patchwork or mosaic of vegetation types created by the Aboriginal burning regime provided some protection from large high intensity wild fires, the maintenance of firebreaks was also considered necessary. Aboriginal people in Arnhem Land will lightly burn around the hollow grave posts erected in the earth that contain the bones of their dead, in order to provide protection from larger fires.[45] In the Top End, other places requiring such firebreaks around them include rainforest pockets that are associated with spiritual Ancestors and that contain specific food sources. In the Kakadu region, the deliberate burning of the grasslands fringing the patches of jungle and paperbark forest helped to protect fruits and yams.[46] Firebreaks set around Aboriginal camps and major pathways also provide protection from major fires, as well as serving to clear away unwanted brush and thorns.[47]

Aboriginal people were conscious of their role in upholding the vegetation pattern. There is the record of Gunei people in central Arnhem Land having been appalled that the traditional 'owners' of a neighbouring area had not maintained fires in the cooler seasons, leading to a devastating fire during hot dry weather that had killed off a northern cypress pine grove.[48] There were protocols to be observed when setting fires for game drives. In the southwest of Western Australia, medical officer Scott Nind, stationed at King George Sound in 1827, reported that the 'presence of the [Aboriginal] owner of the ground is considered necessary when they fire the country for game'.[49] Across tropical Australia it was considered a serious offence to burn without the approval of senior 'land owners'.[50]

Throughout Australia, the major advantage of frequent fires for the local environment under the indigenous regime was the suppression of fuel loads. Furthermore, the matrix of vegetation patterns produced by their burning limited the spread of natural fires resulting from lightning strikes. These factors prevented widespread and high intensity fires developing in the event of natural ignition. The fire regime introduced by Europeans in the north to control stockfeed has encouraged large fires at the end of 'the dry', and has suppressed most fires at other times. This shift has irreversibly altered tropical ecosystems. In some areas of northern Australia, rainforest started to return once the Aboriginal fire regime had ceased.[51] Similarly, the Central Australian acacia shrublands, dominated by fire-sensitive species such as mulga and gidgee, are presently being replaced by arid grasslands in areas burnt two or more times within a ten to fifteen year period.[52] Fire and vegetation each determine the other, with past Aboriginal hunters and gatherers having actively exploited this relationship.

Some plant food sources benefited greatly from being burnt. The removal of the forest canopy gives extra light, while the nutrients released into ashes combines to increase plant growth.[53] The fodder for game species, like kangaroos and wallabies, benefit greatly from low intensity fires. Leichhardt described the ashes from the early Aboriginal-lit seasonal fires in the grasslands as 'manure' to the sweet young grass that shoots up after the rains.[54] Elderly Aboriginal men in central Arnhem Land maintain that much of their pre-European style 'fire-stick farming' was concerned with managing the kangaroo population.[55] This is supported by evidence from the Kimberley and Cape York Peninsula regions.[56]

Too much burning in the hot dry season will damage some foods, particularly edible fruits that have a limited season. In the case of yams, burning the green tops from these underground food sources can make finding them extremely awkward. Anthropologist Ian Crawford commented that in the Kalumburu area of the northern Kimberley, 'The valleys were burnt later [after July], if at all, because the fires destroyed the leaves and stems of the root crops and made the women's task of locating plant foods more difficult'.[57] By taking control of the fire regime, Aboriginal custodians of the land were able to minimise the negative impacts of burning on their favoured resources, and turn it to moulding and maintaining the landscape in forms that best suited their local hunting and gathering economy.

Temperate Fires

Aboriginal control of fires in southern Australia ended soon after the commencement of European settlement. In reconstructing a model of 'fire-stick farming' for the temperate zone we must rely almost entirely upon on historical records. The seasonal timing and spatial arrangement of Aboriginal burning practices here is imperfectly known. In many parts, the coldest and wettest times of the year tend to occur together, making the setting of fires in the bush impossible during the southern winter. Aboriginal people would have found starting fires difficult in the more densely vegetated areas until early summer, when the hot winds coming from inland Australia had created generally drier conditions. Fires lit early in the fire season would have greatly reduced the severity of late summer fires.

The early British colonists were astounded at the regular and frequent Aboriginal burning of the landscape. In July 1788 at Sydney in New South Wales, Captain John Hunter observed about a hectare of fires in the surrounding hills that he believed were lit by Aboriginal hunters and gatherers. Hunter said that the colonists:

> conjectured that these fires were made for the purpose of clearing the ground of the shrubs and underwood, by which means they might with greater ease get at those roots which appear to be a great part of their subsistence during the winter. We had observed that they generally took advantage of windy weather for making such fires, which would of course occasion their spreading over a greater extent of ground.[58]

Victorian Aboriginal people were also recorded as using fire as an aid to hunting and gathering. James Dawson noted that 'In summer, when the long grass in the marshes is dry enough to burn, it is set on fire in order to attract birds in search of food, which is exposed by the destruction of the cover; and, as the smoke makes them stupid, even the wary crow is captured when hungry'.[59]

Tasmanian Aboriginal people set ablaze the vegetation around their camps, along pathways and when hunting in manners similar to mainlanders.[60] James B. Walker claimed that in Tasmania:

> It appears that the blacks were accustomed to take considerable pains, by means of periodical burnings, to keep down the scrub and promote the growth of grass

on their favourite hunting grounds. Many open plains, especially in the north, which were formally [*sic*] known as favourite resorts of the blacks, subsequently became overgrown with forest through the discontinuance of these annual burnings.[61]

Although some types of vegetation burnt relatively easily, many temperate rainforest areas could only be fired after severe drying through droughts. Once fires had opened up tracts through the rainforest, further fire episodes produced sclerophyll forests. The existence of each vegetation type depends largely on fire frequency.[62]

Through firing, Tasmanians actively retained an open landscape, as it was more useful for their hunting and gathering lifestyle. Over the last few thousand years, sclerophyll forest, which is favoured by frequent burning, may have only existed on this comparatively moist southern island because the fire regime was generally controlled by humans. The more remote rainforest regions of the inland mountainous region were difficult to burn and consequently largely ignored for foraging. Tasmanian use of 'fire-stick farming' practices had modified much of the island's vegetation pattern to such an extent that it was no longer a product of nature, but a cultural artefact, by the time Europeans first arrived.

A pattern of seasonal fires emerges from the South Australian historical records. In Pastor William Finlayson's reminiscences, he records his first view of the Adelaide Hills from the deck of the ship on which he arrived from England in 1837, a year after South Australia was founded:

> at the distance inland of twelve or fifteen miles [19 to 24 km] a grand range of hills rose before us, white and glistening with the long dry grass of summer, and well wooded. Before next day's sunrise a great change took place in the landscape before us. The watchers on deck beheld a fire on one of the hills, which seemed to spread from hill to hill with amazing speed. All on board were now awake and on deck looking at this grand, and yet to us, who knew not its cause, fearful conflagration, as it seemed as if the whole land was a mass of flame. In the morning a great change had taken place; the whole range was as black as midnight, except where trees were burning, and shortly after we landed the mystery was explained. At the end of summer as this was, the natives had set fire to the long dry grass to enable them more easily to obtain the animals and vermin on which a great

part of their living depends.[63]

These fires were not haphazardly organised events. Apart from the hunters being able to predict animal behaviour, they would have taken into account the type of the vegetation and its fuel loading, as well as the prevailing humidity, wind direction and the recent history of burning in the surrounding area.

A newspaper report in 1841 from Port Lincoln in South Australia stated that 'Independently of the danger which follows in the wake of a tribe of natives carrying fire-sticks through ripe grass, two or three feet [about 60 to 90 cm] high, they always set fire to scrubby places, whenever a small patch is found, in order to hunt'.[64] This method of hunting required much strategy and planning. Another report from Port Lincoln described the problems that European landowners had in 1851 with Aboriginal hunters burning the farm stations, which is their 'customary mode of hunting game'.[65] The regular burning off of the Lakes area of the Lower Murray region was apparently a sufficient enough threat to the local farmers for it to be reported in the Aboriginal Protector's Report of 1850.[66] Here, it was noted some landowners were offering incentives, in the form of goods, to Aboriginal people if they could get through the dry season without causing a serious bushfire.

Analysis of the historical records from the southwest of Western Australia shows a similar pattern of Aboriginal bush burning in order to catch game and to produce fresh grass.[67] European settlers in this region had major concerns over Aboriginal burning practices threatening their property.[68] Nind recorded that Aboriginal people here would commence firing the country in sections for game in late December.[69] He reported different classes of fire: men created larger fires to capture kangaroos and wallabies, while women working separately would generally set more contained fires for capturing smaller mammals, such as bandicoots.[70] These deliberate early summer burnings lessened the impact of the fires occurring later in the season, when the land was much drier. George Grey noted that Aboriginal people in the southwest of Western Australia would burn the tops off the bulrushes, which die off in winter, and he referred to this practice as a 'sort of cultivation'.[71]

Desert Fires

In the arid zone, as with elsewhere, fire was a powerful foraging tool. Western Desert groups would strategically use smoke and flames during hunting drives.[72] Biologist Hedley H. Finlayson described how Aboriginal hunters conducted a hare-wallaby drive in the Musgrave Ranges of Central Australia during the early 1920s.[73] He stated that this could only be done when the wind was suitable. Desert dwellers ensured that campsites and travel corridors were burned every year, while favoured hunting and gathering areas were set alight on a cycle of several years.[74] Burning vegetation increased surface run-off into crucial water sources. Whether intended or not, the Aboriginal practice of not burning around some sacred sites would have provided refuges for certain plant and animal species.[75]

The majority of the fires desert people lit would have gone out during the cool of the night, particularly when the vegetation mosaic was in place. Desert dwellers would burn throughout the year, although the frequency of both natural and human-made fires would have been higher in the period following good rains due to increased plant growth. Ecologist Peter Latz claimed that fires could occur at most times in country dominated by spinifex grass.[76] The only exception was during the worst of the droughts, when there was not enough fuel available to maintain a fire. At other times, lightning and Aboriginal fire-sticks competed as causes of fires in Central Australian spinifex country.

Many plant resources desirable to desert dwellers benefited from being seasonally burnt. Latz remarked: 'I estimated the amount of fruit produced by a colony of *Solanum centrale* [desert raisins] near Alice Springs to be 20 kg during the first growth season after a bushfire. Three years later production had dropped to 0.26 kg and five years later no fruit was produced, as most of the plants were dead.'[77] Anthropologist Richard Gould recorded that Western Desert people considered spinifex grass firing to have the benefits of both increasing the resin yield and producing secondary growth as fodder for kangaroos.[78] Wild tobacco is another plant resource that responds well to burning.[79] Burning frequency is the driving force behind the succession of arid zone plant communities.

Much of what is known about Aboriginal fire regimes in the desert is derived from observations of environmental changes during the decades since they had ended. In order to protect grazing fodder for cattle, European settlers discouraged Aboriginal groups from burning all year round. The cessation of Aboriginal 'fire-stick farming' in the desert has had serious implications for some desert plant and animal communities. Latz described the current land management problem in the deserts: 'After several very good seasons the amount of flammable material can build up to such an extent that a single wildfire, initiated by lightning in the height of summer, can sweep over huge areas of the desert destroying everything in its path.'[80] Among the animals that rely on the protection of the mosaic vegetation pattern are the hare-wallaby and the bilby, both of which are now rare and threatened with extinction.

Tropical Fires

The Australian tropics are notable for having fire seasons that last from seven to eight months, which is long when compared with other parts of the world at the same latitude.[81] Explorer Ludwig Leichhardt observed that northern Australian Aboriginal people frequently used fire. On 5 November 1845 in southern Arnhem Land he remarked, 'Smoke from the natives' fires was seen from the range in every direction, and their burnings invariably led us to creeks.'[82] Explorer Carl S. Lumholtz claimed that on the grassy plains of southeast Cape York Peninsula during the 1880s, the hunting of wallabies by burning the grass was a 'sport most dear to the men.'[83] Modified Aboriginal burning practices continues today in a few parts of tropical Australia.

In the early twentieth century, scientists and anthropologists were able to observe fire being used as a foraging tool in many remote northern regions. Museum researcher Norman B. Tindale visited Groote Eylandt in the western Gulf of Carpentaria in 1921–22. In his detailed account of Aboriginal hunting there, he recorded that:

Ngalia man blowing smouldering tinder after using a fire drill. From start to finish, making the fire took 65 seconds. *(Norman B. Tindale, Mount Liebig, Central Australia, 1932. South Australian Museum Archives.)*

> Another method is to fire a semicircular area of dry-grass country, watchers being stationed at the unburnt side. As the frightened wallabies and other animals attempt to escape they are speared. Dogs are also used to catch the smaller creatures that appear, such as bandicoots, rats ('orandinda'), and lizards ('dungalua').[84]

Such events would have required the participation of at least several community members, for spearing game and controlling dogs.

Anthropologist Ursula H. McConnel worked in the Wik area of northwest Cape York Peninsula from the 1920s to the 1940s. She also recorded hunting and gathering practices involving fire:

> After the wet season, when the grass is rank and tall, game is hard to see. When dry enough it is burned off. Fires sweep through the country and smoke rises in all directions. The men stand before the flames and spear the wallaby as it tries to escape, and women follow in the wake of the fire to dig out small game, bandicoots, snakes, iguanas, etc., which have taken refuge in their holes.[85]

Due to the retention of some hunting and gathering practices in the more remote parts of northern Australia until recent times, we know more about vegetation burning practices in the tropical region than for the temperate and desert zones.

An ecological study by Christopher D. Haynes through the 1970s has provided deep insights into how Aboriginal burning practices are attuned to vegetation types and to the seasons. Haynes studied the land management practices of the Gunei people living in the Upper Cadell Valley of central Arnhem Land. The Gunei recognise six main seasons in their calendar, although the length of each season may vary from year to year. The general seasonal pattern is as follows.[86] *Duludu* is from early October to late November, and is when the early storms happen. *Gadjagdung* is monsoon rain time, 'the wet', commencing in late November to early December and continuing through to late March. From this time through to early May is *ganirringgan*, a period when 'knock 'em down' rains occur. The next season, *yegerr*, is the first part of what Europeans refer to as 'the dry', when it is becoming cool. *Wurrgeng*, from mid June to late August, is the season for really cold weather. The hot weather during the season of *walirr*, referred to in Australian English as the 'build up', begins in early September and continues through to the early storms in *duludu*.

Firing in central Arnhem Land commences after a short break when *gadjagdung*, the monsoon time, comes to an end around late March. In the following *ganirringgan* season the burning of vegetation surrounding camping places is targeted first. When the 'knock 'em down' storms are over and the floods begin to recede, the newly exposed grass and sedge lands are fired, as well as some parts of the woodland. These early burnings create a series of firebreaks, the burnt areas protecting rainforest enclaves from natural fires started by lightning. At this time, the fires typically burn out with the onset of late afternoon humidity, or when the fire front encounters an existing firebreak or swamp. Kangaroos, wallabies and other mammals converge on the newly burnt grasslands for the fresh green growth, even before it appears, while waterfowl seek out the recovering sedges. Although the Gunei fire the lowlands every year, the burning of upland sections occurs only on cycles of two to four years.

The Gunei use wind direction to control their fires, lit at midday. When the winds switch to coming from the southeast, it is blustery. Deliberate burning of the woodlands commences in the *yegerr* season (around May), and by the start of *wurrgeng* (in mid June), the woodlands

Wik man making fire with a drill. The long sticks provide additional torque. *(Ursula H. McConnel, northwestern Cape York Peninsula, northern Queensland, 1930s. South Australian Museum Archives.)*

are prime for burning. The strong winds keep the flames bent, protecting the crowns of flowering trees. The dampness during the night stops many fires. By burning in the early cold weather, major food sources are protected. Plant parts at risk are the flower buds of fruit species like the green plum, lady apple and wild pear, and the terminal shoots of the northern kentia palm and the Carpentarian palm.[87] By late June, Aboriginal people are burning when fires caused by lightning are not possible

due to prevailing cold weather and lack of storms. Such low intensity fires also minimise harm to the northern cypress pines.

When 'the dry' heats up in early September, during the *walirr* season, the Gunei burn the woodlands and upland savannahs in broad patches. By restricting fires from entering the pockets of rainforest, the foods within, such as yam tubers, gulf plum seeds and black plum fruit, are protected. Kangaroo and wallaby drives are organised at this time. Hunters also search the ashes for goannas and snakes. Landscape features, such as cliffs, gorges and old burns are exploited for their effect of directing or limiting the progress of the fires they light. The deliberate burnings are curtailed when the evening humidity is no longer present to act as a control.

Archaeologists Betty Meehan and Rhys M. Jones, who lived during 1972–73 with one community of Gidjingarli speaking people at the mouth of the Blyth River in central Arnhem Land, noted that, 'fire was used in a quite systematic and continuous way, and from our records, there were only about two months at the height of the wet season that fires were not lit. And sometimes there might be 20 or 30 fires lit continuously on this land.'[88] Across Arnhem Land, most of the grassland and savannah areas are burnt each year, with between a quarter and a half of the woodland and forests fired too. Parts of the floodplain were burned twice in a year. The central Arnhem Land people would fire all areas, with the exception of the rainforest pockets, at least once within a three or four year cycle. Although the rainforests were generally left unburnt, the surrounding fires would have limited their expansion. By burning each patch of vegetation as it becomes flammable, Aboriginal hunters and gatherers maintained their foraging zones.

Fires mark the main Aboriginal travelling routes in northern Australia, and are burnt every year. Hunting in dense grass is hazardous because of the snakes. After burning, these and other reptiles are more easily seen and caught. There is evidence to suggest that Aboriginal burning in the tropics contributed to the transformation of rainforest into *Eucalyptus* woodland, as well as helped to create large stands of cycad palms.[89] In the case of cycads, fire not only increases seed production, but also synchronises their fruiting season, thereby making them a more reliable Aboriginal food source.[90] This factor is important to Aboriginal people when planning ceremonies, as large numbers of people will assemble and require feeding. In northern Australia, some cycads are referred to locally as 'fire-fern'.

Since the late twentieth century, a deeper understanding by Europeans of the active roles that hunter-gatherers have had in managing the Australian environment has challenged earlier views of passive Aboriginal lifestyles and simple economies. To Australian foragers, fire was probably the single most important technology they utilised. Aboriginal Australia was comprised of cultural landscapes where the controlled use of fire increased the productivity of the environment for the benefit of the people who lived within it. While little is known about more ancient burning practices in the millennia long before Europeans arrived in Australia, it is thought that Aboriginal firing over this time would have had a profound impact upon the Australian flora and fauna.

PART THREE: ABORIGINAL PLANT USES

Chapter 6
Planning Ahead

Aboriginal diets were based on an immense variety of food that changed constantly as sources came in and out of season. Aboriginal foragers applied their detailed knowledge of the land to enable them to make the most of their resources. In response to the seasons, they spread themselves out across the landscape in order to minimise their impact upon the environment. Aboriginal foragers possessed strategies for taking advantage of surplus plant foods and for getting through the year.

Staple Foods

The seasonal fluctuation of resources, even in relatively high rainfall areas, resulted in some hard times for Aboriginal foragers. Apart from bad droughts, these periods of hardship were probably brief. According to Grey, Aboriginal people in the southwest of Western Australia only suffered from lack of food twice a year — at the height of summer and depth of winter.[1] In better seasons, he claimed that Aboriginal foragers could collect enough food within two or three hours to last them the whole day. The severity of the worse periods would have set limits on the optimum size of the Aboriginal population.

To hunt large and wide-ranging animals, such as kangaroos and emus, successful Australian hunters had to know their habits intimately, being what missionary the Reverend Friedrich W. Albrecht described as 'accomplished naturalists'.[2] The required knowledge also stretched to other organisms as, sooner or later, as the seasons worsened, Aboriginal foragers would turn to most sources of animal food. Horn Expedition member Edward Stirling summed up Aboriginal animal foods in the better watered parts of Central Australia by stating that to 'mention the names of all [the animals] that are eaten would be largely to recapitulate the zoology of the district and I believe entirely so in the case of the mammalian fauna'.[3] For plant foods, he simply listed those few for which he had direct observations, as a full list he claimed would have been too lengthy.[4]

The majority of plant foods have an optimum period of use due to seasonal availability. Fruits, seeds and greens are highly seasonal, with nectars and gums also tending to flow in certain seasons. Some food sources are linked to cycles of fire and rain. Although underground parts of plants, like rhizomes and tubers, are generally available for long periods, there are times when they are not collected. Aboriginal gatherers avoided roots when they were small during reproduction or when the ground was too hard for digging. What Aboriginal people ate at particular times of the year was also the outcome of cultural factors, such as food preferences and band movements.

It is difficult to classify staple foods on the basis of the frequency of use alone when dealing with the subsistence of hunter-gatherers. Due to marked seasonal differences and constantly changing diets, there can be no true staple food species in terms of regular Aboriginal use throughout the year. When they could get favoured foods, such as meat and fruit, these were eaten to the exclusion of more reliable or longer lasting foods, like grass seeds and yams.[5] For this reason, Aboriginal staple foods are often more easily identified for particular seasons. In times of hardship, such as severe drought, emergency sources normally avoided were of paramount importance when everything else was exhausted.

Temperate South

Aboriginal hunter-gatherers in the temperate zone relied heavily upon plant resources associated with wetlands at the coast and along inland river systems.[6] These regions, which are rich in fish, tortoises, bird life, shellfish and plants, seasonally supported large Aboriginal populations. When in season, fruits and greens would have attracted large numbers of people to particular areas. However, in the south roots were mainstays of the Aboriginal diet.[7] Depending on the area, temperate root foods included the bulrush, marsh club rush, early-nancy, milkmaid, various orchids (like the greenhood, onion and potato orchids) and many plants called lilies (such as bulbine lily, chocolate lily, flax lily, fringe lily, grass lily, gymea lily and pale vanilla lily).[8]

In southeastern Australia, most historical records of edible roots that are described as being like a radish probably relate to the yam-daisy.[9] Although growing densely when the settlers first arrived, this plant is no longer common, apparently having suffered from the introduction of grazing animals such as sheep and cattle, and from competition with exotic grasses and herbs. The tubers of the marsh club rush were extensively used across southeastern Australia, particularly in autumn, and were commonly found in abundance on river flats.[10] Eyre described them as walnut-sized and prepared by being roasted and pounded between stones into a thin cake.[11]

Backhouse observed Aboriginal use of the warran yam tubers in the Swan River district of southwest Western Australia. He

> Examined some holes, where the Natives had been digging for roots of a *Dioscorea*, or Yam, for food. This plant climbs among bushes, in a strongish soil, and the Natives have a tradition, respecting its root having been conferred upon them, in which there are traces of the deluge.[12]

These tubers penetrate about half a metre down into the soil before enlarging into a thick cylindrical structure. Archaeologist Sylvia Hallam found that for those Aboriginal groups which relied on the warran yam grounds, it was 'not a matter of digging out a root here and there, but of returning regularly to extensively used tracts'.[13] Grey described the warran as tasting 'like a [cultivated] sweet potato'.[14]

Many of the southern Australian records for edible roots, particularly those described as growing on riverbanks or being pulled from the water, refer to a reed that is known by various Australian English names, such as bulrush, cat-tail, cumbungi and flag.[15] In the southwest of Western Australia, settler George F. Moore recorded that:

> The natives dig the [bulrush] roots up, clean them, roast them, and then pound them into a mass, which, when kneaded and made into a cake, tastes like flour not separated from the bran. This root is in season in April and May, when the broad leaves will have been burned by the summer fires, by which the taste, according to native ideas, is improved.[16]

Early naturalist Gerard Krefft claimed in relation to bulrushes, that on the New South Wales/Victorian section of the Murray River:

> at a certain period, I believe January and February to be the months, the women enter these swamps, take up the roots of these reeds [bulrushes], and carry them in large bundles to their camp; the roots thus collected are about a foot to eighteen inches [about 30 to 46 cm] in length, and they contain besides a small quantity of saccharine matter, a considerable quantity of fibre. The roots are roasted in a hollow made into the ground, and either consumed hot or taken as a sort of provision upon hunting excursion.[17]

Eyre stated that 'In all parts of Australia, even where other food abounds, the root of this reed [bulrush] is a favourite and staple article of diet among the aborigines'.[18]

Deserts

Desert dwellers sought and ate a large range of dispersed plant and animal species.[19] Although animal food was highly desirable, it is likely that the bulk of the daily Aboriginal food in arid Australia was derived from plants. Sturt, who explored Central Australia between 1844 and 1846, remarked that 'In many parts of the country in which I have been I feel satisfied they can seldom procure animal food, as they would not otherwise resort to the use of some things which no time could, I should imagine, make palateable [*sic*]'.[20] The wide variety of plants eaten by Desert people led Roth to remark in his description of the plant foods at Boulia in southwest Queensland that 'Indeed, it is difficult under this heading to know what is refused'.[21]

In Central Australia, the yalka is a sedge that has tubers with a wide season of use and the only time Aboriginal people did not eat them was when they were germinating to form new plants.[22] The desert sweet potato, which grows as a bushy climber, was another dependable desert food source, with tubers that could grow to several kilograms in weight.[23] For the Warlpiri people of the Tanami Desert, patrol officer Gordon Sweeney reported in 1947 that:

> The swollen tubers [of the desert sweet potato] eighteen inches [46 cm] to three feet [92 cm] below the surface are discovered by small cracks in the surface soil. The harvesting is done by the native women, digging with their yam sticks and using their wooden food vessels as a shovel. In favoured localities, tubers up to the size of a man's head are obtained. The tubers have a slightly sweet taste and a good percentage of moisture. They can be harvested at any time of the year. Yala is one of the most valuable food supplies of the desert native.[24]

Anthropologist Theodor G.H. Strehlow also thought that the desert sweet potato was a key Aboriginal food reserve. In 1933, when on a camping trip to the country north of Mount Liebig in Central Australia, he came upon a group of nineteen Ngalia people who had stayed at one camp in sandhills for many weeks, largely living by eating desert sweet potato.[25]

When seasons turned difficult for desert dwellers, they were forced to shift towards less palatable or more labour intensive foods. In northern and Central Australia, the tar-vine root, which would be ignored when there was plenty of other food available, was a useful 'hard time' food — at its best when the plants have stopped actively growing.[26] The fibrous root of the common reed, found in waterholes, was a desert food source that requires considerable effort in collecting and processing.[27] Central Australian missionary Louis Schulze claimed in the late nineteenth century that food sources such as marsupials, caterpillars and honey are highly desired by the Finke River people. But:

> When nothing else is to be had, the roots of various grasses and shrubs are collected, as, for example, those of the common reeds, &c. These are roasted and pounded with stones to soften them somewhat and make them less fibrous. They are swallowed in pieces, for chewing has no effect, as they remain wood-like. A real 'bread of misery'.[28]

Bush plum (northern sandalwood or plum-bush) fruits are edible, while the leaves and bark are widely used medicinally. *(Philip A. Clarke, Seven Mile Creek, northeast of Lake Eyre, Central Australia, 1987.)*

Similarly, Albrecht said that, 'In creek beds roots

of reeds are dug up and used, and there is a bush [possibly a mallee] called "erimati" whose roots are long and tough, but when broken up and mixed with water can be eaten. But this is not a sustaining food, for children living on it in a native camp soon look like mere skeletons.'[29]

Some desert fruits remain edible long after they have fallen from the bush or tree, preserved in the arid environment. In Central Australia, the fruit of rock (or desert) figs appear on the trees around waterholes after rain.[30] Dried figs were collected from the ground and made into paste before eating. According to Western Desert tradition, rock fig fruit is never cooked.[31] At extreme drought times, desert people were forced to rely on local resources around permanent waters.[32] This meant more heavily utilising foods that require grinding, such as nardoo fern sporocarps and grass seed.[33] Foods such as these were rarely touched if more favourable sources were available. Although Anmatyerre and Pintupi people ate the horse dung

fungus while still young and tender, it was generally considered by most Central Australian people a 'hard time' food.[34] Under harsh environmental conditions, a resource that generally contributes little to the total Aboriginal diet throughout the year may be a critical emergency food.

Tropical North
Tropical northern Australia has a rich variety of fruit and nut trees, as well as a number of high-yielding yams species. Here, the boundaries to Aboriginal hunting and gathering territories were more precisely delineated than was the case for desert people, where supplies of food and water were more thinly spread and less reliable.[35] In the tropics, vegetable foods were generally lacking during the height of the wet season, from January to March.[36] Botanist Raymond L. Specht noted the seasonal cycle for gathering plant food in Arnhem Land. He stated that, 'Fruits from the monsoon forests and savannah woodlands form a large part

Kangaroo apples are only edible when yellow. Tasmanians buried them in sand to help them ripen. *(Philip A. Clarke, Lake Condah, western Victoria, 1988.)*

of the aborigines' diet throughout the wet season, whereas underground storage organs from the freshwater swamps are mature during much of the dry season'.[37]

In the tropics, as with the arid zone, some fruits remain edible long after they have fallen. The fruit of the nonda plum generally ripens on the ground. Northern Aboriginal foragers considered it to be 'emu food' when still on the tree, as it is too astringent for humans to eat.[38] When required more quickly than natural ripening allowed, it was an Aboriginal practice to pluck the fruit and then bury it for a few days to hasten the process. Nonda plums were also left on shelter roofs to ripen and dry. The fruit pulp was ground and then baked into a loaf. In the Wik Ngathan language spoken in northwest Cape York Peninsula, the dried nonda plums are known by a different name from that which applies to fresh fruit.[39]

The dark fruits of conkerberry in northern Australia appear on bushes from May to August, although Aboriginal people extend the season by retrieving desiccated fruits from the ground and soaking them before they are eaten.[40] The cheesefruit tree is widespread across tropical Australia and is in fruit for most of the year.[41] Although many consider the odour of the ripened fruit repulsive, the fruit does have a pleasant taste. It has a slight anaesthetic effect upon the throat when eaten.

Aboriginal people in the tropics ate a large variety of tubers, many of them, such as the Kurlama yam and the elephant yam (bush pumpkin), requiring extensive preparation to remove toxins.[42] Women and children spent many hours with digging sticks following the creeping stems of yam vines down to their tubers over a metre below in the sand.[43] The tubers of the spike rush or water chestnut, which were gathered from northern Australian lagoons, required less processing and were widely collected and eaten.[44] They are also a favourite food of magpie geese, which Aboriginal people hunt. The tubers collected from the crops of killed magpie geese are considered a delicacy.[45]

Food Storage

Many of world's hunter-gatherers used the strategy of storing their surplus food to extend the season of use.[46] In Aboriginal Australia it was a widespread practice which helped foragers get through harsh periods when resources became generally scarce.[47] By taking advantage of those periods of abundance, food reserves could also be accumulated to eventually feed large groups of people at ceremonial feasts.

In arid regions, where desert people depended on milled seeds and nardoo sporocarps during poor seasons, food was usually stored in wooden containers or in bags of woven string or skin that were cached in dry caves or buried in the sand.[48] According to Alfred W. Howitt, who led the Burke and Wills Relief Expedition (1861–62), Aboriginal people at Cooper Creek in Central Australia would store munyeroo seed as a survival strategy. It was:

> collected in large quantities by the natives after rains. It is even sometimes collected in such quantities as to be preserved for future use. Near Lake Lipson, one of my party found about two bushels contained in a grass case daubed with mud. It looked like a small clay coffin, and was concealed. ... The 'Manyoura bowar' [munyeroo] tastes like linseed-meal, and is by no means unpleasant when baked in ashes and eaten hot.[49]

While Diyari men from Cooper Creek were visiting an ochre quarry near Brachina Creek in the Flinders Ranges, they lived on nardoo and seeds stockpiled by the local Adnyamathanha women.[50]

In southeastern Australia, the fruits of the nurp (monterry) were mashed and dried into cakes for later use and trade.[51] Fish flesh was sometimes added to the cakes before drying. Various solanum species were major fruit sources in the desert, although some species are poisonous.[52] Thomson reported finding on top of abandoned brushwood shelters at Lake Mackay, on the border between Western Australia and the Northern Territory, some dried solanum fruit skewered on twigs stripped of bark.[53] Here, Pintupi people were keeping these for later use, when the dried fruits would be softened in water before eating. Similarly, the fruit of the black plum is highly regarded in the tropics, being dried and stored for later use.[54]

Adnyamathanha people of the arid Flinders Ranges collected surplus amounts of edible wattle gum and quandong fruit for storing in skin bags kept in dry caves.[55] The quandong, which is also known as the wild peach, was a highly sought after food in arid regions.[56] When it was in season, Aboriginal foragers in the southern deserts ate the fleshy outer layer of this fruit.[57] The kernel was only eaten when all food was scarce, and at these times even quandong seeds that had passed through the gut of an emu would be cracked open and eaten.[58] Anthropologist Charles P. Mountford recorded a collection method for quandong fruit from Adnyamathanha people during a fieldtrip in the 1930s.[59] It involved the construction of a high platform, covered with branches, under particularly large fruiting trees. The platforms collected the falling fruits before they reached the ground, where emus got most of them. The quandong fruit gathered in this manner was dried and stored. When later required for a meal, wattle gum and dried quandongs were reconstituted in water. Bush plums (northern sandalwood) were similarly used, the small trees that bear them being found widely across the Australian arid zone and north in the tropics.[60]

An early colonist from the Darling River in western New South Wales, Simpson Newland, provided an example of root storage. He said that, 'The sandhill country was equally prolific [as the river area] after rain, and from both plains and highlands the roots of the wild geranium and other plants were collected, cooked, and after being trampled into a pulp in their coolamans (a wooden basin made out of the elbows of hollow box limbs), were kneaded into large balls and kept for future use'.[61] In the Roper River area of the Top End, Alawa people stored water lily roots in caves on paperbark sheets.[62] These roots will apparently keep for several years if properly prepared by being sun-dried and rubbed with red ochre. Wik people on Cape York Peninsula kept tubers from long yams stored in the sand for months.[63] In Central Australia, the larva-bearing roots of the witchetty-bush were collected and stored until fresh grubs were required for eating.[64]

Plant Food Feasts

The super abundance of favoured plant foods enabled Aboriginal people to assemble in large numbers in good seasons. Wilhelmi was visiting the southern Eyre Peninsula region of South Australia in 1851 when he noted that local Aboriginal foragers treated the karkalla (pigface or wild fig) as highly desirable:

> Pressing the fruit between their fingers, they drop the luscious juice into the mouth. During the karkalla season, which lasts from January till the end of the summer, the natives lead a comparatively easy life: they are free from any anxiety of hunger, as the plant grows in all parts of the country, and most abundantly on the sandy hills near the sea. The men generally gather only as much as they want for the moment, but the women collect large quantities for eating after supper.[65]

Summer along the southern coasts was generally a time of plenty, with fish and edible fruits available in a period of relatively mild weather. In southeastern Australia, the prolific availability of fruit, such as the nurp, triggered the coming together along the coasts of many Aboriginal groups for feasting.[66] In southwest Victoria, settler Gideon S. Lang stated, 'There is also the nurp, a sort of raspberry, which grows in large quantities over the sandhills on a run which I took up on the Glenelg. All the neighbouring tribes had the right to go there, and did so in large numbers when the fruit was in season,'[67]

In southern Eyre Peninsula, seeds of the nondo-bush were of great economical importance. In the 1840s, missionary Clamour W. Schürmann observed that the 'nondo bean' was:

> much prized by the natives, grows in abundance among the sandhills between Coffin and Sleaford Bays, where it every attracts a large concourse of tribes, and generally gives occasion for a fight. As a proof how much this bean is valued it may be mentioned that the Kukata [Kokatha] tribe, notorious for ferocity and witchcraft, often threaten to burn or otherwise destroy the Nondo bushes in order to aggravate their adversaries.[68]

The 'nondo bean' has been specifically identified as the green seedpod of the coastal wattle (nondo-bush).[69] Given that wattle seeds have a very hard coating when ripe, some explanation is required. During the 1980s, Aboriginal people consulted by me in southern South Australia referred in Aboriginal English to the pods of the coastal wattle as 'beans'.[70] It was stated that they would be eaten green, before they became dry and hard. This assertion is supported by other historical accounts of wattle seed use in the south. Backhouse recorded

The dried fruits of the rock fig (*ili*) can be found for many months lying on the ground under the trees, which occur around rockholes. *(Philip A. Clarke, Mutitjulu, Uluru, Central Australia, 1997.)*

Wangkangurru man Chippy Flash collecting desert gooseberry fruit. *(Philip A. Clarke, near Innamincka, Cooper Creek, Central Australia, 1986.)*

The tops, leaves, and stalks of a kind of cress, gathered at the proper season of the year, tied up in bunches, and afterwards steamed in an oven, furnish a favorite, and inexhaustible supply of food for an unlimited number of natives. When prepared, this food has a savoury and an agreeable smell, and in taste is not unlike a boiled cabbage. In some of its varieties it is in season for a great length of time, and is procured in the flats of rivers, on the borders of lagoons, at the Murray, and in many other parts of New Holland.[75]

It is likely that the seasonal availability of foods, like greens growing on river flats, coincided with an abundance of other food sources, particularly fish and freshwater crayfish.

Gums were easily dried and stored. In the southwest of Western Australia, wattle gum was made into cakes and eaten as required, probably by softening it in water.[76] Grey remarked that here the '*Kwon-nat* is the kind of gum which most abounds, and is considered the nicest article of food. … In the summer months the acacias, growing in swampy plains, are literally loaded with the gum, and the natives assemble in numbers to partake of this favourite esculent.'[77] In this region, flat cakes of gum from the raspberry jam wattle were stored for hard times.[78]

In coastal central Western Australia, the yam grounds of the bush potato (round yam) and warran attracted many Aboriginal bands to them for annual feasts.[79] During these concentrations of people, such cultural activities as the organising of trade fairs, dispute resolutions, marriages and religious ceremonies occurred. Across northern Australia, yams and cycad nuts were collected and prepared as sanctified food in religious rituals, when extra visitors for ceremonies put pressure on normal food sources.[80] Cakes made from cycad nuts can last for many months. Thomson claimed that these nuts, which were chiefly gathered by the women, form 'the most important staple food in Arnhem Land, the annual harvest of which can be measured in tons'.[81]

The bunya pine was a significant food plant for many Aboriginal groups in southeast Queensland, who came from far away to feast upon its nuts.[82] It is thought that the Australian English name is derived from a Yagara word, *bunya-bunya*, from around Brisbane.[83] The fruit containing the bunya

that the Tasmanian Aboriginal cooks 'were in the habit of collecting the ripening pods of *Acacia Sophora* or the Boobialla [coastal wattle], and, after roasting them in the ashes, they picked out the seeds and eat them. This is a common shrub, growing from 6 to 15 feet [1.8 to 4.6 m] high, on the sand-hills of the coast.'[71] In Tasmania, the seed of lightwood wattle, which was said to be like 'French bean', was roasted and eaten.[72] In the mallee areas of Victoria, the green pods of eumong wattle were laid on the campfire, and then seeds picked out for eating.[73]

Crucifers, such as cress, were an abundant source of edible young leaves that came into season during August.[74] Eyre described them as a key food source along the Murray River:

nuts is similar in size and shape to a large pineapple. Bunce described the taste of the nuts as 'equal, if not superior, to a mealy potato'.[84] The fruiting season lasts from January to March.[85] Burying raw nuts in well-drained sand extended the season of use by several months.[86] In the southern ranges of coastal Queensland, colonist John Mathew noted that, 'In laying up a store of bunyas, the Blacks exhibited an unusual foresight. While the fruit was in season, they filled netted bags with the seeds, and buried them generally about the beds of creeks, to be ready for use when the season was long past'.[87]

The fruiting of the bunya pine was a factor that influenced Aboriginal movement patterns. In 1843 Leichhardt visited an Aboriginal 'Bunya feast' and recorded the experience:

> The black-fellows go up to the top of these giants of vegetation with a simple brush-vine and which they put round the tree and which they push higher with every step they take upwards. They break the cones, almost a foot [30 cm] long and ¾ [23 cm] in diameter, and throw them down. ... The black-fellows eat an immense quantity; and indeed, it is difficult to cease, if one has once commenced to eat them. ... The black-fellows thrive well on them ... It seems, indeed, that these trees bear very good fruit only every three years'.[88]

Colonist and historian Samuel Bennett also reflected on the impact of the nut harvest upon the local Aboriginal population:

> the supply is vastly larger than can be consumed by the tribes within whose territory the trees are found. Consequently, large numbers of strangers visit the district, some of them coming from very great distances, and all are welcome to consume as much as they desire, for there is enough and to spare, during the few weeks which the season lasts.[89]

Protocol demanded that when the visitors were in the bunya-bunya country, they could only eat this nut and they were not to disturb any game. European colonists observed that young people often returned from the 'Bunya feast' with boils, which were caused by them being jabbed by the sharp leaf spikes on the trunk and branches when climbing the trees to collect the fruit.[90] On one occasion, Aboriginal people threatened to attack local settlers when the bunya was in season, as there would then be enough food to support a large fighting force.[91]

Angular pigface (karkalla or wild fig) is a source of edible leaves and fruit. In the mallee region, pigface was sometimes carried as a portable water source. *(Philip A. Clarke, Kingston, southeastern South Australia, 1986.)*

Drinks from Plants

Aboriginal foragers were attracted to a range of heavy flowering plants for their sweet nectar. Particularly rich are the bottlebrushes, dryandras, grasstrees, grevilleas, hakeas, red-devils, teatrees and wild honeysuckles. These were highly seasonal food sources. Nectar was liquid refreshment, as well as a source of highly desired sugar and energy. In the tropics, children suck the 'honey' out of flowers from the weeping paperbark, or dunk them in water to produce 'cool drink'.[92] The nectar from the golden grevillea is collected by shaking it into a container or by dunking the flowers into water.[93] Nectar collecting is an early morning activity, done before the flowers have become dry by the sun's heat or have been drained by nectar loving birds. In the north, swamp banksia cones and Kimberley bauhinia flowers are rubbed between the hands and the sweet nectar is then sucked out or soaked in water to produce a drink.[94] Other flowers are tapped across the open palm, and the nectar licked off.

In Central Australia, corkwood nectar is

collected in containers in the early morning.[95] Nectar from the desert thryptomene freezes into flakes on frosty nights, and Western Desert people then gather it into wooden bowls by beating the bushes.[96] The nectar from bloodwood trees is sucked directly from the blossoms.[97] A widely used method of nectar extraction involved soaking the flowers overnight in a wooden dish.[98] In the southwest of Western Australia, Aboriginal people obtained nectar from the round-fruited banksia by soaking the flower cones in water held by a skin cloak stretched over a hole dug in the ground.[99] In western Victoria, crushed honeysuckle seeds were added to infusions of nectar to make a strong flavoured drink.[100]

Foragers utilised nectar-loving birds to help them with nectar collection. In western Victoria, colonist James Dawson claimed that Aboriginal boys often stole nectar from 'parakeets'.[101] The nests of these birds, probably lorikeets, were visited often and the young nestlings pulled out and dangled by their feet until they had disgorged their food into the mouths of their captors. In this area also, the wild honeysuckle cob was used as a filter when drinking water. Dawson stated that the Aboriginal people, 'When obliged to drink from muddy pools full of animalculae [probably zooplankton and algae], ... put a full-blown cone of the banksia tree into their mouths, and drink through it, which gives a fine flavour to the water and excludes impurities'.[102] The Kaurna people of the Adelaide Plains in South Australia were said to often carry a bunch of the fragrant eucalypt blossoms with them, to suck out the nectar as they walked along.[103]

Particular eucalypts were sources of edible sap syrup. Settler Ethel Hassell recorded that in the inland region of Bremer Bay, in southwest Western Australia:

> The yate is a species of Eucalyptus from which the sap was secured by [Aboriginal gatherers] scraping pieces of bark stripped from the tree. The sap is thick, purplish syrup, which is very sweet. It was carried in containers made of bark by curling in the sides and bending up the ends. It was often eaten like honey and tastes like molasses'.[104]

Wattles produce edible gum in the temperate zone during the warmer months, often flowing from borer holes in tree trunks.[105] The gum was dissolved in water to make a drink. In 1839, Bunce was travelling with an Aboriginal group through the Dandenong area of Victoria when he recorded that:

> The native women sometimes went out by themselves, and returned with a quantity of the liquid amber gum, which exudes from the *Acacia decurrens*, or black wattle tree. This gum they call *korong*. They prepare it as a relish for their food in the following manner: having formed, of a sheet of wattle bark, a trough to hold water (*willum*), the women soak the gum until it assimilates with the water, and forms a thin glutinous liquid; a little sugar, or manna, is then added to make it palatable.[106]

The pale gums from wattles are more palatable than those of a deep red colour, which have higher tannin content and therefore make unpleasant drinks.[107]

Aboriginal hunter-gatherers in the arid zone, who often ranged many kilometres away from waterholes, obtained drinking water from tree roots. The main Central Australian species used for this purpose were the needle-bush (water-tree), desert kurrajong, desert oak, silver-leaved water-bush, coolibah, inland bloodwood and the twin-leaved mallee.[108] Various eucalypts were used as root water sources in the southern desert regions, and the mallabie in coastal central Western Australia.[109] Across the southern mallee region, from southwestern Australia to western Victoria, surface water is often scarce, even when rainfall is comparatively high. Here, Aboriginal sources of water came from roots of the yorrell (white mallee), red mallee, congoo mallee and sheoak.[110] At the west coast of South Australia, Aboriginal children dug up and ate the watery tuberous roots of the shaking grass.[111]

In the case of mallee trees, it is the lateral roots running just beneath the surface of the soil that store water.[112] These roots can be found by looking for a slight rise or crack in the ground where its rapid growth, as it absorbed water left by the last significant rainfall, has compressed the earth. These roots range from a centimetre in diameter to about the size of a person's wrist. Once located, Aboriginal people scraped the soil away from the whole length of the root with a wooden shovel, and then prised it off at the trunk end with a yam-stick or spear point. The root was then broken into sections between half a metre and a metre long, and the pieces leant against the trunk with the ends inside a container such as a wooden dish, wallaby skin bag or a simple trough made from bark removed from the roots. Blowing the root from the top end helped the dripping water along.

The water produced from roots kept desert people alive during most droughts. On several occasions during David W. Carnegie's exploration of central Western Australia in the 1890s he came across piles of discarded mallee roots that desert dwellers had used to obtain drinking water.[113] Horne and Aiston reported that, 'Quite a quantity of fluid is yielded that has been stored up by these plants. It is not very nice to the taste, but in that dry sandy desert any fluid that is drinkable is good.'[114] One long mallee root reputedly satisfied the wants of two or three thirsty men. The root ends can also be sealed with clay for transporting water over long distances. A 30 centimetre long section of root can produce over 200 millilitres of water.[115] In drought times, a desert kurrajong tree would be felled by stone axe and the leafy crown set on fire to force water to ooze out of the cut trunk into a bark container.[116]

The ability to extract water from roots and trunks would have enabled hunter-gatherers to extend their range further away from permanent waters, thereby minimising their overall impact upon the land. Desert dwellers would depend upon plant water almost entirely when travelling long distances between rock holes and soakages. At times of severe hardship, the Kokatha people in the desert country to the north of Eyre Peninsula in South Australia were forced to travel towards springs and wells nearer the coast.[117] Aboriginal mobility in the arid zone depended upon water gained from roots.

The historical literature contains examples of the life-saving properties of tree roots. An Aboriginal woman and her family travelling from Mingan, west of Kalgoorlie in central Western Australia, to Daisy Bates' camp at Ooldea on the eastern edge of the Nullarbor Plain in South Australia, were reported to have survived by drinking water from mallee roots.[118] A young male Aboriginal companion, whose name is not recorded, once saved explorer William H. Tietkens and himself during an expedition to the Ooldea region by finding and digging up desert oak roots to ease their thirst.[119] Only during the height of the worst droughts would these plant-based water supplies begin to falter.

Desert dwellers ate the leaves and stems of succulent plants, such as the small ground covering parakeelya bush, to quell their thirst.[120] They also ate the sweet white gummy substance that comes out of 'sheoak apples' or 'cones' for relief from light-headedness caused through lack of drinking water.[121] In the Top End, the inner bark of the kapok-bush was chewed on long walks to relieve thirst.[122] Similarly, in the Victoria River area of the Northern Territory, Aboriginal travellers chewed the leaves and bark of the Kimberley bauhinia tree when in need of water to 'save you from perishing'.[123] In the tropics, the bud casings of the native roselle (red sorrel) plant have an acidic flavour and are a source of moisture.[124] In the southwest of Western Australia, the bush potatoes (round yams) were not only eaten as food, but were used as thirst-quenchers.[125]

Parts of plants also served as straws to suck up drinking water. Warm layers of water often blanket still ponds, covering the colder layers towards the bottom. Aboriginal people living in the Cambridge Gulf region of northern Western Australia used the long hollow stalk of the giant water lily leaf as a straw to suck up the cooler water towards the bottom of the waterhole.[126] In hot regions, this would have had a refreshing effect on the drinkers.

Large trees sometimes have cavities, caused by storm damage, insect borers and rot, where rainwater pools.[127] Desert people removed a cylinder of bark from a quandong tree branch to use as a tube for sucking water accumulating in natural hollows, like in tree trunks and rock holes.[128] Aboriginal foragers in the mallee regions similarly used reed straws for gaining access to water in deep crevices.[129] More recently, access to the water held inside trees was gained by using a

Pencil yams (small yams) are generally collected after the surface parts of the plants die off, some months after rain. The tubers are cooked in hot sand and ashes. *(Philip A. Clarke, near Innamincka, Central Australia, 1986.)*

The bull banksia was a source of nectar. Aboriginal people made refreshing drinks by leaving the cones soaking overnight in water. *(Philip A. Clarke, near Albany, southern Western Australia, 1987.)*

steel axe to chop an entrance hole. In stony scrub country of northern Queensland, Aboriginal people gained water from the Queensland bottletree. Nineteenth-century gardener and plant collector, Anthelme Thozet, recorded that:

> The natives refresh themselves with the mucilaginous sweet substance afforded by this tree, as well as make nets of its fibre. They cut holes in its soft trunk, where the water lodges and rots them to its centre, thus forming so many artificial reservoirs. On their hunting excursions afterwards, when thirsty, they tap them one or two feet [30 or 60 cm] below the old cuts and procure an abundant supply.[130]

In western Victoria, a water tree 'is readily distinguished by bushmen, owing to the dis-colouration of the bark caused by the overflowing of the water from the cavity down the outside of the bole of the tree'.[131] Grass, tied to the end of a

Bundle of mallee roots from which Aboriginal foragers obtained over a litre of drinking water. The use of such sources enabled foragers to range far from their waterholes. *(Norman B. Tindale ethnographic collection, Penong, west coast of South Australia, 1928. South Australian Museum Aboriginal Artefact Collection.)*

Gathered fruit of the zamia palm containing nuts that are edible only after processing. The seasonal availability of this food enabled large numbers of people to assemble to hold ceremonies. *(Norman B. Tindale, Tinaroo, near Cairns, northern Queensland, 1972. South Australian Museum Archives.)*

Desert raisins (*kampurarpa*). When dry they become brown and wrinkled, and in this condition they are pounded, moistened and kept in balls for future eating. *(Norman B. Tindale, Musgrave Ranges, Central Australia, 1960. South Australian Museum Archives.)*

Bunya pine nuts are in season between January and March, and formerly attracted Aboriginal groups from a wide area to feast upon them. They taste like mealy potato. *(Philip A. Clarke, southeastern Queensland, 2004.)*

Munyeroo (common pigweed) is a succulent creeper that bears edible seed that is as fine and black as gunpowder. The leaves and stems were used by desert dwellers as thirst quenchers. *(Philip A. Clarke, Goyder Lagoon, Central Australia, 1987.)*

spear, would be used as a sponge to soak up the hard-to-get drinking water.[132]

In the Kimberley region, the root of the boab (bottletree) is a source of water, as is the pith of the tree trunk.[133] Basedow claimed that the tops of boab trees sometimes collected water:

The branches of this species surround the 'gouty' stem in a circle at the top, like the heads of a hydra, and by this

Finding water by digging up the lateral roots of the needle-bush (water-tree). The use of such water sources was crucial during droughts. *(Norman B. Tindale, Pandi Pandi, near Birdsville, Central Australia, 1934. South Australian Museum Archives.)*

means form a concavity between them, which is capable of storing a considerable volume of cool, clear rain-water. To reach this water, the natives construct ladders by simply driving a series of pointed pegs into the soft bark of the tree one above the other.[134]

In northern Australia, the swellings on the trunk of the cajuput-tree can be tapped for drinking water.[135] Although labour-intensive, the ability to extract water from trees would have saved many Aboriginal people from death due to dehydration. It also gave them access to parts of their territory that were remote from permanent water sources. The diet of Aboriginal hunter-gatherers was characterised by an immense diversity, with few foods available or eaten for very long periods. When large numbers of people converged at a single place during feasts and ceremonies, certain staple foods were utilised. By storing food, much of it derived from plants, the severity of the 'hard times' could be reduced. Emergency sources were often labour intensive to process, but crucial in maintaining the Aboriginal community through difficult times. The ability to obtain drinking water away from permanent water sources greatly extended the range of hunter-gatherers. In the long term, the effectiveness of such strategies to preserve food and water sources would have dictated the size of local Aboriginal populations.

Alyawarra woman grinding native millet grass seed for baking. The receiving bowl for the wet ground meal is typically placed under the right hand side of the grindstone. At the rear of the woman is a wooden container of seed; while on her left she keeps the water. Desert people relied on milled grass seed during poor seasons. *(Norman B. Tindale, Macdonald Downs, Central Australia, 1930. South Australian Museum Archives.)*

Chapter 7

Plant Food Technology

Australian hunter-gatherers relied upon a few key food technologies in order to provide a surplus for feasts, and to survive periods of hardship due to lack of readily obtained food. Much of the desert was only inhabitable in the long term with the use of seed and nardoo grinding technology. In the tropics, and in parts of the temperate zone, the leaching of poisons was a major technology for food production. Aboriginal occupation of Australia became more intensive over the past 10,000 years or so, with cultural changes supporting large numbers of people coming together for ceremonial events. This would have led to certain emergency food sources, such as grass seed, nardoo, 'cheeky' yams and cycad nuts, being intensively harvested for short periods in good seasons. For Aboriginal foragers, the abilities to gain nourishment from hard-coated grass seed and nardoo, and to remove toxins from yams and cycad nuts, greatly extended their range of food for both 'hard times' and ceremonial gatherings.

Grinding Seed

The first European explorers to push into the arid zone of inland Australia remarked upon the predominance of Aboriginal grass seed collecting activities. On 9 March 1846, explorer Major Thomas L. Mitchell was at Narran River in central New South Wales, when he noted the Aboriginal harvesting of native millet grass:

Dry heaps of this grass that had been pulled expressly

for the purpose of gathering the seed lay along our path for many miles. I counted nine miles [14 km] along the river, in which we rode through this grass only, reaching to our saddle-girths and the same grass seemed to grow back from the river, at least as far as the eye could reach, through very open forest. I had never seen such rich pasturage in any other part of NSW. Still it was what supplied the bread of the natives.[1]

Native millet was widely used across the arid zone.[2] August C. Gregory, who was leader of the North Australian Exploring Expedition (1854–58), remarked: 'On Cooper's Creek, the natives reap a Panicum grass [native millet]. Fields of 1,000 acres [405 ha] are there met with growing this cereal. The natives cut it down by means of stone knives, cutting down the stalk half way'.[3] In Central Australia, native millet grass grows on flood plains that collect water after the northwest monsoonal rains have fallen in summer.[4]

Desert dwellers were notable for their extensive use of grindstones for preparing small seeds into meal to make loaves. Newland stated that along the Darling River in western New South Wales:

The river supplied abundance of fish and water fowl, as well as immense quantities of 'parper' on the low lands after the subsidence of floods. ... 'Parper' is a term applied to many kinds of grass or herb seed. It was collected by the lubras [Aboriginal women] and children, put into bags or skins and ground between two stones when required. One large flat stone was laid on the ground, some seed put upon it and a smaller stone worked round with the hands, water occasionally being added; when finished it had much the appearance of our gruel.[5]

Gregory stated that Cooper Creek people of Central Australia collected native millet, then:

> beat out the seed, leaving the straw which is often met with in large heaps; they winnow by tossing seed and husk in the air, the wind carrying away the husks. The grinding into meal is done by means of two stones — a large irregular slab and a small cannon-ball-like one; the seed is laid on the former and ground, sometimes dry and at others with water into a meal.[6]

Seeds from other grasses, such as arm grass millet, hairy panic and mulga grass, were also ground to make a meal for baking into biscuit-like loaves. Although some of these species are also present in tropical and temperate regions, the desert dwellers were the main users of grass seed. It was a practice that made them distinctive.[7]

Some grasses have seed that is not easily removed from the stalk and so require special treatment. Roth described the threshing of star grass seed in the Boulia district of western Queensland:

> A sufficient quantity having been collected — a woman always preparing all plant food — it is more or less broken up with the hands, next brushed into a heap, and then put into a circular hole in the ground ... Within this hole, about 12 inches [30.5 cm] in diameter and 7 or 8 [17.8 or 20.3 cm] in depth, the woman stands: pressing alternately one foot upon the other ... she exerts a sort of rotary motion into which she throws all her weight, with the result that the grass upon which she treads becomes more and more disintegrated, the seed itself gradually working its way to the bottom. To throw all her weight upon the legs, she either supports herself on a sort of tripod of forked sticks erected in front of her, or else, when it happens to be handy, some low-lying limb of a tree.[8]

This technique was widely used with other grass species, such as the naked woollybutt grass.[9] After the seed is separated from the stalk, it is collected from the hole and placed into wooden containers for winnowing. After winnowing the seed is ground on stone slabs, before being baked into 'damper'. At Boulia, ray grass was cut down, tied into bundles, soaked in water for a few minutes, dried again, and then the seed stripped off by hand.[10] Desert people also collected the loose and already partially cleaned grass seeds of various species from around the entrance holes of 'harvesting' ant nests.[11]

The munyeroo or common pigweed is a creeping succulent annual herb that was also a major source of edible seed.[12] Mitchell stated that in Outback New South Wales the munyeroo was:

> the same reed-stalked coral-like plant, also mentioned as having been observed in similar heaps, on the banks of the Darling, during my journey of 1835 ... I now ascertained that the seed of the latter is also collected by the natives and made into paste. This seed was black and small, resembling fine gunpowder when shaken out. Nevertheless it was sweet and pleasant to the taste, possessing a nutty flavour.[13]

Stirling noted the Aboriginal use of munyeroo in the desert country south and west of Alice Springs:

> It is collected in large quantities by the females in the 'Pitchis' or wooden boat-shaped receptacles. The seeds are cleverly winnowed from the husks by pouring them from one vessel to another in the wind, or by blowing. They are then ground on a large flat bedstone by the to-and-fro movements of a hard rounded, or flattened, waterworn pebble held in the hand, water being added from time to time. The resulting paste may be eaten raw, but is more usually baked in the ashes and converted into a kind of cake. This is very insipid, but it must possess good nutritive properties, as, in many camps, 'Munyeru' seemed to be the chief article of diet.[14]

Although the seeds are very small, women were easily able to collect large amounts in their bark or wooden containers.[15]

The nardoo waterfern has pea-shaped growths, known as sporocarps, which are cases that bear spores. The nardoo sporocarp, which is edible after extensive preparation, was a major 'hard time' food in many parts of arid Australia.[16] In spite of its dietary importance in the desert, nardoo was largely ignored by Aboriginal people living in the temperate and tropical zones, where it is also seen growing in shallow water with its clover-like leaves forming a dense mat. For use by desert foragers, Howitt claimed that nardoo 'may be called their "stand-by" when other food is scarce. In many places, miles of the clay flats are thickly sprinkled with the dry seeds [sic — sporocarps]'.[17] Horne and Aiston claimed that in the northeast of South Australia the nardoo sporocarps were 'collected by sweeping them up into a *pirrha* or wooden bowl with a bunch of twigs. They are flattened from side to side and about .5 cm in diameter. If the thick, smooth casing is removed they are seen to be full

Alyawarra woman using her feet, with standing support from a tree, to remove the husks of native millet grass seed put into a stamping hole. *(Norman B. Tindale, Macdonald Downs, Central Australia, 1930. South Australian Museum Archives.)*

of a yellowish powder which has a rather bitter taste.'[18] In the semi-arid Darling River district of western New South Wales, where the Barkindji used grass seed as a major food source, nardoo appears to have been ignored completely.[19]

Nardoo requires a process of grinding, washing and baking into cakes to purge it of toxins.[20] Mounted constable Samuel T. Gason, who was stationed at Lake Hope on the western side of the Strzelecki Desert in South Australia from 1865 to 1871 to help pacify relationships between graziers and Aboriginal groups, observed the use of nardoo. He described it as 'A very hard fruit [*sic* — sporocarps], a flat oval, of about the size of a split pea; it is crushed or pounded, and the husk winnowed. In bad seasons this is the mainstay of the natives' sustenance; but it is the worst food possible, possessing very little nourishment and being difficult to digest.'[21] The trans-Australian explorers Robert O'Hara Burke and William J.

Wills died at Cooper Creek in 1861 while existing on nardoo food, which they appear to have improperly prepared.[22]

For desert dwellers, the availability of seed and nardoo, and the ability to grind them, enabled them to live in country that experienced long dry periods. Apart from low growing plants, edible seed was also collected from shrubs and trees. In the Pilbara region of Western Australia and the Tanami Desert of the Northern Territory, seeds from the green crumbweed bush were a major food source.[23] To gather the seed, bundles of the plant were scorched to make the pods open, before threshing in wooden bowls. Many wattles were sources of edible seed. In the desert this was collected from bramble wattle, mulga and witchetty-bush, and then processed by being ground into a mash with water before roasting.[24] In the southwest of Western Australia, Aboriginal women ground the seeds of the manna wattle and raspberry jam wattle into flour in order to make damper.[25] In the Murray Valley of the temperate zone, small millstones were used for dry pounding and crushing wattle and other shrub seed, possibly when still green.[26] Aboriginal cooks would sometimes mix their foods. In the Great Victoria Desert, north of the Nullarbor Plain, termites were kneaded into wattle seed dough, before being made into cakes and cooked.[27]

In the desert some of the smallest edible seeds came from the largest plants. Scientists Thomas Harvey Johnston and John B. Cleland recorded the following account of harvesting the fine gritty seed from coolibah trees growing along watercourses in Central Australia:

> The branches are broken off and taken to a claypan, where the seed becomes liberated from the capsules in about five days' time. The seed and debris are collected and placed in a coolamon, winnowed in a strong wind, soaked all night in water in the coolamon, and then rubbed with the hands to clean and dry the seed. The latter is then treated in the same way as that obtained from grasses. About two handsful are placed on a large lower millstone with a groove along one side, and ground with a smaller stone till very fine. The moist mass is then collected into a dish (Pitchi) held below the edge of the lower stone. This paste (Paua bilu) may be eaten dry, but the main portion is usually cooked in hot ashes.[28]

In the Boulia district of southwest Queensland and in the adjacent southeast part of the Northern Territory, the seeds of the grey box were similarly utilised.[29]

Grindstone technology enabled desert dwellers to use sources of food that would otherwise be unavailable to them.[30] The archaeological record suggests that Aboriginal use of grindstones in the arid zone has grown over the last 5000 years, probably due to a mixture of climatic and social reasons.[31] Today, large grindstones left behind by their Aboriginal users are found from western New South Wales, across Central Australia, through the Western Desert to the Pilbara in central Western Australia.[32]

The main part of a large grindstone (or millstone) set is the lower slab, which is typically a flattish piece of hard coarse rock about 50 to 80 cm in length, 50 cm across and about 4 cm thick. The milling is performed by pushing a smaller upper stone, usually shaped to fit inside the hand, across seed or sporocarps on the lower slab, which may have one or two troughs on each side. Aboriginal toolmakers conserved their grinding stone resource. Examination of specimens held in the South Australian Museum show that some of the upper stones bear the signs that they were once part of a lower stone. A few of the heavily used lower stone slabs are worn right through at the bottom of the troughs.

For Aboriginal women, there were long periods when the use of grindstones was essential to their daily routine. During droughts, there was a much greater reliance upon plant food sources that required grinding, like stored nardoo sporocarps and munyeroo seed. In the Diyari language of the northeast of South Australia, *pita-ru* was the lament of hardworking women, meaning 'always-pounding'.[33] It referred to their increased reliance during drought time upon small seeds and the sporocarps, laboriously picked out of the dried mud, to provide the bulk of their sustenance. Since water was generally applied to the ground material during milling, grindstones are typically found at localities where both the food source and water supply are available nearby.[34]

Being fairly large, most grindstones were not carried around by their owners. Aboriginal bands moved around seasonally, so the amount of moveable property they could take with them was limited. They therefore left behind their bulky implements, and perhaps a store of food, at their camps. At Mungeranie, east of Lake Eyre, Horne and Aiston remarked that when Aboriginal women went away from camp to collect food, their large '*Nardoo* and *munyeroo* stones lay about haphazard. No one would dream of taking them. These munyeroo stones were always in pairs, the upper and the lower stone invariably being the same sort of stone.'[35]

Aboriginal women coveted good grindstones, with Horne and Aiston claiming that, 'A lot of friendly rivalry was shown over the smaller *piddinies* [upper grindstones]. The blackfellow who had the smoothest and cleanest-shaped *piddinie* was a person of some little conceit.'[36] Necessity placed a high value on grindstones, and Aboriginal bands either gained them through trade or travelled great distances to quarry sites where suitable stone could be obtained.[37] Once grindstones had been placed at favourite camping spots, they became vital assets to the groups that regularly camped there. Visiting American archaeologist Richard A. Gould described how Western Desert women he worked with in the 1960s were annoyed when they discovered that Europeans passing through their country had removed grindstones as souvenirs.[38]

Poison Removal

Early European explorers and settlers sometimes sampled plant foods, such as yams and cycad nuts, without first ascertaining the Aboriginal method for preparing them. In some cases, due to the toxic properties of the plants, they became violently ill. Certain species of yam require extensive treatment to render them edible, but due to their abundance and reliability they were formerly fallback sources during harsh seasons or used as food during ceremonies when large numbers of people needed to be fed.

In the Australian tropics, the tubers of the long yam taste like cultivated potato after preparation and were widely used by Aboriginal people.[39] Nutritionists, who collected data on the bushfoods of the Top End in the early 1980s, described the Aboriginal gathering technique for tubers from long yams:

> Locate the thick (25 mm) vine that climbs around the trees — it may reach 20 m above the ground. Prod the ground with a stick in an area 2 m around the base of the vine. You can tell where the yams are by the sound when prodding. A fuller deeper sound is heard above the yam.[40]

Northern Aboriginal people refer to the long yams in Aboriginal English as 'cheeky', meaning that they have a hot taste and are toxic without proper preparation. This is removed from long yams by cutting the tubers and soaking them in water.

The elephant yam and air potato of the tropics are also 'cheeky' and require at least a day of baking.[41] One Aboriginal method of preparing the Polynesian arrowroot was to mash the roots, soak the material through several changes of water, and then cook it.[42] Another way was to cover the roots with ashes or ground burnt seashells and coral, then bake them for 24 hours. The thick roots of the Australian wild grape, even after extended roasting and preparation, would still burn the mouth.[43] Cunjevoi roots are very poisonous, but were still used by northern Aboriginal people after extensive preparation.[44] Although some species of bindweed are known as 'sweet yams', meaning that they are not toxic or 'hot', others in this group require lengthy preparation.[45] Across northern Australia, the small roots of the bush carrot or arda were eaten after cycles of soaking and cooking.[46]

One of the main Aboriginal sources of food recorded at King George Sound in southern Western Australia was the long tuber of the bloodroot, which is a grass-like plant. According to Backhouse, for Aboriginal people the bloodroot was 'poor fare, it truly is, occasioning their tongues to crack grievously: it is prepared for eating by being roasted, and beaten up with the earth, from the inside of the nest of the White Ant.'[47] It has been suggested that the use of earth in the preparation of this food reduces its toxicity.[48] Bloodroot causes dysentery when eaten alone.

Some plant food toxins can be removed simply by baking. The tops of the Australian stinging nettle (scrub nettle) are edible, if first cooked to destroy the irritants.[49] According to colonial artist George French Angas, in the southeast of South Australia, 'A species of stinging nettle grows abundantly amongst the reeds; and especially in times of scarcity, it is eaten by the natives, who bake it between heated stones.'[50] In the western coastal region of South Australia, Annie Richards reported on the Afghan thistle or porcupine solanum:

> The native name of this plant is 'walga'. The blacks use the fruit for food, but only with the pounded and baked bark of the mallee [congoo mallee] root called 'congoo' by them. Before using the fruit they take off the shell (the dry prickly calyx) and remove the seeds. This leaves a pulpy skin about the thickness of that of a native peach [quandong]; the fruit and bark are then made into a cake. ... The natives told me, when opening the fruit for the seeds, not to eat the fruit, as it would make my throat sore, nor yet to touch my eyes with my fingers. The fine prickles and juice got into my fingers and produced a good deal of pain and inflammation for a short time.[51]

This food, even when properly prepared, causes sickness if consumers overindulged.[52]

At Cleveland Bay in the Townsville area of northern Queensland, it was recorded that Aboriginal cooks first baked the fruit of the white mangrove tree, then placed it in a hole and poured water over it before eating.[53] This was done to reduce the high tannin content. A longer process

Ngaatjatjarra woman Tjiwina Porter collecting wattle seed, which, after separation from the pods, is made into a paste by a process of roasting and grinding. *(Thisbe Purich, Tjukurla, southeastern Gibson Desert, Western Australia, 2000. Ara Irititja collection.)*

was recorded at both Broome in northern Western Australia and at Borroloola near the mouth of the McArthur River in the Northern Territory, where the white mangrove fruit was first soaked in water for three days prior to cooking.[54] At Groote Eylandt, the Warnindilyakwa people avoided eating this fruit, although it may still have been a 'hard time' food.[55] In northern Australia, the seeds of the screw palm can be eaten raw, but the fruit requires cooking if eaten at all.[56]

European settlers had more opportunities than explorers did to investigate the process of removing the toxins from plant food sources, such as zamia palm nuts, to render them edible. When visiting New South Wales in 1835, Backhouse and his party were a few miles east of Sydney when they noted:

In a bushy hollow, we met with *Zamia spiralis* [burrawang], a singular, Palm-like plant, in fruit. The whole fruit has some resemblance to a Pine-apple; but large nuts, in red coats, are fixed under the scales forming the outside. The Blacks, place these nuts under stones, at the bottom of water, in order to extract some noxious principle from them; they are afterwards converted into food.[57]

He added that Aboriginal people prepared the nuts by roasting, pounding and then leaving the resulting mass for two or three weeks in water to leach out the bitterness before eating.[58]

The zamia palms are cycads, occurring in clumps of small trees within the inland forests of eastern and southwestern Australia. Northern Australian cycads are also major Aboriginal food sources, having high yields of nuts that are relatively easy to collect in the latter quarter of the year.[59] The bread made from the nuts is heavy and has a strong odour, but Aboriginal people regarded it as having a pleasant 'cheesy' taste. It is good to eat while walking and will keep well for several months. Cycad nuts, unless aged, require several distinct stages of processing — usually a combination of grinding, leaching, fermenting and baking, to remove poisons such as cycasin and other associated glycosides.[60] Without this process, the eating of fresh seeds will cause severe vomiting, diarrhoea and abdominal cramps. Aboriginal techniques for judging whether the poison has successfully been removed from the cycad nuts include crumbling, smelling and visually inspecting them.[61] Archaeologists believe that the Aboriginal use of this food source, through leaching technology, started becoming more important to the diet during the late Pleistocene, about 13,000 years ago.[62]

Nuts that have aged over many months under the tree generally have fewer toxins and may, if judged safe, be eaten straight away without treatment. It has been suggested that the ability to smell poisons in cycads may be an inherited trait among northern Aboriginal people.[63] Cawte claimed that zamia palm nuts were an example of 'the treachery of Australian food'.[64] In cases of poisoning through consuming poorly processed nuts, northern Aboriginal people treated themselves by eating screw palm root.[65]

Thozet described the extensive preparation for the matchbox bean, which is a tropical climber bearing disc-shaped seeds about 5 centimetres in diameter.[66] His chief information came from James Murrells, a sailor who had lived seventeen years with Aboriginal people after being shipwrecked in the Townsville area of northeastern Queensland. According to Murrells, the seeds of this plant 'are put in the stove oven and heated ... then pounded fine and put into a dilly-bag and left for ten or twelve hours in water, when they are fit for use'.[67] The indigenous people of India prepared the seeds in a similar way.[68] The matchbox bean is widespread across the tropics, due to the ability of the seeds to remain viable after travelling long distances in the ocean.

Another food source that requires extensive processing before it can be eaten is the seed of the black bean, which is found along the eastern coast of Cape York Peninsula and down to Brisbane.[69] Backhouse considered it 'a fine tree, with a profusion of flame-coloured blossom, and with leaves like those of the English Walnut. Some of its pods are ten inches [about 25 cm] long and eight inches; [about 20 cm] round; they contain several seeds ... The Blacks roast them, and soak them in water, to prepare them for food'.[70] The main season for the nuts is from May to October.

In the northern and Central Australia regions, the seeds of various species of kurrajong also require processing, to remove a coating of hairs that cause severe irritation if eaten.[71] Aboriginal foragers collected desert kurrajong seeds, preserved inside crow dung around waterholes. These crow-processed seeds had lost most of their irritating cover.[72] Crawford described their use in the northern Kimberley being 'As the kurrajongs ripen at the beginning of the wet season [about late December], the baked seeds could be stored as emergency supplies on days when hunting was unsuccessful. Where kurrajongs were abundant, baked seeds were cached away.'[73]

Cunjevoi tubers are poisonous, but northern Aboriginal people ate them after extensive preparation. *(Philip A. Clarke, Mt Coot-tha, southeastern Queensland, 2004.)*

Cooking

There was some regional variation in cooking style, particularly in relation to meat.[74] In desert regions, grass seed was ground and cooked as 'damper', meaning biscuits or loaves, on the open fire. While smaller meats, such as small marsupials, lizards, molluscs, witchetty grubs and small birds could be broiled in ashes, larger meat was baked in earth ovens, which can reach high temperatures if the fire is large. Greens, like munyeroo and mustard grass, were also steamed in ovens.[75] Western Victorian colonist James Dawson described the Aboriginal cooking as follows:

> Ovens are made outside the dwellings by digging holes in the ground, plastering them with mud, and keeping a fire in them till quite hot, then withdrawing the embers and lining the holes with wet grass. The flesh, fish or roots are put into baskets, which are placed in the oven and covered with more wet grass, gravel, hot stones, and earth, and kept covered until they are cooked.[76]

He goes on to say that larger animals, such as emus, wombats, bush turkeys and kangaroos, are cooked in the same manner, but with stones placed at the bottom of the oven.

Holes dug into clay soils hold heat better than those in sand. Ovens are dug in soils that will not taint the food. Some types of stone, such as lumps of shell grit, have heat-retaining properties that are essential for underground cooking ovens.[77] Other types of rock were avoided. Moandik man Ron Bonney told me in the mid 1980s that in the southeast of South Australia it had been a practice for Aboriginal campers to avoid using limestone in ovens or as hearthstones. He explained that this was because these stones might contain flint nodules, which tend to explode when heated. At places where suitable rocks were unavailable, cooking stones were sometimes made from baked clays gathered from the ground, termite mounds, or mud-dauber wasp nests.[78] Specific woods, which provide a pleasant taste to the foods, are sought to make the ashes and coals of cooking fires. Digging-sticks or a pair of small sticks were employed as tongs to move small items of food through the heat of the fire.

Although prolonged boiling was not possible before Europeans introduced metal containers, water was warmed to make drinking more pleasant. A recorder of Aboriginal culture from the late nineteenth and early twentieth century, Robert H. Mathews, stated that:

> Some of the old blackfellows belonging to the Shoalhaven River and other parts of the south-east coast of New South Wales, have told me that in the winter time, when the water was very cold, they used to warm it by means of a hot stone. Water was brought in a native vessel made of bark or wood, and one or more stones were heated in the fire and lifted into the water with a forked stick, to take the chill off it, in order that the natives could drink it with comfort. My informants also stated that wild honey was sometimes added to the water to make a palatable and nutritious drink.[79]

In 1856, Gregory recorded the cooking of fish using small holes in clay ground at Victoria River in the Northern Territory.[80] Putting in fire-heated stones apparently warmed the water. Mathews suggested that some small and modified rockholes in the Hawkesbury area of eastern New South Wales might have been used in a similar way to heat water.[81] In some northern coastal regions, large seashells placed in the hot ashes of a fire were used as containers to warm water, heat fat and resins, and for making oil.[82]

Aboriginal cooks, when using earth ovens, often utilised different plant parts as wrapping, avoiding those that may impart a bad taste. In northern Australia, fish and red meats are wrapped in paperbark before placement in an earth oven, thereby keeping the flesh clean.[83] In the Kimberley region, Aboriginal people employ the large leaves of the elephant-ear wattle to wrap up food for cooking in 'bush ovens' or on the open fire.[84] At Groote Eylandt in the Gulf of Carpentaria, Warnindilyakwa people use the peanut-tree leaves to cover fish and red meat in earth ovens.[85] Such leaves, when fresh, resist burning during cooking and impart a sweet flavour to the food. The moisture in plants is also a source of steam. Wik people on Cape York Peninsula place bloodwood leaves in earth ovens filled with wallaby or wild pig meat.[86] Central Australian people steamed their food with the foliage of the twinleaf plant.[87]

Plants are used to season meat cooked in earth ovens. In the Victoria River area of the Northern Territory, Aboriginal cooks place large wads of

Wik woman baking cycad palm nuts to remove poisons. Many Aboriginal food sources are poisonous, the eating of them first requiring extensive preparation. *(Ursula H. McConnel, Archer River, northwestern Cape York Peninsula, northern Queensland, 1930s. South Australian Museum Archives.)*

Wik woman grinding cycad palm nuts into a paste for cooking. The seasonal abundance of nuts and yams allowed people to congregate in large numbers for ceremonies. *(Ursula H. McConnel, Archer River, northwestern Cape York Peninsula, northern Queensland, 1930s. South Australian Museum Archives.)*

Mustard grass plants were pulled up and cooked by steaming in earth ovens. They are available for much of the year. *(Philip A. Clarke, Wild Dog Hill, near Innamincka, Central Australia, 1986.)*

lemon-scented grass in the stomach cavities of kangaroo carcases, before cooking them.[88] Arnhem Land people similarly use foliage from a certain species of wattle, while in the western side of the Top End the leaves of the golden grevillea are used as herb for flavouring meat.[89] Plant gums served as flavour enhancers, used mainly when eating food that was highly acidic. Crawford stated that in the northern Kimberley:

> Aborigines mixed foods to improve their flavours. Additives were gums from kurrajongs and acacias, or water sweetened with honey (nowadays with sugar). *Daranggal* [kurrajong] gum was dissolved in water and then mixed with honey to form a sweet for children. Gums were mixed with the 'bush apples' [eugenia apples] ... or with *gandala* [wild pear] fruit.[90]

South Australian colonist Frederick M. Bailey observed that for local Aboriginal people on the Adelaide Plains in the 1840s, lumps of golden wattle gum 'were used for food, like we use bread

The coastal wattle (boobialla or nondo-bush) has 'beans' that are edible when green. Tasmanian Aboriginal cooks roasted them on the open fire and picked the seeds out of the pods when cooked. *(Philip A. Clarke, Stony Well, Coorong, South Australia, 1984.)*

Black bean (Australian chestnut) nuts are poisonous before processing. As a seasonal indicator, Aboriginal foragers knew that when this food was ready for eating, it was time to catch jungle fowls. *(Norman B. Tindale, Atherton Tableland, northern Queensland, 1972. South Australian Museum Archives.)*

with meat'.[91] Plants were widely used as food additives.

For hunter-gatherers in pre-European Aboriginal Australia the secret of long-term survival was knowing where to find seasonal resources in their country, and how to collect and prepare them. Some key Aboriginal food sources presented obstacles to gathering and preparation, such as being minute and requiring an effort to prepare enough for a meal, or loaded with toxic compounds, or both in the case of nardoo. Grindstone technology and the ability to remove toxins through leaching and baking enabled Australian foragers to get through 'hard times' and also afforded them the means to support large groups assembled to engage in social and cultural activities. Their success in remaining in harsh environments during extreme periods rested upon these technologies.

Chapter 8

The Power of Plants

Due to the uniqueness of the Australian flora, many of the medicinal plant species Aboriginal people have utilised are quite different from those in the rest of the world. The active principles of most herbal remedies are a multitude of chemical substances, but the power of plants was not restricted to physical properties alone, as in many cultures they also have symbolic values in effecting cures. As with human societies throughout the world, Australian hunter-gatherers employed plant-based narcotics and stimulants for ritual and recreational purposes. Such substances were key trade items in the Aboriginal economic system.

Perceptions of Health

At a broad level, people in the world recognise three main categories for the causes of disease: natural, human and supernatural.[1] In many societies, notably those with tribal political structures, the origin of serious illness is generally seen as a mixture of human and supernatural agencies.[2] In the case of the latter, sickness is attributed to such things as sorcery, breaches of sanctions and rules of behaviour, intrusions of spirits and disease-objects, or loss of soul. Aboriginal people generally attributed the swift and inexplicable onset of deadly illness to supernatural reasons. Prior to European arrival, there appear to have been many fewer fatal diseases in isolated parts of the world, such as Australia.[3] In agricultural societies, dense human populations and the close proximity of livestock provide ideal environments for the development of pathogens.[4]

In all human cultures, the manner in which sickness is dealt with is shaped by entrenched cultural beliefs and traditions. Europeans today will consider a headache to be caused by stress, high blood pressure or in worst cases a brain tumour. Traditional Aboriginal notions of feeling sick are quite different from those of contemporary Western Europeans. In many Aboriginal cultures such pain may be explained in terms of a malevolent spirit taking up residence in the head, or perhaps of sorcery. In comparison with Western medicine, the prescientific concepts of the causes of sickness and its treatment in ancient Europe and the Middle East may have had much more in common with indigenous Australian beliefs.[5]

We cannot begin to comprehend the range of Aboriginal medicinal plant use without first having a basic understanding of indigenous concepts of sickness and pain. This can be shown through looking at notions concerning the state of wellbeing held by the Ngarinman people of the Victoria River area in the Northern Territory.[6] These people use the term, *punyu*, to mean 'health', but this also refers to being 'good', 'beautiful', 'safe', 'smart' and 'strong'. All these concepts relate to the ideal human condition, with illness seen as the disruption of *punyu*. It is Ngarinman tradition that serious colds originate from a place associated with the Bad Cold Dreaming.[7] Aboriginal people widely believe that the disruption of the power surrounding Dreaming places or sites also cause serious illnesses.[8]

In desert Aboriginal communities, it is reasoned that people suffering from hunger and thirst will have a hot heart, which can be made cooler by drinking water. Aboriginal man Wiminydji and Father Tony Peile of the Balgo Hills Mission in Western Australia claimed that the 'notion of being cold is the essential concept of Aboriginal health and well-being. This concept is very different to Western ideas where with physiological foundation, a balance — not too warm and not too cold — is considered healthy.'[9] The Gugadja people at the Mission would say *Ngala baldja-riwa dulbu-dju-ra yalda-djura*, meaning 'Eat and become full, it makes the heart cold'.[10] The consuming of animal blood is believed by many Aboriginal groups to generally assist in 'cooling' the body.[11] Related to this belief, red ochre, which is often associated with the 'blood' of Dreaming Ancestors, is combined with fat and applied to the body for a 'cooling' effect. When the heart and spirit is considered 'hot', it is thought that this condition will affect other parts of the body, like the head.

Desert dwellers often express the health condition of individuals in terms of hotness and coldness. Aboriginal people in the northern deserts consider the roots of young 'wild curry' kurrajong trees to be a 'cool food', because eating them makes you feel refreshed.[12] In some parts of Australia, the treatment for headaches caused by hunger, thirst or sickness, is to wrap the head with the stem of snakevine.[13] This plant is a woody climber with milky latex that has a cooling property, which is utilised to treat various ailments.[14] In spite of the differences between indigenous and modern Western European explanations of healing mechanisms, we know that many of the Aboriginal plant medicines have a proven ability to cure people when properly used.

Healers

Aboriginal societies place great faith in their own healers, who they believe have special powers to cure the sick. In many varieties of Aboriginal English, the healers are referred to as 'clever men' or 'powered men', although these terms include other spiritually powerful people too.[15] Healers are considered to have the power to 'see' into the body of their patients. Their equivalent in contemporary Western European healing traditions would be a professional who is both a general practitioner and a psychiatrist. There are many different Aboriginal language terms for healers across Australia, such as *ngangkari* in the Western Desert, *marrnggitj* in northeast Arnhem Land and *garraaji* around Sydney.[16]

Most healers are men, although people of both genders have a wide general knowledge of efficacious plants. Women also perform ceremonies that promote the general health and wellbeing of their families. In pre-European times, all adults in the community would know about basic medicines, although healers were recognised as having greater access to spiritual and Dreaming powers and assistance. This use of a healer's set of special skills was considered fundamental for treatment in cases where sickness was blamed upon supernatural things, such as sorcery, contact with spirits and the breaking of taboos. In Aboriginal English, some places or areas that make people ill are referred to as 'sickness country'.[17] 'Devil devil business' is often the stated cause for the most serious and otherwise unexplained illnesses.[18]

In the southern Kimberley today, the Aboriginal 'doctorman' is often the first healer that an Aboriginal person approaches when feeling sick.[19] In 1999, while on a fieldtrip to the northwest of South Australia, I met and travelled with a *ngangkari* (traditional healer) who had come across from Jigalong in Western Australia. In each settlement we visited, families brought along their sick members to be looked at and treated by him. The *ngangkari* would speak about the patient's spirit, and in a few instances he related the sickness to sorcery. He was generally paid for his services with lodging, food and travel assistance. After helping his patients with the aid of his own rituals, the healer recommended to those most seriously ill that they see a Western-style medical doctor or nurse as soon as possible. The *ngangkari* proved

Arrernte man, as a newly graduated healer. The sacred designs painted on him were intended to increase his healing powers. *(Francis J. Gillen, Alice Springs, Central Australia, 1890s. South Australian Museum Archives.)*

to be a skilled observer and communicator. Today, Aboriginal people see such healers as having a role in maintaining the health of their extended community, without necessarily entirely replacing the need for Western medicine.

There are many ways in which Aboriginal people become healers.[20] It often comes through special training, commencing when still a youth, into the methodology and rituals related to discerning causes of illness, and involves spiritual revelation. The role of healer is rarely passed down directly from father to son. While they are considered to be individuals who have access to powers derived from Dreaming forces and who possess highly developed social skills and an aptitude for learning, they otherwise generally lead relatively normal lives.

The identity of the healer's clan has an impact on some of the methods employed in treating the sick. In 1846, Dresden missionary Heinrich A.E. Meyer at Encounter Bay in South Australia claimed that Ramindjeri people had 'doctors' who drew their healing power from an object, animal or plant that was the totemic 'friend' or spirit familiar of his clan.[21] One such person used a snake and others an ant or seaweed. In the case of seaweed, Meyer recorded the term *parraitye-orn*, which was translated by him to mean 'sea-weed man' or 'doctor'. This person was said to be he who

> pretends to cure diseases by chewing a small piece of a red-coloured species of sea-weed, which he gives to the patient, bidding him to conceal it about his person. As soon as the sea-weed becomes dry it is supposed the disease will have evaporated with the moisture.[22]

From its description, the seaweed was probably one of the coralline algae, commonly found in rock pools around the southern coasts.

In the southern Kimberley and Western Desert, a traditional 'doctor' receives his power from dreams or by obtaining magical charms, *maban*, from other recognised living 'doctors'.[23] The *maban* are power objects, some of which are considered invisible, while others are small trinkets like shells and tektites. Aboriginal healers observe a number of specific taboos in order to maintain their powers. In northeast Arnhem Land, some healers cannot submerge themselves in saltwater.[24] In many regions, particularly Central Australia and parts of the Kimberley, healers avoid such things as bites from large ants, excessive eating of fat and the drinking any hot beverages, through their fear of losing power.[25] It was a custom in western New South Wales that 'medicine men' could never eat their individual totemic animal or plant.[26] Across southeastern Australia, 'clever men' were said to lose their psychic and healing abilities, such as knowing in advance who was about to arrive, through drinking too much alcohol.[27]

Treatments

The healer's job is to diagnose problems, advise on remedies, suggest and perform ritualised healing procedures, and importantly to reassure their patients. When sickness is diagnosed as being caused by foreign objects entering the body, the healers will treat the patient with singing, massage and sucking to 'remove' the offending articles, which may be revealed as a fragment of wood, bone, shell, stone or even wire or glass.[28] In some situations, special objects, or *maban*, belonging to the healer are 'inserted' into the patient to affect a cure. From a contemporary Western European perspective, 'bush medicine' in Aboriginal English embraces a continuum: from substances that are demonstrably effective due to pharmacological properties, to others that work solely on a psychological basis.

Plants feature prominently as bush medicines that are chiefly used to treat symptoms such as fever, congestion, headache, skin sores, tired or swollen aching limbs and digestive problems.[29] Treatment may involve drinks, washes, massage and aromatherapy. The drinks are made by heating water with plant additives, and are commonly referred to in Aboriginal English as 'tea'. Washes are prepared more recently by boiling plants, with the liquid applied externally after it has cooled. Some plants are heated, then rubbed or massaged into swollen parts of the patient's body. The aroma of plants is generally transferred to the patient through contact with steam and smoke.

Since Aboriginal hunter-gatherers seasonally moved through different habitat zones in the landscape, it was necessary for them to possess knowledge of a broad range of plant medicines. It was also important to know the seasonal efficacy of each species. Today, I find that Aboriginal people prefer to use bush medicines prepared from plants that actually grow in their own traditional estate or 'country', often travelling large distances to obtain them.[30] They consider that treatment from such medicines, with which they share a Dreaming affinity, is fundamental to the maintenance of their health. When I have conducted ethnobotanic surveys, most Aboriginal people have only talked with authority about medicinal plants when we are visiting their own traditional country. Regardless of the healing mechanism, all remedies perform best in situations when the patient has confidence in the treatment.

The Aboriginal community used their traditional medicines, with mixed success, when Europeans introduced into Australia virulent diseases, including measles, tetanus, chicken pox, mumps, smallpox, syphilis, gonorrhoea and influenza.[31] They modified their healing practices after contact with outsiders, such as the Asian seafarers and European settlers, who brought in metal pots. This enabled Aboriginal people to increase the effectiveness of some medicines by boiling the source plants. Before metal containers were available in the Kimberley, Aboriginal healers used bark containers, or 'bush billies', to hold water when making medicine.[32] Water contained in clay pits or very small rockholes was warmed by the immersion of heated stones.[33] After European settlement, glass bottles with tops provided a means to store medicines. I know Aboriginal people today who prepare bush medicine from emu-bush and keep it sealed in containers for future use.

In Aboriginal communities across northern and Central Australia, people still actively seek their own traditional treatment, even when being treated by Western-style health systems, without any apparent sense of contradiction. In 1973, a psychiatrist with the Northern Territory Medical Service, H.B. (Don) Eastwell, remarked that, 'Forty years of Western medicine, twenty of them intensive, have not resulted in the disappearance of the traditional Aboriginal medical practitioner'.[34]

More recently, psychiatrist John Cawte described his challenge as a Western medical practitioner in remote Aboriginal communities:

> During a lifetime of medical care of Aborigines, I developed the view that sound medicine is not enough. If suffering individuals are to be reached, the doctor should try to grasp the patient's language, religion and basic beliefs. Unless the cultural gulf is narrowed in this way, there will be limited compliance with care.[35]

Rather than Europeanising indigenous health systems, medical experts such as Eastwell, Cawte and others have argued that responsibility for community health in these remote areas must be shared by both Aboriginal and European practitioners.[36] Here, the use of indigenous medicines, particularly those derived from local plants, should remain a component of a contemporary health system.

Bush Medicines

The following descriptions are only selected examples of an immense body of living oral tradition concerning the Aboriginal pharmacopoeia. It is not recommended that laypeople try any of these herbal remedies. Even plants of the same species may vary considerably in the levels of chemicals present. There is comparatively little known about medicinal plants from southern regions, because of knowledge loss within indigenous communities through the impact of European colonisation. More detailed information has been obtained in desert and tropical regions.

Skin Infections

A large variety of plants were used to treat sores, boils and burns. In northern Australia, the inner bark of the cocky-apple tree was used to make a red liquid for pouring over such wounds.[37] Ethnobotanist Dulcie Levitt provided an account from Groote Eylandt in the Gulf of Carpentaria of a toddler, who had acid burns around the mouth from licking a battery, being successfully treated with juice from mashed cocky-apple roots.[38] Burns from sleepers rolling into campfires would have been common injuries in pre-European times. In the Sydney region of New South Wales, the thick stems of the rock orchid were chewed as food, but also rubbed onto burns and sores.[39]

Foliage and stems from the small-leaved clematis (old man's beard) were widely employed across the temperate zone as a poultice in the treatment of skin problems and for aching limbs.[40] During fieldwork in the southeast of South Australia in the 1980s, Aboriginal people often warned me that prolonged exposure to this plant caused severe blistering to the skin. In eastern New South Wales, the leaves and sap of the inkweed were similarly applied to external infections.[41] Wood ashes were extensively used to treat skin ailments.[42] It was recorded that a common remedy of Tasmanians suffering from sores thought to be caused from having eaten too many young mutton-birds was to lie in the ashes of a fire behind a windbreak.[43] In Central Australia, thorns from plants, like the straggly corkbark and dead finish wattle, are inserted into the base of warts to make them disappear.[44]

In northern Australia, leaves from the giant water lily are crushed and then rubbed over the body to discourage leeches.[45] Here, stings from stonefish, catfish and stingrays, as well as bites from snakes and spiders, are treated with applications of heated leaves from the purple beach convolvulus and various mangroves.[46] In Central Australia, irritated skin, especially from scabies, is treated with washes made from caustic-vine stems and the caustic-weed.[47] On my fieldtrip to the Diamantina River of Central Australia in 1987, Wangkangurru man Chippy Flash stated the hairy caustic-weed was used to treat a wide range of bites. To support his claim, he said that the goanna would eat the hairy caustic-weed after fighting with a snake.

On several occasions through the 1980s, I was told by Aboriginal people living in the southeast of South Australia of treatment for itches caused by bites from 'ti-tree lice', ticks and insects.[48] According to Ngarrindjeri woman Lola Cameron-Bonney and Moandik man Ron Bonney, a herbal remedy for itches was a wash made from slabs of sheoak bark that were cut, dried and then boiled in a kerosene-tin bucket. For treating ant stings, Cape Barren Islanders in Tasmania applied the juice from young bracken fronds and pigface leaves.[49] Across northern Australia, the leaves of the soap-bush are rubbed together to make a lather, which is used to clean hands and bodies.[50]

Tonics and Digestive Problems

In northeast Arnhem Land, Yolngu man Stingray Spine described how eating the growing tip of palms 'lubricates a man's sexual strength and smoothness'.[51] Such preparations, intended for improving a person's general health and body function, rather than as a remedy for an existing ailment, are strictly speaking tonics and not medicines. Plant gums were widely employed as sources of tonics and medicines. In the Lower Murray region, Ngarrindjeri woman Laura Kartinyeri described for me in 1987 the use of golden wattle gum as both a tonic and a medicine for treating general stomach disorders, such as indigestion.[52] When needed, it was dissolved in water, and in between uses the gum was kept fresh by wrapping it in eucalypt leaves. In Tasmania, pigface leaves were used as a purgative.[53] Northern Aboriginal people treated diarrhoea with external applications of asparagus-fern roots and by eating the raw taproot of the medicine bean.[54]

Plants that Western Desert people have often described to me as a source of their bush medicine are members of the *Eremophila* genus, generally known in Australian English as native fuschia, poverty-bush and emu-bush.[55] In the Northern Goldfields during my fieldtrip in 2002, Pintupi woman Sunshine Williams pointed out a 'medicine bush', which was an *Eremophila*, growing at a waterhole. She stated that you 'Boil it. Put it in bottle. Drink it. Made [you] better. Cure cancer'. *Eremophila* species are commonly encountered as large shrubs in the western parts of the arid zone. Although these desert plants are employed in a variety of ways, the most common method is to make a 'tea' from the leaves, either fresh or dried, which is then drunk as a tonic. It is used to combat stomach disorders and also to treat colds, coughs and fever. Medicine made from emu-bush is one of the few that will keep well when stored in containers for later use.

The thick stems of the rock orchid (rock-lily) were chewed, then rubbed into burns and sores. These starchy stems were also roasted and eaten as food. *(Philip A. Clarke, Sydney area, New South Wales, 2005)*

Emu-bush. Desert people boiled the leaves to make medicine and tonic. *(Philip A. Clarke, Flinders Ranges, South Australia, 1983.)*

The application of milky sap from the hairy caustic-weed is an Aboriginal treatment for skin sores. In Wangkangurru tradition, a goanna will eat this plant after fighting with a snake. *(Philip A. Clarke, Diamantina River, Central Australia, 1987.)*

The gummy kino from eucalypts was widely used to make medicines. In western Victoria, it was used to treat tooth decay. *(Philip A. Clarke, Adelaide Plains, South Australia, 2004.)*

The needle-like leaves of the dead finish wattle are inserted into warts to make them disappear. *(Philip A. Clarke, Macdonnell Ranges, Central Australia, 2004.)*

Respiratory Ailments

Some medicinal plants can be used in a wide variety of methods. Inhaling vapour from the lemon-scented grass of northern Australia, crushed between the hands, will clear nasal passages, while a liquid preparation produced by boiling it is used for treatment of scabies, cuts, headaches, fever and other respiratory problems.[56] In Central Australia, toothed ragwort is used to make a 'sniffing and rubbing medicine' as a decongestant.[57] These daisies are utilised in several ways: a fresh twig may be worn through the pierced nasal septum, as a wash, or placed under the bedding of a sick baby. A powder made by grinding up the dried plant is rubbed onto the chest.

Cough medicines are made for both internal and external use. At Broome in northern Western Australia, Aboriginal people treat coughs with a warm 'tea' drink, made by boiling a bunch of chopped up leaves from bunch spear grass.[58] At

Groote Eylandt, leaves of the star boronia are crushed by hand, then soaked in water to produce a solution which is poured over the head and body for the relief of influenza aches and pains.[59] Screw palm aerial roots and the white soft inner portions at the bases of new leaves are used to make a wash to treat colds, high fevers and headaches.[60] In tropical Australia, leaves from varieties of paperbark and teatree are used to make medicine that is drunk to relieve coughs and colds.[61] To make paperbark or teatree 'tea', the aromatic leaves are crushed and then soaked in water.

In temperate mainland Australia, steam baths were used to treat patients with breathing problems.[62] The apparatus for these baths was comprised of a wooden platform built over smouldering aromatic foliage, such as eucalypt leaves. The sufferer sat on top and was covered by a skin cloak to catch the steam. Eucalypt kino or 'gum' was widely used to make a drink for treating colds and fevers.[63] Tasmanian Aboriginal people also used aromatherapy, hanging branches of wattle blossoms inside their huts to induce sleep.[64]

Head Problems

Aboriginal people used plants to relieve pain. In the Darling River district of western New South Wales, Barkindji people treated a headache by tying a small bunch of heated native fuschia leaves to their forehead.[65] In Tasmania, indigenous healers used a wash made from the Cape Barren tea plant to treat facial nerve pain.[66] Western Victorian people used eucalypt kino as a plug that was inserted into the hollow of a decayed tooth for relief.[67] On Groote Eylandt, the Warnindilyakwa treatment for a bad toothache is to insert a heated twig from the digging-stick tree into the tooth cavity, and then keeping it there until the pain is gone.[68] In the Cooktown area of northern Queensland, Aboriginal people dealt with toothache by gargling a solution made from the bark and wood of the soap-tree.[69]

The Warnindilyakwa on Groote Eylandt clear up ear infections by pouring into the ear canal a solution made by soaking the hammered young shoots of beach spinifex grass in seawater con-tained in a baler shell.[70] Here, an Aboriginal treatment for sore eyes was squeezing into them juice from the young growing tips of the whipvine.[71] Excessive smoke from campfires often made Aboriginal campers sick. The kino, or 'gum', from a variety of eucalypts is widely used across Australia to make a solution to drink for washing sore eyes, as well as for putting on wounds.[72] In Central Australia, toothed ragwort was used as a wash for inflamed skin around the eyes.[73]

Cuts and Breaks

In the tropics, various species of tree orchid and bracket orchids have juice that is sticky enough to hold together the edges of gaping wounds, and also to cover open sores.[74] In Arnhem Land, woody bracket fungus was used to heal wounds, and ensured very smooth scar tissue.[75] The fungi were prepared by lightly charring them on the fire, then by washing in water. Fresh inner bark removed from a wide variety of tree roots and trunks was used for making bandages.[76] In Central Australia, the stiff root bark of dead finish wattle was flattened and wrapped around a broken limb.[77] It was left in place to strengthen healing fractures. On Elcho Island off the coast of northeast Arnhem Land, the stems of the lolly-bush, which are straight and strong, are used as splints.[78]

In northern Australia, the sharp edges of screw palm leaves were formerly employed to make the 'tribal marks' cut into the skin of a person's stomach, arms and upper body.[79] Another marking method of body scarring was to use a burning stem of a burr to burn into the skin.[80] In the Kimberley region, the sap from the fruit of caustic-tree was used to inhibit the healing of decorative flesh cuts, thereby making them become more prominent with raised scar tissue.[81] In the Top End, the green fruit of a related plant, which is also a grevillea, was similarly used.[82] Cuts to the flesh of the arms and upper body were also packed with kino from the ghost gum and smooth-stemmed bloodwood, which provided protection from flies.[83]

Postnatal

In the northern deserts, turpentine wattle is used for postnatal therapy.[84] It is employed in a smoking treatment, aimed to soothe mother and baby and to give them strength. Leaves and termite mound fragments are layered over hot coals. Both patients then lie on or near the leaves, and sleep with the smoke passing over them. Similarly, in the north of Western Australia, northern sandalwood (bush plum) leaves and stems are used in aromatherapy to make a newborn baby strong and placid.[85] Bleeding by the mother after childbirth was treated in a number of ways. At Groote Eylandt, Warnindilyakwa midwives heat the leaves of the green plum and apply them to the abdomen, while in the past a soaked fruit from the styptic-tree would be inserted into the vagina.[86]

In the Kimberley, when a mother is lacking milk for nursing her baby it is a practice to put caustic-vine sap on her breasts.[87] On Groote Eylandt, mother's breast milk is induced to come by using a compress of warm green plum leaves.[88] In central New South Wales, heated native willow leaves were once used for this purpose.[89] Arnhem Land people use the smoke from burning the cladode pea to stop women lactating.[90]

Mood-altering Substances

Before European settlement, Aboriginal hunters and gatherers harvested, prepared and used a range of plant-based narcotics and stimulants. Narcotics are substances that work to blunt the senses for the purpose of pain relief, sleep inducement and to cause insensibility. Stimulants act to temporarily quicken processes of the mind and body. The Aboriginal community had social controls over the use of these drugs. Narcotics and stimulants were the basis of extensive trade networks.

Fermented Beverages

Most early European observers failed to note the traditional Aboriginal use of narcotics and stimulants in temperate Australia.[91] Nevertheless, there are a few records that demonstrate the widespread use of such substances here. Bunce noted that in Tasmania the cider gum:

> at certain seasons, yields a quantity of slightly saccharine liquor, resembling treacle, which the [European] stockkeepers were in the habit of extracting, and using as a kind of drink. The natives had also a method, at the proper season, of grinding holes in the tree, from which the sweet juice flowed plentifully, and was collected in a hole at the bottom, near the root of the tree. These holes were kept covered over with a flat stone, apparently for the purpose of preventing birds and animals coming to drink it. When allowed to remain any length of time, it ferments and settles into a coarse sort of wine or cider, rather intoxicating if drank to excess.[92]

The sweetness of the liquid also added to its attraction. Presumably, the Europeans adopted their use of cider gum from the Tasmanian Aboriginal people.

In the southwest of Western Australia, the nectar from wild honeysuckle trees and grasstrees was the basis of a favourite narcotic drink.[93] Roth claimed that Aboriginal people placed loads of the flower cones into boat-shaped bark vats and let the resulting solution ferment into 'mead', the drinking of which apparently produced 'excessive volubility' in the drinkers.[94] He stated that in a local Aboriginal language the cones and the drink were referred to by the same name, 'mangaitch'. Bates described a similar practice:

> In the South Perth district, where once the banksia grew most abundantly, a fresh water spring on the Melville water side was widened and deepened as soon as the banksia flowers had ripened. The flowers were then gathered by the men and soaked in water, where they fermented slightly, the drink thus obtained having a rather heady effect.[95]

Similarly used was a mixture of red bauhinia blossom and wild honey in the Diamantina River region of Central Australia.[96]

In eastern New South Wales, Aboriginal people used poison corkwood as a narcotic. It was reported by a nineteenth century botanist, Reverend Dr William Woolls, to have 'an intoxicating property. The aborigines make holes in the trunk and put some fluid in them. Which, when drunk on the following morning, produces stupor.'[97] Lake Boga people of central Victoria used root and bark of the ming (bitter quandong) tree to prepare a stupefying drink.[98] The Tatiara people in the southeast of South Australia frequently used an unidentified plant root, which may also have been the ming, dug up from the scrub to cause intoxication.[99] In the Top End, it has been reported that there was an Aboriginal practice of making 'toddies' by bashing

While Aboriginal people considered the fruit and seeds of the native willow (native apricot) too bitter to eat, the leaves were used in a warm compress to induce a mother to lactate. *(Philip A. Clarke, Sturts Meadows, western New South Wales, 2004.)*

Paperbark menstrual pad. As a universal wrapper, this material was also used for making tools, clothing and bandages. *(Ursula H. McConnel ethnographic collection, Archer River, northwestern Cape York Peninsula, northern Queensland, 1930s. South Australian Museum Aboriginal Artefact Collection.)*

The Broughton willow wattle was a source of alkaline ash, produced by burning the leaves and stems, to mix with pituri to make quids. *(Philip A. Clarke, Pandi Pandi, near Birdsville, Central Australia, 1986.)*

Pituri was used as a narcotic, as well as to hunt game animals. Aboriginal hunters stupefied emus by placing pituri into waterholes, thereby making these large birds easier to catch. *(Philip A. Clarke, Coongie Lakes, Central Australia, 1987.)*

screw palm fruit between stones and leaving the pulp to ferment in a wooden container of water.[100] The solution was drunk in considerable quantities during large gatherings of people.

True Pituri

In the deserts, drugs had major economic value. Pituri, in particular, was a highly prized trade item in eastern Central Australia, with the superior leaves and sticks coming from southwestern Queensland.[101] Botanists know the plant as *Duboisia hopwoodii*, and it grows widely across the arid zone.[102] It is believed that the common name of the plant was derived from southwestern Queensland, where *pijiri* is a word for the plant in the Pitta Pitta language.[103] Apart from Aboriginal recreational uses, pituri was said 'to excite their courage in warfare' and was given to male initiates before ceremonies to heighten their sense of revelation.[104] As a stimulant, it was claimed to create sensations of wellbeing and as a narcotic to suppress hunger and thirst, such as that experienced during protracted hunting expeditions.

Early European visitors to the desert became well aware of the effects of pituri. In 1861, members of the tragic Burke and Wills expedition at Cooper Creek used pituri that was supplied to them by local Aboriginal people.[105] In the Channel Country of Outback Queensland, Roth claimed that, 'Among the aboriginals themselves everywhere as great a craving appears to exist for pituri as alcohol for Europeans, a fact which is put into practical and economical effect by drovers, station-managers, and others ... [And] when on the Mulligan the supply of [commercial] tobacco runs out the aboriginals will smoke pituri in their pipes.'[106] A specimen of chewed pituri in the South Australian Museum has a collector's label which says it was 'Grasped from behind the ear of a native whom I had watched made comatose by the chewing there of'.[107] Northern Territory medical officer Herbert Basedow remarked 'It cannot be denied, once a person starts chewing pituri, he soon develops a craving for it, like a habitual smoker does for tobacco'.[108]

Pituri, which comes from a large bush, requires preparation prior to use.[109] The twigs and leaves were dried over a fire before being broken down into fine fragments. At this stage it was often put into bags for trading purposes. The fragments were mixed with wood ash to make a lump, called a 'quid' or 'plug' in English, which is the size and shape of a small biscuit. Animal hair was sometimes added to help bind the material together. The main psychoactive chemicals in pituri are alkaloids: nicotine and nor-nicotine.[110] The ash, which is alkaline, is thought to increase the absorption of the alkaloids into the bloodstream through sensitive areas of skin.[111]

The trees or bushes chosen to provide the

Pituri was not originally smoked, but chewed. Although widespread across arid Australia, Aboriginal people considered that only pituri plants in certain areas were suitable for this use. *(George Aiston, Central Australia, early twentieth century. South Australian Museum Archives.)*

Wangkangurru woman Linda Crombie with a pituri bag from the South Australian Museum. Pituri is a narcotic that was once the basis of a major trade economy in eastern Central Australia. *(Chris Nobbs, near Birdsville, Central Australia, 1999. Personal collection.)*

wood to make the ash were generally wattle species, such as the Broughton willow, umbrella-bush, river cooba and Murray wattle.[112] Wood and bark from the limestone senna, coolibah, sandhill spiderflower and turpentine-bush could also be used as sources of ash.[113] The toxic plant, rock isotome, was sometimes added to pituri to increase its effect.[114] Once made, the pituri quids were chewed repeatedly by the men and were kept behind their ear or stored in a pouch when not required. Only adult men were generally allowed to use pituri.[115]

For travelling purposes, pituri was packaged into bags woven from string or made from marsupial skin. The trade was extensive — covering the whole Lake Eyre Basin region, which straddles the state borders of Queensland, South Australia and the Northern Territory.[116] Although the pituri bush is widespread across arid Australia, the main source of treated material was the Mulligan River area of southwestern Queensland. It is likely that the quantity of psychoactive chemicals in the plants varies considerably in other areas and was shunned due to unpredictable or unwanted side effects. Stirling noted during the Horn Expedition that although the pituri plant grows in the region around Lake Amadeus and Uluru (Ayers Rock), it did not appear to be collected there for use as a human drug.[117] Similarly, Latz claimed that desert dwellers in Central Australia west of Lake Eyre avoided using true pituri plants, which they dismissed as 'only good for Emu poison', in preference to chewing wild tobacco.[118] When European colonisation caused the collapse of the pituri trade in eastern Central Australia, those dependent on it turned to various forms of tobacco.

Wild Tobaccos

After European settlement, the term 'pituri' came to mean in Australian English all desert species of chewable wild tobacco (of the genus *Nicotiana*), which are generally prepared in a similar way to that described above for true pituri (*Duboisia hopwoodii*).[119] Although several species are involved, the most valued by Central Australian people today are the tobacco species now commonly known by Europeans as sandhill pituri and rock pituri.[120] Thomson provided an account of Pintupi men in the Western Desert preparing the sandhill pituri. He described how, after the whole bush had been pulled up:

> The freshly gathered tobacco plants were taken to camp where the men would sit down at once and make a fire — even before they had cooked the game collected in the desert. One of the men would cram as many of these plants into his mouth as possible, chewing them into a compact mass, which was then removed from his mouth, rolled in the white, powdery caustic ash that had been obtained by burning the green leaves of the *Grevillea* [sandhill spiderflower] gathered on the dunes. The quid of tobacco, called *mannagarratta*, was passed round the group of men sitting by the fire and chewed with evident satisfaction, and finally tucked behind the ear of one of the men for further use.[121]

As shown by this quote, wild tobaccos had social uses. They were also employed when performing love magic,[122] which ensured that it was a major trade item.[123] During fieldwork in 1966, Tindale collected hand-sized rolling stones that Anangu Pitjantjatjara men used to prepare tobacco.[124]

In the Western Desert, the Pitjantjatjara and Pintupi people utilise mingkulpa tobacco for chewing.[125] In the Tanami Desert of the Northern Territory, Warlpiri people use tjuntiwari tobacco, as do desert groups living along the Canning Stock Route further west into northern Western Australia.[126] In the Pilbara region of central Western Australia, Aboriginal people chew tobacco quids made from talara tobacco.[127] In the past, when these species were not available, others types, such as round-leaf tobacco and velvet tobacco, were chewed instead.[128] Desert people use the roots of the small flower tobacco, but only when preferred tobacco species are in short supply.[129] All these species are plants that benefit from bushfires. To enhance the effect of both wild and commercial chewing tobaccos, desert people mix them with ash made by burning the bark of trees such as inland bloodwood, coolibah, corkwood, river red gum and silver box.[130]

In remote parts of northern Australia, Aboriginal smokers mix commercial chewing tobacco with fine white ashes gained from a number of plant species. Across the Kimberley to the Top End, Aboriginal

Aboriginal people in northern coastal areas smoked wild tobacco with Macassan-style pipes. Elsewhere in Aboriginal Australia, tobacco was originally just chewed. *(Norman B. Tindale, Groote Eylandt, Northern Territory, 1922. South Australian Museum Archives.)*

tobacco chewers generally burnt eucalypt bark for this purpose.[131] At Belyuen, southwest of Darwin in the Northern Territory, they use bark from the northern black wattle.[132] In the Broome area of northern Western Australia, ashes are obtained from the supplejack-tree.[133]

Prior to Europeans arriving, Asian seafarers introduced into northern Australia the practice of smoking tobacco in opium-style pipes, while the Papuans brought in the communal smoking pipe.[134] Across the north, austral tobacco was used in pipes fashioned from special types of wood. In the Arnhem Land region, Aboriginal men made their smoking-pipes from the hollow stems of the smartweed growing in the swamps.[135] At Groote Eylandt, the pipebush was employed for this purpose.[136] During fieldwork at Princess Charlotte Bay in 1927, Norman Tindale was told that local Aboriginal smokers made their pipes from bamboo lengths that had floated all the way down from New Guinea on a special ocean current that runs around December.[137]

Other Drugs

Formerly, when pituri and wild tobacco were in short supply, Central Australian Aboriginal groups were drawn to use other narcotic plants, such as leaves and stems from the serrated goodenia, sneezeweed, speedwell, desert gooseberry, stiff goodenia and bush vicks (aromatic daisy).[138] In the northern deserts, the dried ground leaves of toothed ragwort was prepared for chewing and is said to taste similar to 'Log Cabin Tobacco'.[139] When austral tobacco was unavailable in the coastal Northern Territory and northern Queensland, other indigenous sources of 'bush tobacco' (that were not *Nicotiana*) were smoked, including granadilla, heliotrope, toothed ragwort and witchweed.[140] The leaves of the emu-berry were formerly smoked, and it has more recently been used when mixed with 'whitefella (commercial) tobacco'.[141] In the Kimberley, bunch spear grass, bunu bunu, fruit salad-bush, lobelia and toothed ragwort were a fallback instead of chewing tobacco.[142] The rock isotome was sometimes

Pitjantjatjara man Andy Tjilari collecting mingkulpa tobacco. The leaves are dried over a fire or in the sun, before being ground up, mixed with wood ash and made into a quid for chewing. *(John Dallwitz, northern Mann Ranges, northwestern South Australia, 1993. Ara Irititja collection.)*

taken as a substitute for pituri and chewing tobacco, and was regarded as a 'strong chew'.[143] Isotome contains the chemical lobeline, which has a physiological action similar to that of nicotine.[144] After European settlement, many northern Aboriginal people used opium, which they obtained from Chinese settlers, by mixing the ashes with water and drinking it.[145]

Some of the drugs traditionally used in the Aboriginal community were highly toxic and required strict controls. In 1897, Roth claimed that in northern Queensland, 'At certain of the corrobborees on the lower Tully River some of the blacks will chew, and spit out again, the leaves of the "stinging-tree," … The immediate effect is apparently a condition of frenzy, in which the individual may take violent action on his mates.'[146] At Broome in northern Western Australia, stems

from a particular bush are soaked in water, which is then given to hunting dogs as a drink to make them chase kangaroos faster.[147] Although the use of fungi as a hallucinogen was globally widespread, there are no such records from anywhere in Aboriginal Australia.[148]

The Aboriginal health system is based upon cultural beliefs of the causes of sickness and the powers of plants. While Western European scholars see charms, medicines, narcotics and stimulants falling into distinct use categories, for Aboriginal users, as for many other of the world's non-European people, the distinctions are either blurred or non-existent. Although some plant uses have chiefly symbolic importance, pharmacologists can demonstrate a scientific basis for the effectiveness of many Aboriginal plant uses.

Chapter 9

Plants as Tools

The artefacts Aboriginal people make and use vary from region to region, influenced in design by such things as climate, topography, availability of materials and cultural mores. Aboriginal technologies are deceptively simple, but well suited for the challenge posed by living in the variable Australian environment. Aboriginal hunters and gatherers required their portable implements to be lightweight and few in number. This stands in marked contrast to the sedentary horticulturalist societies in nearby Indonesia and Papua New Guinea, which have more extensive material cultures. Although there is not a shared set of tools for the whole of Australia, there are broad regions within which the same hunting and gathering strategies were employed, leading to the similar types of artefacts being used.

Artefacts from Plants

In gaining a living, Aboriginal foragers made tools from a wide variety of materials, many of them incorporating parts of plants that were either gathered by the makers or obtained through trade. The archaeological record, as found in the ground, tends to favour the preservation of objects made from stone, bone and shell, while remains of those chiefly comprised of plant fibre, wood, fur, hair and skin are rarely preserved.[1] Stone tools were not universally important in Aboriginal Australia. When the British settlers first arrived, stone technology was heavily utilised in parts of

the Kimberley and Central Australia, but was less significant in most other regions. In the coastal areas of northern Cape York Peninsula, stone was largely ignored in favour of shell, bone and wood.[2]

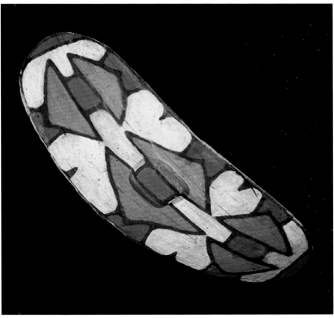

Shield made from timber chopped from the flanged root of a fig tree. Wooden artefacts provide a 'canvas' for Aboriginal artists to carve or paint their own Dreaming designs, varying widely across the country. Within the limits of regional styles, an individual shield expressed the owner's visual connection to their Dreaming. This is decorated with the scorpion totemic design of the Gonggandji people. *(Unknown artist, collected by A.M. Lea, Cairns, northern Queensland, early twentieth century. South Australian Museum Aboriginal Artefact Collection.)*

Given the extensive range of materials from which it is known that hunting and gathering artefacts were made, it is wrong to think of any cultures in the world as in the 'stone age'. It is misleading because while there are people who use stone to make artefacts — such as Australian Aboriginal people — the concept of the 'stone age' also implies ancient times ancestral to our modern times. Yet, as studies of indigenous peoples have shown, many of these cultures are of the present and in this sense are as contemporary as any other culture present in the world today.

Wood

Timber was the base material utilised in the manufacture of many types of weapons, implements and ceremonial objects.[3] Aboriginal toolmakers generally carved out of green wood, which is easier to cut than dried timber.[4] In 1788, Captain Watkin Tench of the Marines in New

Slab being removed from a beantree to make a shield. Wooden artefacts were generally made from green timber, which was then hardened over the fire and rubbed with animal fat. *(Norman B. Tindale, Cockatoo Creek, Central Australia, 1931. South Australian Museum Archives.)*

Trunk scar showing where bark was once removed to make a carrying dish. *(Norman B. Tindale, Coombah, western New South Wales, 1976. South Australian Museum Archives.)*

South Wales observed Aboriginal men making weapons in the Sydney area. He claimed that, 'On the bark of a tree they mark the size of the shield, then dig the outline as deep as possible in the wood with hatchets, and lastly flake it off as thick as they can, by driving in wedges'.[5] The use of living wood, which is more easily cut, is necessary when using stone tools, which require frequent reworking to maintain their sharpness.[6] The curing of the finished piece over the fire gave a harder edge that was resistant to wear and damage.[7] Wooden artefacts were treated with animal oil to protect them from weathering.

Aboriginal artefact makers, particularly in the temperate and tropical zones, had a large number of different tree species from which to choose their timber, far more than can be adequately described here.[8] Such an extensive range of timber permitted Aboriginal artefact-makers to select species with specific properties — such as strength, durability, resistance from termites and decay, carving quality, and the ability to make fire or to float. Even in arid Central Australia, it is estimated that at least 33 different types of timber were formerly used.[9]

Striking weapons like clubs and fighting staves need to be hard, tough and heavy, so dense

Carving a dugout canoe from a single log. The Aboriginal use of dugout canoes, which were originally obtained from foreign fishermen, made offshore reefs and islands more accessible to foragers. *(Norman B. Tindale, Groote Eylandt, Northern Territory, 1922. South Australian Museum Archives.)*

Using fire and steam to finish making a dugout canoe. After government authorities stopped Macassans from coming to northern Australia around 1906, Aboriginal people made their own. *(Norman B. Tindale, Groote Eylandt, Northern Territory, 1922. South Australian Museum Archives.)*

Kamilaroi man Charlie Dennison cutting river red gum bark to make a canoe. The selected tree had a curved trunk with a 'proper belly'. *(Norman B. Tindale, Boggabilla, Macintyre River, northeast New South Wales, 1938. South Australian Museum Archives.)*

wood from various eucalypt trees and wattles are favoured.[10] Similar properties are required for digging-sticks and club-parrying shields. For some boomerangs, strength, but not heavy weight, is paramount in the chosen timber. When making Western Desert hunting spears, two different woods are generally employed to make a single object.[11] The shafts, which need to be light and flexible, are usually manufactured from straightened stems of spearwood bush or eucalypt sapling, while the spearheads are generally made from the harder and heavier mulga wood, which

keeps its sharp edge. Spears were made in two or three sections on Cape York Peninsula, which gave them optimal levels of strength, flexibility and lightness of weight.[12] In southern South Australia, the lightweight stems of dried grasstree flower spikes were used as a main shaft, while the stone barbs at the head were gum-mounted onto a fore-shaft of black cypress pine.[13]

The properties of the available wood have influenced the development of some regional artefact styles. In Central Australia, Latz contrasted the large softwood shields made by the Arrernte people from the light weight wood of beantrees (grey corkwoods) growing in the Macdonnell Ranges with the more compact form fashioned from heavier mulga wood that the neighbouring Pitjantjatjara people obtained from the Western Desert plains.[14] A similar contrast existed in other object types, such as wooden containers.[15] Latz claimed that the distribution of the wood sources was responsible for the difference in artefacts between these people.

Macassans, in their praus, brought to coastal northern Western Australia and the Top End the use of dugout canoes, consisting of a single hollowed-out log.[16] There were at least three or four canoes carried on each prau when it arrived in Australia. These were essential for collecting trepang on offshore reefs. They were traded or lent to Aboriginal people, who also occasionally acquired them by theft. After the Macassans were barred from Australian waters by government in 1906, Aboriginal people continued to use dugout canoes, but had to manufacture their own. In the early twentieth century, the practice of making dugouts was said to be spreading south along the Kimberley coast at the rate of 80 to 100 kilometres per Aboriginal generation.[17] Anthropologist Ursula McConnel linked the use of the dugout to the expansion of Papuan type cultures down Cape York Peninsula.[18] On the eastern side of the Cape, the northern influence penetrated further south due to the greater accessibility of dugout canoes to the seas along this coast. In the tropics, the use of ocean-going watercraft was fundamental to the hunting and gathering lifestyle of Aboriginal people living along the coast and in the islands.

A 'canoe tree' in a river red gum forest. This tree had a slab of bark removed for making a canoe. It was later ring-barked by settlers wanting to clear the land for pasture. *(Philip A. Clarke, near Cummeragunja, New South Wales, 1988.)*

Bark Slabs

Tree bark was widely used across Australia, particularly in forested areas of the temperate south and tropical north.[19] Bark removed from eucalypt trees can be heated over a fire and moulded into various shapes, such as bark shields and containers.[20] Bark from the messmate stringybark, which is stiff and robust, was used for roofing, water carriers, shelter wall material and for bark paintings.[21] Paperbark sheeting, which is relatively soft and layered, was used as a universal wrapper across northern Australia.[22] Many of the paperbark species were sources of material for shelter roofs, clothing, toilet paper, water and food containers, bandages, torches, burial coverings, pouches, mats and liners for baby cradles.[23]

In southeastern Australia, slabs of river red gum bark were removed for making large canoes. Along inland waterways, ancient trees with long scars down their trunks are prominent reminders of former Aboriginal occupation.[24] Although other temperate tree species were used to make temporary canoes, only river red gum bark was said to resist the weather and not curl up or split.[25] On the northern Adelaide Plains of South Australia a local newspaper reported in 1908 that:

the natives made the Little Para famous by their tribal ceremonies. There are few localities where better evidence of the popularity of the place as a native resort can be found than along the banks of the serpentine watercourse, and even trees bear testimony to the boat building industry of the coloured race. There are huge

Desert dwellers using a wooden wedge and a stone to remove a slab from a mulga tree to make into a spearthrower. (*Norman B. Tindale, Cockatoo Creek, Central Australia, 1931. South Australian Museum Archives.*)

Wik woman collecting paperbark, which was widely used across northern Australia as a universal wrapper. *(Ursula H. McConnel, Archer River, northwestern Cape York Peninsula, northern Queensland, 1930s. South Australian Museum Archives.)*

gums [river red gums], from which the bark has been stripped in one canoe shaped piece, but the indentations are becoming overgrown with new bark, so that in a few years there will be practically nothing visible of the solid wood from which nature's covering was removed over 60 or 70 years ago for the purpose of canoe building.[26]

Many of the large scars created for canoe making in the Murray–Darling Basin remain more than 100 years after the bark was removed. Along the Murray Valley and adjacent southern Fleurieu Peninsula region, I have found many examples of 'canoe trees'. Many of these are still alive, bearing prominent scars where the main slab was peeled off, and in a few cases even the footholds made on either side for the climbers.

Bark canoes would only last a few seasons. Colonist Peter Beveridge claimed in the Riverina district of New South Wales and Victoria that, 'After the lapse of two years or a little more the canoe becomes heavy and sodden, therefore correspondingly unwieldy, so the owner in his many rambles keeps his eyes about him with the view of discovering a suitable tree from which he can take a canoe wherewith to replace his now frail craft.'[27] In Tasmania, canoes were made from bundles of rushes and bark removed from the trunks of swamp teatrees and various eucalypts, such as messmate stringybark and mountain ash.[28] In the coastal areas of the Northern Territory and northern Queensland, bark canoes were made from stringybark and used for both inland and marine environments.[29] Some northern bark canoes were used to travel to offshore islands in favourable conditions.

Fibre Sources

Plants provide Aboriginal people with fibre for producing cord and for making baskets and mats. In temperate Australia, bulrush roots were a major fibre source for string.[30] These roots were chewed as food and then the fibres scraped off from the remains, by using freshwater mussel shells, and collected for the

Wik woman making baskets from the many-flowered mat rush. The fibres were softened in water before being worked. *(Ursula H. McConnel, Holroyd River, northwestern Cape York Peninsula, northern Queensland, 1930s. South Australian Museum Archives.)*

String bag, used for holding food, was made from a combination of different cords: native verbine plant (light coloured) and human hair (black coloured) *(Johann G. Reuther ethnographic collection, east of Lake Eyre region, Central Australia, about 1900. South Australian Museum Aboriginal Artefact Collection.)*

Spiny-headed mat rush. The leaves were used as a source of fibre to make string and baskets. *(Philip A. Clarke, southeast Queensland, 2004.)*

Australian hollyhock stems were widely used in southern and Central Australia as a source of fibre for string making. The roots are also edible. *(Philip A. Clarke, near Innamincka, Central Australia, 1986.)*

Moandik man Ron Bonney demonstrating how, as a child, he had assisted his mother in basketmaking by splitting each stem of the sticky sword sedge (*kukandu*). *(Philip A. Clarke, Sandy Hut Swamp, southeastern South Australia, 1986.)*

This 'sister basket' is made from hoary rapier sedge (*pinki-moranyi*). Comprised of two 'sister' halves, it held small items like food morsels and tools. Baskets and mats made in the coiled-bundle technique from sedges and grasses were a distinctive feature of southeastern Australia. *(Ethel Watson of the Moandik people, Kingston, southeast of South Australia, 1931. South Australian Museum Aboriginal Artefact Collection.)*

After good desert rains, the Australian hollyhock, also known as the flood mallow, grows prolifically in the channels of the Diamantina River. *(Philip A. Clarke, near Birdsville, Central Australia, 1986.)*

Child's sandal made from stems of birdflower-bush. Western Desert people needed footwear to protect the soles of their feet from hot rocks and thorns. *(Calvert Expedition ethnographic collection, Great Sandy Desert, Western Australia, 1897. South Australian Museum Aboriginal Artefact Collection.)*

purpose of making string for bags, fishing lines and nets.[31] In Victoria, the bark of the hemp-bush was processed into cord, while black kurrajong trees provided the source fibre in eastern New South Wales.[32] Colonist James Bonwick described a Tasmanian woman making string: 'She got hold of some fine fibres, bared her thigh when squatting on the ground, and began to twist the threads by rolling the material up and down her thigh'.[33] This plant was identified as the Melville kurrajong, although grasses were also similarly treated.[34] Other fibre sources for cord making in southeastern Australia included the Australian hollyhock (flood mallow) and kangaroo grass.[35]

Within the temperate zone, the practice of making baskets and mats from fibres woven or stitched together was restricted to the region from the Lower Murray in South Australia, through Victoria and Tasmania, and across into eastern New South Wales.[36] Backhouse recorded how Tasmanians made baskets. He was 'watching a woman making oval bags of open work, used in fishing, &c. of the leaves of a sedgy plant, which she split with great dexterity, and after having divided them into strips of proper width, softened by drawing through the fire'.[37] The temperate zone species used in basket and mat-making include the hoary rapier sedge, spiny-headed mat rush, spiny-headed sedge, sticky sword sedge, tussock grass and wire rush.[38] Tasmanians made water-carrying vessels from a large piece of bull kelp gathered from the sea.[39]

In the Western Desert, the birdflower-bush was a source of bark fibre used to make cord for the slings that women used to carry heavy loads between their arms and waist.[40] When kangaroo sinew was not available, the fibre was also made into lashings for spear barbs.[41] In the northern deserts, strips of bark from the birdflower-bush were made into sandals, necessary to protect the feet from the extremely hot ground, as well as from burrs and thorns.[42] In the Cooper Creek and Diamantina River region of northeast South Australia and southwest Queensland, large fishing nets and carry bags were made from string.[43] The plant fibre generally used came from the bark of native verbine, which is a small bush that grows along watercourses and on flood plains. The native verbine was prepared by placing stems, which were tied in a large bundle, in the sun to dry for three or four days.[44] The bundle was then made tighter by twisting the stems around each other, after which it was left in water overnight to loosen the bark. After being rubbed in sand, the stems were pulled through the hand to remove the bark. This bark was kept for making fibre with a spindle, while the stems were discarded.

Across Australia, cordage was a key component of the kit that Aboriginal toolmakers used for their artefacts in pre-European times. In tropical northern Australia, the fibre from the inner barks of a large number of trees and bushes provided raw material for string making. Plants used include the boab, cocky-apple, cottontree, cottonwood, kapok-bush, kurrajong, peanut-tree, sand palm, screw palm (pandanus) and various types of wild fig-tree.[45] Plant fibres are employed to make a variety of woven and threaded baskets, from coastal Northern Territory across to northern and eastern Queensland.[46] The main sources are screw palm, various sedges and grasses. In Arnhem Land, women collect young screw palm leaves in the early dry season to strip for making into baskets and mats.[47]

At Darwin in the Top End, Aboriginal people made water carriers from folded palm leaves.[48] In the northwest of Western Australia region, it was mainly bark, rather than leaf fibre, which was used to make containers, although the Bardi people in the southwest Kimberley formerly made shoes from screw palm leaves.[49] The Tiwi people on Melville and Bathurst Islands used cotton from the fruit of the kapok-tree (silk cottontree) to line coffins and Iwaidja people at Port Essington used it to stuff their pillows.[50]

Gums and Resins

Grasstree and Australian cypress pine resins were extensively used across temperate Australia as an adhesive in tool making, providing firm cement for the attachment of stone axe heads and knife blades to their wooden handles.[51] Suitable hafting gums were also collected from the late black wattle, golden wattle and silver wattle.[52] In the

Murrumbidgee River area of New South Wales, the dark resin that exuded from the sugarwood was used to attach spearheads to their shafts, as well as for fixing stone axe blades to handles.[53]

For desert dwellers, the main source of cementing material used in making and mending artefacts was obtained from spinifex (porcupine grass).[54] In the 1890s, Stirling obtained the following account of its preparation from Frank J. Gillen, who was based at the telegraph station in Alice Springs, Central Australia:

> The leaves and stems are pounded into fine shreds; as much as possible of this fibrous material is discarded, while the sticky residue is collected and melted by holding close to it a burning stick or bunch of burning grass. The mass is then placed on a heated flat stone and well kneaded with another hot stone, which is held between two pieces of wood. It is then ready for use, or, if allowed to harden, it can be re-melted when required. I was told that use is made of the masses of this exudation which accumulate at the bases of burnt porcupine [grass].[55]

Spinifex resin is used for cementing the stone blades onto adzes, axes and spearthrowers.[56] It was also moulded or used in the manufacture of ornaments, and kept on sticks for storage and trading purposes.

In desert areas where spinifex resin was not available, other plants were used to make adhesive. Aboriginal people from the Macdonnell Ranges and the Diamantina River areas are known to have extracted a 'pitchy substance' from the roots of the tangled leschenaultia shrub to use in making artefacts such as knives, axes and adzes.[57] Stirling outlined how Arrernte people produced it:

> The root is heated in the ashes, and, by rubbing it on to a stick, a plastic substance detaches itself from the bark which hardens as it cools. When in the plastic condition it is moulded and hammered so as to form a cementing union, or rather moulding, for the point of junction of objects which were to be united.[58]

In spite of his own record, Stirling doubted that it was needed, as the artefacts collected during the Horn Expedition only had cement derived from spinifex resin. Gum from beefwood, gidgee and grasstree was also employed as hafting cement in the arid zone, but again usually when spinifex gum was in short supply.[59]

In northern Australia, dark gum obtained from northern ironwood was made into an adhesive when attaching spearheads to shafts and pegs to spearthrowers.[60] Toolmakers extracted the "cement" by cutting the roots into strips, then heating them over a fire. The gum was scraped off and put on to a stick, where it cooled and hardened. When required, it was reheated and made pliable. In the Kimberley, the growing point of a bush gardenia branch was hammered, which produced gum for making artefacts.[61] When making or fixing spears, Wik men on Cape Yorke Peninsula used a wooden palette knife for smoothing hot gum onto the head to hold the barbs in place, as well as for junctions between the shaft and fore-shaft.[62]

Plant adhesives were not just employed to make artefacts. In his list of plants that Tindale collected in 1933 during an expedition to Pitjantjatjara country in Central Australia, he recorded the tar-vine as 'a sticky plant, and is used as a tangle-foot to trap small birds. It is spread around waterholes.'[63] In southeastern Australia, plant resin was placed on fingertips to help catch hair being plucked from the bodies of initiates.[64] Plants had what may seem as other bizarre uses too. In southern Victoria, Bunce described the use of plants to help locate the hive of native bees. A bee 'was caught and marked by the boy with the feather-like seed of a composite [daisy] plant, and followed to its home in a neighbouring gum tree; this betraying the little industrious community of which it formed a member'.[65] In this case, plant resin had probably been used to stick the marker onto the bee. Aboriginal toolmakers sometimes used beeswax, instead of plant gum and resin, as artefact cement.[66]

Plants as Decoration

For body decorations, Central Australian Aboriginal people collected the cotton-like down produced by the foliage of slender pigweed, an erect herb.[67] It was applied either in its natural white state or could be stained red or yellow with ochre. Down from the sand sunray daisy was also utilised for body painting.[68] Arrernte and Warlpiri people in Central Australia used daisy down on ground paintings, as it is more easily obtained

Trunk of a grasstree showing resin deposits. Aboriginal toolmakers used this resin as cement when repairing damaged artefacts and for fixing stone flakes onto spearheads. *(Philip A. Clarke, Mount Barker, South Australia, 1989.)*

Scented sundew. The bulb of this plant has a red covering, which Aboriginal people crushed to make dye. *(Philip A. Clarke, Aldgate, Mount Lofty Ranges, South Australia, 1986.)*

During play, Aboriginal children paint their bodies with the black spores of the stalked puffball fungus. *(Philip A. Clarke, Tjuntjuntjara, Western Australia, 2006.)*

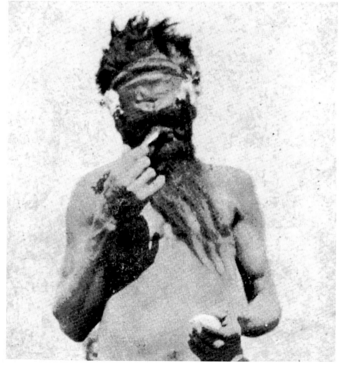

Desert dwellers used the spores of the stalked puffball fungus as a 'powder puff' to darken grey whiskers and for body painting. The spores may also have been used to repel flies. *(Herbert M. Hale, Mount Liebig, Central Australia, 1932. South Australian Museum Archives.)*

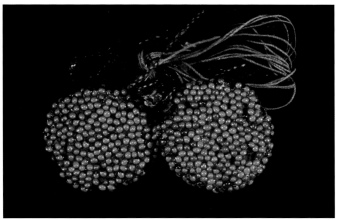

Ornament made by Tiwi people. The cord is made from human hair and vegetable fibres. The red seeds from the gidgee gidgee (jequirity) shrub, which are mounted in resin, are extremely poisonous if swallowed. *(David M. Sayers ethnographic collection, Melville Island, South Australian Museum, about 1900. South Australian Museum Aboriginal Artefact Collection.)*

in large amounts than feather down, which is preferred for smaller creations. In the northern Kimberley, the 'cotton wool' used to decorate the bodies of performers for a dance was obtained by pounding the woolly sundew plant.[69]

Aboriginal artists formerly used plant-based pigments, obtained from charcoal, fruits, saps and puffball fungal spores, to decorate their bodies and artefacts.[70] Across the Top End and parts of northern Queensland, a variety of plants are boiled to make the dye for colouring screw palm leaf strips used in making baskets and mats in the coiled bundle technique.[71] Here, tubers from the redroot plant are used as a source of red/brown dye, while hibbertia bush leaves and twigs produce colours ranging from blue to green, the inner bark of the colour-tree makes yellow/orange, and leaves and twigs of the black currant-tree produce a blue.[72]

Although Aboriginal people usually made red paint by grinding ochre and mixing it with water or animal oil, it could also be made from plants. Administrator and historian Thomas Worsnop recorded that when settlers arrived in South Australia during the 1830s and 1840s:

The native tribes around Adelaide obtained a brighter red pigment from the bulbous roots of the small sundew [scented sundew] plant, which contains a small red

Eucalypt nuts hanging as ornaments from the hair of a young woman. They were fastened onto strands of hair by the seed valves on the nuts, which were closed by moistening them. *(Herbert M. Hale, Mount Liebig, Central Australia, 1932. South Australian Museum Archives.)*

pustule [blister-like swelling] between the brown outer skin and the white inner bulb. This red pustule they used to scrape off and mix with fat for colouring the fillet of opossum hair-twine which they bound round their heads.[73]

The Kaurna people of the Adelaide Plains also appear to have used this source of paint for decorating their bark shields, as colonist Edward Stephens records that during their manufacture they 'received a coating of pipeclay or lime, and then ... ornamented with red bands made from the juice of a small tuber which grew in abundance on the virgin soil'.[74] Pitjantjatjara women made paint from the milky latex sap of the caustic-vine (milk-bush) and the desert spurge.[75] This was used to make white decorative spots on the breasts of young women to imitate milk, as a magical charm to help make them pregnant. These two plants are called *ipi-ipi* — *ipi* referring to both the breast and milk. In the north, the white sap taken from wax-plants and milkwoods was employed in the preparation of ceremonial paints, although in the case of the latter the sap can cause blindness if it got into the eyes.[76]

In the tropics, painters made a paint fixative from the sticky juice of the bracket orchid for ochre drawings done on bark slabs and human torsos.[77] Similarly, the stems and bulbs from the bracket orchid and the inland tree orchid were once crushed to make a green liquid to fix pigments on bark paintings.[78] Nowadays, commercial wood glues are mixed with pigments as a fixative when painting objects. During the Kurlama initiation ceremony on the Melville and Bathurst Islands, Tiwi people rubbed the latex-like sap of the banyan fig tree into the beard and body hair of participants, then rubbed red ochre into it.[79] When dry, and at the appropriate time of the ceremony, the sap was forcibly pulled off along with the coloured hair. Across northern Australia, the central core from the dry flower cone of the swamp banksia was used as a paintbrush when applying paint to human bodies, and could also be used as a hair comb.[80]

Colour is also provided by the presence of seeds in ornaments. The bright 'bush beads', which are the red seeds from the gidgee gidgee (jequirity) shrub, are widely used in the tropics for a variety of body ornaments, necklaces and pendants, and for decorating artefacts.[81] They are extremely poisonous if eaten. Quandong fruit stones and sections of reeds were also extensively used to make ornaments.[82] At Broome in northern Western Australia, Aboriginal performers in ceremonies wear the leafy branches of the croton.[83] Apart from the spectacular visual display it produces, the foliage produces a rustling sound when the wearers stamp their feet.

Plants as Poisons

Poisons that affect the nervous system of fish and mammals, thereby making them easier to catch, are technically stupefacients. In small waterholes, where it was not practical to use fishing nets due to snags, Aboriginal fishers often used poisons. The use of plants in this manner is widespread across the world, and as Australian scientists Ronald Hamlyn-Harris and Frank Smith remarked, 'the method did not even escape the notice of the wily English poacher.'[84] Plants were also used to fend away sharks. At Broome, Aboriginal turtle-hunters wear branches of the Wickham wattle through their waist belts when swimming, which they believe acts as a shark repellent.[85]

The Bangerang people of the Murray River in northern Victoria poisoned small lagoons when fishing, by casting in fresh eucalypt boughs.[86] The fish died in a few hours and floated to the surface from their underwater refuges. Poison corkwood and hickory wattle have been used for a similar purpose on the coast of New South Wales.[87] In the case of the poison corkwood, one early European observer in New South Wales noted that, 'Branches of this shrub are thrown into pools for the purpose of intoxicating the eels and bringing them to the surface. I have known an instance in which giddiness and nausea have arisen from remaining in a close room where branches of it have been placed.'[88]

In the western interior of New South Wales, Aboriginal fishers used boughs of the Broughton willow wattle to poison fish in waterholes, making them float to the surface as if the water had been dynamited.[89] There does not appear to be any reliable accounts of poisonous plants being employed to stun fish in the southwest of Western Australia, although it is possible that early European observers overlooked this practice here.[90] Tasmanians apparently did not eat fish at all when Europeans first arrived.[91] In northern Australia, a large variety of plants were put into small pools to poison fish. Examples include Burdekin plum, damson plum, derris, emu-apple, fern-leaved tamarind, fishkiller-tree, forest siris, freshwater mangrove, Flinders River-poison, gidgee gidgee, indigo-rouge, Leichhardt-tree, soap-tree and tulican.[92] The crushed tubers, leaves and bark are the main plant parts used. Even crocodiles in lagoons can be stunned or killed by such plant poisons.[93]

Gonggandji men crushing the red fruit of tulican for fish poisoning. The yellow pulp causes blistering if it comes into contact with the user's skin. *(Norman B. Tindale, Oombundgie, Cape Grafton Peninsula, northern Queensland, 1939. South Australian Museum Archives.)*

In the arid zone, poisonous plants were used to help capture emus. Newland, reported:

On the Finke [in Central Australia] the aboriginals used to practise another method of capturing them [emus] — by poisoning small waterholes. During my late visit to the north a blackfellow showed me a bush, the leaves of which they used for the purpose ... I believe a few bullocks were poisoned by drinking on one occasion from a waterhole prepared in this way for emus by the aboriginals.[94]

It is likely that this technique was only used when desert dwellers knew they had enough drinking water available to afford poisoning a waterhole. For the desert country of Central Australia, west and south of Alice Springs, Spencer reported that:

The chief use of the Pituri plant in this neighbourhood (apart from its value as an article of barter) seems to be that of making a decoction for the purpose of stupefying and then catching the emu. The leaves are pounded in

water and the decoction is placed in a wooden vessel where the emu is likely to come across it, or else a small pool or a fenced portion of a larger one is used for the purpose. After drinking it up the animal becomes so stupefied that it falls an easy victim to the blackfellow's spear.[95]

Spencer gave no indication as to whether kangaroos and wallabies were caught by this method. It is probably that for catching large numbers of these particular animals at a single time, Aboriginal hunters relied mainly on drives using fire.

Albrecht provided further details on the use of pituri as emu poison in Central Australia:

The twigs are cut or broken into short lengths, then with a little water the juice is squeezed into one of the open waters, and all the leaves and signs of this removed, as emus know this poison plant and will go away if they see signs of it. However, if everything is clear, the animals will come at night and drink, when they are poisoned and die. Natives may eat the meat, provided they remove the eyes and intestines. Old men report that they have caught as many as seven emus in one night in this way.[96]

Records of Aboriginal hunters using true pituri as emu poison cover much of its natural range: from central Western Australia, and Mount Liebig and the Finke River in the Northern Territory, to Ooldea in western South Australia.[97] In northern Western Australia, wild indigo leaves were used to poison waterholes.[98]

In the Goldfields region of Western Australia, Aboriginal people formerly used desert poplar branches and leaves to make a poison to kill wild dogs and possibly other game.[99] It was put into the drinking water held in claypans. The carcases of poisoned animals had the entrails and stomach discarded before the flesh was eaten. Central Australian desert dwellers have also employed camel-poison, gyrostemon, native wallflower and stiff goodenia to poison game.[100] The Warlpiri people of the Tanami Desert scatter the dried and crushed leaves of the striped mint-bush over the surface of waterholes to stupefy game birds.[101]

Before Europeans arrived, Aboriginal hunter-gatherers possessed technologies based upon detailed environmental knowledge. This was not expressed, as in the case of Melanesians and Europeans, with conspicuous material items. For Aboriginal people, their survival was based upon knowing the physical resources for making tools in their country — where to find them, how to collect them, the impact of seasons on supply, and the ways to prepare them. Plants, as sources of fibre, gum, bark and wood, were incorporated into the making of artefacts. The use of plant poisons extended the efficiency of Aboriginal hunting strategies.

PART FOUR: PEOPLE, PLANTS AND CHANGE

Chapter 10

The Old and the New

Australia has seen many changes since the beginning of the period commencing with the arrival of the ancestors of modern Aboriginal people, some 50,000 years ago. Variations in world climate have led to the rise and fall of sea levels, which have changed the shape of, and distance between, the landmasses.[1] Along with direct hunting and gathering pressure, early human impacts upon the environment included the introduction of exotic plants, animals and diseases. The cumulative effect of all this change has been the extinction of many of the large vertebrate species during this period.[2] Contacts between Australia and human populations in the rest of the world continued through the last 50,000 years, albeit infrequently. In Australia, the most devastating human impact upon the land occurred in 1788, with permanent European settlement.

Exotic Northern Influences

The Aboriginal ancestors came to Australia's northern shores as South-East Asian immigrants, finding on this continent what were to them strange animals, but at least some familiar plants.[3] Australia back in the Pleistocene period had megafauna, such as the world's largest known marsupial, the *Diprotodon*, and a giant goose-like bird, *Genyornis*.[4] Early Aboriginal rock paintings and engravings depict many of these now-extinct animals.[5] The first human arrivals would have been able to utilise the jungle flora occurring in pockets around the northern coast, before acquiring the environmental knowledge and technology to conquer the more arid interior. The first human colonists encountered the Australian landscape as a *tabula rasa* — a blank slate waiting to be etched.

In spite of scholars once assuming that Australian Aboriginal people remained an isolated population of hunter-gatherers until the arrival of Europeans in the late eighteenth century, there is ample evidence that this was not entirely so. The introduction of the dingo to Australia about 5000 years ago is proof that organic material was being brought in from South-East Asia or Melanesia.[6] In the case of this terrestrial carnivore, there is no apparent way for them to have crossed sea barriers without human assistance. Timing of the arrival of the dingo corresponds to the expansion of Austronesian people across the Pacific.[7]

There are species of Aboriginal food, like the air potato (bitter yam) and lotus lily (sacred lotus), which appear to have originated in South-East Asia, from where they have been widely dispersed by humans long before European settlement of Australia.[8] It has been suggested that Asian seafarers introduced bamboo plants into Arnhem Land.[9] The ulcardo melon growing in tropical and arid regions of Australia may also have originated in Africa, having been brought across via Asia.[10] Aboriginal beliefs in the spiritual significance of banyan fig trees may have been influenced by

Trepang processing. Before European settlement in northern Australia, coastal Aboriginal people collected and dried trepang for the Macassans. From the early twentieth century, Europeans controlled the Australian industry. *(Louis Keipert, Goulburn Island, Northern Territory, early 1920s. South Australian Museum Archives.)*

related beliefs in South-East Asia.[11] Future human DNA research may one day indicate the extent of contact between Australia's hunter-gatherers and their northern neighbours over the last 50,000 years.[12]

For a few centuries prior to British settlement, the northern Australian coast was part of the zone of economic activity for South-East Asian peoples. Asian seafarers undertook annual expeditions to northern Australia and Papua New Guinea to collect a wide range of trade materials, particularly trepang, turtle shell, trochus shell and bird of paradise feathers.[13] Trepang was probably the most valuable cargo they gained from the Australian shores. It is an edible 'sea slug', also known as 'bêche-de-mer' and 'sea cucumber', and is a distant relative of the sea urchin.[14] Aboriginal labour was employed to help collect and process the trepang. After being dried, then coloured using mangrove bark, it was transported to markets as far away as China. In terms of plant materials, Asian visitors loaded their praus for the return voyage with northern ironwood and northern cypress pine timber for building construction and boat repairs, as well as northern sandalwood for the manufacture of incense sticks to burn in temples.[15] They also collected root bark from the cheesefruit tree, to make red dye, and possibly Australian nutmeg as a spice too.[16]

Among the earliest Asian visitors to Australia were probably the Buginese, and then later the Macassarese, both groups based in southern Sulawesi.[17] By the nineteenth century, the people involved in the trepang industry of northern Australia were culturally mixed. In 1844, geographer George Windsor Earl observed the collecting and processing of trepang during his visit to the Top End:

> Indeed, about the month of April, when the prahus [praus] congregate at Port Essington, the population of the settlement became of a very motley character, for then Australians of perhaps a dozen different tribes might be seen mixed up with natives of Celebes and Sumbawa, Bajus [Bajaus] of the coast of Borneo, Timorians [Timorese], and Javanese, with an occasional sprinkling of New Guinea Negroes.[18]

In spite of the diversity of groups represented among the Asian seafarers, the Europeans often referred to them simply as 'Malays' or 'Macassans'. Similarly, to many Aboriginal people they became known as 'Malayu' or 'Makassa'.

Many of the Asian seafarers who visited Australia were Islamic traders, and, although they came with each monsoon, they appear never to have made an attempt to settle permanently. We can gain some insight into the organising of their trading expeditions from biologist Alfred Russel Wallace's published account of his South-East Asian experiences. He was on a trading prau that travelled from Macassar to the Aru Islands in the Arafura Sea during the wet season of 1856–57.[19] Such expeditions were focused on business, rather than colonial expansion. Wallace claimed that, 'Even by the Macassar people themselves, the voyage to the Aru Islands is looked upon as a rather wild and romantic expedition, full of novel sights and strange adventures'.[20] The promise of good fishing brought other visitors to northern Australia. It is reported that the Bardi Aboriginal people of Dampier Peninsula on the southern Kimberley coast sometimes encountered Timorese fishermen working the reefs around Sunday Island.[21]

The arrival in northern Australia of the Buginese and Macassarese at the beginning of each monsoon season was a significant cultural and economic event for local Aboriginal groups. Between the northern visitors and Aboriginal Australians there was a two-way exchange of ideas and technology. Asian trepang fishermen introduced the opium-style pipes into northern Australia.[22] Biological anthropologist Neville White speculated that 'the Indonesian fishermen, the Macassans, who were also intent on bringing back trade goods to sell to Chinese merchants, were interested in procuring herbal remedies, and it's possible that Aborigines learnt of some of these from Indonesians'.[23] It was a common practice for each Macassan prau to carry two or three Aboriginal workers from the Top End when in Australian waters.[24]

The annual Asian visitors to the northern coasts of Australia left behind botanical traces. In 1818, Phillip Parker King's expedition to the north reached the coast of western Arnhem Land, where they found physical evidence of trepang expeditions. King reported that, 'Among the relics were old broken joints of bamboo, which the Malays use to carry their water in, some worn out cordage and a coca-nut, which had perhaps been left behind by accident'.[25] In the same year, King's expedition was at Croker Island, off the coast of Cobourg Peninsula, north of Darwin, when they came across an unusual group of tall palms, which:

> were at first supposed to be cocoa-nut trees that had been planted by the Malays; but on examining them closer, they proved to be *areca*, the tree that produces the betel-nut and the toddy, a liquor which the Malays and the inhabitants of all the eastern islands use. Some of these palms were from thirty to forty feet [about 9 to

12 m] high, and the stem of one of them was bruised and deeply indented by a blunt instrument.[26]

Betel nut palm occurs widely across the Pacific, where the nut is consumed as a recreational drug, and as such is the basis of an extensive industry.[27] In Java, the root of these palms is crushed and boiled to make an invigorating tonic that men drink to make them feel stronger.[28] The concoction is also used as a treatment for internal parasites and for indigestion. Although thought by botanists to have originated from wild plants occurring somewhere in Malaysia or the Philippines, betel nut palms are now grown widely in tropical regions across the world.

Coconut palms are widespread across tropical Asia and the Pacific. In northern Australia, Asian seafarers planted coconut palms at their trepang processing sites.[29] During Tindale's expedition to Groote Eylandt (1921–22) in the western Gulf of Carpentaria and to the adjacent part of eastern Arnhem Land, he noted that:

> Coconuts ('kalukwa') are much appreciated among the Ingura and Balamumu [people]. The sea currents at certain periods of the year bring great numbers of drift coconuts to their coasts; they sometimes germinate, but owing to the improvident nature of the inhabitants, no palm has ever become established. Young nuts planted by our party were invariably dug up, and the tender portions eaten.[30]

Coconuts appeared seasonally in a similar way further east. Aboriginal informants told Tindale on his expedition to Princess Charlotte Bay (1926–27) in northeast Cape York Peninsula that coconuts drifted down the coast all the way from New Guinea.[31]

In northern coastal areas of Australia today, coconut palms are often found growing around towns and settlements. They are highly visible along the eastern coast of northern Queensland.[32] At Groote Eylandt, missionary and ethnobotanist Dulcie Levitt remarked that in the 1970s, 'Coconuts that drifted ashore were broken open and the kernel eaten. The milk was usually lost when the nut was opened and was not used. A popular food but, owing to the uncertain supply, not important. It is still eaten.'[33] Here, the black oil obtained by heating mature coconuts over the fire was rubbed

The lotus lily or sacred lotus is widespread across northern Australia and South-East Asia. Formerly an Aboriginal source of edible seed, it is now grown in botanical parks and gardens. *(Philip A. Clarke, Adelaide Botanic Gardens, South Australia, 2004.)*

onto the head and body to treat dryness caused by the sun and wind.[34] The Tiwi people on Melville and Bathurst Islands have different names for the male and female coconut plants, respectively *purumatingurrupuwa* and *alupwa*.[35] They use the leaves as brooms in their yards and houses.

Another plant still present in coastal northern Australia and linked to the Asian visitors is the tamarind tree.[36] It was the practice of Indonesian seafarers to take with them tamarind pods as part of their supplies on long voyages.[37] The sticky brown pulp of the fruits, which has been described as tasting like sour apricot, is used widely in Asian curries.[38] In terms of nutrients, the fruit yields a relatively high amount of energy.[39] Top End Aboriginal people generally know the tamarind as *djambang*, which linguists think is a word

Ulcardo melons form on a vine. While the pulp of the fruit is edible, the astringent skin is best avoided. This species occurs in many countries, possibly originating in tropical Africa and arriving in Australia through Asia. *(Philip A. Clarke, Diamantina River, Central Australia, 1987.)*

A row of banyan fig trees in East Timor. These plants occur in northern Australia, as well as widely across South-East Asia and the southern Pacific. The Timorese and northern Australian Aboriginal people treat particular trees in their country as sacred. *(Philip A. Clarke, Dili, East Timor, 2005.)*

borrowed from a Malaysian language.[40] From my own experience, tamarind trees are commonly found growing along the shores of Timor.[41] In spite of wild populations in South-East Asia, botanists believe that the tamarind's association with humans begins in tropical Africa, where it probably has its indigenous origins.[42]

On Groote Eylandt, the Warnindilyakwa people consider the tamarind a popular fruit, which is ready for picking in September when the stringybarks have stopped flowering.[43] The fruit has a tart taste and requires added sugar when made into a drink. When eating the fruit, the seeds are discarded. Tamarinds were used medicinally in a number of ways. On Groote Eylandt the fruits are rubbed over aching muscles experienced after a long walk or from paddling a canoe.[44] Here, it is also used for headaches — the tamarind fruits are rubbed over the hands, which are then used to massage the forehead. A solution made from the pulp is drunk to relieve coughs, diarrhoea and colds and the green fruit is eaten as a laxative.[45] Another fruit species that has been suggested as a likely Asian introduction to Australia is the wild gooseberry.[46] This plant is widespread across the Australian tropics and also occurs widely in other tropical zones in the world, where it is used medicinally.

The impact of exotic cultures and their plants in northern Australia is not restricted to the distant past. During the 1980s, the kava narcotic, which is derived from the root of the pepperbush, arrived at Yirrkala in northeast Arnhem Land.[47] Missionaries brought it in from Fiji, Tonga and other Christianised Pacific countries, where kava is extensively used in traditional ceremonies and for social occasions.[48] Kava is valued by Pacific Islanders as a medicine and it is widely sold for this purpose. Its use by indigenous communities in Arnhem Land is secular, with Aboriginal people and authorities elsewhere deciding not to allow it in.

Altered Environments

The first British colonists in Australia used a few Aboriginal foods and medicines in times of need, but mainly before the agricultural transformation of the landscape was much advanced.[49] Later,

they largely forgot most of their earlier uses of indigenous plants. In many cases, the bush that had sustained them either no longer existed or was heavily transformed through such things as land clearance, drainage, altered fire regimes and the invasion of foreign organisms. British settlers wanted to transform what they saw as an Australian wilderness into an ordered European-style landscape — filled with agriculturally useful plants and animals.

The economic plants that Europeans brought out with them to Australia, such as wheat and cultivated potato, had already undergone substantial genetic enhancement through hundreds and even thousands of years of selective breeding.[50] In comparison with these agricultural species, the colonists considered wild Australian food plants to be generally poor in taste and difficult to collect and process. Many of the indigenous foods also contain copious amounts of fibre, while others have toxins that require removal processes before they are consumed. Once the Europeans had firmly established themselves on the land, their use of Aboriginal foods became redundant.

European explorers believed that the Australian bush could be improved for human use, and with this in mind they actively introduced what they thought would be useful plants wherever they went. Early nineteenth century plant hunter, Allan Cunningham, once told a British scientist that with his imported seeds, 'whenever I find a piece of good soil in the wilderness I cause it to be dug up and drop in a few in the hope of providing a meal for some famished European … or some hungry blackfellow'.[51] In doing this, he was acting like the famous John Chapman (alias Johnny Appleseed) of North America, who in the early nineteenth century spread apple seedlings widely in that country with the intention of improving the land.[52] To early plant hunters, the Australian landscape would have been full of botanical wonders, but nevertheless was considered to need substantial improvement through the introduction of more 'useful' plants and animals.

Cunningham's plant introduction program was practised during most of his trips with explorers across Australia. Travelling through inland New

South Wales, Oxley noted that the plant hunter was sowing acorns, quince seeds, peach and apricot stones.[53] Cunningham provided a list of what he planted at Goulburn Island during his trip to the Top End of northern Australia with King. Planted were apricot, lemon, coconut, marrowfat pea, long-padded bean, scarlet runner, large-horned carrot, parsley, celery, parsnip, cabbage, lettuce, endives, spinach, broad-leaved Virginian tobacco, sweet and everlasting pea, Spanish broom and milk-vetch.[54] On the same trip, Cunningham noted at King George Sound in southern Western Australia that ground was cleared near a water hole to plant European fruits.[55]

Cunningham's actions were consistent with those of the first Europeans to reach Australia. Early maritime explorers, such as James Cook, Matthew Flinders and Nicholas Baudin, had introduced into the Australasian and Pacific regions a range of animals, such as pigs and goats, and were in the habit of leaving behind gardens, containing plants including lemons and leeks.[56] Botanist Ferdinand von Mueller also had an active interest in new plant introductions.[57] These explorers and botanists all believed that they were doing their bit in preparing the land for future visits by sailors and settlers. The plants they established, plus others that inadvertently came with them and early colonists as weeds, have led to disputes among botanists about whether or not some species are indigenous to Australia.[58]

In the 1860s, most of the Australian colonies formed acclimatisation societies to facilitate the introduction of exotic species for the purposes of 'improving' the landscape.[59] The total ecological impact of these organisms upon local floras and faunas has been enormous.[60] By spreading introduced plants and animals, the explorers started the process of rapid landscape trans-formation that continues today.

Blended Traditions and Innovations
Change within the physical Australian landscape, at the hands of European invaders, is evident in documented cases of the deliberate introductions of new organisms, as discussed above. It is often less obvious in circumstances when indigenous

people have taken on new plant uses, either directly or indirectly from outsiders, and used them as a part of their hunting and gathering economy. The adoption of different practices, whether the result of a blending of ideas or as innovations, can lead to the creation of modified or entirely new cultural traditions.[61]

Aboriginal uses of plant species that have a cosmopolitan distribution have caused confusion for ethnobotanists looking for strictly pre-European practices. This is best illustrated with the example of the sow or milk thistle. This was one of the first European weeds to arrive along with British colonists in various parts of the world, having originated somewhere in Europe and central Asia.[62] When British settlement in Australia commenced, Aboriginal people appear to have incorporated this plant into their diet almost immediately.[63] Colonist Edward Stephens remembered that in the first few years of South Australian settlement he once encountered a group of Kaurna people who were returning to Adelaide from a fight with some Murray River people. They had come across:

> about a quarter of an acre of luxuriant sow thistles on our land. Some of them asked if they might have them. I obtained the requisite permission, and told them they could take the lot. In a moment they had climbed the fence, and this little plot was one seething mass of men, women and children. Ten minutes later the ground was bare of thistles, and the tribe passed on gratefully devouring the juicy weed.[64]

Similarly, Dawson also recorded Aboriginal people eating sow thistles in colonial western Victoria.[65]

During the 1980s, when I was conducting ethnobotanical work in southern South Australia and western Victoria, the sow thistle was described by elderly Aboriginal people, such as Dick Koolmatrie and Laura Kartinyeri, as 'black-fellow's salad'.[66] Related thistle species, which included prickly species thought to be Australian, were largely ignored. Sow thistle leaves were stripped away and the tasty succulent stems were eaten 'like celery'. They even had a name for it, *thalgi*, which was part of the Ngarrindjeri language of the Lower Murray. On several occasions Aboriginal people demonstrated to me how they were still using sow thistles medicinally, by applying the 'milk' or sap to cuts and abrasions. It was also being eaten as 'blood medicine' — seen as a tonic that made them feel better.

The Aboriginal use of recently introduced plants posed a problem for some botanists.[67] In the early twentieth century, the medical doctor and botanist, John B. Cleland, watched an insane Aboriginal person in an Adelaide institution eating a sow thistle.[68] He used this observation to reason that at least one species of thistle, if not the sow thistle itself, was present in Australia before Europeans arrived. Cleland appeared unwilling to believe that Aboriginal hunters and gatherers would independently develop new uses of plants through experimentation. An alternative explanation, and one preferred by me, is that when Aboriginal foragers first came across a newly arrived edible plant, that was similar in form and taste to an existing item of theirs, they simply incorporated it into the diet. Since Aboriginal hunter-gatherers in temperate Australia relished eating greens, the adoption of sow thistles may have been straightforward.

The fact that sow thistle has been allocated Aboriginal language terms is not in itself strong evidence of a pre-European origin in Australia. During the Cleland and Tindale Central Australian fieldtrip (1956–57), the Aboriginal people they interviewed in the Haast Bluff area insisted that the sow thistles found growing there, which they called *ulburulbura*, 'Came with the white man.'[69] In the past, many scholars considered, incorrectly, that people in hunting and gathering cultures have actively resisted all innovations, with most major changes forced upon them bringing on cultural collapse.[70] In reality, Aboriginal hunters and gatherers had a lifestyle that adapted to constant changes, from short to long term, within their physical environment.

Not all new uses of plants are necessarily borrowed from other peoples. Aboriginal people appear to have experimented with plant species, in isolation from the direct influences of foreign cultures. Scientists Ronald Hamlyn-Harris and Frank Smith provided an illustration of Aboriginal innovation from coastal Queensland, between Townsville and Proserpine, when they reported in 1916 that 'the recent use as a poison of the exotic *Asclepias curassavica* [red-headed cottonbush from tropical South America] by natives on the Don River, and which may be supposed to be frequently efficacious from its botanical association with other Asclepiadeae [Asclepiadaceae], is an instance of the extension of aboriginal poison lore, probably as a result of experience.'[71] These scientists also noted that Aboriginal people in the Pennefather district, near Weipa in northern Queensland, incorporated some part of the red-headed cottonbush into love-charms.

During my ethnobotanical studies of temperate Australia in the 1980s, there were foreign plant species like horehound, small nettle and wormwood, which Aboriginal people were using medicinally.[72] Aboriginal people living in modified landscapes have also come up with new seasonal practices. In the Lower Murray, Ngarrindjeri people warn their children not to swim in the lakes until the dandelions, which are exotic plants, have stopped flowering in October.[73] By adhering to this rule, they avoid 'dandelion fever' brought on by contact with chilly water. The fact that these were plants that had been introduced to their country by Europeans was immaterial to them. For Aboriginal people, changes in the landscape since European settlement have caused many of their earlier traditional sources of plant medicine and plant seasonal indicators to become extremely rare, or at least no longer readily accessible.

There are other early accounts of Aboriginal foragers utilising plants that were probably introduced by Europeans. Famous author and journalist, Dame Mary Gilmore, remembered as a child growing up in rural New South Wales seeing Aboriginal people chewing the fresh leaves and stems of a variety of centaury (pink-stars) for medicinal purposes.[74] This group of plants occurs around the world and, as with thistles, it is debatable how many species were already present in Australia when the Europeans arrived, even though it is known that several species came in later as weeds.[75] Gilmore described centaury as a little pink flower on a plant that grew in open grassy areas. Apparently, Aboriginal travellers carried it with them in dried bundles, along with other herbs, when it was no longer in season. European settlers also used this plant as a medicine, especially for diarrhoea and dysentery, and as material to make a 'slightly tonic beer', hanging it up to dry from a roof beam.[76] European men travelling through the bush would take some with them as a medicine.

In northern Australia, Aboriginal people living at the Belyuen settlement, southwest of Darwin, use ringworm-bush as a medicine to treat fungal infections.[77] This species came from Asia, where it is similarly used, some time after European settlement. Another plant use adopted by Aboriginal people at Belyuen is that of making their traditional style string bags from fibre obtained from sisal hemp leaves.[78] This material is apparently preferred over local indigenous fibres because of its easy preparation and good colour absorption. The Chinese introduced the use of sisal hemp to the Australian tropics in the early twentieth century. The species originated from Yucatan in Mexico and has been introduced to many other tropical parts of the world.

Levitt gave an instance of a likely adopted plant use on Groote Eylandt. She suspected that Aboriginal use of essential oils from paperbarks for the treatment of colds had come about through observing the European use of aromatic eucalypt leaves.[79] This appears to be a possibility, as it is recorded that missionaries may have taught the Maori of New Zealand the medicinal uses of leaves from southern blue gum trees that had been imported from Australia.[80] However, Levitt's explanation is problematic, given the records from elsewhere in the Australian tropics of the Aboriginal use of both paperbarks and eucalypts.[81] In the examples of centaury, ringworm-bush, sisal hemp and paperbark, the plant use traditions of Aboriginal and non-Aboriginal peoples have merged to such an extent that it is not possible or even practical to classify them today as being wholly indigenous or introduced.

'New' Food

The types of food people prefer to eat are part of their cultural identity. British settlers generally found the wild plant food in Australia to be unpalatable and only suitable to get them through severe hardship.[82] Their use of most Aboriginal foods was therefore abandoned after the frontier period had passed. Other reasons for Europeans not permanently adopting Aboriginal foods into the Australian national diet include cultural biases and the fact that many of the wild sources are unsuitable for agriculture. Today, a rare exception is the macadamia-nut (bopple-nut), in terms of a commercially developed food originating in Australia with an international market.[83]

It is apparent that when Aboriginal people first discovered European food, they also found that it tasted very different from their own. Stephens remarked upon Aboriginal food preferences in the earliest years of South Australia. For the Kaurna people in Adelaide, 'if some bread and meat were given to them they would consume the meat, but on getting a little distance from the house, after smelling the bread they would deliberately throw it away'.[84] In 2003, I received a related account from elderly Mardudjara man Dusty Stevens in central Western Australia, who could remember back to when his family came out of the interior of the Western Desert in the 1940s and first met Europeans. At this time, in addition to clothes, they were given white flour rations, which they cooked as a damper on the open fire. The result tasted so unpleasantly sweet to the Stevens family, in comparison to their own ground seed sources, that they spat it out. Europeans have produced foods with enhanced flavours which, to the Aboriginal palate, tasted strong in comparison to that of many wild plant foods.

While Aboriginal people on the frontier initially found some new foods to be distasteful, other aspects of European life were attractive to them. During the phases of British settlement and expansion across Australia, Aboriginal hunter-gatherers were often drawn towards Europeans by the lure of access to new goods and technologies. The Aboriginal desire for European tobacco caused some remote Aboriginal groups to move more or less permanently into settlements.[85] In many areas, Aboriginal groups had little choice but to come in, as they no longer had unrestricted access to the places where their traditional foods and materials could be gathered. Mission stations became institutions that protected Aboriginal people from the atrocities, at the hands of Europeans, occurring in the surrounding country.[86] The rations given to Aboriginal people living under the care of the authorities in remote regions tended to be basic things — like sugar, flour and tea.[87] This new diet was far less diverse than that gained from hunting and gathering.

A factor influencing Aboriginal people in colonial times adopting goods produced by European agriculture was their comparative reliability. In comparing European and indigenous food sources in New South Wales, Backhouse reported in 1836 that his Aboriginal guide Beerabahn, whom Europeans knew as M'Gill,

> thought [cultivated] potatoes were better than most vegetables they [Aboriginal foragers] used: he said, the Blacks, in this neighbourhood [Newcastle], had 'thrown away' the use of fern-root. These people find maize, potatoes, bread, and other articles produced by the industry of white people, so much better than their own native articles of diet, that they stay much about the habitations of the European population, and do little jobs, for which they get these articles in return: they also find this kind of provision more certainly to be relied upon, which induces them to keep near to the usurpers of their country, notwithstanding the abuse and indignity they sometimes meet with, and their liability to be fired upon, if seen helping themselves among the growing Indian corn.[88]

There are records of the Aboriginal theft of crop foods, such as cultivated potatoes, from fields established by settlers.[89] It is likely that in many of these cases the Aboriginal people involved would have considered that they had the right to gather all plant foods they found growing within their traditional estates.

Soon after European colonisation, Aboriginal foraging practices generally turned away from foods that took much effort to process.[90] Archaeologist Anne Clarke summed up the situation for former hunter-gatherers as being one where 'Pre-contact strategies were seen to include a wide range of environments, a varied diet and a marked seasonality, whilst post-contact strategies were confined to a narrower range of environments with a less varied diet and a concentration on permanent food sources'.[91]

A Country Transformed

The change in the physical environment has, for Aboriginal people, brought about a further gap between the present and the pre-European past. The issues surrounding indigenous responses to environmental change are complex. The continuing transformation of the landscape is not just restricted to 'settled' Australia, as it is happening in more remote regions too. Invasive organisms, such as the cane toad from South America and buffel grass from Africa, are currently spreading across northern and Central Australia respectively at alarming rates.[92] In the north, the growth in crocodile numbers over recent decades due to government hunting bans has increased the danger of Aboriginal foraging activities around billabongs.[93] Here also, the European introduction of water buffalo and pigs has resulted in habitat destruction, most apparent in the ecologically fragile wetlands.[94]

The cessation of Aboriginal vegetation firing practices has led to profound environmental changes all over Australia, including in regions where few exotic plant species have yet to become established. The structure of the vegetation is not the only thing to have been altered by the new fire regime. According to early settlers, the ground changed too through the combination of reduced fire frequency and the introduction of hoofed animals, which have both compacted the soil.[95] Across Australia, wild cattle often moved ahead of the European frontier, establishing themselves in remote areas long before colonists, or even explorers, had arrived.[96] In southern Australia, increasing soil salinity and erosion have resulted from excessive vegetation removal and altered water movement.[97] Today, plants that have economic and cultural values to indigenous people may require conservation in threatened environments.

For many Aboriginal communities, particularly in remote regions, a hybrid economy exists that incorporates some of the former hunting and gathering traditions with practices derived from the European-dominated system.[98] Aboriginal people no longer eat foods that are difficult to collect and that require substantial labour to

To encourage sedentary lifestyles, missionaries taught Aboriginal people in the tropics how to grow recognised agricultural plants, such as coconut palms, bananas, mangoes, pawpaw and pineapples. *(Louis Keipert, Goulburn Island, Northern Territory, early 1920s. South Australian Museum Archives.)*

prepare, instead relying on shop food. In northern Australia, some root foods, such as from the various 'cheeky yams' and water lilies, are now rarely gathered and consumed.[99] A flow on effect is that the distinctive string bags essential for leaching yam tubers are no longer made. Other types of artefacts are also disappearing, such as spears and clubs which are giving way to rifles. The movement of the Aboriginal population away from being solely hunter-gatherers towards having more sedentary lifestyles has altered their plant use practices.

In some areas, the Aboriginal community has come to terms with the new arrangement of plants and animals living in their country. As a result, Aboriginal people are often not in favour of pest eradication of introduced species, such as buffalo and goats, as they see them as game suitable for hunting.[100] This, in part, compensates them for the widespread extinctions of herbivores since Europeans first arrived.[101] Hunting remains an important economic and cultural activity for the Aboriginal population located away from the cities.[102]

Influence of Art

From the nineteenth century, the indigenous art and craft trade has spurred on further development of artefact styles, which has impacted directly on plant uses. Examples include the spread of 'old time' practices, such as bark paintings, and making boomerangs, baskets and mats, into parts of Aboriginal Australia where they did not previously exist. Aboriginal people now use a broader range of art and craft media.[103] These changes are brought about through the influences of expanded cultural contacts, as well as by the availability of imported European materials, such as canvas and acrylic paint, and the introduction of new tools, such as chain saws, steel hatchets and metal rasps. In most cases, the finished products are primarily for sale to non-Aboriginal people, even though the makers place importance on such activities preserving their old traditions and helping to maintain their local identity.[104]

The change in Aboriginal lifestyle and economy, along with the introduction of different technologies, has created a new range of uses for plants. From the early twentieth century,

Tropical water lilies have many edible parts. Today, the actions of introduced pigs and water buffalos threaten them in their swamp environments. European plant collectors grow these highly decorative plants in glasshouses. *(Philip A. Clarke, Adelaide Botanic Gardens, South Australia, 2004.)*

Basketry aeroplane made from hoary rapier sedges (*pinki-moranyi*). The maker made a model of the first aircraft she had ever seen. Aboriginal artists and craftspeople have adapted traditional skills and materials to make new ranges of objects. *(Janet Watson of the Moandik people, Kingston, southeastern South Australia, about 1920.)*

Aboriginal basketmakers in the Top End and northern Queensland adopted 'mission' style crafts from other parts of Australia and the Pacific Islands.[105] They have produced new ranges of baskets, mats, armlets and ornaments from

Ngarrindjeri man Lindsay Wilson making a hunting club from mallee wood, using a broken plate as a scraper. Today, Aboriginal people consider that maintaining knowledge of 'old time' plant uses and the making of traditional artefacts help maintain their regional indigenous identities in a rapidly changing landscape. *(Philip A. Clarke, Coorong, South Australia, 1990.)*

pandanus and palm leaves. In the Western Desert, the greater accessibility of metal woodcarving tools in the late nineteenth century led to the Aboriginal production of new material culture items for sale, such as carved wooden animals that they refer to as *punu*.[106] More recently, this cultural region has seen the growth of an extensive craft industry, with women making baskets and bags for the first time from spinifex grass and wool.[107]

In some art traditions the media used have changed, while the basis of the art styles and themes has largely remained the same. While Aboriginal men in Central Australia tend to paint themes from their Dreaming traditions, the artwork of female painters generally focuses on their own gathering activities, such as the plants they collect and the associated toolkit.[108] The cultural background of the artists is proving a rich source of themes for painters to use. Although the artists have primarily painted to engage in commercial activity, such artwork still provides insights into Aboriginal relationships with their country, and often with the flora. Many Aboriginal community art organisations have an internet web presence, which includes a catalogue of artworks for on-line sales.

The art produced within the bark painting tradition of Arnhem Land looks very different from Desert dot painting art, although much of this artwork still features the activities of Dreaming Ancestors, as well as cataloguing the plants and animals that live in the artist's country.[109] Although originally restricted to Arnhem Land in the pre-European period, bark paintings are now painted across northern Australia and sold extensively in the art and tourism markets.[110] The growth of the Aboriginal art industry has led to further descriptions of plant use, through the documentation of artworks. The labels stuck on the backs of bark paintings, or written in ink on the reverse side of canvas paintings, often contain unique ethnographic information that was compiled by art advisers directly from the painters. Aboriginal artists convey plant use information in their art, a fact that some ethnobotanic book publications have utilised.[111] The involvement of Aboriginal people in the art industry will continue to encourage the painting of plant use themes as an expression of regional identity.

Over the millennia since their ancestors arrived in Australia, Aboriginal hunter-gatherers have possessed lifestyles that have adapted to change within their physical environment. They have been able to adopt uses of plants from other cultures, as well as experiment with newly introduced species. There are species of tropical food plants in northern Australia that are also found in other countries, such as Indonesia, from where they may have originated. For hundreds of years before the British arrived, Asian seafarers visited northern Australia each monsoon season to collect trepang and other goods. Aboriginal Australia was not totally isolated from the influences of other cultures before British settlement. The action of foragers adopting new plant uses, to the extent that it has transformed the original hunter-gatherer economy, reflects significant physical and cultural changes within the landscape.

Chapter 11

Appreciating Aboriginal Uses of Plants

Since the 1980s, the general public has developed a greater awareness of Australian land, environment and heritage, which is expressed in the renewed academic and popular interest in the properties of the indigenous flora. The more recent and present day concern for the plants previously used by Aboriginal hunter-gatherers is not just antiquarian. Australian ethnobotany has the potential to help better describe Aboriginal cultural landscapes, both past and present.

From Ecotourism to New Foods

Ever since European settlement of Australia began in the late eighteenth century, the investigation of indigenous plant uses has been a vehicle for exploring the potential applications of wild plant species for the broader community. During the twentieth century, Australians gradually stopped seeing the indigenous flora as impoverished and started appreciating its uniqueness. From the early 1980s, a number of popular publications on useful Australian plants have appeared, chiefly drawing upon information derived from empirical research, augmented by existing Aboriginal ethnobotanical data.[1] These books nurture an appreciation of pre-European Aboriginal relationships with the Australian flora.

Tourism

Tourism in northern Australia draws heavily upon the Aboriginal cultural landscape, as seen for example in the way Aboriginal rock art is promoted to visitors of National Parks. In 1991, the Conservation Commission of the Northern Territory produced for the popular market two pocket sized booklets, the *Bush Tucker Identikit* and the *Bush Medicine Identikit*, that are concerned with Top End Aboriginal plant uses.[2] It is stated on the inside cover of the former publication that: 'This identikit highlights the importance of not only conserving the plants themselves, but also conserving the traditional Aboriginal knowledge of our flora for future generations'. With this style of ethnobotany, the cultural and environmental concerns of the plants are heavily interwoven.

Ecotourism encourages an appreciation of the Australian landscape through an understanding of Aboriginal ethnobotany. The Nyinkka Nyunyu Art and Culture Centre at Tennant Creek in the Northern Territory provides an excellent overview, in the form of a garden, static displays and brochures, of the desert plants used by the local Warumungu people.[3] At Uluru there are commercially run indigenous guided tours that give visitors to Central Australia insights into the Anangu Pitjantjatjara cultural landscape, including local plant uses. The Adnyamathanha community runs 'bushtucker' walks from their cultural centre at Iga Warta in the northern Flinders Ranges of South Australia.[4] Similarly, the Brambuk Aboriginal Cultural Centre, situated in the Grampians of western Victoria, showcases traditional Aboriginal plant uses in the region.[5] There are many Aboriginal-run venues across Australia that display local use of plants.[6]

Since the 1980s, government-funded botanical gardens and parks around Australia have established Aboriginal plant use trails through their living botanical collections. Apart from informative signage, these tracks are generally accompanied with leaflets that give visitors an explanation of the significance of various plants.[7] Tours conducted by teachers and indigenous guides along these plant use trails add much to the cultural experience. This type of information is also starting to appear on the printed colour labels that accompany native plants sold in nurseries. Aboriginal plant uses are becoming a marketing factor in the selling of plants to home gardeners.

In northern Australia, ecotourism has led to the production over the last few decades of a number of published guides to Aboriginal use of the flora.[8] Government funded publications, such as by the Northern Territory Heritage Commission and the Parks and Wildlife Commission of the Northern Territory, have provided detailed regional case studies in the tropics and northern deserts.[9] The scope of these works covers the traditional interests of ethnobotany: food, medicines, material culture, linguistics and cultural traditions. A practical application of Aboriginal plant use data is the incorporation of this knowledge into survival courses run by biologists and environmentalists for the benefit of the armed forces.[10]

Food and Health

Anthropologists pay much attention to the cultural aspects of what people eat. Mary Douglas described food as a system of communication — meaning that what and how we eat is heavily influenced by our cultural perceptions of food in general.[11] Peter Farb and George Armelagos stated 'that by knowing how people eat, anthropologists can know much about them and their society'.[12] The permanent replacement of foods does not happen quickly, even when people are colonising a 'new' land. For instance, European Australians have been relatively conservative when it comes to adopting food used by Aboriginal hunter-gatherers.[13] In spite of the bushfood industry being likely to grow significantly over the coming years, it is doubtful that any of the plants formerly consumed by Aboriginal people are about to completely replace staple foods already being used in the households of the Western world.

Nutritionists have approached Aboriginal plant use in a way that is similar to pharmacologists, by investigating the dietary attributes of many indigenous foods and by producing masses of quantitative data.[14] Some Australian food sources contain significant levels of vitamins. The billygoat plum (Kakadu plum) contains the highest known amount of vitamin C for a fruit in the world, with just one of these fruit containing the equivalent of up to eight oranges.[15] These are pale green when ripe, about two by one centimetre, and are usually gathered after they have fallen onto the ground from their tall slender trees. Around Broome, an Aboriginal drink is made from billygoat plum by pounding the fruit up and soaking them in water.[16] Such fruit are therefore nutritionally superior to Northern Hemisphere counterparts, but with their acidic green plum taste they lack what European-Australians would consider a desirable flavour.

Nutritional research has indirectly influenced the menus of restaurants specialising in 'bushfood' cuisine.[17] In Australian supermarkets there are a growing number of products sold under the label of 'bushfoods'. Examples include crispy baked bread sticks infused with wattle seed, and breakfast cereals flavoured with seasoning of roasted wattle seeds, macadamia-nuts, rosella-bush flowers, strawberry gum leaves, lemon-scented myrtle and aniseed myrtle leaves. There are also excellent cooking sauces that incorporate wild limes. Research into Aboriginal 'bushfoods' potentially offers Australians a wide range of new food additives as condiments from which to develop new cooking styles.

There is further scope for Aboriginal plant uses to become commercialised, but to begin with mainly in niche markets, particularly 'bushfood' restaurants and novelty food shops.[18] The main venues for selling indigenous spices, sauces and jams are hotels, railway and airport cafes, gift stores, museum/art gallery shops and other tourism

Aboriginal people made cakes from dried monterry (*manthri*) fruit and traded these for stone axe heads. Monterry fruit is commonly used in contemporary Australian 'bushtucker cuisine', particularly for jams and tarts. *(Philip A. Clarke, Kingston, southeastern South Australia, 1987.)*

Pitjantjatjara and Yankunytjatjara students collecting honey grevillea (*ultukunpa*) flowers for their nectar during an excursion from the Fregon Primary School. *(Heather Alcorn, west of Fregon, northwestern South Australia, 1979. Ara Irititja collection.)*

outlets. In such places there is already a strong market for monterry tarts, rosella bush relish, bunya-bunya toffee and quandong preserves.[19] There are Aboriginal communities involved in the collecting of wild foods for restaurants and food outlets.[20] As the bush has only a limited capacity for the harvesting of its bushfoods on a commercial scale, the successful adoption of most 'new' foods will probably lead to some form of cultivation to boost supply. Such developments will also allow horticulturalists to develop superior plant strains in response to the market. This is what happened with Queensland's macadamia-nut, although in Hawaii, not Australia.[21]

Apart from investigating commercial opportunities, the results of nutritional studies of wild food have the potential to help authorities manage Aboriginal health problems. In compar-ison to contemporary Aboriginal usage of European-style foods, 'bushtucker' is widely recognised as being of more nutritional benefit to them.[22] This is most relevant for Aboriginal people living in remote areas, such as in outstation communities in the Western Desert and Arnhem Land, where wild food of one kind or another is still accessible and therefore able to become even more significant to Aboriginal diets.[23] In arid and tropical Australia, European settlement and agriculture has struggled

Australian Aboriginal Cultures Gallery. Aboriginal uses of plants feature prominently in exhibitions of hunter-gatherers. *(Grant Hancock, South Australian Museum, Adelaide, 2000.)*

in comparison to the temperate south. In the Centre and the north, Aboriginal food sources may yet gain economic value beyond their hunting and gathering uses, particularly within the indigenous sphere. Aboriginal medicinal plants will continue to be used by indigenous health practitioners, and may also provide clues for the development of new cures for the rest of the world.[24]

Land Management

There are strong economic and social arguments for Aboriginal people to use their community-owned knowledge of the environment in their involvement with management of the land and the coastal zone.[25] Communities of former hunter-gatherers, that have maintained a close relationship with the land, still possess considerable ecological

Don A. Campbell and his children at their bag shelter camp along the Murray River. Originally from the Aboriginal mission at Cummeragunja in New South Wales, Campbell was a returned soldier. Until the late twentieth century, many Aboriginal 'fringe dwellers' in rural areas gained a living from the environment to supplement their income. *(H. Anthony Stevens, Mannum, South Australia, 1931. South Australian Museum Archives.)*

knowledge of their country, which is of interest to scientists.[26] The reintroduction of the Aboriginal fire regime, or something approaching it, has been attempted in some of the National Parks in arid and tropical areas, and there are compelling ecological reasons to do this more where possible.[27] There is still much that remains unknown about past Aboriginal firing practices. Within the last two decades, some insightful work on burning practices has been done with indigenous people from northern and Central Australia, although even here fire patterns have been affected by changes in Aboriginal relationships to the environment since European settlement.[28]

The reinstatement of Aboriginal firing regimes in most temperate areas within Australia would be extremely difficult, because of both the threat it poses to property and the lack of understanding. The maintenance of a system of diverse habitats requires detailed local knowledge within the Aboriginal community that in many cases, particularly in southern Australia, has vanished. Today, Aboriginal people do not possess the high movement patterns and dispersed population densities they had when living solely as hunter-gatherers. The new relations that Aboriginal people have with the land are strongly influenced by the infrastructure of settlements and the broader Australian economy.[29] Aboriginal people in many parts of Australia no longer have direct and easy access to all sections of the land for which they once had custodianship.

Contemporary Cultural Landscapes

Culture shapes the way people experience the spaces within which they live. People from varying cultural backgrounds see the same country quite differently. In Australia, descendants of British settlers have been relatively conservative with what they have absorbed from indigenous cultural landscapes, tending to interpret the land they live on in predominantly European terms. Indigenous Australians have different relationships to their country and therefore do not read the landscape in the same way.[30] There are Aboriginal cultures in remote regions that continue many of their pre-European traditions and practices, in spite of European intrusion into their country.

European Australians have also been slow in adopting any of the elements from the many Aboriginal seasonal calendars operating in Australia. In 1964, anthropologist Adolphus P. Elkin recognised the conservatism of British culture when commenting on the diversity of Aboriginal systems for recognising seasons: 'But each [indigenous] calendar is a local one. We stick to our four seasons wherever we are, like plum-pudding for Christmas on the equator or in the Antarctic, although we know that in some regions this is often an unreal division of the year'.[31] But today there are signs of the grafting of traditions. For example, the use of sheoak, eucalypt and wattle saplings for Christmas trees, instead of the European fir tree.[32] Also, Australians are beginning to replace their chocolate Easter Bunnies with Easter Bilbies (rabbit-eared bandicoots). Neither development diminishes Christian traditions, but instead gives them greater force in a 'new' landscape.

The recognition and limited adoption by European Australians of Aboriginal models of seasonal change is beginning to occur in monsoonal Australia. Here, this knowledge is increasingly being used to better inform the managers of National Parks.[33] The aim of sharing a single calendar in a country that has such diverse climates and landscapes as Australia will only serve to maintain a system that fits poorly. The increasing awareness, through the study of indigenous calendars, of Australian seasonal cycles will help provide a greater sense of belonging with land for people at the local level. Australia requires the equivalents of Northern Hemisphere traditions based upon the autumn leaves fall, the groundhog winter predictions, and the arrival

of spring heralded by the swallows. Greater appreciation of the diversity of seasonal systems in Australia will hopefully lead to better appreciation and management of the environment by all.

In recent years, many of Australia's indigenous people have continued to work closely with European scholars in systematically recording their plant uses.[34] As mentioned above, the Northern Territory government has published detailed case studies of regional ethnobotany, and the primary authors of these are generally botanists who recorded the data and classified the plants. Often, the names of the Aboriginal people who were major sources and compilers of the information are included as secondary authors. These texts help to describe indigenous affinities to specific landscapes, and provide unique insights into the social aspects to hunting and gathering activities, methods of plant preparation and seasonality. The depth of such data itself further discredits early European notions of 'poor' Australian flora and 'primitive' Aboriginal culture.

The importance of acknowledging the Aboriginal heritage of the country is not just of scholarly interest, since it impacts upon the ways the land is developed and maintained. It is a characteristic of governments worldwide to structure their budgets around concepts of national identities and cultural landscapes. For instance, the English persistently regard themselves as a rural-based society, despite all evidence to the contrary.[35] This is largely supported through the British media. The result is a rather generous government subsidy to the farming sector, which enables the rural landscape to be preserved.

Much of this book has concerned the use of plants by Australian hunter-gatherers at the time Europeans first arrived in their country. And yet Aboriginal people living in rural and urban settings today still have unique relationships to flora. Some of the modern uses of plants reflect on the contemporary identity of Aboriginal people. During September and October 1999, while doing fieldwork in the environs of Aurukun in northwest Cape York Peninsula, I observed Wik women and children in the settlement throwing boomerang-shaped lumps of wood and bent iron high up into the branches of street trees, in order to dislodge mango fruit for eating on the spot and for taking to school. Mangoes are originally from India, but are now grown widely as plantation fruit in the tropics of the world. An analysis of food eaten by people living in Aurukun, and probably in many other northern Aboriginal settlements, would have to include the introduced mangoes. The situation observed was both Aboriginal and urban in character, albeit in a landscape that was remote from other towns and pastoral stations. Newly developing Aboriginal traditions are bound to incorporate some non-Aboriginal elements.

In many Aboriginal communities, indigenous-run social history projects have produced accounts of the historical past that are flavoured by references to the local flora. In 'settled' Australia, Aboriginal people have been involved in recording plants once used by their hunter-gatherer ancestors, as well as their own reminiscences of the species that were formerly used by them as part of 'fringecamp' and 'station life'.[36] Knowledge of plants displayed in these situations reflects the life history of the individuals giving the information. In a study of plant use at Wreck Bay in New South Wales, Aboriginal woman Donna McLeod reminisced that when she and her friends were children they 'never used to worry about lollies — lots of kids lived on mylong [apple-berry] and geebung and other things'.[37]

Part of my ethnobotanical research has centred on Aboriginal harvesting practices of temperate Australia during the twentieth century, when many people were living in rural fringecamps and mission stations until the 1960s. I often recorded how Aboriginal children on the way to school had seen wild food, such as fruits and gums, as edible treats.[38] Bushfoods helped supplement the rations given to them. Similarly, it has been my experience that adults in the Central Australian Aboriginal communities have fond memories of the times when, as schoolchildren, they had refreshed themselves by drinking the 'honey' (nectar) from honey grevillea. Such personal accounts are part of the rich social history of people who are asserting their indigenous cultural identity. Ethnobotanical studies therefore have potential for documenting

Aboriginal links to their lands and cultures since European settlement.

Ethnobotanical researchers, and a few indigenous people, have more recently argued for the wider and greater recognition of indigenous ownership of botanical knowledge, claiming that in the past ethnobotanical research has often not been of direct or long-term benefit to people who gave the information.[39] In spite of this, it has been acknowledged that, while there are moral obligations for the researcher to compensate adequately the indigenous person who provides the data, intellectual property rights on cultural or community-owned knowledge are often difficult to grant and enforce in cross-cultural situations.[40] Being a custodian of ethnobotanical information does not translate to being the owner of it. But there are situations when certain information is closely associated with an individual. The level of botanical knowledge of persons within each community varies considerably. As artist and ethnobotanist John Kean explained:

> The acquisition and retention of such information would be affected by many factors — regions traversed, sex, age and even individual spiritual associations with particular areas of land and associated totems. Accordingly, knowledge can be viewed as either an individual or a community/cultural attribute.[41]

Regardless of who 'owns' ethnobotanical data, it is reasonable to expect that the relevant cultural group gains appropriate benefits in cases where the acquisition of Aboriginal plant use knowledge leads to commercial exploitation.

The Future of Australian Ethnobotany

Ethnoscience can be described as a scholarly field that encompasses the study of the physical and cultural relationships that indigenous people have with their physical environment. The indigenous studies literature contains other ethnosciences, such as ethnobiology, ethnocosmology, ethno-ecology and ethnozoology. Yet ethnobotany is better known as a field, primarily because of the longstanding European tradition of a wide range of scholars studying the flora. It is also because plants are present and highly visible in most landscapes and therefore relatively easy to investigate, whether or not the researcher has a good grasp of indigenous languages. The same ease of study could not be said for most of the other ethnosciences, which require a higher level of basic training. All cultural groups have relationships to plants that ethnobotanists could study, given the appropriate techniques. In northern Australia, for example, anthropologist David Trigger has considered the symbolic role of introduced plants for European pastoralists making their home in the wild bush.[42]

There are researchers with scientific and economic concerns with the indigenous use of environmental resources who have treated ethnobotany as a study of the physical properties of plants and their potential for application outside the Aboriginal arena. This is a continuation of the type of interest shown in Australian plants by Joseph Banks and his plant hunters back in the late eighteenth and early nineteenth centuries. In contrast, anthropologists and cultural geographers have taken ethnobotany as a study that highlights the importance of plants within particular indigenous cultures. Both physical and cultural approaches are valid and can sometimes be used simultaneously, as I have tried to do with my own ethnobotanical researches. An emerging field of research is being undertaken between the chiefly scientific and cultural extremes, by ecologists studying indigenous environmental knowledge for its application to issues both within and outside the indigenous domain.[43]

Until the late twentieth century, most scholars wrongly used the nature of the flora to help explain the apparent 'primitive' condition of Australian hunter-gatherers.[44] Although climate and natural resources were probably factors influencing whether or not a community adopted agriculture on its own accord, the environment alone cannot explain why some indigenous people in the world retained a hunting and gathering lifestyle into the twentieth century. Cultural isolation also does not provide an adequate explanation for the lack of agriculture in Australia before European settlement. Papua New Guinea is in close proximity to Australia and has had agriculture for perhaps as long as the last 9000 years.[45] Archaeologist John M. Beaton described Papua New Guinea as the 'Pleistocene vegetable garden of Australia'.[46] The issue of why some hunter-gatherer societies resisted the adoption of agriculture should be inverted. The more appropriate question, which is beyond the scope of this book, is what combination of cultural, environmental and demographic factors are required to induce a society to become pastoralists or horticulturalists?

Areas of Australian ethnobotany that invite further study include the role of plants in indigenous calendars, the further description of Aboriginal plant uses (past and present), as well looking at the application of Aboriginal ethnobotanical knowledge in future environmental management. Cultural change and landscape transformation will continue to form the backdrop of Australian ethnobotanical investigations. Since ethnobotany is a field of study, rather than a discrete discipline, it is a topic that will continue to be enriched by the different, but complementary, approaches that various specialists bring to it.

Notes

Preface

1 Hallam (1975) and Williams & Hunn (1986).
2 For examples of the view of Aboriginal people being 'primitive' see Durkheim (1915 [1976, pp. 1, 95–6]), Fison & Howitt (1880), Frazer (1890), Lang (1905), Lubbock (1870) and Ratzel (1896, chapters B & C). See discussion by Hiatt (1996), Moorehead (1968, pp. 62–75) and Mulvaney (1985).
3 Woods (1879, pp. vii–viii).
4 White & Hicks (1953, p. 281).
5 Cleland (foreword in Albrecht, 1959).
6 Elkin (1964, p. 51).
7 Bicchieri (1972), Lee & de Vore (1968) and Williams & Hunn (1986).
8 The age of Aboriginal settlement of Australia is still a matter of academic debate, with new dates likely to be refined over the next few years (Adcock et al., 2001; Allen, 1998a, 1998b, 2000; Clarke, 2003a, chapter 1; Gillespie, 2002; Lourandos, 1997; Mulvaney & Kamminga, 1999; Roberts et al., 2001).
9 Clarke (2006 ms), Lemmon (1968) and Whittle (1970).
10 Clarke (2003c).
11 Anderson & Gale (1992), Baker (1999), Clarke (1994), David (1998, 2002), Head (2000a, 2000b) and Young (1992).
12 Cosgrove (1984), Duncan & Duncan (1988), Gosden (1995), Gosden & Head (1994), Jackson (1989), Ley (1983) and Meinig (1979).
13 Australian Biological Resources Study (1981–2002).
14 Clarke (1985a, 1985b, 1986a, 1986b, 1987, 1988, 1994, 1996a, 1996b, 1996c, 1997, 1998a, 1998b, 1999, 2001, 2002, 2003b, 2003c).
15 Australian Plant Name Index (http://www.anbg.gov.au).
16 Refer to Haddon (1904–35), Harris (1977), McNiven & Quinnell (2004), Moore (1979) and Sharp (1993, 2002) for a description of Torres Strait Islanders and their environment

Chapter 1

1 Head (2000a, chapter 4), MacKenzie (1997) and Thomas (1983, pp. 17–25).
2 Brown (1986), Duranti (2001), Foley (1997) and Lakoff (1987).
3 Berlin (1992), Brown (1986), Crawford (1982, pp. 16–7), Heath (1978), Kean (1991), Laramba Community Women (2003, pp. vii–ix), McKnight (1999), Smith & Kalotas (1985, p. 326), Waddy (1979, 1982, 1988) and Walsh (1993).
4 Blake (1981), Henderson & Nash (2002), Schmidt (1993), Thieberger & McGregor (1994) and Yallop (1982).
5 Clarke (2003a, pp. 198–200, 204–5, 218; 2006 ms) and Finlayson (1952, pp. 57–8, 71).
6 Stirling (1896, p. 37). Reference cited by Stirling is Schulze (1891, p. 216).
7 Mühlhäusler (2003, pp. 50, 61–2).
8 Robinson (2 July 1831 [cited Plomley, 1966, p. 369]). Also see Plomley & Cameron (1993, pp. 5–7, 15, 20, 23) and Robinson (1829–31 [cited Plomley, 1966, pp. 61, 139, 190, 369, 386, 490, 492–3, 601]).
9 McKnight (1999, p. 136).
10 Latz (1995, pp. 75–6). See also Crawford (1982, pp. 16–7) and Nash (1997).
11 Mühlhäusler (2003), Povinelli (1990) and Waddy (1982, 1988).
12 Wiminydji & Peile (1978, p. 506).
13 Goddard & Kalotas (1988, pp. 14–5), Johnston & Cleland (1942, pp. 95, 102),

Thomson (1962, pp. 272–3), Tindale (1978, pp. 160–2) and Wilhelmi (1861, p. 172).
14 Henderson & Dobson (1994, pp. 445, 476, 495, 558) and Turner (1994, p. viii). Schulze (1891, pp. 231–4) identified the same food categories, but used the spellings 'garra' (kere), 'ntjaba' (tyape), 'mana' (merne) and 'unkuala' (ngkwarle).
15 For instance, refer to Akerman (1978), Davis (1989, pp. 34–5), Heath (1978, pp. 44), Mathews (1904, pp. 227, 237), O'Connell et al. (1983, p. 83), Sutton (1995, p. 154) and Wilhelmi (1861, p. 172).
16 McKnight (1999, pp. 136–40).
17 Memmott et al. (2006, p. 31).
18 McKnight (1999, p. 125).
19 Rudder (1978–79, p. 353).
20 Clarke (2003a, pp. 34, 186), Russell-Smith (1985, pp. 244–5), Warner (1958, pp. 135–6) and Yunupingu (1995, p. 12). Mathews (1904, pp. 294–5) recorded a similar system, which divided plant species into moieties (phratries), from western Victoria.
21 Smith (1991, p. 27) and Smith et al. (1993, p. 24).
22 Goddard (1992, pp. 21, 99, 176) and Goddard & Kalotas (1988, pp. 116–9).
23 Heath (1978, pp. 52–3). See also Levitt (1981, pp. 111–2) and Wightman, Roberts et al. (1992, p. 36).
24 Warner (1958, pp. 278–9). Refer to Capell (1962), Mathews (1903) and O'Grady (1956) for descriptions of Aboriginal 'secret' languages.
25 Mühlhäusler & Fill (2001) and Mühlhäusler (2003) provided overviews of the study of language and environment.
26 Heath (1978, p. 46).
27 A.R. Peile (1980 [cited Carr & Carr, 1981, p. 8]). In the quote, 'Calytrix microphylla' is an earlier name for C. exstipulata.
28 Cleland & Johnston (1937–38, pp. 208–9, 211, 213), Goddard (1992, p. 125) and Goddard & Kalotas (1988, p. 15). See also Cleland (1936, p. 8) and Johnston & Cleland (1942, p. 95) for related categories.
29 Meyer (1843, p. 70).
30 Yunupingu (1995, p. 49) and Yunupingu & Williams (1995, p. vi). The species of 'bush potato' here refers to Ipomoea graminea.
31 Levitt (1981, pp. 32, 39, 145). See also Smith & Kalotas (1985, p. 337) and Specht (1958, pp. 483, 501). The name is sometimes written as Triglochin procera.
32 Latz (1995, pp. 296–7). See also Bindon & Gough (1993, p. 14), Cleland (1957, pp. 152, 155), Cleland et al. (1925, p. 115), Cleland & Johnston (1933, p. 121), Cleland & Tindale (1954, p. 84; 1959, p. 135), Hiddins (2001, p. 135), Latz (1995, pp. 296–7), O'Connell et al. (1983, pp. 84–6), Roth (1897, pp. 92–3), Turner (1994, p. 21), Wightman, Dixon et al. (1992, p. 33) and Wightman, Gurindji elders et al. (1994, p. 53).
33 Willie MacKenzie (Winterbotham, cited Symons & Symons, 1994, p. 16).
34 Berndt (1940, p. 173), Berndt & Berndt (1993, pp. 124, 237, 452–3) and South Australian Department of Education, Training and Employment (2001, pp. 20–3). During the 1980s, I also received several related accounts from Ngarrindjeri people.
35 Johnston & Cleland (1942, p. 97).
36 Goddard (1992, p. 60).
37 Common name derivation discussed by Ramson (1988, p. 646).
38 Bunce (1859, p. 71; see also p. 74).

39 Frankel (1982), Gott (1983), Gott & Conran (1991, pp. 6–7), Low (1989, pp. 104, 108) and Zola & Gott (1992, pp. 7–9).
40 Dawson (1881, pp. 101, xxxiii).
41 Tunbridge (1985b, p. 3; 1987, p. 4).
42 Hercus & Simpson (2002, p. 16).
43 Dawson (1881, p. lxxix).
44 Dawson (1881, p. lxxx). Identification by Gott (1985a, p. 14).
45 Dawson (1881, p. lxxxi). Recorded words for pigface include *puuyuupkil* in Gundidjmara around Portland in western Victoria (Zola & Gott, 1992, p. 20), *booyeup* in the Lake Boga language of central Victoria (Stone, 1911, p. 444), *buyub* in the Djadjala dialect of Wergaia language in northwest Victoria (Hercus, 1986, p. 275) and *poo-yup* in southeast South Australia (Cameron-Bonney, 1990, p. 21).
46 Dawson (1881, p. lxxxi). Gott (1985a, p. 14) was not able to identify this plant. This name appears related to the Aboriginal words recorded from the Adelaide region, 'parngutta' – 'native root; potatoe' (Teichelmann & Schürmann, 1840, pt.2, p. 37), 'parangota' — 'potato' (Wyatt, 1879, p. 174) and 'pernuta' — 'potato' (Williams, 1839, p. 64).
47 Beveridge (1884, p. 74), Clark & Heydon (2002), Smyth (1878, vol. 2, pp. 174–220) and Wesson (2001). See discussion of Aboriginal placenames by Harvey (1999), Hercus et al. (2002) and Ryan (2002).
48 Tunbridge (1985b, p. 12).
49 Black (1920, p. 86).
50 Bindon (1996, p. 165), Douglas (1988, pp. 2, 7, 267, 291) and Smith & Smith (1999, pp. 25–7). Douglas wrote the Western Desert Aboriginal name as *karlkurla*, whereas Bindon and Smith & Smith wrote the name as said by Aboriginal people at Kalgoorlie as *kalkula*. Parker (1980, p. 42) listed the name used for this at Leonora as *kalkula*.
51 Blake et al. (1998, p. 22).
52 Mollison (1974, section 7.1).
53 Dousset (1997), Howie-Willis (1994), Howitt (1904, pp. 736–40), Latz (1995, p. 76), McConnel (1930, pp. 14–5), Meggitt (1962, pp. 144–5, 148, 278–9), Roth (1897, pp. 65–66), Spencer & Gillen (1899, Appendix A; 1927, vol. 2, Appendix B) and Warner (1958, pp. 26, 42–3, 62, 88–9, 102, 457).
54 Stanbridge (1861, p. 290).
55 Meggitt (1962, p. 279).
56 Bunce (1859, p. 27).
57 Robinson (cited Plomley, 1987, p. 805).
58 For example, see Warner (1958, pp. 4, 380).
59 Teichelmann & Schürmann (1840, pt.2, pp. 4, 75). See Gara (1998) for a biography of Mullawirraburka.
60 Willsteed et al. (2006, p. 4).
61 S. Klose (cited Simpson, 1998, p. 4). See Clarke (2003a, pp. 115–6) for other similar examples.
62 Tindale (1976, p. 26). Peterson (1976) discussed the relationship between natural and cultural areas.
63 Von Brandenstein (1988, pp. 19, 165).
64 Angas (1847, p. 92). Meyer (1843, p. 98) recorded the Ramindjeri word *timbelin*, which is possibly another rendering of 'chembillin', as 'licking with the tongue'.
65 Tindale (1974, pp. 99–102, 106; 1977).
66 Clarke (2003a, pp. 49–50) and Latz (1995, p. 76).
67 Hawker (1841–45, pp. 101–2). Eyre (1845, vol. 2, pp. 354–5) gave another account of the same example. King Tenberry was also recorded as 'Tenbury'.
68 Holden (1879, p. 23).
69 Wightman & Smith (1989, p. 17).
70 Robinson (1831 [Plomley, 1966, pp. 369–70]). Robinson's sketch is included within Plomley's text.
71 Robinson (1831 [Plomley, 1966, p. 369]). The peppermint trees were probably the Risdon peppermint (*Eucalyptus risdonii*), the stringybarks would be messmate stringybark (*E. obliqua*) and the honeysuckle is most likely to be the white honeysuckle (*Banksia integrifolia*).
72 Cook & Armstrong (1998), Myers (1986a, chapter 5; 1986b), Rigsby (1998), Sutton (2003, chapter 1), Sutton & Rigsby (1986) and Williams (1986).
73 McKnight (1999, pp. 136–7).
74 Dawson (1881, p. 21). Gott (1985a, p. 8) identified the species.
75 Basedow (1925, p. 155).
76 Grey (1841, vol. 2, p. 298).
77 Gregory (1887, pp. 131–2).
78 Grey (1841, vol. 2, p. 289), Meagher (1974, p. 24) and Nind (1831, p. 34).
79 Clarke (2003a, p. 111) and Tindale (1974, p. 60).
80 Thomson (1975, p. 4).
81 White (1983, p. 2).
82 Levitt (1981, pp. 32, 39, 145). See also Smith & Kalotas (1985, p. 337) and Specht (1958, pp. 483, 501). The name is sometimes written as *Triglochin procera*.
83 Basedow (1925, p. 148), Berndt (1981, pp. 174–7; 1982b, pp. 42–51), Clarke

84 Roheim (1974, pp. 48–51).
85 Meggitt (1962, pp. 307–8) and Warner (1958, pp. 278–9).
86 Meggitt (1962, pp. 274–5).
87 Clarke (2003a, pp. 48–50, 64, 125), F. Rose (1987, pp. 145–6), Tunbridge (1991, pp. 36–8), Warner (1958, pp. 58, 277–80) and Worsnop (1897, pp. 8–9).
88 Backhouse (1843, Appendix D, p. xl), Cleland (1934–35, pp. 204, 209), Gunn (1842, pp. 48–9), Kalotas (1996, pp. 284–6), Kennedy et al. (1984), Robinson (1831 [cited Plomley, 1966, pp. 369, 490, 492–3]), Roth (1899, pp. 95, 97) and Walker (1888–99, pp. 256–7). See the *Adelaide Observer*, 10 July 1909, p. 18. The 'native bread' was formerly known as *Polyporus mylittae*.
89 Smyth (1878, vol. 1, p. 48).
90 Mitchell (cited Smyth, 1878, vol. 1, p. 48). See also Basedow (1925, p. 69) for a similar record.
91 Berndt (1940, p. 167). See also Berndt & Berndt (1993, p. 146).
92 Kalotas (1996, p. 288) and Latz (1995, p. 257). Also known as orange shelf fungus and previously known as *P. coccineus*.
93 Webb (1960, p. 108).
94 D. Bird Rose (1987).
95 Basedow (1925, p. 76). Basedow's identification of *Spinifex hirsutis* [= *S. hirsutus*] is probably more correctly *S. longifolius*.
96 Silberbauer (1971, p. 35).
97 Clarke (2003a, pp. 44–5). Aboriginal artefact collection, South Australian Museum.
98 Basedow (1925, p. 77).
99 Cleland (1966, pp. 123, 129, 131), Cleland & Johnston (1937–38, pp. 210, 337) and Goddard & Kalotas (1988, p. 22).
100 Thomson (1983, p. 20, plate 4132).
101 Crawford (1982, p. 63).
102 Latz (1995, pp. 196, 255–6).
103 Berndt & Berndt (1985, pp. 91–106), Edwards (1988, pp. 42–64) and Jacob (1991, pp. 80–145).
104 Berndt (1940, pp. 286–8), Berndt & Berndt (1970, p. 106) and Howitt (1904, pp. 773–7).
105 Teichelmann (1841, p. 9). For other descriptions of gender division of labour, refer to C.H. Berndt (1981, pp. 174–7; 1982b, pp. 42–51), Clarke (2003a, pp. 47–9, 57, 59, 69–70, 113, 153, 169), Earl (1846, p. 251), Kaberry (1939) and Meagher (1974, p. 14).
106 Berndt (1981, pp. 174–7; 1982b, pp. 42–51), Clarke (2003a, pp. 47–9, 57, 59, 69–70, 113, 153, 169), Laramba Community Women (2003, pp. vii–viii) and Wallace (1983).
107 Webb (1960, p. 105; 1969a, p. 84).
108 Clarke (2003a, pp. 47–50), Keen (1994, part 2) and Maddock (1982, chapter 3).
109 Goddard (1992, p. 61) and Latz (1995, p. 211).

Chapter 2

1 Arthur (1996, pp. 27–8), Clarke (2003a, chapter 2), Maddock (1982, pp. 105–20), Rose (1992, pp. 42–57), Spencer (1896, part 1, p. 50), Stanner (1953) and Sutton (1988b, pp. 14–9).
2 Account from eastern Gunwinggu man, Long Paddy, Djamargula (told in Berndt & Berndt, 1989, pp. 56–7).
3 Tunbridge (1988, pp. 47–51).
4 Young (1992, p. 257).
5 Latz (1995, p. 191).
6 Cleland (1952).
7 Mathews (1904, pp. 343–4). Mathews spelled the Ancestor's name as 'Dhurramulan'.
8 Berndt (1974, p. 26), Berndt & Berndt (1993, pp. 177–8), Clarke (1999, p. 54), Howitt (1904, p. 674), Mathews (1904, p. 333) and Taplin (1874 [1879, p. 17]).
9 Hercus (1992, p. 13). See also Strehlow (1970, pp. 94–5).
10 Brooks (2003) provided examples of sacred trees in the landscape surrounding Alice Springs in Central Australia.
11 Strehlow (1968, p. 35). See also Strehlow (1970, pp. 102–5).
12 Gillen (cited Mulvaney et al., 1997, pp. 1, 171, 191, 233, 343, 349, 506–7), Hiatt (1996, pp. 105–6), McConnel (1930, pp. 17–8, 20) and Spencer & Gillen (1899, chapter 6; 1927, vol. 1, chapter 8).
13 Horne & Aiston (1924, p. 53).
14 Dix & Lofgren (1974).
15 Tindale (1936, p. 58).
16 Crawford (1968, pp. 128–9).
17 Worsnop (1897, p. 26).
18 Etheridge (1918), Howitt (1904, fig.31, p. 540; p. 594) and McCarthy (1940a).
19 Mathews (1904, pp. 239–52).

20   Leichhardt (1847, p. 232).
21   Cawte (1996, p. 61) and Levitt (1981, pp. 52–3, 107).
22   Zola & Gott (1992, p. 29).
23   Robinson (1832 [Plomley, 1987, p. 241]) and Walker (1888–99, p. 253).
24   Backhouse (1843, p. 542).
25   Hassell (1936, p. 709).
26   Tunbridge (1988, p. 46).
27   Blandowski (1855, p. 72).
28   Blandowski (1855, p. 72).
29   Leichhardt (1847, pp. 22, 110–1 .
30   Leichhardt (1847, pp. 23–4).
31   Cawte (1996, p. 17).
32   Blake et al. (1998, p. 85).
33   Levitt (1981, p. 147) and Puruntatameri (2001, pp. 61, 142).
34   Wightman, Dixon et al. (1992, p. 30).
35   Smith (1991, p. 16), Wightman, Roberts et al. (1992, p. 14) and Wightman
     & Smith (1989, p. 15).
36   Refer to Bonney (1994, p. 23) for the southeast of South Australia, Berndt &
     Berndt (1954, p. 37) and Cawte (1996, p. 23) for Arnhem Land, and Tindale
     (1938–39, vol. 1, p. 37) for the Darling River. See also the vocabulary card for
     the Tangani word, *mulba katal*, from the Coorong (N.B. Tindale collection,
     South Australian Museum Archives).
37   See the vocabulary card for the Potaruwutji word, *katalemelba*, from the
     southeast of South Australia (N.B. Tindale collection, South Australian
     Museum Archives).
38   Bates (1912 [1992, p. 19]). Bates wrote *djanga* as 'janga'.
39   Bates (1938 [1992, pp. 153–4]).
40   Clarke (1997, p. 128; 2003a, pp. 25–9) and Johnson (1998, pp. 13–6).
41   Mathews (1904, pp. 270–4).
42   Smith (1880, p. 30). Mathews (1904, pp. 281–2) described a similar myth
     from Victoria. For an account of Odin in Germanic and Norse mythology,
     see Simek (2003, pp. 233, 235–9). Bates (2002) considered pre-Christian
     pagan tree worship in Europe.
43   Blake et al. (1998, p. 72) and Yunupingu (1995, p. 42).
44   Chaloupka (1993, pp. 32, 35, 66).
45   Brennan (1986, p. 19). The plant, *Platysace arnhemica*, does not have a
     widely recognised common name.
46   Bardon (1999, pp. 80, 100, 109, 120, 122–3, 139), Sutton (1988a, pp. 222–3)
     and Warlukurlangu Artists (1992, pp. 40–51). Both the Bush Potato and Big
     Yam Dreamings probably refer to the desert sweet potato (*Ipomoea costata*)
     or a related species. The Bush Tomato Dreaming is most likely based upon
     Solanum chippendalei. Sugarleaf refers to the sweet exudate produced by
     insects living on plants, such as mulga.
47   Howitt (1904, pp. 794–5). Howitt uses the language name 'Yantruwunta'.
     Kimber (1984, p 17) presented an overview of other Nardoo Dreaming
     accounts from surrounding areas. McBryde (1987, pp. 271–3) provided a
     Grinding Stone Dreaming from Wangkangurru people further west.
48   Clarke (2005), Smith (1986) and Tindale (1977).
49   Brandl (1988, p. 174), Chaloupka (1993, pp. 89, 138–41), Flood (1997, pp.
     280, 283–5, 295, 324) and Morwood (2002, pp. 19, 21, 160–1, 171, 194).
50   Bindon (1996, p. 102), Blake et al. (1998, p. 61), Hiddins (2001, p. 134), Levitt
     (1981, pp. 41, 136–7), Puruntatameri (2001, pp. 8, 44, 143–4), Rae et al.
     (1982, p. 45), Roth (1901b, p. 12), Smith (1991, p. 21), Smith & Wightman
     (1990, p. 12), Sutton (1994, pp. 37, 45), Wightman, Roberts et al. (1992, p.
     18), Wightman & Smith (1989, p. 16) and Yunupingu (1995, p. 35). The long
     yam is sometimes referred to as the 'pencil yam'.
51   Arthur (1996, pp. 92–3).
52   Berndt (1951, pp. 20–1, 45, 92–3, 135, 191–2, 198–9; 1952, pp. 98, 100–1,
     109, 115–6, 121, 131, 227–8, 235, 238, 247, 250, 261, 276, 286, 298).
53   Goodale (1971, chapter 7; 1986, pp. 205–8), Hiatt (1996, chapter 9),
     Mountford (1958, pp. 124, 130–43), Puruntatameri (2001, pp. 43–4, 143–4),
     Sims (1978) and Smith (1990, pp. 57–8).
54   Mountford (1958, chapter 4) and Smith (1990, pp. 57–8).
55   Mountford (1958, p. 134 & plate 44D). See also Goodale (1971, pp. 190–1,
     203, 223–5).
56   Puruntatameri (2001, p. 24).
57   Puruntatameri (2001, pp. 43–4, 147).
58   Goodale (1971, p. 181).
59   Bradley (1995).
60   Charles White in the *Adelaide Observer*, 14 January 1905, p. 39. See also
     Stanbridge (1857, p. 139).
61   Mountford (1956, p. 482).
62   Mathews (1904, p. 280).
63   For examples see Chaloupka (1993, p. 231) and Thomson (1932).
64   Howitt (1904, p. 429). Turrbal is the language of the Yuggera (Jagara) people
     living between Ipswich and Brisbane (see Tindale, 1974, Tribal Map).
65   Robinson (1830–31 [Plomley, 1966, pp. 266, 300, 509]).
66   Latz (1995, p. 68).
67   In 1977, Kim McKenzie (producer & editor) made a film, *A Walbiri Fire
     Ceremony — Ngatjakula*, which was shot in 1967 at Yuendumu, Northern
     Territory. It is available through the library of the Australian Institute of
     Aboriginal Studies (LV0010). See also Elkin (1964, pp. 206–7), Morphy
     (1998, pp. 193, 196–8), Nicholson (1981, pp. 64–5), Peterson (1970) and
     Spencer & Gillen (1904, pp. 375–92).
68   Morphy (1998, p. 196).
69   Clarke (2003a, p. 61).
70   Sutton (1994, p. 48), Wightman, Dixon et al. (1992, p. 16) and Wightman,
     Roberts et al. (1992, p. 20).
71   Taplin (26 April 1862 [1859–79, p. 151]; 1874 [1879, p. 137]; 1879, p. 127).
72   Elkin (1964, pp. 246–8), Hallam (1975, chapters 12 to 14), Maddock (1970),
     Menzies (2003), Mowaljarlai & Malnic (1993, pp. 166–8) and Pyne (1991,
     chapter 7).
73   Isaacs (1980, pp. 102–8), Mountford (1969, pp. 40–3; 1970, pp. 26–7; 1971,
     pp. 36–9; 1976, pp. 9–13), Parker (1953, pp. 39–42), Roberts & Roberts
     (1975, pp. 26–35), Smith (1930, pp. 67–9, 71–8) and Thomas (1943, pp.
     65–9).
74   Meyer (1846 [1879, pp. 202–4]). See also Clarke (2001, pp. 22–7).
75   Maddock (1970, pp. 175–86) discussed Crocodile and Rainbird Dreamings,
     Dawson (1881, p. 54) recorded Raven and Firetail Bird mythology, and
     Hercus (1986, addition to vol. 1, p. 2) provided an account of the Water Rat
     and Hawk Ancestors.
76   For example, see Bardon (1999, pp. 60, 75), Morphy (1998, pp. 99, 150) and
     Sutton (1988a, pp. 114, 123, 224–5).

Chapter 3

1   Tasman (1898 [1998, p. 25]).
2   Robinson (1830–31 [Plomley, 1966, pp. 190, 208, 368, 372, 381–2, 385–6,
     388, 531, 557; 1987, pp. 263–4]), Roth (1899, pp. 98–101) and Walker
     (1888–99, p. 286).
3   Hunter (1793, pp. 61, 520–1), Mathews (1904, p. 271) and Oxley (1820, p.
     172).
4   Oxley (1820, p. 164).
5   Oxley (1820, p. 169).
6   Cunningham (1827, cited Lee, 1925, pp. 548, 552, 556, 569, 579).
7   Cunningham (1827, cited Lee, 1925, p. 569). The species of 'box' tree involved
     is unclear.
8   Hunter (1793, pp. 520–1). Jacques Arago (1822, cited Rolls, 2002, pp. 69–70)
     and Tench (1788–92, p. 197) described tree climbing around Sydney. See
     also paintings by Joseph Lycett (1820–22 [1990, plates 1 & 2]).
9   Howitt (1904, p. 262). A 'waddy' is an Australian English word for an
     Aboriginal club, possibly derived from the Dharug (Dharruk) word 'wadi'
     for wood (Dixon et al., 1992, pp. 181–2; Ramson, 1988, p. 705; Troy, 1994,
     p. 72).
10   Urry (1985, pp. 52–4).
11   F. Barrallier (1802, cited Flannery, 1998, pp. 90–3) described his attempts
     at procuring a specimen of the native 'monkey' (koala) in the Blue
     Mountains.
12   Bevan & Vaughan (1978, p. 8).
13   Cleland (1957, p. 151).
14   Maiden (1889, p. 40).
15   Hassell (1936, p. 691).
16   Anderson (1996, p. 71) and Lumholtz (1889 [1980, pp. 97–9, 125]).
17   Brennan (1986, p. 30), Levitt (1981, pp. 42–3), McConnel (1930, p. 19), Rae
     et al. (1982, p. 46), Smith & Kalotas (1985, p. 347), Specht (1958, p. 497)
     and Wightman, Roberts et al. (1992, p. 22, 24), Lands (1987, pp. 32–4),
     Puruntatameri (2001, p. 47–52, 144) and Wightman, Jackson et al. (1991,
     pp. 13, 16, 19) listed additional tree species that are noted for 'sugar-bag'.
18   Goodale (1971, p. 162).
19   Bellchambers (1931, p. 108).
20   Cawte (1996, p. 16), Eyre (1845, vol. 2, p. 305) and Levitt (1981, p. 14).
21   Pyne (1991, p. 90).
22   Hahn (1838–39 [1964, p. 133]).
23   Hunter (1793, p. 150; see also p. 153).
24   Clarke (1988, pp. 66–7) provided ethnographic references to the use of this
     species.
25   Kalotas (1996, p. 271, 273–5).
26   Thomson (1975, p. 102).
27   Cunningham (1827, cited Lee, 1925, p. 569).
28   Campbell (1926, p. 408), Conway (1990), Croll (1937), Devitt (1986), Tindale
     (1966, pp. 180–1; 1974, p. 103 & colour pl.42) and Turner (1994, p. 8).
29   Brokensha (1975, p. 53), Clarke (2003a, pp. 69–70), McConnel (1953, pp. 8,
     28) and Thomson (1975, p. 99).
30   For descriptions of Aboriginal fish-traps and weirs, see Clarke (2002, pp.
     154–7; 2003a, p. 63, 124–5), Coutts et al. (1978), Mulvaney & Kamminga
     (1999, p. 34) and Worsnop (1897, pp. 99–102, 104–7). Soakages and wells
     are discussed by Basedow (1925, pp. 96–7), Clarke (2003a, pp. 69, 141–3),

Gara (1994, p. 46) and Worsnop (1897, pp. 102–4). For quarrying practices see Clarke (2003a, pp. 108–11), Jones (1984), McBryde (1987, pp. 259–62, 269–71), Peterson & Lampert (1985), Sagona (1994) and Worsnop (1897, pp. 97–9).

31 Batey (1909–10, cited Frankel, 1982). For earth mound construction see also Etheridge (1893), Gott (1982a, p. 65; 1983, pp. 11–2) and Hallam (1975, pp. 12–3, 72, 74).

32 Grey (1841, vol. 2, pp. 11–2).

33 Giles (1889, vol. 2, p. 286).

34 Crawford (1982, pp. 5–6).

35 Stirling (1896, p. 60). For use of yalka see also Albrecht (1959), Bindon (1996, p. 97), Cleland (1957, p. 155), Cleland & Johnston (1933, pp. 115, 118; 1937–38, pp. 213, 335; 1939b, p. 172), O'Connell et al. (1983, pp. 84–5), Pate & Dixon (1982, p. 151), Roth (1897, p. 91), Scott (1972, p. 95), Sweeney (1947, p. 291), Turner (1994, p. 22) and Wightman, Dixon et al. (1992, p. 14). In the past, this plant was often identified as *C. rotundus*.

36 Basedow (1925, p. 149).

37 Latz (1995, pp. 158).

38 Gott (1982a, p. 65).

39 Tindale (1974, p. 96). The 'yams' involved were *Dioscorea* species. See also Chaloupka (1993, p. 139) and Specht (1958, p. 481) for other references for replanting roots in the tropics.

40 Gregory (1887, p. 131). See also Irvine (1970, p. 278) and Sutton (1994, p. 41).

41 Pate & Dixon (1982, p. 163).

42 Jones (1969). See discussion by Clarke (2003a, pp. 66–7, 147, 186) and Roth (1887, pp. 120–2).

43 Laramba Community Women (2003, pp. 27–28, 39–46) and Tindale (1966) provided an overview of Aboriginal use of insects.

44 Barr et al. (1988, pp. 220–1), Campbell (1926, p. 409–10), Clarke (2003a, pp. 86, 148, 153, 155), Dixon et al. (1992, pp. 108–9), Johnston & Cleland (1943b, pp. 306–7), Palmer (1999b, pp. 54–9) and Tindale (1952; 1966, pp. 179–80, 182–3; 1974, pp. 103–4). See McEntee (1988, pp. 12–3) for an explanation of the term, *varti (vati)*. Hercus (1989) discussed grass witchetty grubs.

45 Basedow (1925, p. 125).

46 Cleland (1936, p. 9).

47 Beveridge (1884, pp. 38–40), Cann et al. (1991), Clarke (2003a, pp. 67, 87, 123, 202, 220), Etheridge (1893), Meehan (1982), Mulvaney & Kamminga (1999, pp. 19–23, 276–7, 280–1, 286–7, 349–50), Smyth (1878, vol. 2, pp. 238–44) and Stanbridge (1861, pp. 294–5).

48 Angas (1847, p. 90).

49 Angas (1847, p. 58), Beveridge (1889, p. 71), Dawson (1881, p. 20), Roth (1899, Appendix F, p. lxxii) and Thomas (1906, p. 116).

50 Beveridge (1884, p. 39).

51 *The Advertiser* (Adelaide), 5 November 1908, p. 8.

52 *South Australian Register*, 22 April 1926.

53 Cribb et al. (1988) and Mulvaney & Kamminga (1999, pp. 280–1).

54 Gott & Conran (1991, p. 34), commenting upon Beveridge (1884, p. 39).

55 Cleland (1957, p. 154), Eyre (1845, vol. 2, p. 271), Low (1989, pp. 53–4, 69–70), von Mueller (cited Smyth, 1878, vol. 1, p. 215), Wilhelmi (1861, p. 173) and Zola & Gott (1992, p. 26). Name written as '*N. billardieri*' by earlier sources.

56 Wilhelmi (1861, p. 173).

57 Wilhelmi (1861, p. 9).

58 White (1994, p. 167).

59 Kimber (1984, p. 17) and Symon (1979, p. 327).

60 Clarke (2003a, pp. 108, 113–4, 199–200, 211, 219) and Hardy (1969, p. 15).

61 Cunningham (1817, cited Lee, 1925, p. 352).

62 Leichhardt (1847, pp. 139, 157, 207, 246, 251, 257, 261–3, 265, 276–7, 282, 286–7, 317, 320, 326, 333–4, 336).

63 Leichhardt (1847, p. 131).

64 W.K. Mallyon in the *Adelaide Observer*, 31 December 1910, p. 46. See also Clarke (1994, p. 107), Tolcher (2003, p. 23) and Worsnop (1897, p. 97).

65 Grey (1841, vol. 2, pp. 12–3). See also Hallam (1975, pp. 12, 14, 39).

66 Grey (1841, vol. 2, pp. 19–20).

67 Pyne (1991, p. 125).

68 Robinson (1829–34 [Plomley, 1966]) has many references to Aboriginal pathways. See also Tindale (1974, pp. 75–6).

69 Hale & Tindale (1933, pp. 68–9 & fig.3).

70 Robinson (1831 [Plomley, 1966, p. 368]).

71 Clarke (1996b, p. 76; 2003a, pp. 113–4, 199–200), Jones (1974, p. 321), Robinson (1831 [Plomley, 1966, p. 520]) and Tindale (1974, p. 148).

72 Clarke (2003a, pp. 65, 219–21) and Symons & Symons (1994, p. 2).

73 Tasman (1898 [1998, pp. 25–6]).

74 Cook (1893, cited Blainey, 1976, p. 68). For other fire references see Cook (1893, pp. 315, 332, 339, 342, 361–2).

75 Flinders (1814 [2000, pp. 91–4]).

76 Flinders (1814 [2000, p. 95]).

77 Caley (1802, cited Else-Mitchell, 1939, p. 467).

78 Caley (1804, cited Currey, 1966, pp. 101–2).

79 King (1827, vol. 1, pp. 6–7). See also the painting by Joseph Lycett (1820–22 [1990, plate 17]) of an Aboriginal kangaroo hunt involving the use of fire around Sydney.

80 Cunningham (1817, cited Lee, 1925, pp. 275–6).

81 Cunningham (1828, cited Lee, 1925, p. 598).

82 Cunningham (1817, cited Lee, 1925, p. 227).

83 Cunningham (1818, cited Lee, 1925, p. 378).

84 Cunningham (1818, cited Lee, 1925, p. 382).

85 Giles (1889, vol. 1, p. 18).

86 Giles (1889, vol. 1, p. 81).

87 Tietkens (1891, p. 3; see also pp. 18–20).

88 Giles (1889, vol. 2, p. 318).

89 R.M. Jones (1995).

Chapter 4

1 Blainey (1976, title of chapter 11).

2 For the dating of human occupation, see the discussion by Allen (1998a, 1998b, 2000), Dodson et al. (1992), Kershaw (1995), Kohen (1995, chapter 2), Mulvaney & Kamminga (1999, chapters 7–9) and Pardoe (1995). Roberts et al. (2001) used the extinction of the megafauna to suggest a date for the arrival of people in Australia some time, within a thousand years or so, before 46,000 BP.

3 Lourandos (1997, chapter 6) and White (1994).

4 Chappell (1983) and Chappell & Thom (1977).

5 See Cameron (1981), Cunningham et al. (1981), Galbraith (1977), Harden (1990–93), Jessop & Toelken (1986), McCann (1989), Paczkowska & Chapman (2000) and Specht (1972).

6 Carter (1964, pp. 232–6), Fenner (1931, pp. 126–7), Linacre & Hobbs (1977, chapter 19), Meagher & Ride (1980, p. 68) and Seddon (1972, pp. 20–6). See also Commonwealth Bureau of Meteorology (http://www.bom.gov.au/climate/).

7 Clarke (2002; 2003a, pp. 54–6, 62–3, 118, 123–6) and Coutts et al. (1978).

8 Kershaw (1995), Lourandos (1997, pp. 296–302), Ross et al. (1992) and White (1994).

9 Clarke (2003a, pp. 136–56), Lawrence (1968, pp. 43–8) and Van Oosterzee (1995).

10 Kalma & McAlpine (1983) and Newsome et al. (1996).

11 Beard (1981), Cunningham et al. (1981), Erickson et al. (1979), Goddard & Kalotas (1988, pp. 10–3), Harden (1990–93), Jessop (1981), Jessop & Toelken (1986), Kutsche & Lay (2003), Mitchell & Wilcox (1994), Urban (1993) and Van Oosterzee (1995).

12 Chappell (1983), Chappell & Thom (1977), Clarke (2003a, chapter 1), Diamond (1998, pp. 297–308) and Kershaw (1995).

13 The flora of tropical Australia is covered by Brennan (1986), Brock (1988), Clark & Traynor (1987), Clifford & Ludlow (1972), Harris (1980), Petheram & Kok (1983), Stanley & Ross (1983–89) and Wheeler (1992).

14 Forrest (1875, p. 78).

15 Gott (1984) commented on this in relation to plant uses.

16 Butlin (1993, Chapter 15), Clarke (2003a, chapters 12 & 13) and Crosby (2004, pp. 142, 198–9, 205–7).

17 Butlin (1993, pp. 98–139), Campbell (2002), Clarke (2003a, pp. 192–6, 197, 208–9, 217–8), Crosby (2004, pp. 197–208, 233, 309–11), Lawrence (1968, pp. 185–7) and Smith (1980).

18 Allen et al. (1977), Lourandos (1997) and Mulvaney & Kamminga (1999).

19 Abbie (1976, p. 46), Black (1966, p. 97), Brown (1918, pp. 230–1), Clarke (1994, pp. 57–63; 2003a, pp. 54–6), Hallam (1975, chapter 16), Lawrence (1968, pp. 71–3), Lourandos (1997, pp. 35–8, 63, 74, 325, Table 2.1, p. 37), Mulvaney (2002), Mulvaney & Kamminga (1999, pp. 68–9) and Smith (1980, chapter 6).

20 Elkin (1932, p. 297), Hiscock & Kershaw (1992, p. 44), Lourandos (1997, pp. 35–8), Mulvaney & Kamminga (1999, p. 68), Stanner (1936, p. 187) and Warner (1958, p. 16).

21 Carr & Carr (1981, pp. 9–12), Clarke (2003a, pp. 111–4, 131–5, 151–6, 165–74), Elkin (1964, pp. 34–7), Jones et al. (1997), McGhee (2006) and Reid (1995a, 1995b).

22 Smyth (1878, vol. 1, p. 141).

23 Rudder (1978–79, p. 352).

24 For example, refer to Silberbauer (1981, chapter 5) for the central Kalahari Desert in Africa.

25 Clarke (1997, p. 137; 2003a, pp. 25–9, 90–1, 111–4), Johnson (1998, chapter 3) and Jones et al. (1997) and Reid (1995a, 1995b).

26 Robinson (1830 [Plomley, 1966, p. 300]). See also Robinson (1834 [Plomley, 1966, pp. 892–3]).

27 Robinson (1832 [Plomley, 1966, p. 633]). See also Robinson (1832 [Plomley, 1966, p. 645]).

28 Reminiscences recorded by E. Davies in the *Mail* (Adelaide), on 25 March

1952. The 'ti-trees' were probably black paperbarks (black tea-tree).

29 Beveridge (1884, pp. 62–3) mentioned seasons for the Riverina, while Bates (1901–14 [1985, pp. 240–1]), Bindon & Whalley (1992), Hallam (1975, pp. 38–40), Meagher (1974, pp. 28–41) and Clarke (2003a, pp. 131–5) discussed the perception of seasons in the southwest of Western Australia.
30 Bindon & Gough (1993, pp. 14–5), Clarke (2003a, pp. 151–6), Kalma & McAlpine (1983) and Mutitjulu Community & Baker (1996, chapter 1).
31 Kalma & McAlpine (1983, pp. 49–57).
32 Goddard (1992, pp. 39, 97, 116, 247), Henderson & Dobson (1994, pp. 92, 585, 613–4), Mutitjulu Community & Baker (1996, pp. 1–5, 51) and Tindale (1933, 1957, 1959, 1972, pp. 228–38; 1974, pp. 62–3; 1978, pp. 158–9; 1981, pp. 1867–8).
33 Clarke (2003a, pp. 140–4).
34 Elkin (1977, pp. 11, 22, 102, 118, 121, 127) and McCarthy (1953).
35 Latz (1995, pp. 58, 258).
36 Latz (1995, pp. 58, 150).
37 Clarke (2003a, pp. 165–74). For Aboriginal calendars based in northern Queensland refer to Aurukun School and Community Calendar (1985), Chase & Sutton (1981), McConnel (1930, pp. 6–10), Roberts et al. (1995, p. 7) and Sutton (1995, pp. 31–2, 151, 169, 179–80). For the Top End see Baker (1999, p. 47), Blake et al. (1998, p. 21), Breedan & Wright (1991, p. 109), Brennan (1986, p. 5), Davis (1989), Hiatt & Jones (1988, pp. 8–9), Levitt (1981, pp. 12–3 & chapter 4), Lucas et al. (1997), McCarthy & McArthur (1960), Povinelli (1993, pp. 233–6), Puruntatameri (2001, pp. 7–11), Rae et al. (1982), Reid (1995a, p. 4), Russell–Smith (1985, p. 246), Specht (1958, p. 480) and Thomson (1949, p. 16; 1950). Kimberley calendars are discussed by Crawford (1982, pp. vii–viii, 17–23, 27–8, 35–6), Kaberry (1939, pp. 11, 409–10) and Smith & Kalotas (1985, pp. 322–5).
38 Winterbotham (cited Symons & Symons, 1994, p. 16).
39 Roberts et al. (1995, p. 7).
40 McKnight (1999, p. 136).
41 Lands (1987, p. 55) and Smith & Kalotas (1985, p. 344).
42 Yunupingu & Williams (1995, p. vii) and Yunupingu (1995, p. 13). Plant is referred to as *Abutilon indicum*.
43 Basedow (1925, chapters 12–3), McConnel (1930, p. 10) and Tindale (1974, pp. 55–6).
44 Poiner (1976, pp. 201–3).
45 Roth (1901b, p. 7).
46 Meehan (1982, p. 26).
47 Berndt (1981, pp. 174–7; 1982b, pp. 42–51), Clarke (2003a, pp. 47–9) and Kaberry (1939, p. 15).
48 Lampert & Sanders (1973, pp. 101–2) and Poiner (1976).
49 Clarke (1996b, pp. 74–6; 2003a, p. 112), Ellis (1976, pp. 116–7) and Tindale (1974, pp. 60–1). For a similar pattern among neighbouring groups, see Clarke (2002, pp. 160–1) and Tindale (1938, p. 21; 1974, pp. 61–2).
50 Tindale (1938, p. 21; 1974, pp. 61–2).
51 Refer to Hallam (1975, pp. 23–4, 29–31, 34, 108–9), Meagher (1974, p. 27) and Nind (1831, pp. 28, 36) for the southwest of Western Australia. See Coutts (1970, p. 2) and Hope & Coutts (1971, p. 110) for the Gippsland in Victoria; and for Tasmanian examples refer to Jones (1974, pp. 322, 328–36, 339, 342, 345, 348, 350, 352) and Walker (1888–99, pp. 268–9).
52 Wilhelmi (1861, p. 178).
53 Teichelmann (1841, p. 7).
54 Walker (1888–89, p. 254).
55 Kimber (1976, pp. 143–4), O'Connell et al. (1983, p. 82), Strehlow (1970, p. 96) and Tindale (1972, p. 234; 1974, p. 62).
56 C. Strehlow, correspondence to the Inspector, 1908 (cited Hill, 2002, p. 31).
57 Tindale (1974, p. 65).
58 Sweeney (1947, p. 297). Sweeney referred to the 'Warlpiri' as the 'Wailbri'.
59 Meggitt (1962, pp. 49–50).
60 Cleland (1966, pp. 141–2).
61 Horne & Aiston (1924, p. 18).
62 Gould (1969, pp. 8–10, 76–88).
63 Albrecht (1959), Cleland (1957, p. 152), Howard (1978–79, p. 298) and Long (1989).
64 Evans-Pritchard (1949).
65 Berndt & Berndt (1942, p. 325), Cane (2002), Elkin (1940) and Lawrence (1968, pp. 41–3).
66 Sweeney (1947, p. 297).
67 Thomson (1939a, p. 209).
68 Leichhardt (1847, p. 216). See also McConnel (1953, p. 9).
69 Basedow (1925, pp. 103–4).
70 Levitt (1981, pp. 13, 49).

Chapter 5

1 Flannery (1994), Frakes (1999), Hill (2004), Hope (1994) and Singh et al. (1981).
2 Blainey (1976, p. 75).
3 Arthur (1996, p. 32).
4 Cleland (1957, p. 150), Kingdon (2003, pp. 271–3, 276–8), Pyne (1991, pp. 72–9) and Tattersall & Schwartz (2000, pp. 70, 155–6, 169, 211).
5 Blainey (1976, pp. 70, 72), Clarke (2003a, pp. 42, 84–5, 119, 124, 153, 170), Hassell (1936, pp. 692, 702), McConnel (1930, p. 10), Nicholson (1981, pp. 62, 65), Rose (1996, chapter 6), Sutton (1994, p. 35) and Thomson (1932).
6 Basedow (1925, pp. 110–2), Calley (1957), Clarke (2003a, pp. 12, 65, 69, 76–7, 84–5, 110), Davidson (1947), Howitt (1904, pp. 770–3), Levitt (1981, pp. 14–5), Mountford & Berndt (1941), Pyne (1991, pp. 86–8) and Sutton (1994, p. 35).
7 Kalotas (1996, pp. 279–80), Meagher & Ride (1980, p. 76) and Robinson (1831 [Plomley, 1966, p. 366]).
8 Examples of 'kerosene-grasses' are delicate lovegrass, fire grass and hummock grass (Blake et al. 1998, p. 117; Russell-Smith 1985, p. 262; and Wightman, Dixon et al. 1992, p. 16).
9 The 'kerosene-wood' category includes black plum, matchwood (Cooktown kerosene-wood), maytenus, saffron-heart and white-flowered turkey-bush (Anderson, 1996, p. 72; Russell-Smith, 1985, pp. 249, 257, 263, Sutton 1994, p. 35; Wightman, Roberts et al., 1992, p. 20).
10 Clarke (2003a, p. 77) and Stirling (1896, p. 84). Aboriginal artefact collection, South Australian Museum.
11 Beveridge (1884, pp. 67–8), Clarke (2003a, pp. 84–5), Eyre (1845, vol. 2, p. 357), Howitt (1904, pp. 770–3), McConnel (1953, pp. 11–2 & plate IX), Petrie (1932, p. 95) and Sutton (1994, p. 35 & fig.4). Aboriginal artefact collection, South Australian Museum.
12 Clarke (2003a, p. 85) and Mountford & Berndt (1941, pp. 343–4).
13 Levitt (1981, p. 14) and Sutton (1994, p. 35).
14 Hassell (1936, p. 692), Robinson (1831–33 [Plomley, 1966, pp. 385, 567, 754; 1987, p. 230]) and Tench (1788–92 [1996, p. 257]).
15 Blake et al. (1998, p. 38), Brennan (1986, p. 62), Puruntatameri (2001, pp. 28, 148), Smith (1991, p. 11) and Yunupingu (1995, p. 21).
16 Bailey (1913, p. 732), Clarke (2003a, p. 85), Cleland (1934–35, p. 12), Robinson (1832 [Plomley, 1987, p. 241]) and Roth (1899, p. 95). See also *Adelaide Observer*, 4 July 1914. Punk bracket fungus earlier known as *Polyporus eucalyptorum*. Ron Bonney (pers. com.) claimed woody bracket fungus was used to carry fire.
17 Sutton (1889, p. 19) and Tindale (1939, p. 10). See also *Adelaide Observer*, 27 November 1886, p. 36.
18 Smith (1991, p. 14) and Wightman, Jackson et al. (1991, p. 9).
19 Reid (1977, p. 23).
20 See Chapter 9, below.
21 Levitt (1981, p. 15) and Robinson (1831 [Plomley, 1966, p. 385]).
22 Gould (1969, p. 124) and Lowe (2002, p. 64).
23 Hassell (1936, p. 681–2).
24 Laramba Community Women (2003, p. 36), Levitt (1981, p. 66), Nyinkka Nyunyu (2003) and Smith (1991, p. 7).
25 Levitt (1981, p. 64).
26 Angas (1847, vol. 1, p. 96) and Bunce (1859, p. 111). Note that while some references have used 'fire-stick' to mean 'fire-brand', others have used it to refer to the fire drill apparatus.
27 This is evident in early colonial paintings of Aboriginal dances, such as by John Glover in Tasmania (Queen Victoria Museum and Art Gallery, Launceston) and George French Angas in South Australia (South Australian Museum Archives).
28 Refer to Howitt (1904, pp. 446–508) and Worsnop (1897, pp. 57–64) for overviews of burial practices. See Robinson (1830 [Plomley, 1966, p. 301]) and Walker (1888–99, p. 259) for accounts from Tasmania and Thomson (1932) for northern Queensland.
29 Browne (1897, pp. 72–3). Browne uses the earlier name, *Xerotes effusa*. Aboriginal artefact collection, South Australian Museum. See related accounts of smoking by Cawthorne (1844 [1926, p. 19]) and Tunbridge (1991, pp. 33, 58).
30 Blake et al. (1998, pp. 120–1).
31 Tonkinson (1978, p. 22). See also Lowe (2002, pp. 60–1), Myers (1986b, pp. 185–6) and Sutton (1994, pp. 35, 37).
32 Curr (1883, p. 88).
33 Jones (1969).
34 Carr & Carr (1981, pp. 35–8), Gill et al. (1991), Hiscock & Kershaw (1992), Nicholson (1981, pp. 66–9), Rose (1995) and White & Flannery (1992).
35 Cleland (1907). See also Cleland (1939, pp. 14–5; 1957, pp. 150–1).
36 Bowman (1991, 1998), Flannery (1994, chapter 21), Head (1989, 1994), Kohen (1995, chapter 4), Lourandos (1997, pp. 95–7) and Mulvaney & Kamminga (1999, pp. 60–2).
37 Blainey (1976, p. 82).
38 Flannery (1990; 1994, chapters 21–22; 2004, chapter 18). Bowman (1991) and Horton (2000, chapters 5–6) challenge Flannery's model of megafaunal extinction.
39 Stocker (1971).

40 Bradley (1995) and Pyne (1991, p. 104).
41 Bindon & Gough (1993, p. 14), Lowe (2002, chapter 7), Lucas et al. (1997, p. 132), Satterthwait & Satterthwait (1983, p. 12) and Young (1992, p. 260).
42 A. Blight (cited Rose, 1996, p. 63). See also Rose (2002, p. 25).
43 Hallam (1975), Haynes (1985, 1991), Jones (1969), Kimber (1983), Lucas et al. (1997, pp. 131–2), Pyne (1991), Rose (1995) and Russell-Smith (1985).
44 Pyne (1991, pp. 122–4).
45 R.M. Jones (1995).
46 Lucas et al. (1997, p. 132).
47 Gould (1969, p. 124) described burning to clear brush around a waterhole.
48 Haynes (1991, pp. 68–9). See also comments recorded in Bowman et al. (2001, p. 62).
49 Nind (1831, p. 32).
50 Baker (1999, p. 50), Bowman et al. (2001, pp. 67–8) and Sutton (1994, pp. 36–7).
51 Dunlop et al. (1975), Stocker (1966), Stocker & Mott (1981).
52 Blainey (1976, p. 80), Cleland (1962; 1966, pp. 123–5) and Latz (1995, pp. 36, 40, 42).
53 Bowman et al. (2001, pp. 63–4).
54 Leichhardt letters, 8 November 1843 and 2 February 1844 (1968, vol. 2, pp. 680, 719). See also Leichhardt letters, 26 October 1842 (1968, vol. 2, pp. 550–1).
55 Bowman et al. (2001).
56 See Crawford (1982, p. 27) for the Kimberley. McConnel (1930, p. 7) and Thomson (1939a, pp. 213–5) mentioned the use of fire for marsupial hunting in western Cape York Peninsula.
57 Crawford (1982, p. 27).
58 Hunter (1793, p. 81; see also pp. 61–2, 507, 524, 546).
59 Dawson (1881, p. 93).
60 Blainey (1976, p. 79), Jones (1974, p. 321), Pyne (1991, pp. 127–9), Robinson (1829–34 [Plomley, 1966, pp. 54, 101, 214, 217, 250, 252, 260, 287–8, 368, 375, 380, 383, 398, 437, 512, 523, 546, 560, 673, 720, 738, 760, 840, 849, 858, 891–2, 902, 904–5]) and Roth (1899, pp. 97–8).
61 Walker (1888–99, p. 268).
62 Bowman & Brown (1986) and Jackson (1968).
63 Finlayson (1903, pp. 40–1).
64 *Adelaide Chronicle and South Australian Literary Record*, 22 December 1841, p. 3.
65 *Adelaide Observer*, 31 May 1851, p. 5.
66 Aboriginal Protectors Report, in *South Australian Gazette and Mining Journal*, 20 April 1850, p. 4.
67 Meagher (1974, pp. 15, 17, 33–4, 38–9), citing evidence from sources such as Grey (1841) and Nind (1831). See also Hallam (1975).
68 Tilbrook (1983, pp. 6–7).
69 Nind (1831, pp. 28, 32).
70 Nind (1831, p. 28).
71 Grey (1841, p. 292).
72 Latz (1995, p. 29) and Lowe (2002, pp. 61–3).
73 Finlayson (1952, p. 45 & plate opposite p. 61). Finlayson gave the Aboriginal name for the hare-wallaby as 'maala'.
74 Pyne (1991, p. 125).
75 Pyne (1991, p. 125).
76 Latz (1995, p. 29).
77 Latz (1995, p. 19).
78 Gould (1971, p. 23).
79 Latz (1995, p. 64).
80 Latz (1995, p. 29).
81 Haynes (1991, p. 61).
82 Leichhardt (1847, p. 304).
83 Lumholtz (1889 [1980, p. 102]).
84 Tindale (1925, p. 80).
85 McConnel (1930, p. 7). See also Anderson (1996, p. 66).
86 Haynes (1991, pp. 65–6 & figure 30).
87 Haynes (1991, p. 68).
88 R.M. Jones (1995).
89 Hopkins et al. (1990, 1993) and Kershaw (1986) discussed creation of eucalypt woodland, while Harris (1977, pp. 428–9), Hiscock & Kershaw (1992, p. 45), Jones (1993, p. 65) and Rose (2002, pp. 31–3) considered cycads.
90 Beaton (1982, pp. 52–4) and Davis (1989, p. 54).

Chapter 6

1 Grey (1841, vol. 2, pp. 261–3). Also see Meagher & Ride (1980, pp. 77–8).
2 Albrecht (1959).
3 Stirling (1896, p. 51).
4 Stirling (1896, pp. 55–63).
5 A. Clarke (1988, pp. 126, 133), Gould (1982, pp. 77–83), Lawrence (1968, pp. 48–51) and Meehan (1977, pp. 526–7; 1982, p. 160).
6 Clarke (2003a, chapter 8) and Lawrence (1968, chapter 4).
7 Bird & Beeck (1988, pp. 115–6, 118), Clarke (1985a, 1988), Gott (1982a, 1983), Meagher (1974, pp. 24–5) and Meagher & Ride (1980, p. 74).
8 Clarke (1988), Gott (1982a, 1983) and Stewart & Percival (1997, pp. 17, 20, 48).
9 Clarke (1988, pp. 68, 72) and Gott (1983).
10 Gott (1982a, pp. 59–62) and von Mueller (cited Smyth, 1878, p. 213). Von Mueller listed the marsh club rush by an earlier name, *Scirpus maritimus*. The record by Angas (1847, p. 101) of a 'triangular species of grass or reed' probably refers to this species.
11 Eyre (1845, vol. 2, pp. 254, 269). Clarke (1988, pp. 66–7, 72) identified the 'belillah' of Eyre's account.
12 Backhouse (1843, p. 540).
13 Hallam (1975, p. 12; see also pp. 13–4, 72–4).
14 Grey (1841, vol. 2, p. 124). See also Bates (1901–14, [1985, p. 261]), Bindon (1996, p. 101), Carr & Carr (1981, p. 14), Hallam (1975, pp. 72, 74), Low (1989, p. 106), Roth (1903b, p. 48) and von Brandenstein (1988, p. 131).
15 Angas (1847, pp. 58–9, 89–90, 92), Beveridge (1884, p. 36; 1889, p. 71), Bindon (1996, p. 259), Clarke (1988, pp. 69–70), Cleland (1957, p. 155), Eyre (1845, vol. 2, pp. 62, 269), Gott (1999), Gott & Conran (1991, p. 8), Hardwick (2001, pp. 117–8), Krefft (1862–65, p. 361), Low (1989, pp. 108–9), Meagher (1974, pp. 25, 35–6, 56, 61–2, 65), Roth (1899, p. 95), Thomas (1906, p. 116), von Brandenstein (1988, p. 136) and Zola & Gott (1992, pp. 8–9, 62–3).
16 Moore (1884, p. 81).
17 Krefft (1862–65, p. 361).
18 Eyre (1845, vol. 2, p. 62). Eyre used the term 'broad flag-reed'. See also Eyre (1845, vol. 2, p. 269).
19 Veth & Walsh (1988) discussed desert plant foods.
20 Sturt (1849 [1984, p. 257]).
21 Roth (1897, p. 93).
22 Henderson & Dobson (1994, pp. 632–3) and Latz (1995, pp. 158, 366).
23 Bindon & Gough (1993, p. 14), Cleland (1957, pp. 152, 155), Cleland & Johnston (1933, pp. 113, 115, 122; 1939a, p. 25), Cleland & Tindale (1954, p. 84), Hiddins (2001, p. 126), Latz (1995, pp. 214–5), O'Connell et al. (1983, pp. 84–6, 97, 99), Scott (1972, p. 95), Turner (1994, p. 23), Wightman, Dixon et al. (1992, p. 25) and Wightman, Gurindji elders et al. (1994, p. 34).
24 Sweeney (1947, p. 296). While Sweeney called the desert sweet potato 'yala', Albrecht (1959) referred to them as 'yalla' yams.
25 Strehlow (1965, p. 125). Strehlow referred to the desert sweet potato as 'jala yams', with 'j' being pronounced as 'y'.
26 Cleland (1957, pp. 152, 155), Cleland & Johnston (1933, pp. 115, 119; 1937–38, p. 209; 1939a, p. 23; 1939b, p. 174), Cleland & Tindale (1954, p. 84; 1959, p. 132), Latz (1995, pp. 130–1), O'Connell et al. (1983, p. 84), Smith (1991, p. 11) and Turner (1994, p. 23).
27 Poiner (1976, p. 197).
28 Schulze (1891, p. 233).
29 Albrecht (1959).
30 Albrecht (1959), Bindon & Gough (1993, p. 14), Cleland (1957, p. 154; 1966, p. 149), Cleland & Johnston (1933, p. 118; 1937–38, pp. 209, 214, 336, 339), Cleland & Tindale (1954, pp. 82–3; 1959, p. 131), Finlayson (1952, p. 64), Hiddins (2000, p. 32; 2001, p. 42), Latz (1995, pp. 196–7), Mutitjulu Community & Baker (1996, p. 38), O'Connell et al. (1983, pp. 93, 95), Tindale (1941, p. 9) and Turner (1994, p. 14).
31 Bindon (1996, p. 143) and Goddard (1992, p. 16).
32 Albrecht (1959), Berndt (1972, pp. 182–3), Clarke (2003a, pp. 140–4, 155–6), Tindale (1981, p. 1864) and Tolcher (2003, pp. 20, 72).
33 Clarke (2005). The main nardoo water fern species used were the common nardoo and short-fruited nardoo.
34 Kalotas (1996, pp. 271, 281–2) and Latz (1995, p. 245).
35 Altman (1987) and Young (1992, p. 257).
36 Irvine (1957, p. 113).
37 Specht (1958, p. 481).
38 Bindon (1996, p. 194), Cribb & Cribb (1982, pp. 48–9), Hiddins (2000, p. 8; 2001, pp. xi, 96) and Sutton (1994, pp. 38, 45).
39 Sutton (1995, p. 164).
40 Hiddins (2000, p. 12; 2001, p. 30), Lands (1987, pp. 46–7), Smith (1991, p. 15) and Wightman, Roberts et al. (1992, p. 14).
41 Hiddins (2000, p. 19; 2001, p. 36), Levitt (1981, pp. 35, 121), Puruntatameri (2001, p. 68), Rae et al. (1982, p. 46), Roth (1901b, p. 14), Smith & Wightman (1990, p. 19), Specht (1958, p. 500) and Wightman & Smith (1989, pp. 10, 17).
42 Puruntatameri (2001, pp. 25, 43–4).
43 Earl (1846, p. 251).
44 Blake et al. (1998, p. 63), Earl (1846, p. 245), Hiddins (2001, p. 5), Levitt (1981, pp. 40, 133–4), Puruntatameri (2001, pp. 8, 45, 144), Smith & Kalotas (1985, p. 331), Specht (1958, p. 484), Wightman, Roberts et al. (1992, p. 20) and Yunupingu (1995, p. 36).
45 Puruntatameri (2001, p. 45),

46 Testart (1982).
47 Clarke (2003a, p. 63), Cleland (1957, p. 153), Kimber (1984, pp. 18–21) and Tunbridge (1985a).
48 Allen (1974), Horne & Aiston (1924, p. 7), Lawrence (1968, p. 57), Tindale (1977, p. 346) and Tunbridge (1985a, p. 14).
49 Howitt (in Smyth, 1878, vol. 2, pp. 302–3). Note that a bushel is a dry measure in the imperial system, equivalent to 8 gallons or 36.4 litres
50 Worsnop (1897, pp. 53–4). Worsnop wrote Brachina as 'Burratchuna'.
51 Clarke (1985b, p. 13), Gott (1982b), McBryde (1986, pp. 133, 136–8, 142, 148–9, 151), Smith (1880, p. 130), Tindale (1981, p. 1879) and Zola & Gott (1992, p. 21).
52 Brokensha (1975, pp. 28–9), Carr & Carr (1981, pp. 23–4), Cleland (1957, pp. 152, 154–5; 1966, pp. 136, 141, 149), Cleland & Johnston (1933, pp. 115, 123; 1937–38, pp. 211, 338, 340; 1939a, pp. 25–6; 1939b, p. 177), Cleland et al. (1925, p. 118), Cleland & Tindale (1954, pp. 82–3, 85; 1959, pp. 127–9, 137–8), Finlayson (1952, p. 64), Goddard & Kalotas (1988, pp. 92–5), Latz (1995, pp. 269–80), O'Connell et al. (1983, pp. 93–5, 99), Tindale (1941, p. 12), Turner (1994, pp. 15, 24), Wightman, Dixon et al. (1992, p. 30) and Wightman, Gurindji elders et al. (1994, p. 49).
53 Thomson (1962, pp. 11–2). See also an account by Sweeney (1947, p. 290) of related practices of the Warlpiri (Wailbri).
54 Blake et al. (1998, pp. 131–2), Brennan (1986, pp. 55, 103), Crawford (1982, pp. 3, 16, 71), Levitt (1981, pp. 33, 130), Puruntatameri (2001, pp. 8, 89, 142), Smith & Kalotas (1985, p. 344), Smith & Wightman (1990, p. 25), Specht (1958, p. 499), Wightman & Smith (1989, p. 24), Wightman, Jackson et al. (1991, p. 27) and Wightman, Roberts et al. (1992, p. 47).
55 Tunbridge (1985a, pp. 12–4). See also Finlayson (1952, p. 63).
56 Cleland (1957, pp. 154, 156; 1966, p. 150), Cleland & Johnston (1937–38, pp. 214–5, 336, 339–41; 1939b, p. 173), Cleland & Tindale (1954, p. 82), Finlayson (1952, p. 63), Latz (1995, pp. 259–60), Goddard & Kalotas (1988, pp. 32–7), Tindale (1941, p. 9) and Turner (1994, p. 14). Formerly known as *Fusanus acuminatus* and *Eucarya acuminata*.
57 Bates (1918, pp. 154, 157; 1947, p. 140), Bolam (1930, p. 107), Cleland (1957, p. 154), Hassell (1936, p. 689), Low (1989, p. 68) and von Mueller (cited Smyth, 1878, vol. 1, p. 213).
58 Tindale (1981, p. 1879).
59 C.P. Mountford (cited Tunbridge, 1985a, pp. 13–4).
60 Cleland (1966, p. 149), Cleland & Johnston (1933, pp. 115, 118; 1937–38, pp. 209, 336, 341), Cleland & Tindale (1954, pp. 82, 84), Finlayson (1952, pp. 63–4), Goddard & Kalotas (1988, pp. 68–71), Hiddins (2000, p. 15), Lands (1987, pp. 17–8), Latz (1995, p. 261), O'Connell et al. (1983, p. 93), Smith & Kalotas (1985, p. 331), Tindale (1941, p. 9), Wightman, Dixon et al. (1992, p. 30) and Wightman, Gurindji elders et al. (1994, p. 45). Hiddins referred to the bush plum as 'quandong', although in this book to avoid confusion that common name is applied only to *S. acuminatum*.
61 Newland (1890, p. 22). The species of 'box' tree concerned is unclear. F.G.G. Rose (1987, p. 58) gave similar references to grass seed storage elsewhere in arid Australia.
62 Wightman, Jackson et al. (1991, p. 21).
63 Sutton (1994, p. 45).
64 Latz (1995, p. 58).
65 Wilhelmi (1861, p. 172). See also Cleland (1966, p. 132) and Schürmann (1844, pt 2, pp. 15, 48). Earlier scientific names for the karkalla are *Mesembryanthemum aequilateras* and *Carpobrotus aequilateras*.
66 Clarke (1985b, p. 13).
67 G.S. Lang (cited Smyth, 1878, vol. 1, p. 219).
68 Schürmann (1846 [1879, p. 217]). See Wilhelmi (1861, p. 173).
69 Clarke (1985b, pp. 10–1; 1986b, p. 43; 1998b, p. 18), Cleland (1966, p. 135) and Wilhelmi (1861, p. 173).
70 Clarke (1985b, pp. 9–10; 1998, pp. 17–8). For other regions see Hardwick (2001, pp. 48–9) and Stewart & Percival (1997, p. 12).
71 Backhouse (1843, Appendix D, p. xxxiii). See also Low (1989, p. 86) and Roth (1899, p. 95). Symons & Symons (1994, p. 38) provided a similar account of the Aboriginal use of this species from around Brisbane, Queensland.
72 Robinson (1834 [Plomley, 1966, p. 840]).
73 Zola & Gott (1992, pp. 26–7).
74 Cleland (1966, p. 134), Coutts (1970, Table 1, pp. 6–7), Hope & Coutts (1971, Table 1, pp. 107–9), Low (1989, pp. 143–4), Tindale (1981, p. 1879) and von Mueller (cited Smyth, 1878, vol. 1, p. 213).
75 Eyre (1845, vol. 2, p. 254).
76 Hassell (1936, p. 689), Low (1989, p. 186) and Meagher (1974, pp. 25–6, 37–8, 56–9, 64).
77 Grey (1841, vol. 2, p. 294).
78 Von Brandenstein (1988, p. 12).
79 For bush potato (round yam) refer to Bindon (1996, pp. 202–3) and Carr & Carr (1981, p. 29). See Grey (1841, vol. 2, pp. 11–2) for a description of the warran.
80 Anderson (1996, p. 66), Beaton (1982, pp. 56–8), Clarke (2003a, pp. 63, 161–

2), Davis (1989, p. 40), Mountford (1958, pp. 129–32), Wightman, Jackson et al. (1991, p. 21) and Yunupingu (1995, p. 31).
81 Thomson (1955).
82 Carr & Carr (1981, pp. 27–9), Cherikoff & Isaacs (1989, pp. 53–6), Low (1989, pp. 82, 85, 89, 94) and Steele (1984, pp. 212–3, 239–40).
83 Dixon et al. (1992, pp. 113–5). While Dixon et al. thought it was a Yagara term, Ramson (1988, p. 109) listed it as possibly a Wiradhuri word from northeast New South Wales.
84 Bunce (1859, p. 113).
85 Leichhardt letters, 27 August 1843 and 6 January 1844 (1968, vol. 2, pp. 670–1, 704).
86 Cherikoff & Isaacs (1989, p. 55).
87 Mathew (1886–87, p. 161).
88 Leichhardt letters, 9 January 1844 (1968, vol. 2, pp. 707–9; see also vol. 2, pp. 675–6).
89 Bennett (1867, cited Smyth, 1878, vol. 1, p. 218).
90 Archer (cited in the Leichhardt letters, 9 January 1844 [1968, vol. 2, p. 708]) and Clements (cited Cherikoff & Isaacs, 1989, p. 55).
91 Day (2001, p. 85).
92 Hiddins (2000, p. 27).
93 Hiddins (2000, p. 30; 2001, pp. ix, 79), Levitt (1981, pp. 38, 118), Rae et al. (1982, p. 45), Wightman, Jackson et al. (1991, p. 17) and Wightman, Roberts et al. (1992, p. 28).
94 Paddy et al. (1987, p. 2), Roth (1901b, pp. 9–10) and Specht (1958, p. 489). For related references see also Crawford (1982, p. 46) and Levitt (1981, pp. 37–8, 117–8).
95 Cleland (1957, p. 158), Cleland & Johnston (1933, pp. 116, 118), Cleland & Tindale (1954, p. 82; 1959, p. 131), Goddard & Kalotas (1988, pp. 20, 50–3), Hiddins (2001, p. 69), O'Connell et al. (1983, p. 96), Turner (1994, p. 10) and Wightman, Dixon et al. (1992, p. 24).
96 Goddard & Kalotas (1988, pp. 88–91) and Mutitjulu Community & Baker (1996, pp. 9–10).
97 Roth (1897, p. 93) and Turner (1994, p. 10). *Corymbia opaca* formerly known as *Eucalyptus opaca*.
98 Angas (1847, p. 150), Cleland (1957, p. 158), Coutts (1970, Table 1, pp. 6–7), Eyre (1845, vol. 2, p. 273), Hope & Coutts (1971, Table 1, pp. 107–9), Maiden (1889, p. 3), Meagher (1974, pp. 25, 54, 58–60), Teichelmann & Schürmann (1840, pt 2, p. 13), Tindale (1978, p. 161), von Mueller (cited Smyth, 1878, vol. 1, p. 213) and Wreck Bay Community & Renwick (2000, pp. 48, 53–4). An account by Hassell (1936, p. 689) of 'Banishia (?)' nectar use probably refers to a *Banksia* species.
99 Bindon (1996, p. 52) and Low (1989, p. 170).
100 Massola (1966, p. 270).
101 Dawson (1881, p. 21).
102 Dawson (1881, p. 22).
103 Wilkinson (1848, p. 205).
104 Hassell (1936, p. 690). See also Bindon (1996, p. 120).
105 Clarke (1986a, pp. 3–5), Cleland (1957, p. 157), Coutts (1970, Table 1, pp. 6–7), Gott & Conran (1991, pp. 44–5, 47), Hope & Coutts (1971, Table 1, pp. 107–9), von Mueller (cited Smyth, 1878, vol. 1, p. 213), Teichelmann & Schürmann (1840, p. 23), Wilhelmi (1861, p. 173), Wilkinson (1848, p. 210), Wreck Bay Community & Renwick (2000, p. 33) and Zola & Gott (1992, pp. 38, 51).
106 Bunce (1859, p. 71).
107 Cribb & Cribb (1982, pp. 185–6).
108 Basedow (1925, pp. 98–9), Carr & Carr (1981, pp. 29–31), Cleland (1936, p. 8; 1939, pp. 8–9; 1957, pp. 159–60; 1966, p. 142), Cleland & Johnston (1937–38, pp. 337, 340; 1939b, p. 177), Cleland et al. (1925, p. 110), Cleland & Tindale (1959, p. 131), Goddard & Kalotas (1988, pp. 22, 54–7), Horne & Aiston (1924, p. 50), Noble & Kimber (1997), O'Connell et al. (1983, p. 97), Reid (1977, p. 122), Stirling (1896, p. 65) and Turner (1994, p. 52).
109 General accounts of eucalypt use as 'water trees' in the southern arid zone were given by Bayly (1999, pp. 22–3), Cleland (1939, pp. 8–9; 1957, pp. 159–60), Cleland & Johnston (1937–38, p. 332), Horne & Aiston (1924, p. 50), Giles (1889, vol. 1, p. 45), Magarey (1894–95, p. 4) and Stirling (1896, p. 65). Bates (1901–14, [1985, p. 263]) referred to use of the mallabie in coastal central Western Australia.
110 Bolam (1930, pp. 50, 118), Clarke (1986a, pp. 7–8; 1988, pp. 67–8), Cleland (1957, p. 159), Eyre (1845, vol. 1, pp. 349–51; vol. 2, pp. 248–9), Massola (1966, p. 270), Smyth (1878, vol. 1, pp. 220–1) and Stanbridge (1861, p. 304). Aboriginal artefact collection, South Australian Museum.
111 Cleland (1957, p. 156). Aboriginal artefact collection, South Australian Museum.
112 Bennett (1883), Gara (1985), Giles (1889, vol. 1, p. 45), Magarey (1894–95, pp. 4–5) and Noble & Kimber (1997, pp. 176–9).
113 Carnegie (1898, pp. 11, 42–3).
114 Horne & Aiston (1924, p. 50).

115 Bolam (1930, p. 49).
116 Basedow (1925, p. 98).
117 Tindale (1981, p. 1865). For a related reference see Berndt & Berndt (1942–43, pp. 317–8).
118 Bates (1947, p. 221). See also Bates (1901–14, [1985, p. 263]).
119 W.H. Tietkens (cited Magarey, 1894–95, p. 6). See also Tietkens (1880, p. 281).
120 Basedow (1925, pp. 91, 149), Cleland (1936, p. 9), Goddard & Kalotas (1988, pp. 120–1), Latz (1995, pp. 56, 134), Lawrence (1968, p. 61) and Stirling (1896, p. 65).
121 Hiddins (2001, p. 72) and Latz (1995, pp. 59–60).
122 Barr et al. (1988, pp. 78–9).
123 D. Bird Rose (1987).
124 Hiddins (2001, p. 43).
125 Bindon (1996, p. 203), Bird & Beeck (1988, p. 116) and Meagher (1974, pp. 26, 57, 65).
126 Basedow (1925, p. 99).
127 Latz (1995, pp. 64–5) and Turner (1994, p. 53).
128 Stirling (1896, p. 65).
129 Massola (1966, p. 270).
130 Thozet (1866, p. 7). Note that this species was formerly recorded in the *Sterculia* genus, but is now considered to be in *Brachychiton*.
131 Mathews (1904, p. 373).
132 Massola (1966, p. 270).
133 Crawford (1982, p. 58) and Hiddins (2000, p. 24; 2001, p. 58).
134 Basedow (1925, pp. 97–8).
135 Davis (1989, p. 7) and Puruntatameri (2001, pp. 66–7, 144).

Chapter 7

1 Mitchell (1848, p. 90).
2 Brokensha (1975, pp. 25–7), Cleland (1957, p. 154; 1966, pp. 137, 148), Cleland & Johnston (1933, pp. 115, 117; 1939b, p. 172), Cleland et al. (1925, p. 108), Cleland & Tindale (1954, p. 83; 1959, p. 130), Goddard & Kalotas (1988, pp. 106–9), Latz (1995, p. 240), O'Connell et al. (1983, pp. 86–7, 89, 92, 99) and Tindale (1981, pp. 1865–6).
3 Gregory (1887, p. 132).
4 Tindale (1977, p. 346).
5 Newland (1890, p. 22).
6 Gregory (1887, p. 132).
7 Chewings (1936, pp. 10, 26), Gregory (1887, p. 131), O'Connell et al. (1983, pp. 89–92) and Spencer & Gillen (1899, pp. 7, 22; 1912, p. 264).
8 Roth (1897, p. 91). See also Cleland (1957, p. 154), Cleland & Johnston (1933, pp. 115, 118; 1939b, p. 172), O'Connell et al. (1983, pp. 86–7, 89, 92), Roth (1901b, p. 12), Scott (1972, p. 94) and Wightman, Gurindji elders et al. (1994, p. 20). Roth referred to star grass as 'button grass'. An earlier name was *Eleusine aegyptiaca*.
9 Cleland (1939, pp. 5–6; 1940, pp. 5–6). Cleland & Johnston (1933, p. 118) referred to this species, 'wonguna', as *E. laniflora*. In the early 1990s, Pitjantjatjara Yankunytjatjara Media Association in Ernabella, northwest South Australia, made a film, *Wangunu Munu Wakati*, which showed Anangu Pitjantjatjara women using this technique to thresh seed.
10 Roth (1897, p. 91; 1901b, p. 15).
11 Cleland & Johnston (1939a, p. 22) and Sweeney (1947, p. 291).
12 Cleland (1939, p. 5; 1957, pp. 152–4; 1966, pp. 146, 148), Cleland & Johnston (1933, pp. 115, 119; 1939b, p. 174), Cleland & Tindale (1954, pp. 83–4; 1959, p. 132), Goddard & Kalotas (1988, pp. 116–9), Hiddins (2000, p. 32; 2001, p. 17), O'Connell et al. (1983, pp. 86–7, 92), Roth (1897, p. 92; 1901b, p. 15), Turner (1994, p. 26), Wightman, Dixon et al. (1992, p. 28) and Wightman, Gurindji elders et al. (1994, p. 44). Species also referred to as 'purslane'.
13 Mitchell (1848, pp. 98–9).
14 Stirling (1896, p. 56).
15 Basedow (1925, pp. 149–50).
16 Bates (1918, p. 160), Cleland (1957, pp. 153–4), Cleland & Johnston (1937–38, p. 335), Cleland et al. (1925, p. 108), Gason (1879, p. 76), Johnston & Cleland (1943a, pp. 151–2), Kimber (1984, pp. 19–20), Roth (1897, p. 92), Spencer (1918) and Worsnop (1897, pp. 81–2). There are two species: common nardoo and short-fruited nardoo.
17 Howitt (in Smyth, 1878, vol. 2, p. 302).
18 Horne & Aiston (1924, pp. 52–3).
19 Newland (1922, pp. 12–4).
20 Basedow (1925, p. 150), Bonyhady (1991, pp. 138, 141), Cherikoff & Isaacs (1989, pp. 131, 184, 190, 195), Earl & McCleary (1994), Horne & Aiston (1924, pp. 52–7, 176), Isaacs (1987, pp. 115, 225), Low (1989, pp. 85, 87, 212), McCleary & Chick (1977) and Murgatroyd (2002, pp. 257–8, 261–3).
21 S.T. Gason (cited Smyth, 1878, vol. 1, p. 216).
22 Daley (1931, p. 29), Thozet (1866, p. 5) and von Mueller (1862, cited Smyth [1878, vol. 1, p. 216]).
23 Bindon (1996, p. 109), Cleland (1957, pp. 153–4), Cleland & Johnston (1933,

p. 119; 1939a, p. 23), Cleland & Tindale (1959, p. 132) and Reid (1977, p. 49). Formerly known as *Chenopodium rhadinostachyum*.
24 Albrecht (1959), Cleland (1957, p. 154), Cleland & Johnston (1933, pp. 115, 120; 1937–38, pp. 210, 329, 337; 1939a, p. 24; 1939b, p. 175), Cleland & Tindale (1954, pp. 83–4; 1959, p. 134), Goddard & Kalotas (1988, pp. 38–40, 58–61), Hiddins (2001, pp. 51, 59), Latz (1995, pp. 85–98, 101–7, 109–12, 114–9, 121), O'Connell et al. (1983, pp. 86–7, 89, 91–3), Scott (1972, p. 94), Smith (1991, pp. 5–6), Sweeney (1947, p. 291), Tindale (1941, p. 10), Turner (1994, pp. 27–8) and Wightman, Dixon et al. (1992, pp. 5–6, 8).
25 Bindon (1996, p. 22), Bird & Beeck (1988, pp. 118–9), Hassell (1936, p. 690), Meagher (1974, pp. 26, 57, 64) and Moore (1884, p. 46).
26 Tindale (1977, p. 347; 1981, p. 1879).
27 Basedow (1925, p. 150).
28 Johnston & Cleland (1943a, p. 155). See also Cleland (1957, p. 153; 1966, p. 146), Cleland et al. (1925, p. 116), Cleland & Tindale (1954, p. 83), O'Connell et al. (1983, pp. 86–7, 93) and Roth (1897, p. 92).
29 Roth (1901b, p. 12) and O'Connell et al. (1983, pp. 86–7). Roth used the earlier name, *Eucalyptus bicolor*.
30 Clarke (2003a, pp. 70, 83–4, 108, 110, 145–8), Cleland (1936, pp. 6–7; 1966, p. 146), Cleland & Johnston (1937–38, p. 208), Latz (1995, pp. 19, 51–6), Smith (1988), Tindale (1981, pp. 1859–60, 1873–4) and Tolcher (2003, pp. 18–9).
31 Lourandos (1997, pp. 55–7, 188–94, 306) and Smith (1986, 1988).
32 Clarke (2003a, pp. 83–4, 110, 120, 144–8, 153), McBryde (1987, pp. 271–3), McCourt (1975, pp. 135–40), Newland (1890, p. 22), Tindale (1977) and Worsnop (1897, p. 98).
33 Reuther (1981, entry no. 2767b).
34 Thomson (1962, p. 13).
35 Horne & Aiston (1924, p. 33).
36 Horne & Aiston (1924, p. 54).
37 McBryde (1987, pp. 271–3).
38 Gould (1969, p. 77).
39 Bindon (1996, p. 102), Blake et al. (1998, p. 61), Hiddins (2001, p. 134), Levitt (1981, pp. 41, 136–7), Lourandos (1997, pp. 49–50), Puruntatameri (2001, pp. 8, 44, 143–4), Rae et al. (1982, p. 45), Roth (1901b, p. 12), Smith (1991, p. 21), Smith & Wightman (1990, p. 12), Sutton (1994, pp. 37, 45), Wightman, Roberts et al. (1992, p. 18), Wightman & Smith (1989, p. 16) and Yunupingu (1995, p. 35). The long yam has also been called the 'pencil yam'.
40 Rae et al. (1982, p. 47).
41 Anderson (1996, pp. 70, 75, 80), Blake et al. (1998, pp. 34–5, 60–1), Brennan (1986, pp. 106–7), Chase & Sutton (1981, pp. 1832–3), Crawford (1982, pp. 2, 8, 16, 21, 44–5), Hiddins (2001, pp. 119, 142), Levitt (1981, pp. 41, 46, 136), Puruntatameri (2001, pp. 5, 8, 24–5, 43–4, 143–4, 147), Roth (1901b, p. 9), Smith (1991, pp. 9, 21), Smith & Kalotas (1985, pp. 341, 347), Smith & Wightman (1990, p. 5), Specht (1958, p. 485), Sutton (1994, pp. 37, 45), Tindale (1974, pp. 95–6, 104–5), Wightman, Roberts et al. (1992, p. 18), Wightman & Smith (1989, p. 17) and Yunupingu (1995, pp34–5). *Dioscorea bulbifera* was formerly known as *Dioscorea sativa*.
42 Anderson (1996, pp. 70–1, 75), Blake et al. (1998, p. 125), Chase & Sutton (1981, p. 1833), Crawford (1982, pp. 8, 21, 43–4), Hiddins (2001, p. 13), Puruntatameri (2001, p. 84), Roth (1901b, p. 16), Smith & Wightman (1990, pp. 3, 25), Specht (1958, p. 487), Sutton (1994, pp. 37, 45), Wightman, Roberts et al. (1992, p. 44) and Wightman & Smith (1989, p. 20).
43 Crawford (1982, pp. 2, 22–3, 56), Hiddins (2000, p. 8) and Levitt (1981, pp. 40, 130).
44 Hiddins (2001, p. 31).
45 Blake et al. (1998, pp. 86–7), Brennan (1986, pp. 69, 73), Crawford (1982, pp. 2, 17, 22–3, 69–70), Hiddins (2001, pp. 129, 132), Levitt (1981, p. 39, pp. 90–1), Puruntatameri (2001, p. 62), Rae et al. (1982, p. 45), Roth (1901b, p. 13), Specht (1958, pp. 486, 498–9), Wightman, Roberts et al. (1992, p. 30) and Wightman & Smith (1989, pp. 10, 15, 20–1).
46 Brennan (1986, p. 65), Levitt (1981, pp. 39, 87) and Low (1989, p. 119).
47 Backhouse (1843, p. 526).
48 Bird & Beeck (1988, p. 116), Meagher (1974, pp. 25, 27, 58–9, 65), Meagher & Ride (1980, p. 75), Reid (1977, p. 15) and von Brandenstein (1988, pp. 19, 77). Barr et al. (1988, pp. 214–9), Levitt (1981, pp. 61, 64), Rowland (2002), Tindale (1981, p. 1862) and Worsnop (1897, p. 84) have discussed the practice of geophagy — the eating of earth.
49 Bindon (1996, p. 260), Clarke (1986a, p. 11), Hardwick (2001, pp. 106–7) and Low (1989, p. 150),
50 Angas (1847, pp. 54–5).
51 A.F. Richards (cited Tate, 1882, p. 137). See also Black (1965, p. 749) and Stirling (1896, p. 59).
52 Cleland (1966, p. 136).
53 Maiden (1889, p. 9) and Roth (1901b, p. 9). Symons & Symons (1994, p. 44) described the cooking technique for the seeds. Maiden and Roth used the name *A. officinalis*.
54 W.E. Harney (cited Specht, 1958, p. 499), Lands (1987, pp. 24–6) and Smith

& Kalotas (1985, p. 349). See also Puruntatameri (2001, p. 26), Smith (1991, p. 11), Sutton (1994, pp. 37, 45) and Wightman & Smith (1989, p. 18).

55 Levitt (1981, p. 84).

56 Anderson (1996, p. 74), Blake et al. (1998, pp. 104–5), Crawford (1982, pp. 37–8), Hiddins (2000, pp. 11, 15; 2001, p. 100), Lands (1987, pp. 54–5), Levitt (1981, pp. 35, 38, 148), McConnel (1930, p. 19), Puruntatameri (2001, pp. 8, 70–1, 143), Roth (1901b, p. 14), Smith & Kalotas (1985, p. 344), Smith & Wightman (1990, p. 19), Specht (1958, p. 483), Sutton (1994, p. 38), Tindale (1925, p. 77), Wightman, Roberts et al. (1992, p. 38) and Yunupingu (1995, p. 61).

57 Backhouse (1843, p. 294). This account is similar to the preparation of the 'nut' described by Hunter (1793, p. 479).

58 Backhouse (1843, pp. 380–1). See Hardwick (2001, pp. 29–31), Low (1989, pp. 83–4) and Wreck Bay Community & Renwick (2000, p. 19) for other records of cycad use in New South Wales. Beaton (1982, pp. 55–6), Lawrence (1968, pp. 149–50), Thieret (1958, pp. 14–7) and Whiting (1963, Table 2, pp. 276–8) summed up preparation methods for cycad seeds.

59 Blake et al. (1998, pp. 55–6), Carr & Carr (1981, pp. 17–22), Cawte (1996, p. 104), Clarke (2003a, pp. 161–2), Crawford (1982, pp. 2–3, 22), Hart & Pilling (1960, pp. 34, 38), Levitt (1981, pp. 38, 44, 48–51, 79–80), Mountford (1958, pp. 129–43), Puruntatameri (2001, pp. 8, 40–1, 143), Roth (1901b, p. 11), Scarlett et al. (1982, pp. 158, 166, 173), Smith (1990, pp. 19, 37), Smith (1991, p. 19), Smith & Wightman (1990, p. 10), Specht (1958, pp. 481–2), Tindale (1925, pp. 76–7) and Wightman & Smith (1989, pp. 2, 21).

60 Anderson (1996, pp. 72–4), Beck et al. (1988), Davis (1989, pp. 39–40), Everist (1981, pp. 226–48), Hiddins (2001, p. 23), Roberts et al. (1995, pp. 23, 29), Smith & Wightman (1990, p. 10), Thieret (1958, p. 22), von Brandenstein (1988, pp. 51, 82) and Wightman & Smith (1989, p. 21).

61 W. Beck (cited Kennedy, 1984), Beck et al. (1988), Hiddins (2000, p. 12) and Shepherdson (1981, pp. 4, 97; see also cover).

62 Beaton (1982, pp. 54, 56), Lourandos (1997, pp. 48–9, 138, 142–3, 238, 303, 306, 314) and Smith (1982, 1996). The main species used in southwestern Australia was the by-yu nut.

63 Beck et al. (1988, p. 143).

64 Cawte (1996, p. 105). Whiting (1963, Table 3, p. 281) summed up the toxic effects of cycads.

65 Cawte (1996, p. 106). Screw palm root is more generally taken orally in the treatment for diarrhoea (Levitt, 1981, p. 63).

66 Thozet (1866, p. 15). See also Anderson (1996, pp. 74–5) and Everist (1981, pp. 422–3). This species previously listed as E. scandens.

67 J. Murrells (cited Thozet, 1866, p. 15).

68 Maiden (1889, p. 24).

69 Anderson (1996, p. 74), Hiddins (2000, p. 6; 2001, p. 55) and Roberts et al. (1995, pp. 8–9).

70 Backhouse (1843, p. 362).

71 Hiddins (2000, p. 26; 2001, p. 89), Lands (1987, pp. 48–9), Levitt (1981, pp. 41, 126), Puruntatameri (2001, pp. 29–30), Smith (1991, p. 12), Smith & Kalotas (1985, pp. 339–40), Smith & Wightman (1990, p. 5), Specht (1958, p. 494), Wightman, Jackson et al. (1991, p. 6) and Wightman, Roberts et al. (1992, p. 10).

72 Tindale (1941, pp. 9, 11; 1972, p. 234). See also Cleland (1939, p. 6; 1940, p. 6; 1957, pp. 153–4; 1966, pp. 139, 146, 148), Cleland & Johnston (1937–38, pp. 330–1, 337, 340) and Wightman, Gurindji elders et al. (1994, p. 13).

73 Crawford (1982, p. 9; see also pp. 21, 23–4, 62–3).

74 Basedow (1925, pp. 108–9), Beveridge (1884, pp. 37–40), Clarke (2003a, pp. 83–7, 119–21, 123–4, 146–7, 160–2), Hackett (1937, p. 297), Jorgenson (1837 [1991, p. 55]), Mowaljarlai & Malnic (1993, pp. 10–1), Palmer (1999a, pp. 32–4), Smyth (1878, vol. 2, p. 187), Sutton (1994, pp. 41–4), Tunbridge (1991, p. 35), Wilhelmi (1861, p. 175) and Worsnop (1897, pp. 82–4). Farb & Armelagos (1980, pp. 51–3) described Aboriginal cooking techniques in a world context.

75 Albrecht (1959), Cleland (1957, pp. 152, 156; 1966, p. 150), Cleland & Johnston (1933, pp. 115, 119; 1937–38, pp. 209, 336; 1939b, p. 174), Cleland & Tindale (1959, p. 133), Latz (1995, pp. 56–7, 219, 249–50) and O'Connell et al. (1983, p. 97). Albrecht referred to munyeroo as 'manjero'.

76 Dawson (1881, p. 4).

77 Angas (1847, pp. 58, 89–90), Bulmer (1887, p. 15), Eyre (1845, vol. 2, pp. 289–92), Sutton (1994, p. 44) and Worsnop (1897, pp. 82–3).

78 Tindale (1981, p. 1869).

79 Mathews (1901, p. 215).

80 A.C. Gregory (cited Mathews, 1901, p. 216).

81 Mathews (1901).

82 Clarke (2003a, pp. 71, 79, 85–6, 162). Aboriginal artefact collection, South Australian Museum.

83 Clarke (2003a, p. 87) and Puruntatameri (2001, p. 66).

84 Crawford (1982, p. 50).

85 Levitt (1981, pp. 32, 127).

86 Sutton (1994, p. 45). The botanical identities of the bloodwoods are uncertain

87 Cleland (1936, p. 6), Cleland & Johnston (1933, pp. 115, 121) and Latz (1995, p. 300).

88 B. David (cited Clarke, 2003a, p. 86).

89 Brennan (1986, p. 58) described the use of the wattle (Acacia gonocarpa), which does not have a widely recognised common name. Hodgson (1988, p. 86) discussed the use of the golden grevillea.

90 Crawford (1982, p. 9). Crawford identified the daranggal gum as coming from Brachychiton paradoxum, which is an obsolete term for a kurrajong. Bindon (1996, p. 58) referred to a kurrajong from this region, with the same ethnobotanical use, as the large-leaf kurrajong (Brachychiton tuberculatus). An earlier genus name for some Syzygium species was Eugenia. See also Crawford (1982, pp. 22, 62, 66), Smith (1991, p. 12) and Smith & Kalotas (1985, pp. 339–40).

91 F.M. Bailey in the Adelaide Observer, 13 June 1914, p. 41.

Chapter 8

1 Clements (1932).

2 For example, see the study of witchcraft and sorcery by Evans-Pritchard (1937) among the Azande of the Sudan in northern Africa.

3 Crosby (2004, chapter 9).

4 Cleland (1953, p. 399), Crosby (2004, p. 285) and Diamond (1998, pp. 87, 92, 164, 195–214, 330, 355, 357).

5 Graves (1966) and Bates (2002, chapter 9) provided examples of the mythological origins of various plant uses in Europe, while Harris (1833) and Zohary (1982) dealt with plants of the Bible.

6 D. Bird Rose (1987, p. 4). For other references in Aboriginal Australia see Reid (1979, 1982).

7 D. Bird Rose (1987, p. 9).

8 Memmott (1982).

9 Wiminydji & Peile (1978, p. 506).

10 Wiminydji & Peile (1978, pp. 506–7).

11 Tonkinson (1982, p. 226).

12 Wightman, Dixon et al. (1992, pp. 10–1).

13 Laramba Community Women (2003, p. 34), Levitt (1981, pp. 55, 101), Nyinkka Nyunyu (2003) and Wiminydji & Peile (1978, p. 509).

14 Barr et al. (1988, pp. 204–7), Collins et al. (1990, pp. 49, 114), Crawford (1982, p. 50), Henshall et al. (1980, p. 10), Lassak & McCarthy (1983, pp. 42–3), Levitt (1981, pp. 54, 101), O'Connell et al. (1983, p. 96), Reid (1977, pp. 6, 112–3), Scarlett et al. (1982, p. 182), Smith & Kalotas (1985, p. 351), Webb (1969b, pp. 142–3), Wightman, Dixon et al. (1992, p. 32) and Wightman, Jackson et al. (1991, p. 27).

15 Arthur (1996, pp. 21–2), Berndt (1947), Beveridge (1884, pp. 68–70), Elkin (1977), Tindale (1974, p. 36) and Tonkinson (1994).

16 For ngangkari references see Elkin (1977, p. 107), Goddard (1992, p. 82), Ngaanyatjarra Pitjantjatjara Yankunytjatjara Women's Council Aboriginal Corporation (2003) and Schulze (1891, p. 235). Elkin used the spelling 'nangari', while Schulze described the 'medicine man' as 'ngankara'. Cawte (1996, pp. 18, 137), Elkin (1977, pp. 117–20) and Reid (1983) discussed the marrnggitj. Elkin used the spelling 'marrngit'. Tench (1788–92 [1996, pp. 146–7]) recorded the role of the garraaji. Tench wrote this name as 'caradyee'.

17 Arthur (1996, pp. 129–30).

18 Cawte (1996, p. 17). For related references see also Cawte (1974, pp. 56–60 and chapter 6), Goodale (1971, pp. 229–36), Levitt (1981, pp. 52–3), Robinson (1831–33, 1837 [Plomley, 1987, pp. 45, 75, 245, 712]) and Roth (1897, chapter 11).

19 Akerman (1979b).

20 Cawte (1974, pp. 30, 41–2, 44, 63–4), Elkin (1977, chapters 3 & 4), Eyre (1845, vol. 2, pp. 359–60), Gason (1879, pp. 78–9), Howitt (1904, pp. 404–13), Spencer & Gillen (1899, chapter 16; 1927, vol. 2, chapter 15) and Roth (1897, pp. 152–3).

21 Meyer (1846 [1879, p. 197]).

22 Meyer (1843, p. 90). See discussion by Clarke (1987, pp. 9–10).

23 Akerman (1979b, pp. 23–4). Bates (1959, pp. 188–90) described Aboriginal use of tektites or 'emu eyes' as healing charms.

24 Warner (1958, p. 200). See broader account by Elkin (1977, p. 9).

25 Elkin (1977, pp. 8–9, 113, 123) and Spencer & Gillen (1904, pp. 480–1).

26 Elkin (1977, p. 91).

27 Elkin (1977, p. 93) and Howitt (1904, p. 409).

28 C.H. Berndt (1982a), R.M. Berndt (1947, pp. 351–5), Berndt & Berndt (1993, chapter 12), Eyre (1845, vol. 2, pp. 359–60), Hardy (1969, pp. 16–7), Roth (1897, chapter 11) and Tonkinson (1982, pp. 234–5).

29 Barr et al. (1988, pp. 22–5), D. Bird Rose (1987, pp. 7–11) and Watson (1994).

30 An example of this is given by Barr et al. (1988, p. 100).

31 Clarke (1987, p. 9; 2003a, p. 194), Denoon & Mein-Smith (2000, pp. 75–6), Lassak & McCarthy (1983, p. 14), MacPherson (1925, pp. 593–4), Plomley (1987, pp. 110–1, 162, 678 & Appendix 2) and Robinson (1839 [Plomley, 1987, pp. 616–7, 785–7]).
32 D. Bird Rose (1987, p. 7).
33 Mathews (1901).
34 Eastwell (1973b, p. 1011).
35 Cawte (1996, p. 9).
36 Cawte (1974, chapter 1), Devanesen (1985, 2000), Eastwell (1973a, 1978), Elkin (1977, pp. 154–61), Maddock & Cawte (1970), Maher (1999), Nathan & Japanangka (1983), Plooij & O'Brien (1973), Reid (1978a, 1978b, 1983), Rose (1988), Soong (1983), Tonkinson (1982), Tynan (1979) and N. White (cited Kennedy, 1984, p. 109).
37 Levitt (1981, pp. 59, 84), Paddy et al. (1987, p. 13), Puruntatameri (2001, p. 73), Scarlett et al. (1982, p. 181) and Smith & Kalotas (1985, p. 340).
38 Levitt (1981, p. 58).
39 Maiden (1889, p. 22) and Stewart & Percival (1997, pp. 16, 24). Also commonly known as 'rock lily', in many books it is referred to by the earlier scientific name, *Dendrobium speciosum*.
40 Bindon (1996, p. 82) and Clarke (1987, p. 6). Similar uses of clematis by the Maori were recorded in New Zealand (Brooker et al. 1987, pp. 200–1).
41 Wreck Bay Community & Renwick (2000, p. 20).
42 Dawson (1881, p. 57) and Eyre (1845, vol. 2, p. 361).
43 Backhouse (1843, p. 90).
44 Barr et al. (1988, pp. 16, 140–1), Reid (1977, pp. 87, 138) and Smith (1991, p. 7).
45 Hiddins (2000, p. 25; 2001, p. 6).
46 Barr et al. (1988, pp. 16, 146–7), Levitt (1981, pp. 56–7, 90), Puruntatameri (2001, pp. 62, 147), Scarlett et al. (1982, p. 178) and Wightman & Smith (1989, p. 21).
47 References to the caustic-vine are Barr et al. (1988, pp. 192–3), Latz (1995, p. 262) and Worsnop (1897, p. 145). Bindon (1996, pp. 135–6) and Latz (1995, p. 195) described use of the caustic-weed.
48 Clarke (1987, p. 5).
49 Mollison (1974, section 7.1.3).
50 Lands (1987, pp. 35–7), Wightman, Jackson et al. (1991, p. 4) and Wightman, Roberts et al. (1992, p. 6).
51 Cawte (1996, p. 79).
52 Clarke (1986a, pp. 3–4; 1987, p. 4). See also MacPherson (1925, pp. 593–4).
53 Backhouse (1843, p. 84). This species previously known as *Mesembryanthemum equilaterale*.
54 Levitt (1981, pp. 116, 145) and Puruntatameri (2001, pp. 75, 147). The asparagus-fern was also known as *Protasparagus racemosus*.
55 Barr et al. (1988, pp. 98–113), Cleland & Johnston (1933, pp. 116, 124), Cleland & Tindale (1959, p. 139), Goddard & Kalotas (1988, pp. 21, 78–81, 84–7), Henshall et al. (1980, p. 6), O'Connell et al. (1983, p. 96), Reid (1977, pp. 114–6, 159), Silberbauer (1971, p. 34), Smith (1991, pp. 23–4) and Wightman, Dixon et al. (1992, p. 16).
56 Barr et al. (1988, pp. 84–5), Henshall et al. (1980, p. 8), O'Connell et al. (1983, p. 96), Reid (1977, p. 21) and Wightman, Gurindji elders et al. (1994, p. 18). An earlier name was *Cymbopogon exaltatus*.
57 Henshall et al. (1980, p. 4), Nyinkka Nyunyu (2003) and Reid (1977, pp. 38–9). Henshall et al. used an earlier name, *Pterigeron odora*, while Reid used the name *Pterigeron odorus*. See also Cleland & Johnston (1933, pp. 116, 124) and O'Connell et al. (1983, p. 96) for related records. The name of *Pterocaulon serrulatum* was formerly *P. glandulosum*. The toothed ragwort is also commonly known as 'bush vicks', as is *Streptoglossa odora*.
58 Reid (1977, p. 23).
59 Levitt (1981, pp. 54, 122).
60 Barr et al. (1988, p. 172), Crawford (cited Reid, 1977, p. 17) and Puruntatameri (2001, pp. 70, 147).
61 Levitt (1981, pp. 62–3, 109–10), Paddy et al. (1987, p. 16), Scarlett et al. (1982, pp. 178–9), Smith & Kalotas (1985, pp. 330, 346), Wightman, Roberts et al. (1992, p. 34) and Wightman & Smith (1989, pp. 11, 16).
62 Clarke (1987, pp. 7, 10), Dawson (1881, p. 56) and Lawson (1879, p. 59). See also D. Miles, *The Sydney Morning Herald*, 14 October 1963, p. 13.
63 Barr et al. (1988, pp. 122–7), MacPherson (1925, pp. 593–4; 1939), Reid (1977, pp. 118–25), Smith (1991, pp. 19–27) and Wightman, Dixon et al. (1992, pp. 16, 18, 20).
64 Robinson (1830 [Plomley, 1966, p. 302]).
65 Bonney (1884, p. 132).
66 Mollison (1974, section 7.1.3).
67 Dawson (1881, p. 57).
68 Levitt (1981, pp. 55, 99).
69 Webb (1969b, p. 143).
70 Levitt (1981, pp. 54, 143–4).
71 Levitt (1981, pp. 65, 138). See also Puruntatameri (2001, p. 54). Whipvine (*Flagellaria indica*) is known as 'supplejack', which is also applied to *Ventilago viminalis*.
72 Barr et al. (1988, pp. 122–7), MacPherson (1925, pp. 593–4; 1939), Reid (1977, pp. 118–25), Smith (1991, pp. 19–27) and Wightman, Dixon et al. (1992, pp. 16, 18, 20).
73 Barr et al. (1988, pp. 184–7).
74 Barr et al. (1988, pp. 94–7), Cawte (1996, p. 106), Levitt (1981, p. 146), Scarlett et al. (1982, p. 176), Smith (1991, pp. 19, 21) and Wightman, Roberts et al. (1992, p. 16). The orchid species referred to includes both the bracket orchid (*Dendrobium affine*) and the inland tree orchid (*Cymbidium canaliculatum*).
75 Kalotas (1996, pp. 277–9) and Specht (1958, p. 482).
76 Barr et al. (1988, p. 25, 35, 60–1, 78–9).
77 Barr et al. (1988, p. 47).
78 Barr et al. (1988, p. 77).
79 Puruntatameri (2001, p. 71). Lumholtz (1889 [1980, pp. 149–51]) and Mathews (1904, pp. 262–70) described body-scarring practices.
80 Worsnop (1897, p. 163).
81 Crawford (1982, p. 47) and Reid (1977, p. 134). An earlier name was *Grevillea viscidula*.
82 Wightman, Roberts et al. (1992, p. 28). The plant is *Grevillea dimidiata*.
83 Levitt (1981, pp. 61, 107) and Smith (1991, p. 25). Smith & Kalotas (1985, p. 347) recorded the medicinal use of kino from ghost gums.
84 Barr et al. (1988, pp. 42–3). See also Wightman, Dixon et al. (1992, p. 6).
85 Barr et al. (1988, pp. 188–9) and Reid (1977, p. 147).
86 Levitt (1981, pp. 57, 81, 85).
87 Crawford (1982, p. 68).
88 Levitt (1981, p. 66).
89 Lassak & McCarthy (1983, pp. 135–6), Reid (1977, p. 131) and Webb (1969b, p. 144).
90 Yunupingu (1995, p. 51).
91 Smyth (1878, vol. 1, p. 222).
92 Bunce (1859, p. 47). See also Carr & Carr (1981, p. 17) and Robinson (1831 [Plomley, 1966, pp. 534, 538–9, 542, 556–7, 569, 580]), who referred to the use of the 'cider tree' and 'cider gum'. Bunce incorrectly referred to this species as *Eucalyptus resinifera*.
93 Brady (1994, p. 41) and Carr & Carr (1981, p. 17).
94 Roth (1903b, p. 49). See also von Brandenstein (1988, p. 15).
95 Bates (1901–14, [1985, p. 241]).
96 Brady (1994, p. 41).
97 Rev. Dr W. Woolls (cited Maiden, 1889, p. 172).
98 Stone (1911, p. 445) and Zola & Gott (1992, p. 29).
99 Angas (1847, vol. 1, p. 73). Angas spelled the group name as 'Tattayarra'. See discussion by Cleland (1966, p. 120).
100 Basedow (1925, pp. 153–4) and Brady (1994, p. 41).
101 Basedow (1925, pp. 155–7), Carr & Carr (1981, pp. 24–7), Cleland (1936, pp. 7–8; 1939, p. 13; 1957, pp. 158–9; 1966, p. 119), Cleland & Johnston (1933, p. 116; 1937–38, p. 338; 1939b, p. 177), Dobkin de Rios & Stachalek (1999), Hardy (1969, p. 14), Helms (1896, pp. 248–9), Hicks (1963), Johnston (1939), Johnston & Cleland (1933–34, p. 168), Latz (1974; 1995), Maiden (1889, pp. 168–72), Peterson (1977), Reid (1977, pp. 159–61), Roth (1901b, p. 31), Smith (1991, p. 22), Smyth (1878, vol. 2, pp. 222–3), Tolcher (2003, pp. 23–4, 83–4, 110), Watson (1983) and Webb (1973, pp. 293–4).
102 Jessop (1981, pp. 324–5).
103 Dixon et al. (1992, pp. 130–1) and Ramson (1988, p. 483). The Aboriginal plant name has also been rendered as 'pitjuri', 'pitcheri', 'pitcherry', 'pitchery', 'pitchury', 'peturr', 'bedgery' and 'pedgery'.
104 Von Mueller (cited Smyth, 1878, vol. 1, p. 223) provided the information on pituri being used to give courage in fighting, while Latz (1995, p. 68) described pituri use for initiatory revelation.
105 Bonyhady (1991, p. 137), Moorehead (1963, pp. 118, 123, 137) and Murgatroyd (2002, p. 253).
106 Roth (1897, p. 100).
107 Specimen A1804, Aboriginal artefact collection, South Australian Museum.
108 Basedow (1925, p. 156).
109 Basedow (1925, p. 156), Roth (1897, p. 100), Smyth (1878, vol. 2, pp. 222–3) and Watson (1983).
110 Bancroft (1872), Everist (1981, pp. 636–9), Hicks & Le Messurier (1935), Maiden (1889, pp. 172–5) and Webb (1948, pp. 8–9; 1969a, p. 83).
111 Latz (1995, p. 234) and Watson (1983, pp. 27–8).
112 Cleland (1936, pp. 7–8; 1939, p. 14), Cleland et al. (1925, p. 113), Cleland & Johnston (1933, pp. 116, 120; 1937–38, p. 210), Goddard & Kalotas (1988, p. 21), Johnston & Cleland (1943a, p. 154). See also Cleland & Tindale (1954, p. 84; 1959, p. 133), Latz (1995, pp. 92–4, 97–8, 105, 114–5), Reid (1977, pp. 79, 84) and Smith (1991, p. 5), who list other *Acacia* species that were also used.
113 Johnston & Cleland (1943a, pp. 155–6) and Reid (1977, p. 73). Reid used an earlier name for the cassia, *Cassia artemisioides*.
114 Cleland & Tindale (1959, p. 139) and Latz (1995, p. 218). The rock isotome

was also chewed alone (Reid, 1977, pp. 105–6; Webb, 1960, p. 104; 1969b, p. 141).

115 King (cited Moorehead, 1963, p. 118) and Watson (1983, pp. 23–4).

116 Clarke (2003a, pp. 61–2, 71, 108, 110), McBryde (1987, pp. 258, 260–2, 265–7, 273) and Watson (1983, chapter 3).

117 Stirling (1896, p. 61).

118 Latz (1974, p. 283).

119 Cleland & Johnston (1937–38, p. 341), Dixon et al. (1992, p. 130), Finlayson (1952, p. 64), Peterson (1977), Symon (2005) and Watson (1983, p. 7). Fumiyo Saitoh et al. (1985) provided an analysis of chemicals contained in *Nicotiana* species. Gately (2001) described the spread of the use of South American tobacco across the world.

120 Brokensha (1975, p. 29), Cleland (1936, p. 7; 1939, p. 14; 1957, p. 159), Cleland & Johnston (1933, pp. 116, 123; 1937–38, pp. 211, 341), Cleland & Tindale (1954, p. 85; 1959, p. 138), Latz (1995, pp. 62–4, 233–5) and O'Connell et al. (1983, pp. 97–8).

121 Thomson (1962, p. 271; see also 1961). Thomson referred to this tobacco species as *Nicotiana ingulba*, which botanists presently consider to be a subspecies of *Nicotiana rosulata*. See related account of tobacco use provided by Bates (1901–14, [1985, p. 262]).

122 Berndt & Berndt (1942–43, p. 274) and Cleland & Johnston (1933, p. 116).

123 Berndt (1972, p. 188), Latz (1995, p. 234), Lumholtz (1889 [1980, p. 115]) and Stirling (1896, p. 62).

124 Aboriginal artefact collection, South Australian Museum.

125 Brokensha (1975, pp. 29–31), Cleland (1936, p. 7; 1939, p. 14; 1957, p. 159; 1966, p. 119), Cleland & Johnston (1937–38, pp. 211, 339–41), Finlayson (1952, p. 64), Goddard & Kalotas (1988, pp. 21, 96–9), Latz (1974, p. 281; 1995, p. 232), Reid (1977, p. 164) and Tindale (1941, p. 12). Aboriginal artefact collection, South Australian Museum.

126 Cleland (1939, p. 14; 1966, p. 119), Cleland & Johnston (1939a, pp. 23, 26), O'Connell et al. (1983, pp. 97–8) and Reid (1977, p. 162). Aboriginal artefact collection, South Australian Museum.

127 Reid (1977, p. 163).

128 Cleland & Johnston (1937–38, p. 211; 1939b, p. 177), Cleland & Tindale (1959, pp. 138–9) and O'Connell et al. (1983, pp. 97–8).

129 W.B. MacDougall (cited Cleland, 1957, p. 159). Aboriginal artefact collection, South Australian Museum.

130 Cleland & Johnston (1939a, pp. 23, 26), O'Connell et al. (1983, pp. 97–8), Smith (1991, p. 25), Wightman, Dixon et al. (1992, pp. 18, 20) and Wightman, Gurindji elders et al. (1994, pp. 24, 26). The inland bloodwood was earlier known as *Eucalyptus terminalis*.

131 Smith (1991, p. 26), Smith & Kalotas (1985, pp. 331, 339), Smith & Wightman (1990, p. 12), Wightman, Jackson et al. (1991, pp. 11, 13, 16) and Wightman, Roberts et al. (1992, p. 22).

132 Smith & Wightman (1990, p. 3).

133 Reid (1977, p. 140).

134 Aboriginal tobacco smoking practices are discussed by Berndt & Berndt (1954, pp. 42, 44–5), Clarke (2003a, pp. 181–2, 185), McConnel (1953, p. 24), Roth (1901b, p. 31), Sutton (1994, pp. 50–1) and Thomson (1939b).

135 Brennan (1986, p. 92).

136 Levitt (1981, p. 97).

137 Tindale (1926–27, p. 101).

138 Johnston & Cleland (1943a, pp. 155–6), Latz (1995, pp. 145, 199, 234, 276, 282), O'Connell et al. (1983, pp. 97–8) and Reid (1977, pp. 105–6).

139 Wightman, Dixon et al. (1992, p. 30) and Wightman, Gurindji elders et al. (1994, p. 45). Cleland & Johnston (1939a, p. 26) described the use of this species by Warlpiri people as an aromatic medicine for head colds.

140 Brennan (1986, p. 66), D. Bird Rose (1987), Roth (1901b, p. 31), Russell-Smith (1985, pp. 260, 266) and Wightman, Roberts et al. (1992, p. 47).

141 Wightman, Roberts et al. (1992, p. 28).

142 Crawford (1982, p. 73), J.R.B. Love (cited Cleland & Tindale, 1954, p. 86), Reid (1977, pp. 23, 41–2, 108) and Smith & Kalotas (1985, p. 339). An earlier name for *Pterocaulon serrulatum* was *P. glandulosum*.

143 Cleland & Tindale (1954, p. 86).

144 Webb (1960, p. 109; 1969a, p. 83; 1973, p. 294).

145 Roth (1901b, p. 31). Rowley (1972a, pp. 2, 37, 181–3, 238, 244) discussed Aboriginal addiction to opium, which is derived from the opium poppy.

146 Roth (1901b, p. 31). Roth used an earlier name, *Laportea* species. Everist (1981, pp. 729–34) outlined the toxicity of stinging-trees.

147 Reid (1977, p. 174). The bush, which has no widely recognised common name, is *Clerodendrum lanceolatum*. Crawford (1982, pp. 70–1) listed 'Clerodendrum ovalifolium' as a chewing tobacco.

148 Kalotas (1996, p. 272).

Chapter 9

1 Overviews of Australian Aboriginal material culture are provided by Akerman (1979a), Allen (1995a), Campbell & Edwards (1966), Clarke (2003a, chapter 5), Davidson (1933, 1934, 1935, 1936, 1947), Hayden (1998), Holdaway & Stern (2004), Luebbers (1975), McCarthy (1940b, 1974, 1976), McCourt (1975), Roth (1901a, 1901b, 1902, 1903a, 1904, 1909, 1910), Worsnop (1897) and Wright (1977).

2 McConnel (1953) and Sutton (1994).

3 Carr & Carr (1981, pp. 33–5), Clarke (2003a, chapters 5 & 6), Kamminga (1988), McCarthy (1974, 1976) and McCourt (1975).

4 Beveridge (1889, p. 19), Brokensha (1975, chapter 6), Horne & Aiston (1924, pp. 87–8), Kamminga (1988, pp. 27–8) and Thomson (1964, 1987).

5 Tench (1788–92, p. 256).

6 Holdaway & Stern (2004, pp. 39, 41–2 & section 6B) and Mountford (1941).

7 Eyre (1845, vol. 2, p. 314).

8 For a general guide of wood types refer to Kamminga (1988). The best detailed accounts are from the tropics. Smith (1991) listed wood use for the Northern Territory. Crawford (1982, p. 34), Paddy et al. (1987, p. 31) and Smith & Kalotas (1985) tabled woods used to make artefacts in the Kimberley. See Puruntatameri (2001, pp. 139–40, 144–5, 148–9) for timber use on Melville and Bathurst Islands. Levitt (1981, chapters 3 & 5) provided description of wood selection for artefacts on Groote Eylandt, while Anderson (1996), McConnel (1953) and Sutton (1994) focused on that from northern Queensland.

9 Latz (1995, p. 65). For studies of Aboriginal use of wood see Barker (2005), Buhmann et al. (1976), Kamminga (1988) and Smith (1991).

10 Brokensha (1975, pp. 57–63) and Levitt (1981, pp. 20–1, 25–31). Aboriginal artefact collection, South Australian Museum.

11 Brokensha (1975, pp. 44–5), Cleland (1957, p. 161; 1966, pp. 120, 125), Cleland & Johnston (1933, pp. 117, 123; 1937–38, pp. 211, 333, 336–8), Cleland & Tindale (1954, p. 85; 1959, p. 139), Goddard & Kalotas (1988, pp. 21, 38, 72–7), Kamminga (1988, p. 50), Latz (1995, pp. 65, 239), Mutitjulu Community & Baker (1996, pp. 39–40), O'Connell et al. (1983, p. 98), Silberbauer (1971, p. 35) and Tindale (1941, p. 12). An earlier name for the Central Australian spearwood was *Tecoma doratoxylon*.

12 McConnel (1953, pp. 10–1, 25–7 & plate VIII) and Sutton (1994, pp. 39–41).

13 Bonney (1994, p. 28), Eyre (1845, vol. 2, pp. 305–7) and Worsnop (1897, pp. 93–4, 124). Black cypress pine formerly known as *Callitris preissii*. Aboriginal artefact collection, South Australian Museum.

14 Latz (1995, pp. 65–6). See also Cleland (1957, p. 161; 1966, p. 120), Cleland & Johnston (1933, p. 121) and O'Connell et al. (1983, p. 98).

15 Basedow (1925, pp. 92–3).

16 Clarke (2003a, pp. 77–8, 181, 185), Tindale (1925, pp. 103–12) and Worsnop (1897, p. 121). Baker (1988) outlined Aboriginal dugout canoe making practices.

17 Tindale (1974, pp. 36–7, 141, 151–3, 262).

18 McConnel (1953, p. 3).

19 Basedow (1925, pp. 93–4) and Clarke (2003a, chapters 5 & 6).

20 Aboriginal artefact collection, South Australian Museum.

21 Anderson (1996, p. 72), Berndt & Berndt (1999, pp. 48, 51, 65, 68, 96, 168, 171), Brennan (1986, p. 51), Crawford (1982, pp. 66–7), Davis (1989, pp. 42–3), Levitt (1981, pp. 17–9, 107–8), McConnel (1953, pp. 10, 12), Mountford (1958, various plates), Puruntatameri (2001, pp. 51, 145–6), Smith (1991, p. 28), Specht (1958, p. 497), Sutton (1994, p. 34), Wightman, Roberts et al. (1992, p. 24), Wightman & Smith (1989, p. 15) and Yunupingu (1995, p. 40).

22 Sheeting from species such as the silver-leaved paperbark, swamp teatree, weeping paperbark and broad-leaved paperbark.

23 Basedow (1925, pp. 95–6), Blake et al. (1998, pp. 94–6), Brennan (1986, pp. 78, 84, 94), Crawford (1982, p. 67), Hiddins (2000, pp. 18, 27; 2001, p. 101), Hodgson (1988, p. 34), Levitt (1981, pp. 17–9, 108–10), McConnel (1930, pp. 9–10; 1953, pp. 9, 12, 30), Paddy et al. (1987, p. 25), Puruntatameri (2001, pp. 66, 146), Roberts et al. (1995, p. 12), Smith & Kalotas (1985, pp. 331, 338, 346), Specht (1958, pp. 497–8), Sutton (1994, pp. 41–3, 45), Symons & Symons (1994, p. 12), Tench (1788–92, pp. 53, 112), Wightman, Jackson et al. (1991, pp. 19, 21), Wightman, Roberts et al. (1992, p. 34) and Wightman & Smith (1989, p. 20). Aboriginal artefact collection, South Australian Museum.

24 Beveridge (1865, p. 22; 1884, pp. 40–2), Black (1947, 1976), Clarke (2003a, pp. 77–8, 85, 124–5, 221), Cleland (1966, p. 120), Edwards (1972), Eyre (1845, vol. 2, pp. 313–4), Gott & Conran (1991, p. 61), Lawrence (1968, p. 153), Mathews (1908), Taplin (1874 [1879, p. 41]), Worsnop (1897, pp. 119–22) and Zola & Gott (1992, p. 14).

25 Beveridge (1884, p. 40).

26 *The Advertiser* (Adelaide), 5 November 1908, p. 8.

27 Beveridge (1884, p. 41).

28 Robinson (1830–31, 1834 [Plomley, 1966, pp. 119, 226, 366, 381, 389, 464–5, 849]) and Walker (1888–99, pp. 259, 284). Walker used the name *Melaleuca decussata* for the source of bark in Tasmania, although this species is not considered to exist there.

29 Baker (1988, pp. 179–81), Levitt (1981, p. 19), McConnel (1953, pp. 9–10,

41) and Mathews (1908).

30 Beveridge (1884, pp. 42–4), Clarke (1988, pp. 69–70) and Zola & Gott (1992, pp. 62–3).

31 Angas (1847, pp. 55, 90), Beveridge (1884, p. 42), Bindon (1996, p. 259), Cleland (1966, p. 138), Taplin (1874 [1879, p. 41]) and Wilhelmi (1861, p. 167).

32 Bunce (1859, p. 75) discussed use of the hemp-bush, which he called *Sida pulchella*. Hardwick (2001, pp. 81–4), Maiden (1889, p. 633) and Stewart & Percival (1997, p. 14) provided an account of black kurrajong use. Maiden used the generic name, *Sterculia*, for kurrajong.

33 J. Bonwick (cited Roth, 1899, p. 143). Crawford (1982, figs.16–9, pp. 59–61) provided photographs of a Kimberley woman demonstrating string making.

34 Roth (1899, p. 143) and West (1999, p. 141). Roth used the common name, 'currijong', and the obsolete name *Plagianthus sidoides*. Walker (1888–99, p. 258) described baskets made from 'native grass'.

35 Beveridge (1884, pp. 43–4), Eyre (1845, vol. 2, p. 311), West (1999, Appendix B, pp. 140–6) and Zola & Gott (1992, pp. 58, 61). Some authors refer to kangaroo grass by an earlier name, *Themeda australis*.

36 Clarke (2003b, pp. 100–1), Cleland (1957, p. 161), Gott & Conran (1991, pp. 53–8), Hardwick (2001, pp. 34–5), Robson (1986), Worsnop (1897, pp. 85–7) and Zola & Gott (1992, pp. 57–60).

37 Backhouse (1843, p. 103). See also Plomley (1976, pp. 346–8) and Robinson (1829–30, 1832 [Plomley, 1966, pp. 58, 266; 1987, p. 244]).

38 Bonney (1994, pp. 12, 29), Carr & Carr (1981, p. 35) and Robson (1986). Plants also identified during my fieldwork in southeastern Australia during the 1980s (Clarke, 1994, pp. 173–4; 2003b, pp. 98–101).

39 Backhouse (1843, p. 102), Robinson (1829 [Plomley, 1966, p. 57]) and Roth (1899, pp. 89, 142 & Appendix F, p. lxxv).

40 Thomson (1975, p. 69).

41 Cleland et al. (1925, p. 114), Latz (1995, p. 67) and Thomson (1962, pp. 266, 277).

42 Bindon & Gough (1993, p. 14) and Thomson (1975, pp. 123–4, 162). Aboriginal artefact collection, South Australian Museum.

43 Clarke (2003a, p. 150), Davidson (1933), Horne & Aiston (1924, pp. 62–4, 68), Lamond (1950, p. 168) and West (1999, pp. 122–5, 137, 146). Aboriginal artefact collection, South Australian Museum.

44 Johnston & Cleland (1943a, pp. 154–5). Plant formerly known as *Psoralea patens*.

45 Anderson (1996, p. 74), Brennan (1986, p. 53), Crawford (1982, pp. 58–62), Hiddins (2000, pp. 18, 20; 2001, pp. 41, 70), Hodgson (1988), Levitt (1981, pp. 17, 19–20, 104–5, 127), McConnel (1953, pp. 12–5, 28–31), Paddy et al. (1987, pp. 4, 26, 31), Puruntatameri (2001, pp. 30, 39, 53–4, 60), Roth (1901a, pp. 8–10), Smith (1991, p. 12), Smith & Kalotas (1985, pp. 329, 339), Smith & Wightman (1990, p. 14), Sutton (1994, p. 49), West (1999, pp. 4–9), Wightman, Jackson et al. (1991, pp. 6, 22, 24), Wightman, Roberts et al. (1992, pp. 10, 38), Wightman & Smith (1989, pp. 10, 16–7, 20) and Worsnop (1879, pp. 90–3).

46 Anderson (1996, pp. 73–4), Davidson (1933, pp. 272–92, 298), Hodgson (1988), McConnel (1953, pp. 12–3, 30–1, 41), Puruntatameri (2001, pp. 70–1), Roth (1901a), Smith & Wightman (1990, p. 19) and Specht (1958, p. 483).

47 Davis (1989, pp. 58–9) and Hodgson (1988, pp. 58–73, 85).

48 Aboriginal artefact collection, South Australian Museum.

49 Lands (1987, p. 55).

50 Puruntatameri (2001, pp. 29, 146) referred to Tiwi use of kapok-tree, while Smith (1991, p. 11) discussed its use by the Iwaidja.

51 Cleland (1939, p. 11; 1966, p. 122), Hassell (1936, p. 694), Meagher & Ride (1980, pp. 76–7) and Wreck Bay Community & Renwick (2000, p. 27). Aboriginal artefact collection, South Australian Museum.

52 Gott & Conran (1991, pp. 44–5, 67).

53 Bennett (1882, pp. 350–1) and Cleland & Johnston (1937–38, pp. 334–5).

54 Carr & Carr (1981, p. 35), Cleland (1936, p. 8; 1939, p. 11; 1957, p. 160; 1966, pp. 120, 122, 146–7), Cleland & Johnston (1933, pp. 113, 117–8; 1937–38, pp. 214, 335), Cleland & Tindale (1954, pp. 83, 85; 1959, p. 130), Goddard & Kalotas (1988, pp. 21–2), Latz (1995, pp. 66–7, 288–93), Maiden (1890), O'Connell et al. (1983, p. 98), Schultze (1891, p. 228), Wightman, Dixon et al. (1992, p. 33) and Wightman, Gurindji elders et al. (1994, p. 53).

55 Stirling (1896, p. 62). See also Spencer (1896, part 1, pp. 71–2).

56 Brokensha (1975, pp. 64–6). Aboriginal artefact collection, South Australian Museum.

57 Cleland (1936, p. 8; 1939, p. 11; 1957, pp. 160–1; 1966, p. 122), Horne & Aiston (1924, p. 53), Johnston & Cleland (1943a, p. 156) and Stirling (1896, pp. 59, 62). Horne & Aiston identified the gum by the Aboriginal name, 'mindrie'. Aboriginal artefact collection, South Australian Museum.

58 Stirling (1896, p. 62).

59 Cleland (1939, p. 11; 1957, p. 161), Cleland & Johnston (1937–38, pp. 214, 334; 1939b, p. 173), Johnston & Cleland (1943a, p. 153) and Latz (1995, pp.

60 Anderson (1996, p. 76), Brennan (1986, p. 52), Levitt (1981, p. 86) and Specht (1958, p. 491).

61 Crawford (1982, pp. 72–3).

62 McConnel (1953, p. 27 & plate X).

63 Tindale (1941, p. 9).

64 Mathews (1900, p. 633).

65 Bunce (1859, p. 77). Eyre (1845, vol. 2, pp. 273–4) provided a similar account for discovering a beehive, involving the use of a bird feather rather than a seed awn.

66 Mountford (1958, p. 97) and Roth (1904, p. 14). Aboriginal artefact collection, South Australian Museum.

67 Cleland (1957, p. 162; 1966, p. 122) and Stirling (1896, p. 63).

68 Latz (1995, pp. 70, 212–3). Latz used an earlier name, *Helipterum tietkensii*.

69 Crawford (1982, p. 50).

70 Cleland (1936, p. 8; 1939, p. 10; 1957, p. 162; 1966, p. 123), Cleland & Johnston (1933, pp. 117, 124; 1937–38, p. 212; 1939a, p. 26), Goddard & Kalotas (1988, p. 22) and Latz (1995, pp. 70, 248–9).

71 Blake et al. (1998, pp. 104–5), Hiddins (2000, p. 15; 2001, p. 100), Hodgson (1988, p. 86), Sutton (1994, p. 46) and Yunupingu (1995, p. 61). Aboriginal artefact collection, South Australian Museum.

72 Anderson (1996, p. 77), Blake et al. (1998, pp. 81, 83), Brennan (1986, p. 67), Hodgson (1988, pp. 73–83), Levitt (1981, p. 145), Puruntatameri (2001, p. 58), Smith & Wightman (1990, pp. 14, 21), West (1999, pp. 9–11), Wightman, Jackson et al. (1991, p. 17), Wightman & Roberts et al. (1992, pp. 30, 40), Wightman & Smith (1989, p. 21) and Yunupingu (1995, p. 46). The hibbertia is *Hibbertia dealbata*. The colour-tree or colour-root has also been known as *Caelospermum reticulatum*.

73 Worsnop (1897, p. 15; also see p. 4). See also F.M. Bailey in the *Adelaide Observer*, 13 June 1914, p. 41.

74 Stephens (1890, p. 487).

75 Cleland & Johnston (1933, pp. 117, 122), Goddard (1992, p. 21), Goddard & Kalotas (1988, pp. 15, 22, 114–5, 139), Silberbauer (1971, p. 34) and Tindale (1941, p. 11). Crawford (1982, p. 68) noted a similar practice in the Kimberley.

76 Brennan (1986, pp. 24, 102), Levitt (1981, pp. 45, 59, 82) and Puruntatameri (2001, p. 24).

77 Cawte (1996, p. 106). An earlier name for the bracket orchid or tree orchid (*Dendrobium affine*) was *D. dicuphum*.

78 Brennan (1986, p. 100), Levitt (1981, p. 146), Mountford (1958, p. 20), Puruntatameri (2001, pp. 41, 146), Smith (1991, pp. 19, 21), Specht (1958, p. 487), Wightman, Roberts et al. (1992, p. 16), Wightman & Smith (1989, p. 13) and Yunupingu (1995, pp. 32–3).

79 Puruntatameri (2001, p. 54).

80 Crawford (1982, p. 46) and Puruntatameri (2001, pp. 28, 146).

81 Anderson (1996, p. 77), Hiddins (2000, p. 12; 2001, p. 128), Levitt (1981, pp. 44–5, 112), McConnel (1953, pp. 11, 15, 28, 34–5), Puruntatameri (2001, p. 20), Smith (1991, p. 5), Smith & Kalotas (1985, p. 348), Smith & Wightman (1990, p. 3), Specht (1958, p. 491), Sutton (1994, pp. 35, 50), Wightman, Jackson et al. (1991, p. 4), Wightman, Roberts et al. (1992, p. 6) and Wightman & Smith (1989, p. 22). Aboriginal artefact collection, South Australian Museum.

82 Worsnop (1897, pp. 87, 158). Aboriginal artefact collection, South Australian Museum.

83 Smith & Kalotas (1985, p. 329).

84 Hamlyn-Harris & Smith (1916, p. 1).

85 Smith & Kalotas (1985, p. 330). The wattle species is *Acacia wickhamii*.

86 Curr (1883, p. 110).

87 Maiden (1889, pp. 149, 172).

88 Rev. Dr Woolls (cited Maiden, 1889, p. 172).

89 T. Mitchell (cited Maiden, 1889, p. 150).

90 Hamlyn-Harris & Smith (1916, p. 1), Meagher (1974, p. 22) and Roth (1903b, p. 47).

91 Horton (2000, pp. 39–52) and Jones (1978).

92 Anderson (1996, p. 70), Brennan (1986, pp. 21, 80), Crawford (1982, pp. 33, 51–3, 64), Everist (1981, Appendix 2), Hamlyn-Harris & Smith (1916), Hiddins (2000, 2001), Levitt (1981, pp. 47, 84), Maiden (1889), Paddy et al. (1987, pp. 14–5), Puruntatameri (2001, pp. 84–5, 146), Russell-Smith (1985, p. 261), Reid (1977, pp. 66–9, 94, 96–7, 99–103, 177), Smith (1991, p. 11), Smith & Kalotas (1985, pp. 330, 332–3, 341, 344), Specht (1958, pp. 491, 495), Stirling (1896, p. 61), Sutton (1994, p. 39), Webb (1948, p. 10; 1960, p. 108; 1969b, p. 144), Wightman, Gurindji elders et al. (1994, p. 50), Wightman, Jackson et al. (1991, pp. 4, 6, 9, 22), Wightman, Roberts et al. (1992, pp. 10, 24) and Wightman & Smith (1989, p. 20). Aboriginal artefact collection, South Australian Museum.

93 Puruntatameri (2001, p. 85).

94 Newland (1890, p. 23).

95 Spencer (1896, part 1, p. 82). See also Cleland & Johnston (1933, p. 116).

96   Albrecht (1959). Albrecht gave the Aboriginal name for the poison as 'monanga', which appears to be equivalent to the 'monunga' specimen of *Duboisia hopwoodii* collected by J.B. Cleland at Mount Liebig in 1932 (Aboriginal artefact collection, South Australian Museum).

97   Basedow (1925, pp. 139, 157), Cleland (1966, p. 120), Cleland & Johnston (1933, p. 123; 1937–38, p. 211), Cleland & Tindale (1954, p. 85), Goddard (1992, p. 178), Goddard & Kalotas (1988, p. 22), Hamlyn-Harris & Smith (1916, p. 1), Hiddins (2001, p. 33), Reid (1977, p. 161) and Webb (1973, p. 294). Aboriginal artefact collection, South Australian Museum. Records of *Duboisia myoporoides* use as a poison in Central Australia are probably referring to *D. hopwoodii*.

98   Basedow (1925, p. 139).

99   Reid (1977, pp. 127–9).

100   Latz (1995, pp. 150, 199, 205) considered uses of gyrostemon, native wallflower and stiff goodenia. Hicks (1963) recorded use of camel-poison. Aboriginal artefact collection, South Australian Museum.

101   Henshall et al. (1980, p. 20).

Chapter 10

1   In terms of the Australian continent, refer to Allen et al. (1977), Chappell & Thom (1977) and White (1994, chapters 14–20).

2   Diamond (1998, chapter 15), Flannery (1994, part 2) and Flannery & Schouten (2001).

3   Golson (1971) and F.G.G. Rose (1987, pp. 52–4).

4   Flannery (1994), Merrilees (1968), Murray (1991), Murray & Vickers-Rich (2003) and Vickers-Rich et al. (1997).

5   Chaloupka (1993, pp. 94–101), Flood (1997, pp. 108–20), McDonald (1983) and Tindale (1972, pp. 240–1; 1978, p. 157).

6   Clarke (2003a, pp. 11–3, 58–9), Corbett (2001, chapter 1) and Flannery (1994, pp. 115, 275–7, 333, 383–4).

7   Clarke (2003a, pp. 13–4), Diamond (1998, chapter 17), Flannery (1994, chapters 14–8) and Thorne & Raymond (1989).

8   Barrau (1958, pp. 43–6), Golson (1971, pp. 202, 208–9, 217, 225, 231, 234), Low (1989, pp. 106, 110), Sauer (1963, pp. 55–8, 60) and Yen (1977, 1995).

9   Favenc (1888, p. 383).

10   Bindon (1996, p. 93) and Jessop & Toelken (1986, p. 885).

11   Therik (2004, pp. 63, 70, 152, 187) described the ritual significance of banyans for the Timorese, while Blake et al. (1998, p. 72) and Yunupingu (1995, p. 42) gave Australian examples of banyans as spirit trees.

12   Olsen (2003), Oppenheimer (2003) and Sykes (2001) provided overviews of the rapidly developing area of human DNA research.

13   Balint (2005, p. 20), Berndt & Berndt (1954, chapters 3–10, 12), Earl (1846, pp. 244–5, 249–50), Favenc (1888, pp. 331–2, 344–7, 382–4), Goodale (1971, pp. 5–7), Macknight (1976), Urry & Walsh (1981, pp. 90–5) and Warner (1958, pp. 456–60).

14   Berndt & Berndt (1954), Clarke (2003a, p. 178) and Thomson (1949, pp. 82–94).

15   Berndt & Berndt (1954, pp. 15, 75–6) and Macknight (1976, pp. 43–44, 46–7). Orchard & Wilson (1999, pp. 447, 451) and Wharton (2005) described the more recent sandalwood (involving *Santalum lanceolatum* and *S. spicatum*) industries dominated by Europeans.

16   Macknight (1976, p. 43) discussed uses of cheesefruit-tree, which Maiden (1889, p. 298) claimed produces 'tints of yellow'. Worsnop (1897, p. 10) recorded the use of Australian nutmeg.

17   Berndt & Berndt (1954), Clarke (2003a, pp. 177–83, 186), Macknight (1976) and Urry & Walsh (1981).

18   Earl (1846, p. 240).

19   Wallace (1890, chapter 28).

20   Wallace (1890, p. 309).

21   Balint (2005, p. 20).

22   Berndt & Berndt (1954, pp. 42, 44–5).

23   N. White (cited Kennedy, 1984, p. 109).

24   Earl (1846, pp. 239–40, 249).

25   King (1827, vol. 1, p. 65).

26   King (1827, vol. 1, p. 80).

27   D.L. Jones (1995, pp. 56, 128).

28   Wightman, Astuti et al. (1994, p. 6).

29   Berndt & Berndt (1954, p. 43).

30   Tindale (1925, p. 78). See also Berndt & Berndt (1954, p. 67).

31   Tindale (1926–27, pp. 66–7).

32   Hiddins (2000, p. 8) and Low (1989, pp. 82–3).

33   Levitt (1981, p. 38).

34   Levitt (1981, p. 147).

35   Puruntatameri (2001, p. 40).

36   Hiddins (2001, p. 110), Levitt (1981, p. 36), Puruntatameri (2001, p. 84), Smith & Wightman (1990, p. 28), Specht (1958, p. 491), Tindale (1925, p. 78), Wightman, Gurindji elders et al. (1994, p. 50), Wightman & Smith (1989, p. 13) and Yunupingu (1995, pp. 9, 72).

37   Cawte (1996, p. 7). Cawte stated that tamarind fruit was high in vitamin C, which is not supported by the analysis in Brand Miller et al. (1993, p. 184).

38   Isaacs (1987, pp. 229, 239), Levitt (1981, p. 36) and Low (1989, p. 75).

39   Brand Miller et al. (1993, p. 184) and Low (1989, pp. 220–1).

40   Blake et al. (1998, pp. 10, 22, 125), Walker & Zorc (1981, p. 126) and Yunupingu (1995, p. 9). Walker & Zorc refer to tamarind as *jambang*.

41   In the Tetum language of Dili in East Timor, the tamarind tree is called *sukaer* (Hull, 1999, p. 338).

42   Popenoe (1974, pp. 432–6) and Ridley (1922–25, vol. 1, p. 636). The 'tamarind' term itself is believed to have originated in India.

43   Levitt (1981, p. 24), Smith & Wightman (1990, p. 25) and Wightman, Roberts et al. (1992, p. 44).

44   Levitt (1981, p. 55).

45   Isaacs (1987, p. 210) and Levitt (1981, pp. 61, 63–4, 86–7).

46   Low (1989, pp. 75–6) and Wightman, Astuti et al. (1994, p. 14). Levitt (1981, p. 35) listed this plant as indigenous on Groote Eylandt, although without an Aboriginal name.

47   Alexander et al. (1987), Cawte (1996, chapter 10) and Mathews et al. (1988). Kava notices, Department of Health and Community Services, Northern Territory Government (http://www.nt.gov.au/health/healthdev/aodp/other/kava.shtml).

48   Barrau (1958, pp. 60–1) and Lebot et al. (1992).

49   Clarke (2006 ms).

50   Diamond (1998, pp. 97, 118, 120, 122–8, 132–3, 137, 145–6, 185, 187) and Pyke (1968, pp. 25–7).

51   Cunningham (cited Lee, 1925, p. 318). See King (1827, vol. 1, pp. 18, 38, 222).

52   Pollan (2002, chapter 1).

53   Oxley (1817 [cited Favenc, 1888, p. 63]; 1820, pp. 50, 59). The acorns planted by Cunningham were presumably from English oak.

54   Cunningham (1818, cited Lee, 1925, p. 361). See also King (1827, vol. 1, pp. 72–3).

55   Cunningham (1818, cited Lee, 1925, p. 318). Other references to this are Cunningham (1817, cited Lee, 1925, pp. 194, 210, 292) and King (1827, vol. 2, pp. 123–4).

56   Bunce (1859, p. 4), Cooper (1954) and Low (1999, chapter 3).

57   Von Mueller (1881).

58   Ridley (1930, p. 630).

59   Griffiths (1997, p. 4), MacKenzie (1997, p. 219), Rix (1978, chapter 1) and Rolls (1984, part 2; 1997, p. 41).

60   Griffiths & Robin (1997, part 1), Low (1999), Parsons (1981) and Rolls (1984).

61   Hobsbawm & Ranger (1983).

62   Crosby (2004, pp. 152, 155, 162, 168, 253, 255), Jessop & Toelken (1986, vol. 3, pp. 1652–4) and Lamp & Collet (1979, pp. 304–5).

63   Clarke (1986a, p. 10; 1986b, p. 43; 1987, p. 9; 2003b, pp. 89, 91), Low (1989, pp. 129, 151–2) and Maiden (1889, p. 59). Similar observations recorded from Maori people in New Zealand (Brooker et al. 1987, pp. 104–8).

64   Stephens (1890, p. 489).

65   Dawson (1881, p. 57). See also Gott & Conran (1991, p. 41).

66   Clarke (1986a, p. 10; 1987, p. 9; 2003b, p. 91).

67   Low (1989, pp. 151–2).

68   Cleland (1957, p. 156). See also Cleland (1966, pp. 132–3) and Cleland et al. (1925, p. 120).

69   Cleland & Tindale (1959, p. 140).

70   For example, Pitt-Rivers (1927).

71   Hamlyn-Harris & Smith (1916, p. 3; see also p. 4).

72   Clarke (1986a, p. 11; 1987, pp. 9, 15).

73   Clarke (1994, p. 123). In South Australia, the species locally called 'dandelion' is elsewhere called 'capeweed' (*Arctotheca calendula*). True 'dandelions' (priest's crown or swine's snout) are also introduced into Australia and belong to the genus of *Taraxacum*, (i.e. *T. officinale*) (Delbridge et al., 1997, p. 548; Lamp & Collet, 1979, p. 317; Turner, 1972, p. 166).

74   Gilmore (1935, pp. 232–3).

75   Jessop & Toelken (1986, vol. 2, pp. 1043–6) and Lamp & Collet (1979, p. 102).

76   Gilmore (1935, p. 233), Lassak & McCarthy (1983, pp. 75, 82–3, 145) and Maiden (1889, pp. 175, 202). The quote is from Gilmore. Maiden used the early name *Erythraea australis*.

77   Smith & Wightman (1990, pp. 23, 27).

78   Hodgson (1988, pp. 6, 38), Smith (1991, p. 8) and Smith & Wightman (1990, pp. 3, 27–8).

79   Levitt (cited Lassak & McCarthy, 1983, p. 12).

80   T.W. Bell, 1890 (cited Brooker et al., 1987, p. 169).

81   Barr et al. (1988, pp. 116–21, 158–65).

82   Clarke (2006 ms).

83   Cherikoff & Isaacs (1989, pp. 47–8, 80, 92–3, 96, 98, 101, 106, 108–9), Cribb & Cribb (1982, pp. 88–9), Isaacs (1987, pp. 79, 225), Low (1988, pp. 9, 27, 119, 183,

211; 1989, pp. 89–90), Maiden (1889, p. 40), O'Hare & Vock (1990), Smith & Smith (1999, pp. 92–3) and Stephenson et al. (1983).

84 Stephens (1890, p. 477; see also p. 484).

85 Cawte (1996, pp. 16, 95, 112), W.J. Darling (cited Plomley, 1987, pp. 991–2), Hardy (1976, p. 79), Lumholtz (1889 [1980, pp. 115, 117]), Read & Japaljarri (1978) and Young (1992, p. 261).

86 Clarke (2003a, pp. 192–6, 200–7, 214–6, 218, 224), Reynolds (1989) and Rowley (1972a, 1972b).

87 Berndt & Berndt (1954, p. 30), Foster (1989) and Rowley (1972a, pp. 82, 204).

88 Backhouse (1843, p. 381).

89 Bassett (1981, pp. 362–3) and Molloy (cited Hasluck, 1955, pp. 144, 164, 121, 214).

90 Clarke (1988, pp. 72–3; 2003b, pp. 90–2) and Levitt (1981, p. 16).

91 A. Clarke (1988, p. 127).

92 Low (1999).

93 Lucas et al. (1997, pp. 131–2).

94 Brennan (1986, pp. 92, 116–7).

95 I. Batey (cited Frankel, 1982, p. 44).

96 Cunningham (cited Lee, 1925, pp. 127, 131–2, 135–7, 139, 284, 286, 291, 554), Favenc (1888, p. 47), Rolls (2002, pp. 257–8) and Taplin (1874 [1879, p. 3]).

97 Beresford et al. (2001), Diamond (2005, chapter 13) and Murray–Darling Basin Commission (2003).

98 Altman (1984, 1987), Clarke (2003b), Meehan (1979), Silberbauer (1971, pp. 24–7, 30–1) and Young (1981).

99 Lucas et al. (1997, p. 131).

100 Wilson et al. (1992, pp. 20–1).

101 Flannery (1994, part 3).

102 Altman (1987, 2001), Altman et al. (1995 & 1997), Bomford & Caughley (1996), Clarke (2003b), Palmer (1999b, pp. 57–9), Sackett (1979) and Wilson et al. (1992).

103 Clarke (1996c, pp. 75–6; 2003b, pp. 98–101), Cochrane (2001), Hodgson (1988), Isaacs (1992a, 1992b) and Morphy (1998).

104 Clarke (1996c, pp. 76–7; 2003b, pp. 98–101), Hodgson (1988), Robson (1986) and Zola & Gott (1992).

105 Aboriginal artefact collection, South Australian Museum. See Allen (1995b, pp. 11–4, 18), Hodgson (1988, pp. 38–9) and Sutton (1994, p. 51).

106 Brokensha (1975), Goddard (1992, p. 123), Goddard & Kalotas (1985, p. 25) and Isaacs (1992a).

107 Aboriginal artefact collection, South Australian Museum. See Allen (1995b, p. 12).

108 Anderson & Dussart (1988, p. 128).

109 Morphy (1998, chapter 4) and Taylor (1996, chapter 9).

110 Berndt & Berndt (1999, chapter 2), Morphy (1998, chapter 1) and Sutton (1988c).

111 For example, Barr et al. (1988, pp. 28–31), Lands (1987) and Laramba Community Women (2003).

Chapter 11

1 Bindon (1996), Cherikoff and Isaacs (1989), Cribb & Cribb (1981a, 1981b, 1982), Gott (2006), Isaacs (1987), Lassak and McCarthy (1983) and Low (1985–86, 1988, 1989, 1991a, 1991b).

2 Wightman & Andrews (1991) and Wightman & Mills (1991).

3 Nyinkka Nyunyu (2003). See also www.nyinkkanyunyu.com.au.

4 See www.igawarta.com.

5 Gib (1999). See also www.brambuk.com.au.

6 Muloin et al. (2001) and Zeppel (1999) provided an extensive bibliography of publications concerning Aboriginal tourism.

7 Adelaide Botanic Gardens (1984), Bindon (1981), Brisbane City Council (no date), Gott (2002), Nash (1994), Olive Pink Botanic Garden (no date), Richardson & Lugg (no date) and Stewart & Percival (1997).

8 Hiddins (1996, 2000, 2001, 2003) and Wightman & Andrews (1991).

9 This extensive literature includes Blake et al. (1998), Marrfurra (1995), Puruntatameri (2001), Raymond and Wightman (1999), Smith et al. (1993), Smith and Wightman (1990), Wightman, Astuti et al. (1994), Wightman, Dixon et al. (1992), Wightman, Gurindji elders et al. (1994), Wightman, Jackson et al. (1991), Wightman, Roberts et al. (1992), Wightman and Smith (1989) and Yunupingu (1995).

10 Hiddins (1981, 1996).

11 Douglas (1982, chapter 4). See also Pyke (1968, chapter 4).

12 Farb & Armelagos (1980, p. 14).

13 Clarke (2006 ms).

14 Brand & Cherikoff (1985a, 1985b), Brand et al. (1982, 1983), Brand & Maggiore (1992), Brand Miller & Holt (1997), Brand Miller et al. (1993), Dadswell (1934), Harwood (1994) and Maggiore (1993). Campbell (1939) studied Aboriginal food in relation to dental conditions.

15 Brand Miller et al. (1993, pp. 17, 186–8), Brennan (1986, p. 56), Hiddins

(2000, p. 26; 2001, pp. viii, 87), Lands (1987, pp. 11, 18), Puruntatameri (2001, pp. 8, 85, 142), Rae et al. (1982, p. 46), Smith & Kalotas (1985, p. 346), Smith & Wightman (1990, p. 25), Sutton (1994, p. 38), Wightman, Roberts et al. (1992, p. 46) and Wightman & Smith (1989, p. 20).

16 Smith & Kalotas (1985, p. 337).

17 Berkinshaw (1999), Bruneteau (1996), Leiper & Hauser (1983) and Palmer (1999a).

18 Berkinshaw (1999), Boland (1997), Cherikoff & Isaacs (1989), Cherikoff & Johnson (2000), Curtis (1974), Gott (1985b, 1997), Graham & Hart (1997), Hegarty et al. (2001), Hele (2003), Herbert (1999), House & Hardwood (1992), Isaacs (1987), Johnson et al. (2002), C.A. Jones (1996), G.P. Jones (1985), King (1997, 1998), Latz (1998), Loneragan (1990), Matthews (1997), Morse (1997), Phelps (1997), Phelps & Phelps (1997), Robins (1996), Roff (1983), Rural Industries Research and Development Corporation (1998) and Thomas (1997).

19 Refer also to the *Australian Bushfoods Magazine* (Maleny, Queensland), which began in 1997 and is now available online. Another relevant journal is *The Australian New Crops Newsletter* (University of Queensland, St Lucia, Queensland).

20 Archer & Beale (2004, pp. 136–8, 252).

21 Cribb & Cribb (1982, p. 87), Low (1988, p. 119) and Orchard & Wilson (1999, p. 439).

22 Devitt (1992), Hodgson & Wahlqvist (1993), Roberts et al. (1980) and Smith & Smith (1999). Thomson & Merrifield (1988) provided a bibliography on Aboriginal health.

23 Altman (1984; 1987, pp. 31–45), Cane & Stanley (1985), Coombs et al. (1980), Head & Fullagar (1991), Hetzal & Frith (1978), Kean (1991, pp. 120–1), Kohen (1995, chapter 9), Meehan (1982, pp. 141–61), Miers (2004) and Wilson et al. (1992). See also Clarke (2003b) for the temperate Australian region.

24 For examples of pharmacological analysis of Aboriginal medicines see Barr et al. (1988), Brouwer et al. (2005), Flower (2000), Prance et al. (1994), Semple (1998), Semple et al. (1998), Stack (1989) and Stern (1984). See Telban (1988) for a New Guinea example of medical ethnobotany.

25 Baker et al. (2001), Gray et al. (2005), Head (2000a, chapters 3 & 8), Kean et al. (1988), Langton (1998), Smyth (1993), Smyth et al. (1986), Wearne & White (1998) and Young et al. (1991). Anderson (1984, 1989) outlined the divergence between Aboriginal and conservation interests.

26 Burbidge et al. (1988), Horstman & Wightman (2001), Newsome (1980), Thomson (1985), Tunbridge (1991), Walsh (1990, 1995) and White & Meehan (1993).

27 Baker (2003), Bowman (1998), Bowman et al. (2001, pp. 76–7), Breedan & Wright (1991), Brennan (1986, p. 120), Davidson (2005), Davis (2003), Griffin & Allan (1986), Hill (2003), Kean et al. (1988), Keen & Merlan (1990), Lawrence (1996), Liddle (2003), Lindenmayer (2003), Mutitjulu Community & Baker (1996, pp. 48–52), Press et al. (1995), Pyne (1991, p. 136; 1997, pp. 24–6), Whelan (2003) and Williams & Baines (1993).

28 Haynes (1991).

29 Rowse (1992, 2002) and Young (1992).

30 Carruthers (2003) and White (2003).

31 Elkin (1964, p. 34).

32 Stapleton (1981).

33 Breedan & Wright (1991), Rose (1996), Smyth (1982) and Williams & Baines (1993).

34 Examples include Lands (1987) and Paddy et al. (1987) for Dampierland, Rose (1984) for the east Kimberley, Levitt (1981) for Groote Eylandt, Kyriazis (1995) for Cape York Peninsula, Henshall et al. (1980) for the Tanami Desert, Goddard & Kalotas (1988) and the Mutitjulu Community & Baker (1996) from the Anangu Pitjantjatjara lands, and McEntee et al. (1986) for the northern Flinders Ranges.

35 Youngs (1985, pp. 145, 163).

36 Clarke (1986b, 2003b), Gott & Conran (1991), Robson (1986), Stewart & Percival (1997), Wreck Bay Community & Renwick (2000) and Zola & Gott (1992).

37 Wreck Bay Community & Renwick (2000, p. 44).

38 Clarke (1994, p. 260; 2003b, pp. 90–2, 103).

39 Barton (1994) and Nabhan et al. (1995).

40 Brown (1998), Langton et al. (2003), Posey (1990) and Williams (1998).

41 Kean (1991, p. 115).

42 Trigger (2003, pp. 4–9).

43 Burrows (2003), Davis (2003), Horstman & Wightman (2001), Rose (2005), Ross & Pickering (2002), Seton & Bradley (2004) and Sveiby & Skuthorpe (2006).

44 For examples refer to Crawfurd (1868), Cleland (1966), Hyam (1943) and Morris (1943).

45 Denham et al. (2003), Golson (1977), Harris (1995), Horton (2000, chapter 4), Swadling & Hope (1992) and Thorne & Raymond (1989, pp. 32–6).

46 Beaton (1982, p. 57).

References

Abbie, A.A. 1976. *The original Australians*. Revised edition. Seal Books, Adelaide.

Adcock, G.J., Dennis, E.S., Easteal, S., Huttley, G.A., Jermin, L.S., Peacock, W.J., Thorne, A. 2001. Mitochondrial DNA sequences in ancient Australians: Implications for modern human origins. *Archaeology in Oceania*. Vol. 36, no. 3, p.163.

Adelaide Botanic Gardens. 1984. *Exhibition of Australian plants used by the Aborigines and early colonists*. Compiled by the staff. Museum of Economic Botany, Adelaide Botanic Garden. Adelaide. 17pp.

Akerman, K. 1978. Ngarla and mei: Living on bush foods in the Central Kimberley. *Earth Gardener*. Vol. 2, no. 3, pp. 20–2.

Akerman, K. 1979a. Heat and lithic technology in the Kimberley, W.A. *Archaeology and Physical Anthropology on Oceania*. Vol. 14, pp. 144–51.

Akerman, K. 1979b. Contemporary Aboriginal healers in the south Kimberley. *Oceania*. Vol. 50, no. 1, pp. 23–30.

Albrecht, F.W. 1959. *The natural food supply of the Australian Aborigines*. Aborigines' Friends' Association, Adelaide.

Alexander, K., Watson, C. & Fleming, J. 1987. *Kava in the north: A research report on current patterns of kava use in Arnhem Land Aboriginal communities*. North Australia Research Unit, Darwin.

Allen, H.R. 1974. The Bagundji of the Darling Basin: Cereal gatherers in an uncertain environment. *World Archaeology*. Vol. 5, pp. 309–22.

Allen, J. 1998a. Antiquity. Pp. 9–12 in T. Murray (ed) *Archaeology of Aboriginal Australia*. Allen & Unwin, Sydney.

Allen, J. 1998b. When did humans first colonise Australia? Pp. 50–60 in T. Murray (ed) *Archaeology of Aboriginal Australia*. Allen & Unwin, Sydney.

Allen, J. 2000. A matter of time. *Nature Australia*. Vol. 26, no. 10, pp. 60–9.

Allen, J., Golson, J. & Jones, R.M. (eds) 1977. *Sunda and Sahul*. Academic Press, London.

Allen, L. (ed) 1995a. *Women's work. Aboriginal women's artefacts in the Museum of Victoria*. Museum of Victoria, Melbourne.

Allen, L. 1995b. Fibrecraft. Pp. 11–8 in L. Allen (ed) *Women's work: Aboriginal women's artefacts in the Museum of Victoria*. Museum of Victoria, Melbourne.

Altman, J.C. 1984. The dietary utilisation of flora and fauna by contemporary hunter-gatherers at Momega Outstation, north-central Arnhem Land. *Australian Aboriginal Studies*. No. 1, pp. 35–46.

Altman, J.C. 1987. *Hunter-gatherers today: An Aboriginal economy in north Australia*. Australian Institute of Aboriginal Studies, Canberra.

Altman, J.C. 2001. *Sustainable development options on Aboriginal land: The hybrid economy in the twenty-first century*. Centre for Aboriginal Economic Policy Research, Australian National University, Canberra.

Altman, J.C., Bek, H.J. & Roach, L.M. 1995. *Native title and indigenous Australian utilisation of wildlife: Policy perspectives*. Centre for Aboriginal Economic Policy Research, Australian National University, Canberra.

Altman, J.C., Roach, L.M. & Liddle, L.E. 1997. *Utilisation of native wildlife by indigenous Australians: Commercial considerations*. Centre for Aboriginal Economic Policy Research, Australian National University, Canberra.

Anderson, C. 1984. *The political and economic basis of Kuku-Yalanji social history*. Postgraduate thesis. University of Queensland, St Lucia, Queensland.

Anderson, C. 1989. Aborigines and conservationism: The Daintree–Bloomfield road. *Australian Journal of Social Issues*. Vol. 24, no. 3, pp. 214–27.

Anderson, C. 1996. Traditional material culture of the Kuku-Yalanji of Bloomfield River, North Queensland. *Records of the South Australian Museum*. Vol. 29, pt 1, pp. 63–83.

Anderson, C. & Dussart, F. 1988. Dreamings in acrylic: Western Desert art. Pp. 89–142 in P. Sutton (ed) *Dreamings: The art of Aboriginal Australia*. Penguin Books, Melbourne.

Anderson, K.J. & Gale, F. (eds) 1992. *Inventing places: Studies in cultural geography*. Longman Cheshire, Melbourne.

Angas, G.F. 1847. *Savage life and scenes in Australia*. 2 volumes. Smith, Elder & Co., London.

Archer, M. & Beale, B. 2004. *Going native: Living in the Australian environment*. Hodder, Sydney.

Arthur, J.M. 1996. *Aboriginal English: A cultural study*. Oxford University Press, Melbourne.

Aurukun School and Community Calendar. 1985. *Seasons and event calendar*. Aurukun Community, Northern Queensland.

Australian Biological Resources Study. 1981–2002. *Flora of Australia*. Volume 1-58A. Bureau of Fauna and Flora, Canberra.

Backhouse, J. 1843. *A narrative of a visit to the Australian colonies*. Hamilton, Adams & Co., London.

Bailey, F.M. 1913. *Comprehensive catalogue of Queensland plants both indigenous and naturalised*. A.J. Cumming, Queensland Government Printer, Brisbane.

Baker, G. 1959. Uses of tektites and their vernacular terminology. Chapter 13 in G. Baker *Tektites*. No. 23, Memoirs of the National Museum of Victoria, Melbourne.

Baker, R.M. 1988. Yanyuwa canoe making. *Records of the South Australian Museum*. Vol. 22, pt 2, pp. 173–88.

Baker, R.M. 1999. *Land is life: From bush to town: The Story of the Yanyuwa people*. Allen & Unwin, Sydney.

Baker, R.M. 2003. Yanyuwa classical burning regimes, indigenous science and cross-cultural communication. Pp. 198–210 in G. Cary, D. Lindenmayer & S. Dovers (eds) *Australia burning: Fire ecology, policy and management issues*. CSIRO Publishing, Collingwood, Victoria.

Baker, R.M., Davies, J. & Young, E. (eds) 2001. *Working on country: Contemporary indigenous management of Australia's lands and coastal regions*. Oxford University Press, Melbourne.

Balint, R. 2005. *Troubled waters: Borders, boundaries and possession in the Timor Sea*. Allen & Unwin, Sydney.

Bancroft, J. 1872. *The pituri poison*. Paper read before the Queensland Philosophical Society. Government Printer, Brisbane.

Bardon, G. 1999. *Papunya tula: Art of the Western Desert*. New edition. J.B. Books Australia, Adelaide.

Barker, J.A. 2005. *A prototype interactive identification tool to fragmentary wood from eastern Australia, and its application to Aboriginal Australian ethnographic artefacts*. Postgraduate thesis. University of Adelaide, Adelaide.

Barr, A., Chapman, J., Smith, N. & Beveridge, M. 1988. *Traditional bush medicines: An Aboriginal pharmacopoeia*. Greenhouse Publications, Melbourne.

Barrau, J. 1958. *Subsistence agriculture in Melanesia*. Bernice P. Bishop Bulletin 219. Bernice P. Bishop Museum, Honolulu, Hawaii.

Barton, J.H. 1994. Ethnobotany and intellectual property rights. Pp. 214–27 in G.T. Prance, D.J. Chadwick & J. Marsh (eds) *Ethnobotany and the search for new drugs*. J. Wiley, Chichester, New York.

Basedow, H. 1925. *The Australian Aboriginal*. F.W. Preece and Sons, Adelaide.

Bassett, M. 1981. Augusta and Mrs Molloy. Pp. 357–73 in D.J. Carr & S.G.M. Carr (eds) *People and plants in Australia*. Academic Press, Sydney.

Bates, B. 2002. *The real Middle Earth: Magic and mystery in the Dark Ages*. Sedgwick & Jackson, London.

Bates, D.M. 1901–14. *The native tribes of Western Australia*. Edited by I. White, 1985. National Library of Australia, Canberra.

Bates, D.M. 1912 (1992). Haunted places of the west. Pp. 14–9. in P.J. Bridge (ed) *Aboriginal Perth and Bibbulmun biographies and legends*. Hesperian Press, Carlisle, Western Australia.

Bates, D.M. 1918. Aborigines of the west coast of South Australia: Vocabularies and ethnographical notes. *Transactions and Proceedings of the Royal Society of South Australia*. Vol. 42, pp. 152–67.

Bates, D.M. 1938 (1992). The tree of souls. Pp. 153–4 in P.J. Bridge (ed) *Aboriginal Perth and Bibbulmun biographies and legends*. Hesperian Press, Carlisle, Western Australia.

Bates, D.M. 1947. *The passing of the Aborigines*. Australian edition. John Murray, London.

Bayly, I.A.E. 1999. Review of how indigenous people managed for water in desert regions of Australia. *Journal of the Royal Society of Western Australia*. Vol. 82, pp. 17–25.

Beard, J.S. 1981. Vegetation of Central Australia. Pp. xxi–xxvi in J.P. Jessop *Flora of Central Australia*. The Australian Systematic Botany Society. Reed Books, Sydney.

Beaton, J.M. 1982. Fire and water: Aspects of Australian Aboriginal management of cycads. *Archaeology in Oceania*. Vol. 17, pp. 51–8.

Beck, W., Fullagar, R. & White, N. 1988. Archaeology from ethnography: The Aboriginal use of cycad as an example. Pp. 137–47 in B. Meehan & R. Jones (eds) *Archaeology with ethnography: An Australian perspective*. Prehistory Pacific Studies, Australian National University, Canberra.

Bellchambers, T.P. 1931. *A nature-lover's notebook*. Nature Lovers' League, Adelaide.

Bennett, K.H. 1882. On *Myoporum platycarpum*, a resin producing tree of the interior of New South Wales. *Proceedings of the Linnean Society of New South Wales*. Vol. 7, pt 3, pp. 349–51.

Bennett, K.H. 1883. Notes on the method of obtaining water from eucalyptus roots, as practised by the natives of the country between the Lachlan and Darling Rivers. *Proceedings of the Linnean Society of New South Wales*. Vol. 8, pt 2, pp. 213–5.

Beresford, Q., Bekle, H., Phillips, H. & Mulcock, J. 2001. *The salinity crisis: Landscapes, communities and politics*. University of Western Australia Press, Crawley, Western Australia.

Berkinshaw, T.D. 1999. *The business of bush foods: Ecological and socio-cultural implications*. Postgraduate thesis, University of Adelaide, Adelaide.

Berlin, B. 1992. *Ethnobiological classification: Principles of categorization of plants and animals in traditional societies*. Princeton University Press, Princeton, New Jersey.

Berndt, C.H. 1981. Interpretations and 'facts' in Aboriginal Australia. Pp. 153–203 in F. Dahlberg (ed) *Woman the Gatherer*. Yale University Press, New Haven.

Berndt, C.H. 1982a. Sickness and health in western Arnhem Land: A traditional perspective. Pp. 121–38 in J. Reid (ed) *Body, land and spirit: Health and healing in Aboriginal society*. University of Queensland Press, St Lucia, Queensland.

Berndt, C.H. 1982b. Aboriginal women, resources and family life. Pp. 39–52 in R.M. Berndt (ed) *Aboriginal sites, rights and resource development*. Academy of the Social Sciences in Australia. Fifth Academy Symposium, 11 Nov. 1981, Proceedings. University of Western Australia Press, Perth.

Berndt, R.M. 1940. Some aspects of Jaraldi culture, South Australia. *Oceania*. Vol. 11, no. 2, pp. 164–85.

Berndt, R.M. 1947. Wuradjeri magic and 'clever men'. *Oceania*. Vol. 17, no. 4, pp. 327–65; Vol. 18, no. 1, pp. 60–86.

Berndt, R.M. 1951. *Kunapipi: A study of an Australian Aboriginal religious cult*. F.W. Cheshire, Melbourne.

Berndt, R.M. 1952. *Djanggawul: An Aboriginal religious cult of north-eastern Arnhem Land*. F.W. Cheshire, Melbourne.

Berndt, R.M. 1972. The Walmadjeri and Gugadja. Pp. 177–216 in M.G. Bicchieri (ed) *Hunters and gatherers today: A socioeconomic study of eleven such cultures in the twentieth century*. Holt, Rinehart & Winston, New York.

Berndt, R.M. 1974. *Australian Aboriginal religion: Fascicle one — introduction; the south-eastern region*. E.J. Brill, Leiden.

Berndt, R.M. & Berndt, C.H. 1942–43. A preliminary report of field work in the Ooldea region, western South Australia. *Oceania*. 1942, Vol. 12, pt 4, pp. 305–30; Vol. 13, pt 1, pp. 51–70; Vol. 13, pt 2, pp. 143–69; 1943, Vol. 13, pt 3, pp. 243–80; Vol. 13, pt 4, pp. 362–75; Vol. 14, pt 1, pp. 30–60; Vol. 14, pt 2, pp. 124–58.

Berndt, R.M. & Berndt, C.H. 1954. *Arnhem land: Its history and its people*. F.W. Cheshire, Melbourne.

Berndt, R.M. & Berndt, C.H. 1970. *Man, land and myth in North Australia: The Gunwinggu people*. Ure Smith, Sydney.

Berndt, R.M. & Berndt, C.H. 1985. *The world of the first Australians*. Rigby, Adelaide.

Berndt, R.M. & Berndt, C.H. 1989. *The speaking land: Myth and story in Aboriginal Australia*. Penguin Books, Melbourne.

Berndt, R.M., Berndt, C.H., with Stanton, J.E. 1993. *A world that was: The Yaraldi of the Murray River and the lakes, South Australia*. Melbourne University Press at the Miegunyah Press, Melbourne.

Berndt, R.M., Berndt, C.H., with Stanton, J.E. 1999. *Aboriginal art: A visual perspective*. Revised edition. Methuen Australia, Sydney.

Bevan, G.A. & Vaughan, M.E. 1978. *Mannum yesterday*. Lutheran Publishing House, Adelaide.

Beveridge, P. 1865. A few notes on the dialects, habits, customs and mythology of the Lower Murray Aborigines. *Transactions and Proceedings of the Royal Society of Victoria*. Vol. 6, pp. 14–24.

Beveridge, P. 1884. A few notes on the dialects, habits, customs and mythology of the Lower Murray Aborigines. *Journal and Proceedings of the Royal Society of New South Wales*. Vol. 17, pp. 19–74.

Beveridge, P. 1889. *The Aborigines of Victoria and Riverina*. Hutchinson, Melbourne.

Bicchieri, M.G. (ed) 1972. *Hunters and gatherers today: A socioeconomic study of eleven such cultures in the twentieth century*. Holt, Rinehart & Winston, New York.

Bindon, P. 1981. Introduction to *Aboriginal trail*. Australian National Botanic Gardens. Government Printer, Canberra.

Bindon, P. 1996. *Useful bush plants*. Western Australian Museum, Perth.

Bindon, P. & Gough, D. 1993. Digging sticks and desert dwellers. *Landscape*. Spring, pp. 11–6.

Bindon, P. & Whalley, T. 1992. Hunters and gatherers. *Landscape*. Spring, pp. 28–35.

Bird, C. & Beeck, C. 1988. Traditional plant foods in the southwest of Western Australia: The evidence from salvage ethnography. Pp. 113–22 in B. Meehan & R. Jones (eds) *Archaeology with ethnography: An Australian perspective*. Prehistory Pacific Studies, Australian National University, Canberra.

Black, E. Couper. 1947. The canoes and canoe trees of Australia. *Mankind*. Vol. 3, no. 12, pp. 351–61.

Black, E. Couper. 1966. Population and tribal distribution. Pp. 97–109 in B.C. Cotton (ed) *Aboriginal man in South and Central Australia. Part 1*. Government Printer, Adelaide.

Black, E. Couper. 1976. Australian canoes and canoe trees. *Journal of the Anthropological Society of South Australia*. Vol. 14, no. 4, pp. 7–8.

Black, J.M. 1920. Vocabularies of four South Australian languages, Adelaide, Narrunga, Kukata, and Narrinyeri, with special references to speech sounds. *Transactions of the Royal Society of South Australia*. Vol. 44, pp. 76–93.

Black, J.M. 1965. *Flora of South Australia. Part 4*. Revised by E.L. Robertson. Handbook of the Flora and Fauna of South Australia. Government Printer, Adelaide.

Blainey, G. 1976. *Triumph of the nomads: A history of ancient Australia*. Sun Books, Melbourne.

Blake, B.J. 1981. *Australian Aboriginal languages: A general introduction*. Angus & Robertson, Sydney.

Blake, N.M., Wightman, G. & Williams, L. 1998. *Iwaidja ethnobotany: Aboriginal plant knowledge from Gurig National Park, Northern Australia*. Northern Territory Botanical Bulletin No. 23. Parks and Wildlife Commission of the Northern Territory, Darwin.

Blandowski, W. 1855. Personal observations made in an excursion towards the central parts of Victoria, including Mount Macedon, McIvor, and Black Ranges. *Transactions of the Philosophical Society of Victoria*. Vol. 1, pp. 50–74.

Bolam, A.G. 1930. *The Trans-Australian wonderland*. Baker & Co., Melbourne.

Boland, D. 1997. Some thoughts about CSIRO research in bushfoods. *Australian Bushfoods Magazine*. Vol. 2, pp. 26–8.

Bomford, M. & Caughley, J. (eds) 1996. *Sustainable use of wildlife by Aboriginal peoples and Torres Strait Islanders*. Australian Government Publishing Service, Canberra.

Bonney, F. 1884. On some customs of the Aborigines of the River Darling, New South Wales. *The Journal of the Anthropological Institute of Great Britain and Ireland*. Vol. 13, pp. 122–37.

Bonney, N. 1994. *Uses of native plants in the south east of South Australia by the indigenous peoples before 1839*. Celebration South East Volume 4. Southeast Book Promotions, Naracoorte, South Australia.

Bonyhady, T. 1991. *Burke and Wills: From Melbourne to myth*. David Ell Press, Sydney.

Bowman, D.M.J.S. 1991. Can we untangle fire-megafauna-climate-human Pleistocene impacts on the Australian biota? *Archaeology in Oceania*. Vol. 26, no. 2, p. 78.

Bowman, D.M.J.S. 1998. The impact of landscape burning on the Australian biota. *New Phytologist*. Vol. 140, no. 3, pp. 385–410.

Bowman, D.M.J.S. & Brown, M.J. 1986. Bushfires in Tasmania: A botanical approach to anthropological questions. *Archaeology in Oceania*. Vol. 21, pt 3, pp. 166–71.

Bowman, D.M.J.S., Garde, M. & Saulwick, A. 2001. Kunj-ken makka man-wurrk: Fire is for kangaroos: Interpreting Aboriginal accounts of landscape burning in central Arnhem Land. Pp. 61–78 in A. Anderson, I. Lilley & S. O'Connor (eds) *Histories of old ages: Essays in honour of Rhys Jones*. Pandanus Books, Canberra.

Bradley, J.J. 1995. Fire: Emotion and politics: A Yanyuwa case study. In D. Bird Rose (ed) *Country in flames: Proceedings of the 1994 Symposium on Biodiversity and Fire in North Australia*. Biodiversity Unit, Department of the Environment, Sport and Territories and the North Australia Research Unit, Canberra and Darwin.

Brady, M.A. 1994. Alcohol and drug use. Pp. 40–2 in D. Horton (ed) *The encyclopaedia of Aboriginal Australia*. 2 volumes. Aboriginal Studies Press for the Australian Institute of Aboriginal and Torres Strait Islander Studies, Canberra.

Brand, J.C. & Cherikoff, V. 1985a. The nutritional composition of Australian Aboriginal food plants of the desert regions. Pp. 53–68 in G.E. Wickens, J.R. Goodin & D.V. Field (eds) *Plants for arid lands*. George Allen & Unwin, London.

Brand, J.C. & Cherikoff, V. 1985b. Australian Aboriginal bushfoods: The nutritional composition of plants of the desert region. *Australian Aboriginal Studies*. No. 2, pp. 38–46.

Brand, J.C., Cherikoff, V., Lee, A. & McDonnell, J. 1982. Nutrients in important bushfoods. *Proceedings of the Nutrition Society of Australia*. Vol. 7, pp. 50–4.

Brand, J.C. & Maggiore, P.M.A. 1992. The nutritional composition of Australian acacia seeds. Pp. 54–67 in A.P.N. House & C.E. Hardwood (eds) *Australian dry-zone acacias for human food*. Australian Tree Seed Centre, Canberra.

Brand, J.C., Rae, C.J., McDonnell, J., Lee, A., Cherikoff, V. & Truswell, A.S. 1983. The nutritional composition of Australian Aboriginal bushfoods. Part 1. *Food Technology in Australia*. Vol. 35, pt 6, pp. 293–8.

Brand Miller, J.C. & Holt, S.H.A. 1997. Australian Aboriginal plant foods: Evolutionary considerations. *Proceedings of the Nutrition Society of Australia*. Vol. 21, p.166.

Brand Miller, J.C., James, K.W. & Maggiore, P.M.A. 1993. *Tables of Composition of Australian Aboriginal foods*. Aboriginal Studies Press, Canberra.

Brandl, E.J. 1988. *Australian Aboriginal paintings in western and central Arnhem Land: Temporal sequences and elements of style in Cadell River and Death Adder Creek art*. Aboriginal Studies Press, Canberra.

Breedan, S. & Wright, B. 1991. *Kakadu: Looking after country — the Gagudju way*. Simon & Schuster, Sydney.

Brennan, K. 1986. *Wildflowers of Kakadu*. Published by author, Jabiru, Northern Territory.

Brisbane City Council. No date. Aboriginal plant trail. In *Brisbane Botanic Gardens — Mt Coot-tha: Self-guiding interpretative walks*. Brochure. Brisbane City Council, Brisbane.

Brock, J. 1988. *Top end native plants*. Publisher by author, Darwin.

Brokensha, P. 1975. *The Pitjantjatjara and their crafts*. Aboriginal Arts Board, Australia Council, Sydney.

Brooker, S.G., Cambie, R.C. & Cooper, R.C. 1987. *New Zealand medicinal plants*. Heinemann, Auckland.

Brooks, D. 2003. *A town like Mparntwe. A guide to the Dreaming tracks and sites of Alice Springs*. Jukurrpa Books, Alice Springs.

Brouwer, N., Liu, Q., Harrington, D., Collins, M., Kohen, J., Vemulpad, S. & Jamie, J. 2005. Ethnopharmacological study of medicinal plants in New South Wales. *Molecules*. Vol. 10, pp. 1252–62. Version available at http://www.chem.mq.edu.au/~jjamie/ethnopharm.htm.

Brown, A.R. (Radcliffe-Brown) 1918. Notes on the social organisation of Australian tribes. *Journal of the Anthropological Institute of Great Britain*. Vol. 48, pp. 222–53.

Brown, C.H. 1986. The growth of ethnobiological nomenclature. *Current Anthropology*. Vol. 27, pt 1, pp. 1–19.

Brown, M.F. 1998. Can culture be copyrighted? *Current Anthropology*. Vol. 39, pt 2, pp. 193–222.

Browne, J.H. 1897. Anthropological notes relating to the Aborigines of the lower north of South Australia. *Transactions, Proceedings and Report of the Royal Society of South Australia*. Vol. 21, pp. 72–3.

Bruneteau, J-P. 1996. *Tukka: Real Australian food*. Angus & Robertson, Sydney.

Buhmann, J., Robins, R. & Chase, M. 1976. Wood identification of spearthrowers in the Queensland Museum. *Australian Institute of Aboriginal Studies Newsletter. New Series*. Vol. 5, pp. 43–4.

Bulmer, J. 1887. Some account of the Aborigines of the Lower Murray, Wimmera, Gippsland and Maneroo. *Transactions and Proceedings of the Royal Geographical Society of Australasia. Victorian Branch*. Vol. 5, pt 1, pp. 15–43.

Bunce, D. 1859. *Travels with Dr Leichhardt in Australia*. Steam Press, Melbourne.

Burbidge, A.A., Johnson, K.A., Fuller, P.J. & Southgate, R.I. 1988. Aboriginal knowledge of the mammals of the Central Deserts of Australia. *Australian Wildlife Research*. Vol. 15, pp. 9–39.

Burrows, N. 2003. Using and sharing indigenous knowledge. Pp. 205–10 in G. Cary, D. Lindenmayer & S. Dovers (eds) *Australia burning: Fire ecology, policy and management issues*. CSIRO Publishing, Collingwood, Victoria.

Butlin, N.G. 1993. *Economics and the Dreamtime: A hypothetical history*. Cambridge University Press, Cambridge.

Calley, M.J.C. 1957. Firemaking by percussion on the east coast of Australia. *Mankind*. Vol. 5, no. 4, pp. 168–71.

Cameron, M. (ed) 1981. *Guide to flowers and plants of Tasmania*. Launceston Field Naturalists Club. Reed, Kew, Victoria.

Cameron-Bonney, L. 1990. *Out of the Dreaming*. South East Kingston Leader, Kingston.

Campbell, J. 2002. *Invisible invaders: Smallpox and other diseases in Aboriginal Australia 1780–1880*. Melbourne University Press, Melbourne.

Campbell, T.D. 1939. Food, food values and food habits of the Australian Aborigines in relation to their dental conditions. *The Australian Journal of Dentistry*, January, February & March 1939 issues.

Campbell, T.D. & Edwards, R. 1966. Stone implements. Pp. 159–220 in B.C. Cotton (ed) *Aboriginal man in South and Central Australia. Part 1*. Government Printer, Adelaide.

Campbell, T.G. 1926. Insect foods of the Aborigines. *Australian Museum Magazine*. Vol. 2, no. 12, pp. 407–10.

Cane, S. 2002. *Pila nguru: The spinifex people*. Fremantle Arts Centre Press, North Fremantle, Western Australia.

Cane, S. & Stanley, O. 1985. *Land use and resources in desert homelands*. Australian National University North Australia Research Unit, Darwin.

Cann, J.H., De Deckker, P. & Murray-Wallace, C.V. 1991. Coastal Aboriginal shell middens and their palaeoenvironmental significance, Robe Range, South Australia. *Transactions of the Royal Society of South Australia*. Vol. 115, pt 4, pp. 161–75.

Capell, A. 1962. Language and social distinction in Aboriginal Australia. *Mankind*. Vol. 5, no. 12, pp. 514–22.

Carnegie, D.W. 1898. *Spinifex and sand: A narrative of five years pioneering and exploration in Western Australia*. 1973 facsimile edition. Penguin Books, Ringwood, Victoria.

Carr, D.J. & Carr, S.G.M. (eds) 1981. The botany of the first Australians. Pp. 3–44 in D.J. Carr & S.G.M. Carr (eds) *People and plants in Australia*. Academic Press, Sydney.

Carruthers, J. 2003. Contesting cultural landscape in South Africa and Australia: Comparing the significance of the Kalahari Gemsbok and Uluru-Kata Tjuta national parks. Pp. 233–68 in D. Trigger & G. Griffiths (eds) *Disputed territories. Land, culture and identity in settler societies*. Hong Kong University Press, Hong Kong.

Carter, G.F. 1964. *Man and the land: A cultural geography*. Holt, Rinehart & Winston, New York.

Cawte, J. 1974. *Medicine is the law*. University Press of Hawaii, Honolulu.

Cawte, J. 1996. *Healers of Arnhem Land*. University of New South Wales Press, Sydney.

Cawthorne, W.A. 1844. *Rough notes on the manners and customs of the natives*. Manuscript held in the Mortlock Library of South Australia, Adelaide. Edited version published in the *Proceedings of the Royal Geographical Society of Australasia. South Australian Branch*, 1926, Vol. 27, pp. 44–77.

Chaloupka, G. 1993. *Journey in time: The world's longest continuing art tradition: The 50,000-year story of the Australian Aboriginal rock art of Arnhem Land*. Reed, Sydney.

Chappell, J. 1983. A revised sea-level record for the last 300,000 years from Papua New Guinea. *Search*. Vol. 14, pts 3–4, pp. 99–101.

Chappell, J. & Thom, B.G. 1977. Sea levels and coasts. Pp. 275–91 in J. Allen, J. Golson & R. Jones (eds) *Sunda and Sahul*. Academic Press, London.

Chase, A. & Sutton, P. 1981. Hunter-gatherers in a rich environment: Aboriginal coastal exploitation in Cape York Peninsula. Pp. 1819–52 in A. Keast (ed) *Ecological biogeography of Australia*. Junk, The Hague.

Cherikoff, V. & Isaacs, J. 1989. *The bush food handbook: How to gather, grow, process and cook Australian wild foods*. Ti Tree Press, Sydney.

Cherikoff, V. & Johnson, L. 2000. *Marketing the Australian native food industry*. Research paper No. 00/061. Rural Industries Research and Development Corporation, Barton, Australian Capital Territory.

Chewings, C. 1936. *Back in the Stone Age: The natives of Central Australia*. Angus & Robertson, Sydney.

Clark, I.D. & Heydon, T. 2002. *Dictionary of Aboriginal placenames of Victoria*. Victorian Aboriginal Corporation for Languages, Melbourne.

Clark, M. & Traynor, S. 1987. *Plants of the tropical woodland*. Conservation Commission of the Northern Territory, Darwin.

Clarke, A. 1988. Archaeological and ethnobotanical interpretations of plant remains from Kakadu National Park, Northern Territory. Pp. 123–36 in

B. Meehan & R. Jones (eds) *Archaeology with ethnography: An Australian perspective.* Prehistory Pacific Studies, Australian National University, Canberra.

Clarke, P.A. 1985a. The importance of roots and tubers as a food source for southern South Australian Aborigines. *Journal of the Anthropological Society of South Australia.* Vol. 23, pt 6, pp. 2–12.

Clarke, P.A. 1985b. Fruits and seeds as food for southern South Australian Aborigines. *Journal of the Anthropological Society of South Australia.* Vol. 23, pt 9, pp. 9–22.

Clarke, P.A. 1986a. Aboriginal use of plant exudates, foliage and fungi as food and water sources in southern South Australia. *Journal of the Anthropological Society of South Australia.* Vol. 24, pt 3, pp. 3–18.

Clarke, P.A. 1986b. The study of ethnobotany in southern South Australia. *Australian Aboriginal Studies.* No. 2, pp. 40–7.

Clarke, P.A. 1987. Aboriginal uses of plants as medicines, narcotics and poisons in southern South Australia. *Journal of the Anthropological Society of South Australia.* Vol. 25, pt 5, pp. 3–23.

Clarke, P.A. 1988. Aboriginal use of subterranean plant parts in southern South Australia. *Records of the South Australian Museum.* Vol. 22, pt 1, pp. 63–76.

Clarke, P.A. 1994. *Contact, conflict and regeneration: Aboriginal cultural geography of the Lower Murray, South Australia.* Postgraduate thesis. University of Adelaide, Adelaide.

Clarke, P.A. 1996a. Early European interaction with Aboriginal hunters and gatherers on Kangaroo Island, South Australia. *Aboriginal History.* Vol. 20, pt 1, pp. 51–81.

Clarke, P.A. 1996b. Adelaide as an Aboriginal landscape. Pp. 69–93 in V. Chapman & P. Read (eds) *Terrible hard biscuits: A reader in Aboriginal history.* Journal of Aboriginal History. Allen & Unwin, Sydney.

Clarke, P.A. 1996c. Aboriginal use of space in the Lower Murray, South Australia. *Conference of Museum Anthropologists Bulletin.* Vol. 28, pp. 74–7.

Clarke, P.A. 1997. The Aboriginal cosmic landscape of southern South Australia. *Records of the South Australian Museum.* Vol. 29, pt 2, pp. 125–45.

Clarke, P.A. 1998a. The Aboriginal presence on Kangaroo Island, South Australia. Pp. 14–48 in J. Simpson & L. Hercus (eds) *Aboriginal portraits of 19th century South Australia.* Aboriginal History Monograph. Australian National University, Canberra.

Clarke, P.A. 1998b. Early Aboriginal plant foods in southern South Australia. *Proceedings of the Nutrition Society of Australia.* Vol. 22, pp. 16–20.

Clarke, P.A. 1999. Waiyungari and his role in the mythology of the Lower Murray, South Australia. *Records of the South Australian Museum.* Vol. 32, pt 1, pp. 51–67.

Clarke, P.A. 2001. The significance of whales to the Aboriginal people of southern South Australia. *Records of the South Australian Museum.* Vol. 34, pt 1, pp. 19–35.

Clarke, P.A. 2002. Early Aboriginal fishing technology in the Lower Murray, South Australia. *Records of the South Australian Museum.* Vol. 35, pt 2, pp. 147–67.

Clarke, P.A. 2003a. *Where the ancestors walked: Australia as an Aboriginal landscape.* Allen & Unwin, Sydney.

Clarke, P.A. 2003b. Twentieth century Aboriginal hunting and gathering practices in the rural landscape of the Lower Murray, South Australia. *Records of the South Australian Museum.* Vol. 36, pt 1, pp. 83–107.

Clarke, P.A. 2003c. Australian ethnobotany — an overview. *Australian Aboriginal Studies.* No. 2, pp. 21–38.

Clarke, P.A. 2005. Aboriginal relationships with grass. Pp. 1–5. *Grasslands conservation and production: Both sides of the fence.* Proceedings of the Fourth Stipa National Conference on the Management of Native Grasses and Pastures, Burra, SA. 11th–13th October 2005. Stipa, Wellington, New South Wales.

Clarke, P.A. 2006 ms. *The European discovery of Aboriginal plants: An Australian ethnobotanical study.* Unpublished manuscript.

Cleland, J.B. 1907. Notes on the resistance of the vegetation of Australia to bushfires, and the antiquity of the Australian Aboriginal. *Proceedings of the Linnean Society of New South Wales.* Vol. 32, pt 3, pp. 554–5.

Cleland, J.B. 1934–35. *Toadstools and mushrooms and other larger fungi of South Australia. Parts I and II.* South Australian Government Printer, Adelaide.

Cleland, J.B. 1936. Ethno-botany in relation to the Central Australian Aboriginal. *Mankind.* Vol. 2, no. 1, pp. 6–9.

Cleland, J.B. 1939. Some aspects of the ecology of the Aboriginal inhabitants of Tasmania and southern Australia. *Papers and Proceedings of the Royal Society of Tasmania.* Issued separately, 1940, pp. 1–18.

Cleland, J.B. 1940. The ecology of the Aboriginal inhabitants of Tasmania and South Australia. *Australian Journal of Science.* Vol. 2, no. 4, pp. 97–101.

Cleland, J.B. 1952. Meteoric crater — native legend. *South Australian Naturalist.* Vol. 27, no. 2, p.20.

Cleland, J.B. 1953. The healing art in primitive society. *Mankind.* Vol. 4, no. 10, pp. 395–411.

Cleland, J.B. 1957. Ethno-ecology. Our natives and the vegetation of southern

Australia. *Mankind.* Vol. 5, no. 4, pp. 149–62.

Cleland, J.B. 1962. Triodia plains, mulga thickets and firing by the natives. *South Australian Naturalist.* Vol. 36, no. 3, p.43.

Cleland, J.B. 1966. The ecology of the Aboriginal in South and Central Australia. Pp. 111–58 in B.C. Cotton (ed) *Aboriginal man in South and Central Australia. Part 1.* South Australian Government Printer, Adelaide.

Cleland, J.B., Black, J.M. & Reese, L. 1925. The flora of the north-east corner of South Australia, north of Cooper's Creek. *Transactions of the Royal Society of South Australia.* Vol. 49, pp. 103–20.

Cleland, J.B. & Johnston, T.H. 1933. The ecology of the Aborigines of Central Australia; botanical notes. *Transactions of the Royal Society of South Australia.* Vol. 57, pp. 113–24.

Cleland, J.B. & Johnston, T.H. 1937–38. Notes on native names and uses of plants in the Musgrave Ranges region. *Oceania.* Vol. 8, no. 2, pp. 208–15; no. 3, pp. 328–42.

Cleland, J.B. & Johnston, T.H. 1939a. Aboriginal names and uses of plants at the Granites, Central Australia. *Transactions of the Royal Society of South Australia.* Vol. 63, no. 1, pp. 22–6.

Cleland, J.B. & Johnston, T.H. 1939b. Aboriginal names and uses of plants in the northern Flinders Ranges. *Transactions of the Royal Society of South Australia.* Vol. 63, no. 2, pp. 172–9.

Cleland, J.B. & Tindale, N.B. 1954. The ecological surroundings of the Ngalia natives in Central Australia and native names and uses of plants. *Transactions of the Royal Society of South Australia.* Vol. 77, pp. 81–6.

Cleland, J.B. & Tindale, N.B. 1959. The native names and uses of plants at Haasts Bluff, Central Australia. *Transactions of the Royal Society of South Australia.* Vol. 82, pp. 123–40.

Clements, F.E. 1932. *Primitive concepts of disease.* University of California Publications in American Archaeology and Ethnology 32, no. 2. University of California Press, Berkeley and Los Angeles.

Clifford, H.T. & Ludlow, G. 1972. *Keys to the families and genera of Queensland flowering plants (Magnoliophyta).* University of Queensland Press, St Lucia, Queensland.

Cochrane, S. (ed) 2001 *Aboriginal art collections: Highlights from Australia's public museums and galleries.* Craftsman House, Sydney.

Collins, D.J., Culvenor, C.C.J., Lamberton, J.A., Loder, J.W. & Price. J.R. 1990. *Plants for medicine: A chemical and pharmacological survey of plants in the Australian region.* Commonwealth and Scientific Industrial Research Organisation, East Melbourne.

Conway. J.R. 1990. Copping it sweet: The honey ant in Aboriginal culture. *Geo.* Vol. 12 no. 3, pp. 54–61

Cook, J. 1893. *Captain Cook's journal during his first voyage round the world made in M.M. Bark 'Endeavour' 1768–71.* Elliot Stock, London.

Cook, P. & Armstrong, G. 1998. Ownership and resource use on islands off the Liverpool River, Northern territory. Pp. 178–91 in N. Peterson & B. Rigsby (eds) *Customary marine tenure in Australia.* Oceania Monograph no. 48. University of Sydney, Sydney.

Coombs, H.C., Dexter, B.G. & Hiatt, L.R. 1980. The outstation movement in Aboriginal Australia. *Australian Institute of Aboriginal Studies Newsletter. New Series.* Vol. 14, pp. 16–22.

Cooper, H.M. 1954. Kangaroo Island's wild pigs: Their possible origin. *South Australian Naturalist.* Vol. 28, pt 5, pp. 57–61.

Corbett, L. 2001. *The dingo in Australia and Asia.* J.B. Books, Adelaide.

Cosgrove, D. 1984. *Social formation and symbolic landscape.* Croom Helm, London.

Coutts, P.J.F. 1970. *The archaeology of Wilson's Promontory.* Australian Aboriginal Studies No. 28. Prehistory and Material Culture Series No. 7. Australian Institute of Aboriginal Studies, Canberra.

Coutts, P.J.F., Frank, R.K. & Hughes, P. 1978. Aboriginal engineers of the Western District, Victoria. *Records of the Victorian Archaeological Survey.* No. 7.

Crawford, I.M. 1968. *The art of the Wandjina: Aboriginal cave painting in Kimberley, Western Australia.* Oxford University Press, Melbourne.

Crawford, I.M. 1982. Traditional Aboriginal plant resources in the Kalumburu area: Aspects in ethno-economics. *Records of the Western Australian Museum Supplement No. 15.* Western Australian Museum, Perth.

Crawfurd, J. 1868. On the vegetable and animal food of the natives of Australia in reference to social position, with a comparison between the Australian and some other races of man. *Transactions of the Ethnological Society of London. New Series.* Vol. 6, pp. 112–22.

Cribb, A.B. & Cribb, J.W. 1981a. *Wild medicine in Australia.* Fontana/Collins, Sydney.

Cribb, A.B. & Cribb, J.W. 1981b. *Useful wild plants in Australia.* Fontana/Collins, Sydney.

Cribb, A.B. & Cribb, J.W. 1982. *Wild food in Australia.* Revised edition. Fontana/Collins, Sydney.

Cribb, R., Walmbeng, R., Wolmby, R. & Taisman, C. 1988. Landscape as cultural artefact: Shell mounds and plants in Aurukun, Cape York Peninsula. *Australian Aboriginal Studies.* No. 2, pp. 60–73.

Croll, R.H. 1937. Yarumpa, the honey-pot: Food in the wilderness. *Walkabout*. Vol. 3, no. 3, p.16.

Crosby, A.W. 2004. *Ecological imperialism: The biological expansion of Europe, 900–1900*. Second edition. Cambridge University Press, Cambridge.

Cunningham, G.M., Mulham, W.E., Milthorpe, P.L. & Leigh, J.H. 1981. *Plants of western New South Wales*. Inkata Press, Melbourne.

Curr, E.M. 1883. *Recollections of squatting in Victoria, then called the Port Phillip District (from 1841 to 1851)*. Second edition. Melbourne University Press, Melbourne.

Currey, J.E.B. (ed) 1966. *Reflections on the colony of New South Wales by George Caley*. Lansdowne Press, Melbourne.

Curtis, B.V. 1974. Spare a spot for the *Santalum. Australian Plants*. June issue. Vol. 7, pp. 337–8.

Dadswell, I.W. 1934. The chemical composition of some plants used by Australian Aborigines as food. *The Australian Journal of Experimental Biology and Medical Science*. Vol. 12, pp. 13–8.

Daley, C. 1931. Food of the Australian Aborigines. *Victorian Naturalist*. Vol. 48, pp. 23–31.

David, B. 1998. Introduction: 'A mountain once seen never to be forgotten'. Pp. 1–26 in B. David (ed) *Ngarrabullgan: Geographical investigations in Djungan country, Cape York Peninsula*. Monash Publications in Geography and Environmental Science No. 51. Monash University, Clayton, Victoria.

David, B. 2002. *Landscapes, rock-art and the Dreaming: An archaeology of preunderstanding*. Continuum, London.

Davidson, D.S. 1933. Australian netting and basketry techniques. *Journal of the Polynesian Society*. Vol. 42, no. 4, pp. 257–99.

Davidson, D.S. 1934. Australian spear-traits and their derivations. *Journal of the Polynesian Society*. Vol. 43, pp. 41–72, 143–62.

Davidson, D.S. 1935. The chronology of Australian watercraft. *Journal of the Polynesian Society*. Vol. 44, pp. 1–16, 69–84, 137–52, 193–207.

Davidson, D.S. 1936. Australian throwing-sticks, throwing clubs, and boomerangs. *American Anthropologist*. Vol. 38, pp. 76–100.

Davidson, D.S. 1947. Fire-making in Australia. *American Anthropologist*. Vol. 49, no. 3, pp. 427–37.

Davidson, S. 2005. Cultural burning revives a Kakadu wetland. *Ecos*. June–July issue., Vol. 125, pp. 14–6.

Davis, J. 2003. Indigenous land management. Pp. 219–23 in G. Cary, D. Lindenmayer & S. Dovers (eds) *Australia burning: Fire ecology, policy and management issues*. CSIRO Publishing, Collingwood, Victoria.

Davis, S. 1989. *Man of all seasons: An Aboriginal perspective of the natural environment*. Angus & Robertson, Sydney.

Dawson, J. 1881. *Australian Aborigines*. Robertson, Melbourne.

Day, D. 2001. *Claiming a continent: A new history of Australia*. Harper Collins Publishers, Sydney.

Delbridge, A., Bernard, J.R.L., Blair, D., Butler, S., Peters, P. & Yallop, C. 1997. *The Macquarie dictionary*. Third edition. Macquarie University, Sydney.

Denham, T.P., Haberle, S.G., Lentfer, C., Fullagar, R., Field, J., Therin, M., Porch, N. & Winsborough, B. 2003. Origins of agriculture at Kuk Swamp in the Highlands of New Guinea. *Science*. Vol. 301, 11 July 2003, pp. 189–93.

Denoon, D. & Mein-Smith, P. 2000. *A history of Australia, New Zealand, and the Pacific*. Blackwell Publishers, Oxford.

Devanesen D. 1985. *Traditional Aboriginal medicine and bicultural approach to healthcare in Australia's Northern Territory*. Proceedings of the 2nd National Drug Institute, Alcohol and Drug Foundation, Canberra.

Devanesen, D. 2000. *Traditional Aboriginal medicine practice in the Northern Territory*. International Symposium on Traditional Medicine. Proceedings of Better Science, Policy and Services for Health Development, held 11–13 September 2000, World Health Organisation Centre for Health Development, Kobe, Japan.

Devitt, J. 1986. A taste for honey: Aborigines and the collection of ants associated with mulga in Central Australia. Pp. 40–44 in P.S. Sattler (ed) *The mulga lands*. Royal Society of Queensland, St Lucia, Queensland.

Devitt, J. 1992. Acacias: A traditional Aboriginal food source in central Australia. Pp. 37–53 in A.P.N. House and C.E. Hardwood (eds) in *Australian dry-zone acacias for human food*. Australian Tree Seed Centre, Canberra.

Diamond, J. 1998. *Guns, germs and steel: A short history of everybody for the last 13,000 years*. Vintage, London.

Diamond, J. 2005. *Collapse: How societies choose to fail or succeed*. Penguin, Camberwell, Victoria.

Dix, W.C. & Lofgren, M.E. 1974. Kurumi: Possible Aboriginal incipient agriculture associated with a stone arrangement. *Records of the Western Australian Museum*. Vol. 3, pt 1, pp. 73–7.

Dixon, R.M.W., Ramson, W.S. & Thomas, M. 1992. *Australian Aboriginal words in English: Their origin and meaning*. Oxford University Press Australia, Melbourne.

Dobkin de Rios, M. & Stachalek, R. 1999. The Duboisia genus, Australian Aborigines and suggestibility. *Journal of Psychoactive Drugs*. Vol. 32, no. 2, pp. 155–61.

Dodson, J., Fullagar, R. & Head, L. 1992. Dynamics of environment and people in the forested crescents of temperate Australia. Pp. 115–595 in J. Dodson (ed) *The naive lands: Prehistory and environmental change in Australia and the south-west Pacific*. Longman Cheshire, Melbourne.

Douglas, M.T. 1982. *In the active voice*. Routledge & Kegan Paul, London.

Douglas, W.H. 1988. *An introductory dictionary of the Western Desert language*. Institute of Applied Language Studies, Perth.

Dousset, L. 1997. Naming and personal names of Ngaatjatjarra-speaking people, Western Desert: Some questions related to research. *Australian Aboriginal Studies*. No. 2, pp. 50–4.

Duncan, J. & Duncan, N. 1988. (Re)reading the landscape. *Environment and Planning D: Society and Space*. Vol. 6, pp. 117–26.

Dunlop, C.R., Latz, P.K. & Maconochie, J.R. 1975. A botanical survey of Elcho Island. *Northern Territory Botanical Bulletin*. Vol. 1.

Duranti, A. (ed) 2001. *Linguistic anthropology: A reader*. Blackwell Publishers, Malden, MA.

Durkheim, E. 1915. *The elementary forms of the religious life*. Second edition translated from the French edition, 1976. Allen & Unwin, London.

Earl, G.W. 1846. On the Aboriginal tribes of the northern coast of Australia. *Royal Geographic Society of London*. Vol. 16, pp. 239–51.

Earl, J.W. & McCleary, B.V. 1994. Mystery of the poisoned expedition. *Nature*. Vol. 368, no. 6473, pp. 683–4.

Eastwell, H.D. 1973a. Co-operating with the medicine man. *Health*. First quarter, pp. 12–4.

Eastwell, H.D. 1973b. The traditional healer in modern Arnhem Land. *Medical Journal of Australia*. Vol. 2, pp. 1011–7.

Eastwell, H.D. 1978. Supporting Aboriginal ethnomedicine. Submission to the House of Representatives Standing Committee on Aboriginal Affairs, Health Problems of Aboriginals. *Hansard*. Pp. 2017–28.

Edwards, R. 1972. *Aboriginal bark canoes of the Murray Valley*. Rigby, Adelaide.

Edwards, W.H. 1988. *An introduction to Aboriginal societies*. Social Science Press, Wentworth Falls, New South Wales.

Elkin, A.P. 1932. Social organisation of the Kimberley division, north-western Australia. *Oceania*. Vol. 2, pt 3, pp. 296–333.

Elkin, A.P. 1940. Kinship in South Australia. *Oceania*. Vol. 10, pt 3, pp. 295–349.

Elkin, A.P. 1964. *The Australian Aborigines: How to understand them*. Fourth edition. Angus & Robertson, Sydney.

Elkin, A.P. 1977. *Aboriginal men of high degree*. Second edition. University of Queensland Press, St Lucia, Queensland.

Ellis, R.W. 1976. The Aboriginal inhabitants and their environment. Pp. 113–20 in C.R. Twidale, M.J. Tyler & B.P. Webb (eds) *Natural history of the Adelaide region*. Royal Society of South Australia, Adelaide.

Else-Mitchell, R. 1939. George Caley: His life and work. *Royal Australian Historical Society Journal and Proceedings*. Vol. 25, pt 6, pp. 437–542.

Erickson, R., George, A.S., Marchant N.G. & Morcombe, M.K. 1979. *Flowers and plants of Western Australia*. Revised edition. A.H. & A.W. Reed, Sydney.

Etheridge, R. 1893. The 'mirrn-yong' heaps at the North-west Bend of the River Murray. *Transactions and Proceedings and Report of the Royal Society of South Australia*. Vol. 17, pp. 21–4.

Etheridge, R. 1918. *The dendroglyths, or 'carved trees' of New South Wales*. Memoirs of the Geological Survey of New South Wales, Ethnological Series No. 3. William Applegate Gullick, Government Printer, Sydney.

Evans-Pritchard, E.E. 1937. *Witchcraft, oracles and magic among the Azande*. Clarendon Press, Oxford.

Evans-Pritchard, E.E. 1949. *The Sanusi of Cyrenaica*. Oxford University Press, London.

Everist, S.L. 1981. *Poisonous plants of Australia*. Revised edition. Australian Natural Science Library. Angus & Robertson, Sydney.

Eyre, E.J. 1845. *Journals of expeditions of discovery*. 2 volumes. Boone, London.

Farb, P. & Armelagos, G. 1980. *Consuming passions: The anthropology of eating*. Houghton Mifflin Company, Boston.

Favenc, E. 1888. *The history of Australian exploration from 1788 to 1888*. Turner & Henderson, Sydney.

Fenner, C.A.E. 1931. *South Australia: A geographical study*. Whitcombe & Tombs, Melbourne.

Finlayson, H.H. 1952. *The red centre: Man and beast in the heart of Australia*. Angus & Robertson, Sydney.

Finlayson, W. 1903. Reminiscences by Pastor Finlayson. *Proceedings of the Royal Geographical Society of Australasia. South Australian Branch*. Vol. 6, pp. 39–55.

Fison, L. & Howitt, A.W. 1880. *Kamilaroi and Kurnai: Group-marriage and relationship, and marriage by elopement drawn chiefly from the usage of the Australian Aborigines: Also the Kurnai Tribe, their customs in peace and war*. George Robertson, Melbourne.

Flannery, T.F. 1990. Pleistocene faunal loss: Implications of the aftershock for Australia's past and future. *Archaeology in Oceania*. Vol. 25, pp. 45–55.

Flannery, T.F. 1994. *The future eaters: An ecological history of the Australasian lands and people.* Reed Books, Sydney.

Flannery, T.F. (ed) 1998. *The explorers.* Introduced T.F. Flannery. Text Publishing, Melbourne.

Flannery, T.F. 2004. *Country.* Text Publishing, Melbourne.

Flannery, T.F. & Schouten, P. 2001. *A gap in nature: Discovering the world's extinct animals.* Text Publishing, Melbourne.

Flinders, M. 1814. *Terra Australis.* Edited and introduced by T.F. Flannery. 2000. Text Publishing, Melbourne.

Flood, J. 1997. *Rock art of the Dreamtime: Images of ancient Australia.* Angus & Robertson, Sydney.

Flower, R. 2000. *Characterisation of anti-viral compounds in Australian bush medicines.* Research paper No. 00/006. Rural Industries Research and Development Corporation, Canberra.

Foley, W.A. 1997. *Anthropological linguistics: An introduction.* Blackwell Publishers, Cambridge, MA

Forrest, J. 1875. *Explorations in Australia.* Sampson Low, Marston, Low & Searle, London. Facsimile edition published by the Libraries Board of South Australia, Adelaide, 1969.

Foster, R.G.K. 1989. Feasts of the full-moon: The distribution of rations to Aborigines in South Australia: 1836–1861. *Aboriginal History.* Vol. 13, pt 1, pp. 63–78.

Frakes, L.A. 1999. Evolution of Australian environments. Pp. 163–203 in A.E. Orchard (ed) *Australian biological resources study: Flora of Australia.* Volume 1. Introduction. Second edition. Bureau of Fauna and Flora, Canberra.

Frankel, D. 1982. An account of Aboriginal use of the yam-daisy. *The Artefact.* Vol. 7, pp. 43–5.

Frazer, J.G. 1890. *The golden bough: A study in comparative religion.* Macmillan, London.

Fumiyo Saitoh, Masana Noma & Nobumaro Kawashima. 1985. The alkaloid contents of sixty *Nicotiana* species. *Phytochemistry.* Vol. 24, pt 3, pp. 477–80.

Galbraith, J. 1977. *Field guide to the wild flowers of south-east Australia.* Collins, Sydney.

Gara, T. 1985. Aboriginal techniques for obtaining water in South Australia. *Journal of the Anthropological Society of South Australia.* Vol. 23, pt 2, pp. 6–11.

Gara, T. 1994. 'Tackling the back country': Richard Maurice's expeditions in the great Victoria Desert, 1897–1903. *South Australian Geographical Journal.* Vol. 93, pp. 42–60.

Gara, T. 1998. The life and times of Mullawirraburka ('King John') of the Adelaide tribe. Pp. 88–132 in J. Simpson & L. Hercus (eds) *Aboriginal portraits of 19th century South Australia.* Aboriginal History Monograph. Australian National University, Canberra.

Gason, S. 1879. The 'Dieyerie' tribe. Pp. 66–86 in G. Taplin (ed) *Folklore, manners, customs and languages of the South Australian Aborigines.* South Australian Government Printer, Adelaide.

Gately, I. 2001. *La Diva Nicotiana.* Simon & Schuster, London.

Gib, W. 1999. *The people of Gariwerd: The Grampians' Aboriginal heritage.* Aboriginal Affairs Victoria, Melbourne.

Giles, E. 1889. *Australia twice traversed: The romance of exploration, being a narrative compiled from the journals of five exploring expeditions into and through central South Australia and Western Australia, from 1872 to 1876.* Sampson, Low, Marston, Searle & Rivington, London.

Gill, A.M., Moore, P.H.R. & Armstrong, J.P. 1991. *Bibliography of fire ecology in Australia.* Department of Bush Fire Services, Sydney.

Gillespie, R. 2002. Dating the first Australians. *Radiocarbon.* Vol. 44, no. 2, pp. 455–72.

Gilmore, M. 1935. *More recollections.* Angus & Robertson, Sydney.

Goddard, C. 1992. *Pitjantjatjara/Yankunytjatjara to English dictionary.* Second edition. Institute of Aboriginal Development, Alice Springs.

Goddard, C. & Kalotas, A. (eds) 1988. *Punu: Yankunytjatjara plant use.* Angus & Robertson, Sydney.

Golson, J. 1971. Australian Aboriginal food plants: Some ecological and culture-historical implications. Pp. 196–238 in D.J. Mulvaney & J. Golson (eds) *Aboriginal man and environment in Australia.* Australian National University Press, Canberra.

Golson, J. 1977. No room at the top: Agricultural intensification in the New Guinea highlands. Pp. 602–38 in J. Allen, J. Golson & R. Jones (eds) *Sunda and Sahul.* Academic Press, London.

Goodale, J.C. 1971. *Tiwi wives: A study of the women of Melville Island, north Australia.* University of Washington Press, Seattle.

Goodale, J.C. 1986. Production and reproduction of key resources among the Tiwi of North Australia. Pp. 197–210 in N.M. Williams & E.S. Hunn (eds) *Resource managers: North American and Australian hunter-gatherers.* Australian Institute of Aboriginal Studies, Canberra.

Gosden, C. 1995. Arboriculture and agriculture in coastal Papua New Guinea. *Antiquity.* Vol. 69 (Special no. 265), pp. 807–17.

Gosden, C. & Head, L. 1994. Landscape — a usefully ambiguous concept.

Archaeology in Oceania. Vol. 29, no. 3, pp. 113–6.

Gott, B. 1982a. Ecology of root use by the Aborigines of Southern Australia. *Archaeology in Oceania.* Vol. 17, pp. 59–67.

Gott, B. 1982b. Kunzea pomifera — Dawson's 'nurt'. *The Artefact.* Vol. 7, pt 1, pp. 3–17.

Gott, B. 1983. Murnong — 'Microseris scapigera': A study of a staple food of Victorian Aborigines. *Australian Aboriginal Studies.* No. 2, pp. 2–17.

Gott, B. 1984. Victorian ethnobotanical records. *Australian Aboriginal Studies.* No. 1, p.56.

Gott, B. 1985a. Plants mentioned in Dawson's *Australian Aborigines. The Artefact.* Vol. 10, pp. 3–14.

Gott, B. 1985b. The use of seeds by Victorian Aborigines. Pp. 25–30 in G.P. Jones (ed) *The food potential of seeds from Australian native plants.* Proceedings of a colloquium held at Deakin University on 7 March 1984. Deakin University Press, Victoria.

Gott, B. 1997. Choosing *Acacia* species for bushtucker. *Australian Bushfoods Magazine.* Vol. 4, pp. 3–5.

Gott, B. 1999. Cumbungi, Typha species: A staple Aboriginal food in southern Australia. *Australian Aboriginal Studies.* No. 1 pp 33–50.

Gott, B. 2002. *Aboriginal plant use walk.* Australian National Botanic Gardens, Canberra.

Gott, B. & Conran, J. 1991. *Victorian Koorie plants: Some plants used by Victorian Koories for food, fibre, medicines and implements.* Yangernnanock Women's Group, Hamilton, Victoria.

Gott, R. 2006. *Bush tucker.* Heinemann Library, Port Melbourne.

Gould, R.A. 1969. *Yiwara: Foragers of the Australian desert.* Collins, London.

Gould, R.A. 1971. Uses and effects of fire among the Western Desert Aborigines of Australia. *Mankind.* Vol. 8, no. 1, pp. 14–24.

Gould, R.A. 1982. To have and have not: The ecology of sharing among hunter-gatherers. Pp. 69–91 in N.M. Williams & E.S. Hunn (eds) *Resource managers: North American and Australian hunter-gatherers.* Australian Institute of Aboriginal Studies, Canberra.

Graham, C. & Hart, D. 1997. *Prospects for the Australian native bushfoods industry.* Research paper No. 97/022. Rural Industries Research and Development Corporation, Canberra.

Graves, R. 1966. *The white goddess: A historical grammar of poetic myth.* Octagon Books, New York.

Gray, M.C., Altman, J.C. & Halasz, N. 2005. *The economic value of wild resources to the indigenous community of the Wallis Lake Catchment.* Centre for Aboriginal Economic Policy Research, Australian National University, Canberra.

Gregory, A.C. 1887. Memoranda on the Aborigines of Australia. *Journal of the Anthropological Institute of Great Britain and Ireland.* Vol. 16, pp. 131–3.

Grey, G. 1841. *Journals of two expeditions of discovery in north-west and Western Australia during the years 1837, 38 and 39 ...* Boone, London.

Griffin, G.F. & Allan, G.E. 1986. Fire and the management of Aboriginal owned lands in central Australia. Pp. 72–7 in B.D. Foran & B. Walker (eds) *Science and technology for Aboriginal development.* CSIRO and Centre for Appropriate Technology, Alice Springs.

Griffiths, T. 1997. Introduction. Ecology and empire: Towards an Australian history of the world. Pp. 1–16 in T. Griffiths & L. Robin (eds) *Ecology and empire: Environmental history of settler societies.* Melbourne University Press, Melbourne.

Griffiths, T. & Robin, L. (eds) 1997. *Ecology and empire: Environmental history of settler societies.* Melbourne University Press, Melbourne.

Gunn, R.C. 1842. Remarks on the indigenous vegetable products of Tasmania available as food for man. *Tasmanian Journal of Natural Science.* Pp. 35–52.

Hackett, C. 1937. Man and nature in Central Australia. Reprinted from *The Geographical Magazine.* Vol. 4, no. 4.

Haddon, A.C. (ed) 1904–35. *Reports of the Cambridge Anthropological Expedition to Torres Straits.* Cambridge University Press, Cambridge.

Hahn, D.M. 1838–1839. Extracts from the *Reminiscences of Captain Dirk Meinertz Hahn, 1838–1839.* Translated by F.J.H. Blaess & L.A. Triebel. *South Australiana.* 1964. Vol. 3, no. 2, pp. 97–134.

Hale, H.M. & Tindale, N.B. 1933. Aborigines of Princess Charlotte Bay, North Queensland. *Records of the South Australian Museum.* Vol. 5, pt 1, pp. 63–116.

Hallam, S.J. 1975. *Fire and hearth: A study of Aboriginal usage and European usurpation in south-western Australia.* Australian Institute of Aboriginal Studies, Canberra.

Hamlyn-Harris, R. & Smith, F. 1916. On fish poisoning and poisons employed among the Aborigines of Queensland. *Memoirs of the Queensland Museum.* Vol. 5, pp. 1–9.

Harden, G.J. (ed) 1990–93. *Flora of New South Wales.* 4 Vols. University of New South Wales Press, Kensington, New South Wales.

Hardwick, R.J. 2001. *Nature's larder: A field guide to the native food plants of the NSW South Coast.* Homosapien Books, Jerrabomberra, New South Wales.

Hardy, B. 1969. *West of the Darling.* Jacaranda Press, Milton, Queensland.

Hardy, B. 1976. *Lament for the Barkindji: The vanished tribes of the Darling River region*. Rigby, Adelaide.

Harris, D.R. 1977. Subsistence strategies across Torres Straits. Pp. 421–63 in J. Allen, J. Golson & R. Jones (eds) *Sunda and Sahul*. Academic Press, London.

Harris, D.R. 1980. Tropical savanna environments: Definition, distribution, diversity, and development. Pp. 3–27 in D.R. Harris (ed) *Human ecology in savanna environments*. Academic Press, London.

Harris, D.R. 1995. Early agriculture in New Guinea and the Torres Strait divide. *Antiquity*. Vol. 69 (Special no. 265), pp. 848–54.

Harris, T.M. 1833. *A dictionary of the natural history of the Bible*. New edition. T.T. & J. Tegg, London.

Hart, C.W.M. & Pilling, A.R. 1960. *The Tiwi of north Australia*. Holt, Rinehart & Winston, New York.

Harvey, M. 1999. Place names and land-language associations in the western Top End. *Australian Journal of Linguistics*. Vol. 19, No. 2, pp. 161–95.

Harwood, C.E. 1994. Human food potential of the seeds of some Australian dry-zone Acacia species. *Journal of Arid Environments*. Vol. 27, pp. 27–35.

Hasluck, A. 1955. *Portrait with background: A life of Georgiana Molloy*. Oxford University Press, Melbourne.

Hassell, E. 1936. Notes on the ethnology of the Wheelman tribe of southwestern Australia. *Anthropos*. Vol. 31, pp. 679–711.

Hawker, J.C. 1841–45. *Journal of an expedition to the River Murray, against the natives, in order to recover sheep taken by them from Messrs Field and Inman on their overland journey from New South Wales to South Australia; also to protect another overland party expected almost immediately*. Transcribed by I. Palios, 1981. State Library of South Australia, Adelaide.

Hayden, B. 1998. Stone tool functions in the Western Desert. Pp. 266–84 in T. Murray (ed) *Archaeology of Aboriginal Australia: A reader*. Allen & Unwin, Sydney.

Haynes, C.D. 1985. The pattern and ecology of *Munwag*: Traditional Aboriginal fire regimes in north-central Arnhem Land. Pp. 203–15 in M.G. Ridpath & L.K. Corbett (eds) *Ecology of the wet-dry tropics*. Proceedings of the Ecological Society of Australia. Vol. 13.

Haynes, C.D. 1991. Use and impact of fire. Pp. 61–71 in C.D. Haynes, M.G. Ridpath & M.A.J. Williams (eds) *Monsoonal Australia: Landscape, ecology and man in the northern lowlands*. A.A. Balkema, Rotterdam.

Head, L. 1989. Prehistoric Aboriginal impacts on Australian vegetation: An assessment of the evidence. *Australian Geographer*. Vol. 20, pt 1, pp. 37–46.

Head, L. 1994. Landscapes socialised by fire: Post contact changes in Aboriginal fire use in northern Australia, and its implications for prehistory. *Archaeology in Oceania*. Vol. 29, no. 3, pp. 172–81.

Head, L. 2000a. *Second nature: The history and implications of Australia as Aboriginal landscape*. Syracuse University Press, New York.

Head, L. 2000b. *Cultural landscapes and environmental change*. Arnold, London.

Head, L. & Fullagar, R. 1991. 'We all la one land': Pastoral excisions and Aboriginal resource use. *Australian Aboriginal Studies*. No. 1, pp. 39–52.

Heath, J. 1978. Linguistic approaches to Nunggubuyu ethnozoology and ethnobotany. Pp. 40–55 in L.R. Hiatt (ed) *Australian Aboriginal concepts*. Australian Institute of Aboriginal Studies, Canberra.

Hegarty, M.P., Hegarty, E.E. & Wills, R.B.H. 2001. *Food safety of Australian plant bushfoods*. Research paper No. 01/028. Rural Industries Research & Development Corporation (Australia) New Plant Products and Development, Barton, Australian Capital Territory.

Hele, A.E. 2003. *Researchers' extension program for the native foods industry*. Research paper No. 03/013. Rural Industries Research and Development Corporation, Canberra.

Helms, R. 1896. Anthropology of the Elder Expedition. *Transactions, Proceedings and Report of the Royal Society of South Australia*. Vol. 16, pt 3, pp. 238–332.

Henderson, J. & Dobson, V. 1994. *Eastern and Central Arrernte to English dictionary*. Arandic Languages Dictionaries Program, Language Centre, Institute for Aboriginal Development, Alice Springs.

Henderson, J. & Nash, D. 2002. *Language in native title*. Aboriginal Studies Press, Canberra.

Henshall, T., Jambijinpa, D., Spencer, J.N., Kelly, F.J., Bartlett, P., Mears, J., Coulshed, E., Robertson, G.J. & Granites, L.J. 1980. *Ngurrju maninja kurlangu: Yapa nyurnu kurlangu = Bush medicine*. Revised edition. Warlpiri Literature Production Centre, Yuendumu, Northern Territory.

Herbert, F. 1999. *Cultivation of bushfoods: Preliminary investment analysis of the commercial cultivation of six bushfoods*. Marketing Economics and Rural Adjustment Service, Perth.

Hercus, L.A. 1986. *The languages of Victoria: A late survey*. Parts 1–2. Australian Aboriginal Studies No. 17, Linguistic Series No. 6. Australian Institute of Aboriginal Studies, Canberra.

Hercus, L.A. 1989. Preparing grass witchetty grubs. *Records of the South Australian Museum*. Vol. 23, no. 1, pp. 51–7.

Hercus, L.A. 1992. *A Nukunu dictionary*. Australian Institute of Aboriginal and Torres Strait Islander Studies, Canberra.

Hercus, L.A., Hodges, F. & Simpson, J. (eds) 2002. *The land is a map: Placenames of indigenous origin in Australia*. Pandanus Books, Australian National University, Canberra.

Hercus, L.A. & Simpson, J. 2002. Indigenous placenames: An introduction. Pp. 1–23 in L. Hercus, F. Hodges & J. Simpson (eds) *The land is a map: Placenames of indigenous origin in Australia*. Pandanus Books, Australian National University, Canberra.

Hetzal, B.S. & Frith, H.J. (eds) 1978. *The nutrition of Aborigines in relation to the ecosystem of Central Australia*. Commonwealth Scientific and Industrial Research Organisation, Melbourne.

Hiatt, L.R. 1996. *Arguments about Aborigines: Australia and the evolution of social anthropology*. Cambridge University Press, Cambridge.

Hiatt, L.R. & Jones, R. 1988. Aboriginal conceptions of the workings of nature. Pp. 1–22 in R.W. Howe (ed) *Australian science in the making*. Cambridge University Press, Melbourne.

Hicks, C.S. 1963. Climatic adaptation and drug habituation of the Central Australian Aborigine. *Perspectives in Biology and Medicine*. Vol. 7, no. 1, pp. 39–57.

Hicks, C.S. & Le Messurier, H. 1935. Preliminary observations on the chemistry and pharmacology of the alkaloids of Duboisia hopwoodii. *Australian Journal of Experimental Biology and Medical Science*. Vol. 13, pp. 175–88.

Hiddins, L.J. 1981. *Survive to live: An analysis of survival and its relationship within northern Australia*. Behavioural Sciences Department, James Cook University of North Queensland, Townsville, Queensland.

Hiddins, L.J. 1996. *Bushtucker man: Stories of exploration and survival*. ABC Books, Sydney.

Hiddins, L.J. 2000. *The bush tucker guide: 60 of the most common species in northern Australia illustrated region-by-region*. Viking Penguin Books, Melbourne.

Hiddins, L.J. 2001. *Bush tucker field guide*. Penguin Books, Melbourne.

Hiddins, L.J. 2003. *Explore wild Australia with the Bush Tucker Man*. New edition. Explore Australia, South Yarra, Victoria.

Hill, B. 2002. *Broken song: T.G.H. Strehlow and Aboriginal possession*. Knopf, Milsons Point, New South Wales.

Hill, R. 2003. Frameworks to support indigenous managers: The key to fire futures. Pp. 175–86 in G. Cary, D. Lindenmayer & S. Dovers (eds) *Australia burning: Fire ecology, policy and management issues*. CSIRO Publishing, Collingwood, Victoria.

Hill, R.S. 2004. Origins of the southeastern Australian vegetation. *Philosophical Transactions: Biological Sciences. Royal Society*. Vol. 359, pp. 1537–49.

Hiscock, P. & Kershaw, A.P. 1992. Palaeoenvironments and prehistory of Australia's tropical Top End. Pp. 43–75 in J. Dodson (ed) *The naive lands: Prehistory and environmental change in Australia and the south-west Pacific*. Longman Cheshire, Melbourne.

Hobsbawm, E.J. & Ranger, T. 1983. *The invention of tradition*. Cambridge University Press, Cambridge.

Hodgson, J.M. & Wahlqvist, M.L. 1993. Nutrition and health of Victorian Aborigines (Kooris). *Asia Pacific Journal of Clinical Nutrition*. Vol. 2, no. 1, pp. 43–57.

Hodgson, R. 1988. *Peppimenarti basketmakers*. The author, Darwin.

Holdaway, S. & Stern, N. 2004. *A record in stone: The study of Australia's flaked stone artefacts*. Museum Victoria and Aboriginal Studies Press, Melbourne.

Holden, R.W. 1879. The 'Maroura' tribe, lower Darling. Pp. 17–28 in G. Taplin (ed) *The folklore, manners, customs and languages of the South Australian Aborigines*. South Australian Government Printer, Adelaide.

Hope, G.S. 1994. Quaternary vegetation. Pp. 368–89 in R.S. Hill (ed) *History of the Australian vegetation: Cretaceous to recent*. Cambridge University Press, Cambridge.

Hope, G.S. & Coutts, P.J.F. 1971. Past and present Aboriginal food resources at Wilsons Promontory, Victoria. *Mankind*. Vol. 8, pt 2, pp. 104–14.

Hopkins, M.S., Ash, J., Graham, A.W., Head, J. & Hewett, R.K. 1993. Charcoal evidence of the spatial extent of the *Eucalyptus* woodland expansions and rainforest contractions in North Queensland during the late Pleistocene. *Journal of Biogeography*. Vol. 20, pp. 357–72.

Hopkins, M.S., Graham, A.W. & Hewett, R.K. 1990. Evidence of late Pleistocene fires and eucalypt forest from a north Queensland humid tropical rainforest site. *Australian Journal of Ecology*. Vol. 15, pp. 345–7.

Horne, G. & Aiston, G. 1924. *Savage life in Central Australia*. Macmillan, London.

Horstman, M. & Wightman, G. 2001. Karparti ecology: Recognition of Aboriginal ecological knowledge and its application to management in north-western Australia. *Ecological Management and Restoration*. Vol. 2, pt 2, pp. 99–109.

Horton, D. 2000. *The pure state of nature: Sacred cows, destructive myths and the environment*. Allen & Unwin, Sydney.

House, A.P.N. & Hardwood, C.E. (eds) 1992. *Australian dry-zone acacias for human food*. Australian Tree Seed Centre, Canberra.

Howard, M.C. 1978–79. Migration and inequality: The socio-cultural significance of Australian Aboriginal internment in southwestern 'native' settlements.

Anthropological Forum. Vol. 4, pt 4, pp. 297–307.

Howie-Willis, I. 1994. Names. Pp. 757–8 in D. Horton (ed) *The encyclopaedia of Aboriginal Australia*. 2 volumes. Aboriginal Studies Press for the Australian Institute of Aboriginal and Torres Strait Islander Studies, Canberra.

Howitt, A.W. 1904. *Native tribes of south-east Australia*. Macmillan, London.

Hull, G. 1999. *Standard Tetum–English dictionary*. Third edition. Allen & Unwin, Sydney.

Hunter, J. 1793. *An historical journal of the transactions at Port Jackson and Norfolk Island with the discoveries which have been made in New South Wales … John Stockdale, London.

Hyam, G.N. 1943. Living off the land. *Victorian Naturalist*. Vol. 59, pp. 171–3.

Irvine, F.R. 1957. Wild and emergency foods of Australian and Tasmanian Aborigines. *Oceania*. Vol. 28, pt 2, pp. 113–42.

Irvine, F.R. 1970. Evidence of change in the vegetable diet of Australian Aborigines. Pp. 278–84 in A.R. Pilling & R.A. Waterman (eds) *Diprotodon to detribalisation*. Michigan State University Press, East Lansing.

Isaacs, J. 1980. *Australian Dreaming: 40,000 years of Aboriginal history*. Lansdowne Press, Sydney.

Isaacs, J. 1987. *Bush food: Aboriginal food and herbal medicine*. Weldons, Sydney.

Isaacs, J. 1992a. *Desert crafts: Anangu Maruku Punu*. Doubleday, Sydney.

Isaacs, J. 1992b. *Aboriginality: Contemporary Aboriginal paintings and prints*. University of Queensland Press, St Lucia, Queensland.

Jackson, P. 1989. *Maps of meaning*. Unwin Hyman, London.

Jackson, W.D. 1968. Fire, air, water and earth — an elemental ecology of Tasmania. *Proceedings of the Ecological Society of Australia*. Vol. 3, pp. 9–16.

Jacob, T.K. 1991. *In the beginning: A perspective on traditional Aboriginal societies*. Ministry of Education, Western Australia, Perth.

Jessop, J.P. (ed) 1981. *Flora of Central Australia*. The Australian Systematic Botany Society. Reed Books, Sydney.

Jessop, J.P. & Toelken, H.R. 1986. *Flora of South Australia. Parts 1–4*. South Australian Government Printing Division, Adelaide.

Johnson, D. 1998. *Night skies of Aboriginal Australia: A noctuary*. Oceania Monograph no. 47. University of Sydney, Sydney.

Johnson, P.R., Robinson, C. & Green, E. 2002. *The prospect of commercialising boab roots as a vegetable*. Research paper No. 02/020. Rural Industries Research and Development Corporation, Canberra.

Johnston, T. Harvey. 1939. Pituri. *Mankind*. Vol. 2, no. 7, pp. 224–5.

Johnston, T. Harvey & Cleland, J.B. 1933–34. The history of the Aboriginal narcotic, pituri. *Oceania*. Vol. 4, no. 2, pp. 201–23; no. 3, pp. 268–89.

Johnston, T. Harvey & Cleland, J.B. 1942. Aboriginal names and uses of plants in the Ooldea region, South Australia. *Transactions of the Royal Society of South Australia*. Vol. 66, pp. 93–103.

Johnston, T. Harvey & Cleland, J.B. 1943a. Native names and uses of plants in the north-eastern corner of South Australia. *Transactions of the Royal Society of South Australia*. Vol. 67, pt 1, pp. 149–73.

Johnston, T. Harvey & Cleland, J.B. 1943b. Aboriginal names and utilization of the fauna in the Eyrean region. *Transactions of the Royal Society of South Australia*. Vol. 67, pt 2, pp. 244–311.

Jones, C.A. 1996. *Selected plant food species and bush food crops*. Ausbushpro, Monarto South, South Australia.

Jones, D.L. 1993. *Cycads of the world*. Reed Books Australia, Chatswood, New South Wales.

Jones, D.L. 1995. *Palms throughout the world*. Reed Books Australia, Chatswood, New South Wales.

Jones, D.S., Mackay, S. & Pisani, A.M. 1997. Patterns in the valley of the Christmas bush. *Victorian Naturalist*. Vol. 114, pt 5, pp. 246–9.

Jones, G.P. (ed) 1985. *The food potential of seeds from Australian native plants*. Deakin University Press, Victoria.

Jones, P.G. 1984. Red ochre expeditions. *Journal of the Anthropological Society of South Australia*. Vol. 22, pt 7, pp. 3–10; Vol. 22, pt 8, pp. 10–9.

Jones, R.M. 1969. Firestick farming. *Australian Natural History*. Vol. 16, pp. 224–8.

Jones, R.M. 1974. Appendix on Tasmanian tribes. Pp. 317–54 in N.B. Tindale 1974. *Aboriginal tribes of Australia: Their terrain, environmental controls, distribution, limits, and proper names*. Australian National University Press, Canberra.

Jones, R.M. 1978. Why did the Tasmanians stop eating fish? Pp. 11–47 in R.A. Gould (ed) *Explorations in ethnoarchaeology*. School of American Research Advanced Seminar Series. University of New Mexico Press, Albuquerque.

Jones, R.M. 1995. Mindjongork. Legacy of the firestick. In D. Bird Rose (ed) *Country in flames: Proceedings of the 1994 Symposium on Biodiversity and Fire in North Australia*. Biodiversity Unit, Department of the Environment, Sport and Territories and the North Australia Research Unit, Canberra and Darwin.

Jorgenson, J. 1837. A narrative of the habits, manners and customs of the Aborigines of Van Diemen's Land. Pp. 47–131 in N.J.B. Plomley (ed) 1991 *Jorgen Jorgenson and the Van Diemen's Land*. Blubber Head Press, Hobart.

Kaberry, P.M. 1939. *Aboriginal woman: Sacred and profane*. Routledge, London.

Kalma, J.D. & McAlpine, J.R. 1983. Climate and man in the Centre. Pp. 46–69 in G. Crook (ed) *Man in the Centre*. CSIRO Division of Groundwater Research, Perth.

Kalotas, A.C. 1996. Aboriginal knowledge and use of fungi. Pp. 269–95 in A.E. Orchard (ed) *Fungi of Australia*. Commonwealth Scientific and Industrial Research Organisation, Melbourne.

Kamminga, J. 1988. Wood artefacts: A checklist of plant species utilised by Australian Aborigines. *Australian Aboriginal Studies*. No. 2, pp. 26–55.

Kean, J. 1991. Aboriginal–acacia relationships in Central Australia. *Records of the South Australian Museum*. Vol. 24, pt 2, pp. 111–24.

Kean, J., Richardson, G. & Trueman, N. (eds). 1988. *Aboriginal role in nature conservation. Emu conference, June 7th–9th 1988*. South Australian National Parks and Wildlife Service, and Department of Aboriginal Affairs, Adelaide.

Keen, I. 1994. *Knowledge and secrecy in an Aboriginal religion: Yolngu of north-east Arnhem Land*. Oxford University Press, Melbourne.

Keen, I. & Merlan, F. 1990. *The significance of the conservation zone to Aboriginal people*. Resource Assessment Commission, Canberra.

Kennedy, B., Kennedy, J., Kanoa, L. & Maher, D. 1984. *Bush tucker: Bush food list of the Murray–Mallee region*. Privately published, Swan Hill.

Kennedy, H. 1984. Food secrets of the Aborigines. *Omega*. July/August 1984, pp. 86–9, 109.

Kershaw, A.P. 1986. Climatic change and Aboriginal burning in north-eastern Australia during the last two glacial/interglacial cycles. *Nature*. Vol. 322, pp. 47–9.

Kershaw, A.P. 1995. Environmental change in greater Australia. *Antiquity*. Vol. 69 (Special No. 265), pp. 656–75.

Kimber, R.G. 1976. Beginnings of farming? Some man-plant-animal relationships in Central Australia. *Mankind*. Vol. 10, pt 3, pp. 142–50.

Kimber, R.G. 1983. Black lightning: Aborigines and fire in Central Australia and the Western Desert. *Archaeology in Oceania*. Vol. 18, no. 1, pp. 38–45.

Kimber, R.G. 1984. Resource use and management in Central Australia. *Australian Aboriginal Studies*. No. 2, pp. 12–23.

King, B. 1997. Acacia — research, field trials and databases. *Australian Bushfoods Magazine*. Vol. 4, pp. 10–1, 14.

King, B. 1998. Muntari — much more than a ground cover. *Australian Bushfoods Magazine*. Vol. 6, pp. 10–1.

King, P.P. 1827. *Narrative of a survey of the inter-tropical and western coasts of Australia: Performed between the years 1818 and 1822 with an appendix containing various subjects relating to hydrography and natural history*. Murray, London.

Kingdon, J. 2003. *Lowly origin: Where, when, and why our ancestors first stood up*. Princeton University Press, Princeton, New Jersey.

Kohen, J.L. 1995. *Aboriginal environmental impacts*. University of New South Wales Press, Sydney.

Krefft, G. 1862–65. On the manners and customs of the Aborigines of the Lower Murray and Darling. *Transactions of the Philosophical Society of New South Wales*. Pp. 357–74.

Kutsche, F. & Lay, B. 2003. *Field Guide to the plants of outback South Australia*. Department of Water, Land and Biodiversity Conservation, South Australia, Adelaide.

Kyriazis, S. 1995. *Bush medicine of the northern peninsula area of Cape York*. Nai Beguta Agama Aboriginal Corporation, Bamaga, Queensland.

Lakoff, G. 1987. *Women, fire, and dangerous things: What categories reveal about the mind*. University of Chicago Press, Chicago.

Lamond, H.G. 1950. Aboriginal net making. *Mankind*. Vol. 4, no. 4, pp. 168–9.

Lamp, C. & Collet, F. 1979. *A field guide to weeds in Australia*. Revised edition. Inkata Press, Melbourne.

Lampert, R.J. & Sanders, F. 1973. Plants and men on the Beecroft Peninsula, New South Wales. *Mankind*. Vol. 9, no. 2, pp. 96–108

Lands, M. (ed) 1987. *Mayi: Some bush fruits of Dampierland*. Magabala Books, Kimberley Aboriginal Law and Culture Centre, Broome.

Lang, A. 1905. *The secret of the totem*. Longmans, Green & Co., London.

Langton, M. 1998. *Burning questions: Emerging environmental issues for indigenous peoples in northern Australia*. Centre for Indigenous Natural and Cultural Resource Management, Northern Territory University, Darwin.

Langton, M. & Ma Rhea, Z., with Ayre, M. & Pope, J. 2003. *Traditional lifestyles and biodiversity use: Regional report: Australia, Asia and the Middle East*. Prepared for the Secretariat of the Convention on Biological Diversity. United Nations Environment Programme, Montreal, Quebec.

Laramba Community Women 2003. *Anmatyerr ayey arnang-akert: Anmatyerr plant stories*. Compiled J. Green. Institute for Aboriginal Development Press, Alice Springs.

Lassak, E.V. & McCarthy, T. 1983. *Australian medicinal plants*. Methuen, Melbourne.

Latz, P. 1974. Central Australian species of Nicotiana. *Australian Plants*. March issue. Vol. 7, pp. 280–3.

Latz, P. 1995. *Bushfires and bushtucker: Aboriginal plant use in Central Australia.* Institute of Aboriginal Development, Alice Springs.

Latz, P. 1998. The desert raisin and other Solanum. *Australian Bushfoods Magazine.* Vol. 5, pp. 8–9.

Lawrence, D.J. 1996. *Managing parks/managing 'country': Joint management of Aboriginal owned protected areas in Australia.* Research Paper, Parliamentary Research Service, No. 2 1996–97. Department of the Parliamentary Library.

Lawrence, R. 1968. *Aboriginal habitat and economy.* Geography Occasional Paper no. 6. Australian National University, Canberra.

Lawson, R. 1879. The Padthaway tribe. Pp. 58–9 in G. Taplin (ed) *The folklore, manners, customs and languages of the South Australian Aborigines.* South Australian Government Printer, Adelaide.

Lebot, V., Merlin, M. & Lindstrom, L. 1992. *Kava: The Pacific drug.* Yale University Press, New Haven.

Lee, I. 1925. *Early explorers in Australia: From the log-books and journals, including the dairy of Allan Cunningham, botanist, from March 1, 1817, to November 19, 1818.* Methuen & Co., London.

Lee, R.B. & de Vore, I. 1968. *Man the hunter.* Aldine Publishing, Chicago.

Leichhardt, F.W. Ludwig. 1842–48. *Dr Ludwig Leichhardt's letters from Australia during the years March 23, 1842, to April 3, 1848.* **C**ollected and translated from the German, French and Italian by M. Aurousseau. 1968. Published for the Hakluyt Society by Cambridge University Press, London.

Leichhardt, F.W. Ludwig. 1847. *Journal of an overland expedition in Australia, from Moreton Bay to Port Essington, a distance of upward of 3000 miles, during the years 1844–1845.* T. & W. Boone, London. Reprinted in 2000 by Corkwood Press, Adelaide.

Leiper, G. & Hauser, J. 1983. *Mutooroo: Plant use by Australian Aboriginal people.* Assembly Press, Brisbane.

Lemmon, K. 1968. *The golden age of plant hunters.* Phoenix House, London.

Levitt, D. 1981. *Plants and people: Aboriginal uses in plants on Groote Eylandt.* Aboriginal Studies Press, Canberra.

Ley, D. 1983. Cultural/humanistic geography. *Progress in Human Geography.* Vol. 7, no. 2, pp. 267–75.

Liddle, L. 2003. Fire in a jointly managed landscape — fire at Uluru-Kata Tjuta National Park. Pp. 187–97 in G. Cary, D. Lindenmayer & S. Dovers (eds) *Australia burning: Fire ecology, policy and management issues.* CSIRO Publishing, Collingwood, Victoria.

Linacre, E.T. & Hobbs, J.E. 1977. *The Australian climatic environment.* John Wiley & Sons, Brisbane.

Lindenmayer, D. 2003. Indigenous land and fire management: A discussion summary. Pp. 224–6 in G. Cary, D. Lindenmayer & S. Dovers (eds) *Australia burning: Fire ecology, policy and management issues.* CSIRO Publishing, Collingwood, Victoria.

Loneragan, O.W. 1990. *Historical review of sandalwood (Santalum spicatum) research in Western Australia.* Department of Conservation and Land Management, Como, Western Australia.

Long, J. 1989. Leaving the desert: Actors and sufferers in the Aboriginal exodus from the Western Desert. *Aboriginal History.* Vol. 13, pt 1, pp. 9–43.

Lourandos, H. 1997. *Continent of hunter-gatherers: New perspectives in Australian prehistory.* Cambridge University Press, Cambridge.

Low, T. 1985–86. Australian wild foods. *Australian Natural History.* Vol. 21, pt 11, pp. 468–9.

Low, T. 1988. *Wild food plants of Australia.* Angus & Robertson, Sydney.

Low, T. 1989. *Bush tucker: Australia's wild food harvest.* Angus & Robertson, Sydney.

Low, T. 1991a. *Wild food plants of Australia.* Revised edition. Angus & Robertson, Sydney.

Low, T. 1991b. *Wild herbs of Australia and New Zealand.* Angus & Robertson, Sydney.

Low, T. 1999. *Feral future: The untold story of Australia's exotic invaders.* Viking, Melbourne.

Lowe, P. 2002. *Hunters and trackers of the Australian desert.* Rosenberg Publishing, Dural, New South Wales.

Lubbock, J. 1870. *The origin of civilisation and the primitive condition of man.* Longmans, Green & Co., London.

Lucas, D., Gapindi, M. & Russell-Smith, J. 1997. Cultural perspectives of the South Alligator River floodplain: Continuity and change. Pp. 120–40 in D. Bird Rose & A. Clarke (eds) *Tracking knowledge in North Australian landscapes: Studies in indigenous and settler ecological knowledge systems.* North Australia Research Unit, Australian National University, Canberra.

Luebbers, R. 1975. Ancient boomerangs discovered in South Australia. *Nature.* Vol. 253, p.39.

Lumholtz, C.S. 1889. *Among cannibals: Account of four years travels in Australia, and of camp life with the Aborigines of Queensland.* Reprinted in 1980 by Australian National University Press, Canberra.

Lycett, J. 1990. *The Lycett album: Drawings of Aborigines and Australian scenery.* The execution of the original drawings dated at between 1820 and 1822. National Library of Australia, Canberra.

McBryde, I. 1986. Exchange in south eastern Australia: An ethnohistorical perspective. *Aboriginal History.* Vol. 8, pt 2, pp. 132–53.

McBryde, I. 1987. Goods from another country: Exchange networks and then people of the Lake Eyre Basin. Chapter 13. Pp. 253–459 in D.J. Mulvaney & J.P. White (eds) *Australians to 1788.* Fairfax, Syme & Weldon Associates, Sydney.

McCann, I.R. 1989. *The Mallee in flower.* Victorian National Parks Association, Melbourne.

McCarthy, F.D. 1940a. The carved trees of New South Wales. *The Australian Museum Magazine.* June 1, 1940, pp. 160–7.

McCarthy, F.D. 1940b. Aboriginal Australian material culture: Causative factors in its composition. *Mankind.* Vol. 2, pp. 241–269, 294–320.

McCarthy, F.D. 1953. Aboriginal rain-makers. *Weather.* Vol. 8, pp. 72–7.

McCarthy, F.D. 1974. *Australian Aboriginal decorative art.* Eighth edition. Australian Museum, Sydney.

McCarthy, F.D. 1976. *Australian Aboriginal stone implements: Including bone, shell and tooth implements.* Second edition. Australian Museum Trust, Sydney.

McCarthy, F.D. & McArthur, M. 1960. The food quest and the time factor in Aboriginal economic life. Records of the American–Australian Scientific Expedition to Arnhem Land. Vol. 2, pp. 145–94.

McCleary, B.V. & Chick, B.F. 1977. The purification and properties of a thiaminase 1 enzyme from nardoo (*Marsilea drummondii*). *Phytochemistry.* Vol. 16, pp. 207–13.

McConnel, U.H. 1930. The Wik-Munkan tribe of Cape York Peninsula. *Oceania* reprint (originally *Oceania.* Vol. 1, pt 1, pp. 97–104, 181–205).

McConnel, U.H. 1953. Native arts and industries on the Archer, Kendall and Holroyd Rivers, Cape York Peninsula, north Queensland. *Records of the South Australian Museum.* Vol. 11, pt 1, pp. 1–42.

McCourt, T. 1975. *Aboriginal artefacts.* Rigby, Adelaide.

McDonald, J. 1983. The identification of species in a Panaramittee style engravings site. Pp. 236–72 in M. Smith (ed) *Archaeology at ANZAAS 1983.* Western Australian Museum, Perth.

McEntee, J.C. (with P. McKenzie) 1988. *Arthropods of the northern Flinders Ranges and adjacent plains with Aboriginal names.* The author, Adelaide.

McEntee, J.C., McKenzie, P & McKenzie, J. 1986. *Witi-ita-nanalpila: Plants and birds of the northern Flinders Ranges and adjacent plains with Aboriginal names.* The authors, South Australia.

McGhee, K. 2006. Calendar plants mark time. *Australian Geographic.* No. 82 (April–June 2006), pp. 20–1.

MacKenzie, J.M. 1997. Empire and the ecological apocalypse: The historiography of the imperial environment. Pp. 215–28 in T. Griffiths & L. Robin (eds) *Ecology and empire: Environmental history of settler societies.* Melbourne University Press, Melbourne.

Macknight, C.C. 1976. *The voyage to Marege: Macassan trepangers in northern Australia.* Melbourne University Press, Melbourne.

McKnight, D. 1999. *People, countries, and the rainbow serpent: Systems of classification among the Lardil of Mornington Island.* Oxford University Press, New York.

McNiven, I.J. & Quinnell, M. (eds) 2004. *Torres Strait archaeology and material culture.* Memoirs of the Queensland Museum Cultural Heritage Series. Volume 3, Part 1. Queensland Museum, Brisbane.

MacPherson, J. 1925. The gum-tree and wattle in Australian Aboriginal medical practice. *Australian Nurses Journal.* December 15. Vol. 23, pt 12, pp. 588–96.

MacPherson, J. 1939. The eucalyptus in the daily life and medical practice of the Australian Aborigines. *Mankind.* Vol. 2, pt 6, pp. 175–80.

Maddock, K. 1970. Myths of the acquisition of fire in northern and eastern Australia. Pp. 174–99 in R.M. Berndt (ed) *Australian Aboriginal anthropology.* University of Western Australia Press, Perth.

Maddock, K. 1982. *The Australian Aborigines: A portrait of their society.* Second edition. Penguin Books, Melbourne.

Maddock, K. & Cawte, J.E. 1970. Aboriginal law and medicine. *Proceedings of the Medico-Legal Society of New South Wales.* Vol. 4, pp. 170–90.

Magarey, A.T. 1894–95. Aboriginal water quest. *Proceedings of the Royal Geographical Society of Australasia. South Australian Branch.* Session 1894–5, pp. 3–15.

Maggiore, P. 1993. Analysis of Australian Aboriginal bush foods. *Australian Aboriginal Studies.* No. 1, pp. 55–8.

Maher, P. 1999. A review of traditional Aboriginal health beliefs. *Australian Journal of Rural Health.* Vol. 7, pp. 229–36.

Maiden, J.H. 1889. *The useful native plants of Australia.* Trubner, London.

Maiden, J.H. 1890. Spinifex resin. *Proceedings of the Linnean Society of New South Wales.* Vol. 14, pt 3, pp. 639–40.

Marrfurra, P. 1995. *Ngan'gikurunggurr and Ngangiwumirri ethnobotany: Aboriginal plant use from the Daly River area, northern Australia.* Northern Territory Botanical Bulletin No. 22. Conservation Commission of the Northern Territory, Darwin.

Massola, A. 1966. The Aborigines of the Mallee. *Proceedings of the Royal Society of Victoria*. Vol. 79, no. 2, pp. 267–74.

Mathew, J. 1886–87. Mary River and Bunya Bunya country. Pp. 159–209, Vol. 3 in E.M. Curr (ed) *The Australian race*. Trubner, London.

Mathews, J.D., Riley, M.D., Fejo, L., Munoz, E., Milns, N.R., Gardner, I.D., Powers, J.R., Ganygulpa, E. & Gununuwawuy, B.J. 1988. Effects of the heavy usage of kava on physical health: Summary of a pilot survey in an Aboriginal community. *Medical Journal of Australia*. Vol 148, pp. 548–555.

Mathews, R.H. 1900. Phallic rites and initiation ceremonies of the South Australian Aborigines. *Proceedings of the American Philosophical Society*. Vol. 39, no. 164, pp. 622–38.

Mathews, R.H. 1901. Rock-holes used by the Aborigines for warming water. *Journal and Proceedings of the Royal Society of New South Wales*. Vol. 35, pp. 213–6.

Mathews, R.H. 1903. Languages of the New England Aborigines, New South Wales. *Proceedings of the American Philosophical Society*. Vol. 42, no. 173, pp. 249–63.

Mathews, R.H. 1904. Ethnological notes on the Aboriginal tribes of New South Wales and Victoria. *Journal of the Royal Society of New South Wales*. Vol. 38, pp. 203–381.

Mathews, R.H. 1908. Aboriginal navigation. *Proceedings and Transactions of the Royal Geographical Society of Australasia, Queensland Branch*. Vol. 23, pp. 66–81.

Matthews, D.J. 1997. The quandong (*Santalum acuminatum*). *Australian Bushfoods Magazine*. Vol. 1, pp. 14–5.

Meagher, S.J. 1974. The food sources of the Aborigines of the south-west of Western Australia. *Records of the Western Australian Museum*. Vol. 3, pt 1, pp. 14–65.

Meagher, S.J. & Ride, W.D.L. 1980. Use of natural resources by the Aborigines of south-western Australia. Pp. 66–80 in R.M. Berndt & C.H. Berndt (eds) *Aborigines of the west: Their past and their present*. University of Western Australia Press, Perth.

Meehan (Hiatt), B. 1977. Man does not live by calories alone: The role of shellfish in a coastal cuisine. Pp. 493–532 in J. Allen, J. Golson & R. Jones (eds) *Sunda and Sahul*. Academic Press, London.

Meehan (Hiatt), B. 1979. Fire to steel: Aboriginal exploitation of pandanus and some wider implications (Gidjingali speaking Aborigines of the Anbarra community). *Occasional Papers in Anthropology, Anthropology Museum, University of Queensland*. Vol. 9, pp. 73–96.

Meehan (Hiatt), B. 1982. *Shell bed to shell midden*. Australian Institute of Aboriginal Studies, Canberra.

Meggitt, M.J. 1962. *Desert people: A study of the Walbiri people of Central Australia*. Angus & Robertson, Sydney.

Meinig, D.W. (ed) 1979. *The interpretation of ordinary landscapes*. Oxford University Press, Oxford.

Memmott, P. 1982. Rainbows, story places, and malkri sickness in the North Wellesley Islands. *Oceania*. Vol. 53, pt 2, pp. 163–82.

Memmott, P., Evans, N., Robins, R. & Lilley, I. 2006. Understanding isolation and change in island human populations through a study of indigenous cultural patterns in the Gulf of Carpentaria. *Transactions of the Royal Society of South Australia*. Vol. 130, pt 1, pp. 29–47.

Menzies, I. 2003. *Aboriginal fire stories*. The author and NSW Fire Brigades, Sydney.

Merrilees, D. 1968. Man the destroyer: Late Quaternary changes in the Australian marsupial fauna. *Journal and Proceedings of the Royal Society of Western Australia*. Vol. 51, pp. 1–24.

Meyer, H.A.E. 1843. *Vocabulary of the language spoken by the Aborigines of South Australia*. Allen, Adelaide.

Meyer, H.A.E. 1846. Manners and customs of the Aborigines of the Encounter Bay tribe, South Australia. Reprinted as pp. 183–206 in J.D. Woods (ed) 1879. *The Native Tribes of South Australia*. E.S. Wigg, Adelaide.

Miers, G. 2004. *Cultivation and sustainable wild harvest of bushfoods by Aboriginal communities in Central Australia*. Research paper No. W03/124. Rural Industries Research and Development Corporation, Canberra.

Mitchell, A.A. & Wilcox, D.G. 1994. *Arid shrubland plants of Western Australia*. Second edition. University of Western Australia Press and Department of Agriculture, Western Australia, Perth.

Mitchell, T.L. 1848. *Journal of an expedition into the interior of tropical Australia, in search of a route from Sydney to the Gulf of Carpentaria*. Longman, Brown, Green and Longmans, London.

Mollison, B.C. 1974. *A synopsis of data on Tasmanian Aboriginal people*. Second edition. University of Tasmania, Hobart.

Moore, D.R. 1979. *Islanders and Aborigines at Cape York*. Australian Institute of Aboriginal Studies, Canberra and Humanities Press, New Jersey.

Moore, G.H. 1884. *A descriptive vocabulary of the language in common use amongst the Aborigines of Western Australia*. Second edition. G.F. Moore, Sydney.

Moorehead, A. 1963. *Cooper's Creek*. Hamish Hamilton, London.

Moorehead, A. 1968. *The fatal impact*. Penguin Books, Melbourne.

Morphy, H. 1998. *Aboriginal art*. Phaidon Press, London.

Morris, P.F. 1943. Some vegetable foods of the Wimmera and Mallee. *Victorian Naturalist*. Vol. 1, pp. 167–70.

Morse, J. 1997. CSIRO on acacias. *Australian Bushfoods Magazine*. Vol. 1, p.28.

Morwood, M.J. 2002. *Visions from the past: The archaeology of Australian Aboriginal art*. Allen & Unwin, Sydney.

Mountford, C.P. 1941. An unrecorded method of manufacturing wooden implements by simple stone tools. *Transactions of the Royal Society of South Australia*. Vol. 65, no. 2, pp. 312–6.

Mountford, C.P. 1956. *Records of the American–Australian Scientific Expedition to Arnhem Land. Vol. 1. Art, myth and symbolism*. Melbourne University Press, Melbourne.

Mountford, C.P. 1958. *The Tiwi: Their art, myth and ceremony*. Phoenix House, London.

Mountford, C.P. 1969. *The dawn of time*. Rigby, Adelaide.

Mountford, C.P. 1970. *The Dreamtime*. Revised edition. Rigby, Adelaide.

Mountford, C.P. 1971. *The first sunrise*. Rigby, Adelaide.

Mountford, C.P. 1976. *Before time began*. Thomas Nelson, Melbourne.

Mountford, C.P. & Berndt, R.M. 1941. Making fire by percussion in Australia. *Oceania*. Vol. 11, no. 4, pp. 342–4.

Mowaljarlai, D. & Malnic, J. 1993. *Yorro Yorro: Aboriginal creation and the renewal of nature: Rock paintings and stories from the Australian Kimberley*. Inner Traditions, Rochester, Vermont.

Mühlhäusler, P. 2003. *Language of environment, environment of language: A course in ecolinguistics*. Battlebridge, London.

Mühlhäusler, P. & Fill, A. (eds) 2001. *The ecolinguistics reader: Language, ecology, and environment*. Continuum, London.

Muloin, S., Zeppel, H. & Higginbottom, K. 2001. *Indigenous wildlife tourism in Australia: Wildlife attractions, cultural interpretation and indigenous involvement*. Wildlife Tourism Research Report Series no. 15. Cooperative Research Centre for Sustainable Tourism, Gold Coast, Queensland.

Mulvaney, D.J. 1985. The Darwinian perspective. Pp. 68–75 in I. Donaldson & T. Donaldson (eds) *Seeing the first Australians*. Allen & Unwin, Sydney.

Mulvaney, D.J. 2002. 'Difficult to found an opinion': 1788 Aboriginal population estimates. Pp. 1–8 in G. Briscoe & L. Smith (eds) *The Aboriginal population revisited: 70 000 years to the present*. Aboriginal History Monograph No. 10. Aboriginal History, Canberra.

Mulvaney, D.J. & Kamminga, J. 1999. *Prehistory of Australia*. Allen & Unwin, Sydney.

Mulvaney, D.J., Morphy, H. & Petch, A. (eds) 1997. *My dear Spencer: The letters of F.J. Gillen to Baldwin Spencer*. Hyland House, Melbourne.

Murgatroyd, S. 2002. *The dig tree: The story of Burke and Wills*. Text Publishing, Melbourne.

Murray, P. 1991. The Pleistocene megafauna of Australia. Pp. 1071–164 in P. Vickers-Rich, J.M. Monaghan, R.F. Baird & T.H. Rich (eds) *Vertebrate palaeontology of Australia*. Melbourne University Press, Melbourne.

Murray, P. & Vickers-Rich, P. 2003. *Magnificent mihirungs: The colossal flightless birds of the Australian Dreamtime*. Indiana University Press, Bloomington.

Murray-Darling Basin Commission. 2003. *Cost of dryland and urban salinity in the Murray-Darling Basin*. Electronic resource. Murray-Darling Basin Commission, Canberra.

Mutitjulu Community & Baker, L. 1996. *Mingkiri: A natural history of Uluru by the Mutitjulu community*. Institute for Aboriginal Development Press, Alice Springs.

Myers, F.R. 1986a. *Pintupi country, Pintupi self*. Australian Institute of Aboriginal Studies, Canberra.

Myers, F.R. 1986b. Always ask: Resource use and land ownership among Pintupi Aborigines of the Australian Western Desert. Pp. 173–95 in N.M. Williams & E.S. Hunn (eds) *Resource managers: North American and Australian hunter-gatherers*. Australian Institute of Aboriginal Studies, Canberra.

Nabhan, G.P., Joaquin, A., Laney, N. & Dahl, K. 1995. Sharing the benefits of plant resources and indigenous scientific knowledge. Pp. 186–208 in S.B. Brush & D. Stabinsky (eds) *Valuing local knowledge: Indigenous people and intellectual property rights*. Island Press, Washington D.C.

Nash, D. 1994. *Aboriginal plant use in south-eastern Australia*. Education Service, Australian National Botanic Gardens, Canberra.

Nash, D. 1997. Comparative flora terminology of the central Northern Territory. Pp. 187–206 in P. McConvell & N. Evans (eds) *Archaeology and linguistics: Aboriginal Australia in global perspective*. Oxford University Press, Melbourne.

Nathan, P. & Japanangka, D.L. 1983. *Health business*. Heinemann Educational, Richmond, Victoria.

Newland, S. 1890. Parkengees or Aboriginal tribes on the Darling River. *Proceedings of the Royal Geographical Society of Australasia. South Australian Branch*. Vol. 2, pp. 20–32. Also booklet, pp. 1–16.

Newland, S. 1922. The annual address of the president. *Proceedings of the Royal Geographical Society of Australasia. South Australian Branch*. Vol. 22, pp. 1–64.

Newsome, A.E. 1980. The eco-mythology of the red kangaroo in Central Australia. *Mankind.* Vol. 12, no. 4, pp. 327–33.

Newsome, A.E., Nicholls, N. & Hobbs, T. 1996. The uncertain climate and its biotic consequences. Pp. 287–304 in S.R. Morton & D.J. Mulvaney (eds) *Exploring Central Australia: Society, the environment and the 1894 Horn Expedition.* Surrey Beatty & Sons, Chipping Norton, New South Wales.

Ngaanyatjarra Pitjantjatjara Yankunytjatjara Women's Council Aboriginal Corporation. 2003. *Ngangkari work — Anangu way: Traditional healers of Central Australia.* Ngaanyatjarra Pitjantjatjara Yankunytjatjara Women's Council Aboriginal Corporation, Alice Springs.

Nicholson, P.H. 1981. Fire and the Australian Aborigine. Pp. 55–76 in A.M. Gill, R.H. Groves & I.R. Noble (eds) *Fire and the Australian biota.* Australian Academy of Science, Canberra.

Nind, S. 1831. Description of the natives of King George's Sound (Swan River Colony) and adjoining country. *Royal Geographical Journal.* Vol. 1, pp. 21–51.

Noble, J.C. & Kimber, R.G. 1997. On the ethno-ecology of mallee root-water. *Aboriginal History.* Vol. 21, pp. 170–202.

Nyinkka Nyunyu 2003. *Mayi: Bush tucker recipes.* Nyinkka Nyunyu Information Series No. 3. Booklet, 8 pp. Nyinkka Nyunyu Art and Culture Centre, Tennant Creek.

O'Connell, J.F., Latz, P.K. & Barnett, P. 1983. Traditional and modern plant use among the Alyawara of Central Australia. *Economic Botany.* Vol. 37, pt 1, pp. 80–109.

O'Grady, G.N. 1956. A secret language of Western Australia — a note. *Oceania.* Vol. 27, no. 2, pp. 158–9.

O'Hare, P. & Vock, N.T. 1990. *Growing macadamias in Queensland.* Department of Primary Industries and Queensland Government Press, Brisbane.

Olive Pink Botanic Garden. No date. *Olive Pink Botanic Garden, Alice Springs.* The authors, Alice Springs.

Olsen, S. 2003. Mapping human history: Genes, race, and our common origins. Mariner Books, Houghton Mifflin, New York.

Oppenheimer, S. 2003. *Out of Eden: The peopling of the world.* Constable London.

Orchard, A.E. & Wilson, A.J.G. 1999. Utilisation of the Australian flora. Pp. 437–66 in A.E. Orchard (ed) *Australian biological resources study: Flora of Australia.* Volume 1. Introduction. Second edition. Bureau of Fauna and Flora, Canberra.

Oxley, J. 1820. *Journals of two expeditions into the interior of New South Wales, undertaken by order of the British Government in the years 1817–18.* John Murray, London.

Paczkowska, G. & Chapman, A.R. (ed) 2000. *The Western Australian flora: A descriptive catalogue.* Department of Conservation and Land Management's WA Herbarium, the Wildflower Society of Western Australia (Inc) and the Botanic Gardens and Parks Authority, Perth.

Paddy, E., Paddy, S. & Smith, M. 1987. *Boonja bardak korn: All trees are good for something.* Community Report 87/1. Anthropology Department, Western Australian Museum, Perth.

Palmer, K. 1999a. *Swinging the billy: Indigenous and other cooking styles of Australian bush cooking.* Aboriginal Studies Press, Canberra.

Palmer, K. 1999b. Favourite foods and the fight for country: Witchetty grubs and the southern Pitjantjatjara. *Aboriginal History.* Vol. 23, pp. 51–60.

Pardoe, C. 1995. Riverine, biological and cultural evolution in southeastern Australia. *Antiquity.* Vol. 69, (Special no. 265), pp. 696–713.

Parker, A. 1980. An ethnobotany of the Western Desert, Leonora, Western Australia, 1977. *Australian Institute of Aboriginal Studies Newsletter. New Series.* No. 13. March 1980. Pp. 37–42.

Parker, K. Langloh. 1953. *Australian legendary tales.* Republished from the 1896 edition as a selection edited by H. Drake-Brockman. Angus & Robertson, Sydney.

Parsons, W.J. 1981. The history of introduced weeds. Pp. 179–93 in D.J. Carr & S.G.M. Carr (eds) *Plants and man in Australia.* Academic Press, Sydney.

Pate, J.S. & Dixon, K.W. 1982. *Tuberous, cormous and bulbous plants: Biology of an adaptive strategy in Western Australia.* University of Western Australia Press, Nedlands, Western Australia.

Peterson, N. 1970. Buluwandi: A Central Australian ceremony for the resolution of conflict. Pp. 200–15 in R.M. Berndt (ed) *Australian Aboriginal anthropology.* University of Western Australia Press, Perth.

Peterson, N. 1976. The natural and cultural areas of Aboriginal Australia. Pp. 50–71 in N. Peterson (ed) *Tribes and boundaries in Australia.* Social Anthropology Series no. 10. Australian Institute of Aboriginal Studies, Canberra.

Peterson, N. 1977. Aboriginal uses of Australian Solanaceae. Pp. 171–88 in J.G. Hawkes, R.N. Lester & A.D. Skelding (eds) *The biology and taxonomy of Solanaceae.* Academic Press, London.

Peterson, N. & Lampert, R. 1985. A Central Australian ochre mine. *Records of the Australian Museum.* Vol. 37, no. 1, pp. 1–9.

Petheram, R.J. & Kok, B. 1983. *Plants of the Kimberley Region of Western Australia.* University of Western Australia Press for the Rangeland Management Branch,

Department of Agriculture, Perth.

Petrie, T. 1932. *Tom Petrie's reminiscences of early Queensland.* Second edition. Angus & Robertson, Sydney.

Phelps, D.G. 1997. *Feasibility of a sustainable bushfoods industry in Western Queensland.* Research paper No. 97/011. Rural Industries Research and Development Corporation, Canberra.

Phelps, W. & Phelps, D. 1997. Desert lime. *Australian Bushfoods Magazine.* Vol. 2, pp. 16–7.

Pitt-Rivers, G.H.L. 1927. *The clash of culture and the contact of races.* George Routledge & Sons, London.

Plomley, N.J.B. 1966. *Friendly mission: The Tasmanian journals and papers of George Augustus Robinson, 1829–1834.* Tasmanian Historical Research Association, Hobart.

Plomley, N.J.B. 1976. *A word-list of the Tasmanian Aboriginal languages.* Author and Government of Tasmania, Launceston, Tasmania.

Plomley, N.J.B. 1987. *Weep in silence: A history of the Flinders Island Aboriginal settlement with the Flinders Island journal of George Augustus Robinson, 1835–1839.* Blubber Head Press, Hobart.

Plomley, N.J.B. & Cameron, M. 1993. Plant foods of the Tasmanian Aborigines. *Records of the Queen Victoria Museum.* Vol. 101, pp. 1–27.

Plooij, D. & O'Brien, G. 1973. *Culture training manual for technical workers in Aboriginal communities: (Mechanics, stockmen, builders and storemen).* School of Social Sciences, Flinders University, Adelaide.

Pollan, M. 2002. *The botany of desire: A plant's-eye view of the world.* Bloomsbury Publishing, London.

Poiner, G. 1976. The process of the year among Aborigines of the central and south coast of New South Wales. *Archaeology and Physical Anthropology in Oceania.* Vol. 11, no. 3, pp. 186–206.

Popenoe, W. 1974. *Manual of tropical and subtropical fruits, excluding the banana, coconut, pineapple, citrus fruits, olive, and fig.* Hafner Press, New York.

Posey, D.A. 1990. Intellectual property rights: What is the position of ethnobiology? *Journal of Ethnobiology.* Vol. 10, pt 1, pp. 93–8.

Povinelli, E.A. 1990. Emiyenggal and Batjemal folk classifications, Cox Peninsula, Northern Territory: 'Figuring' continuity and contingency. *Australian Aboriginal Studies.* No. 2, pp. 53–9.

Povinelli, E.A. 1993. *Labor's lot: The power, history and culture of Aboriginal action.* University of Chicago Press, Chicago.

Prance, G.T., Chadwick, D.J. & Marsh, J. (eds) 1994. *Ethnobotany and the search for new drugs.* J. Wiley, Chichester, New York.

Press, A.J., Lea, D., Webb, A. & Graham, A. (eds) 1995. *Kakadu: Natural and cultural heritage and management.* Australian Nature Conservation Agency and the North Australia Research Unit, Australian National University, Darwin.

Puruntatameri, J. 2001. *Tiwi plants and animals: Aboriginal flora and fauna knowledge from Bathurst and Melville Islands, northern Australia.* Parks and Wildlife Commission of the Northern Territory and Tiwi Land Council, Darwin.

Pyke, M. 1968. *Food and society.* John Murray, London.

Pyne, S.J. 1991. *Burning bush: A fire history of Australia.* Holt, New York.

Pyne, S.J. 1997. Frontiers of fire. Pp. 19–34 in T. Griffiths & L. Robin (eds) *Ecology and empire: Environmental history of settler societies.* Melbourne University Press, Melbourne.

Rae, C.J., Lamprell, V.J., Lion R.J. & Rae, A.M. 1982. The role of bush foods in contemporary Aboriginal diets. *Proceedings of the Nutrition Society of Australia.* Vol. 7, pp. 45–9.

Ramson, W.S. (ed). 1988. *The Australian national dictionary: A dictionary of Australianisms on historical principles.* Oxford University Press, Oxford.

Ratzel, F. 1896. *The history of mankind.* Translated from the second German edition by A.J. Butler. Macmillan, London.

Raymond, E. & Wightman, G.M. 1999. *Wardaman ethnobiology.* Northern Territory Botanical Bulletin No. 25. Parks and Wildlife Commission of the Northern Territory and the Northern Territory University, Darwin.

Read, P. & Japaljarri, E.J. 1978. The price of tobacco: The journey of the Warlmala to Wave Hill, 1928. *Aboriginal History.* Vol. 2, pt 2, pp. 140–8.

Reid, A. 1995a. *Banksias and bilbies: Seasons of Australia.* Gould League, Melbourne.

Reid, A. 1995b. A plan for all seasons. *Habitat Australia.* Vol. 23, no. 2, pp. 14–5.

Reid, E. 1977. *The records of Western Australian plants used by Aboriginals as medicinal agents.* Reprinted 1986. School of Pharmacy, Western Australian Institute of Technology, Perth.

Reid, J.C. 1978a. The role of the *Marrnggitji* in contemporary health care. *Oceania.* Vol. 49, no. 2, pp. 96–109.

Reid, J.C. 1978b. Change in the indigenous medical system of an Aboriginal community. *Australian Institute of Aboriginal Studies Newsletter.* Vol. 9, pp. 61–72.

Reid, J.C. 1979. Health as harmony, sickness as conflict. *Hemisphere.* Vol. 23, pt

4, pp. 194–9.

Reid, J.C. (ed) 1982. *Body, land and spirit: Health and healing in Aboriginal society*. University of Queensland Press, St Lucia, Queensland.

Reid, J.C. 1983. *Sorcerers and healing spirits: Continuity and change in an Aboriginal medical system*. Australian National University Press, Canberra.

Reuther, J.G. 1981. *The Diari*. Volumes 1 to 13. Translated by P.A. Scherer, T. Schwarzchild & L. Hercus. Original in the S.A. Museum Archives. Australian Institute of Aboriginal Studies, Canberra.

Reynolds, H. 1989. *Dispossession: Black Australians and white invaders*. Allen & Unwin, Sydney.

Reynolds, H. 1990. *With the white people*. Penguin, Melbourne.

Richardson, A. & Lugg, J. No date. *Botanical guide to the Adelaide Zoo: Bush food*. Adelaide Zoo, Adelaide.

Ridley, H.N. 1922–25. *Flora of the Malay Peninsula*. 5 volumes. L. Reeve & Co., London.

Ridley, H.N. 1930. *Dispersal of plants throughout the world*. L. Reeve & Co., London.

Rigsby, B. 1998. A survey of property theory and tenure types. Pp. 22–46 in N. Peterson & B. Rigsby (eds) *Customary marine tenure in Australia*. Oceania Monograph no. 48. University of Sydney, Sydney.

Rix, C.E. 1978. *Royal Zoological Society of South Australia, 1878–1978*. Royal Zoological Society of South Australia, Adelaide.

Roberts, J., Fisher, C.J., Gibson, R. & Popp, T. 1995. *A guide to traditional Aboriginal rainforest plant use by the Kuku Yalanji of the Mossman Gorge*. Bamanga Bubu Ngadimunku Inc., Mossman, Queensland.

Roberts, M.J. & Roberts, A. 1975. *Dreamtime heritage*. Rigby, Adelaide.

Roberts, N., Randall, B., Barker, J., Ward, M. & Owen, P. 1980. Wild foods of New South Wales. *Aboriginal Health Worker*. Vol. 4, pt 1, pp. 13–8.

Roberts, R.G., Flannery, T.F., Ayliffe, L.K., Yoshida, H., Olley, J.M., Prideaux, G.J., Laslett, G.M., Baynes, A., Smith, M.A., Jones, R. & Smith, B.L. 2001. New ages for the last of the Australian megafauna: Continent-wide extinction about 46,000 years ago. *Science*. Vol. 292, pp. 1888–92.

Robins, J 1996. *Wild lime: Cooking from the bushfood garden*. Allen & Unwin, Sydney.

Robson, M.K. 1986. *Keeping the culture alive*. Aboriginal Keeping Place, Hamilton and Western District Museum, Victoria.

Roff, D. 1983. Bushtucker. *Geo*. Vol. 5, pt 3, pp. 70–87.

Roheim, G. 1974. *Children of the desert: The western tribes of Central Australia*. Edited with an introduction by Werner Muensterberger. Basic Books, New York.

Rolls, E. 1984. *They all ran wild: The animals and plants that plague Australia*. Angus & Robertson, Sydney.

Rolls, E. 1997. The nature of Australia. Pp. 35–45 in T. Griffiths & L. Robin (eds) *Ecology and empire: Environmental history of settler societies*. Melbourne University Press, Melbourne.

Rolls, E. 2002. *Visions of Australia. Impressions of the landscape, 1642–1910*. Lothian Books, Melbourne.

Rose, D. Bird 1984. *Preliminary report: Ethnobotany in the Bungles*. Centre for Resource and Environmental Studies, Canberra.

Rose, D. Bird 1987. *Bush medicines: A Ngarinman and Bilinara pharmacopoeia*. Australian Institute of Aboriginal Studies, Canberra.

Rose, D. Bird 1988. Ethnobotany. *The Aboriginal Health Worker*. Vol. 12, pt 3, pp. 21–5.

Rose, D. Bird 1992. *Dingo makes us human: Life and land in an Aboriginal Australian culture*. Cambridge University Press, Cambridge.

Rose, D. Bird (ed) 1995. *Country in flames: Proceedings of the 1994 Symposium on Biodiversity and Fire in North Australia*. Biodiversity Unit, Department of the Environment, Sport and Territories and the North Australia Research Unit, Canberra and Darwin.

Rose, D. Bird 1996. *Nourishing terrains: Australian Aboriginal views of landscape and wilderness*. Australian Heritage Commission, Canberra.

Rose, D. Bird 2002. *Country of the heart: An indigenous Australian homeland*. Aboriginal Studies Press, Canberra.

Rose, D. Bird 2005. An indigenous philosophical ecology: Situating the human. *Australian Journal of Anthropology*. Vol. 16, no. 3, special issue 17, pp. 294–305.

Rose, F.G.G. 1987. *The traditional mode of production of the Australian Aborigines*. Angus & Robertson, Sydney.

Ross, A., Donnelly, T. & Wasson, R. 1992. The people of the arid zone: Human-environment interactions. Pp. 76–114 in J. Dodson (ed) *The naive lands: Prehistory and environmental change in Australia and the south-west Pacific*. Longman Cheshire, Melbourne.

Ross, A. & Pickering, K. 2002. The politics of reintegrating Australian Aboriginal and American Indian indigenous knowledge into resource management: The dynamics of resource appropriation and cultural revival. *Human Ecology*. Vol. 30, no. 2, pp. 187–214.

Roth, H. Ling 1887. On the origin of agriculture. *Journal of the Anthropological Institute of Great Britain and Ireland*. Vol. 16, pp. 102–36.

Roth, H. Ling 1899. *The Aborigines of Tasmania*. Second edition. 1968 facsimile. Fullers Bookshop, Hobart.

Roth, W.E. 1897. *Ethnological studies among the north-west-central Queensland Aborigines*. Queensland Government Printer, Brisbane.

Roth, W.E. 1901a. *North Queensland ethnography: String, and other forms of strand: Basketry, woven bag- and net-work. Bulletin 1*. Government Printer, Brisbane.

Roth, W.E. 1901b. *North Queensland ethnography: Food: Its search, capture, and preparation. Bulletin 3*. Government Printer, Brisbane.

Roth, W.E. 1902. *North Queensland ethnography: Games, sports and amusements. Bulletin 4*. Government Printer, Brisbane.

Roth, W.E. 1903a. *North Queensland ethnography: Superstition, magic and medicine. Bulletin 5*. Government Printer, Brisbane.

Roth, W.E. 1903b. Notes of savage life in the early days of West Australian settlement. *Proceedings of the Royal Society of Queensland*. Vol. 17, pp. 45–69.

Roth, W.E. 1904. *North Queensland ethnography: Domestic implements, arts, and manufactures. Bulletin 7*. Government Printer, Brisbane.

Roth, W.E. 1909. *North Queensland ethnography: Fighting weapons. Bulletin 13*. Government Printer, Brisbane.

Roth, W.E. 1910. *North Queensland ethnography: Decoration, deformation, and clothing. Bulletin 15*. Government Printer, Brisbane.

Rowland, M.J. 2002. Geophagy: An assessment of implications for the development of Australian indigenous plant processing technologies. *Australian Aboriginal Studies*. No. 1, pp. 51–66.

Rowley, C.D. 1972a. *The destruction of Aboriginal society*. Pelican, Melbourne.

Rowley, C.D. 1972b. *The remote Aborigines*. Pelican, Melbourne.

Rowse, T. 1992. *Remote possibilities: The Aboriginal domain and the administrative imagination*. North Australian Research Unit, Australian National University, Canberra.

Rowse, T. 2002. *Indigenous futures: Choice and development for Aboriginal and Islander Australia*. University of New South Wales Press, Sydney.

Rudder, J.C. 1978–79. Classification of the natural world among the Yolngu, Northern Territory, Australia. *Ethnomedicine*. 1978–79, pp. 349–60.

Rural Industries Research and Development Corporation. 1998. *R & D plan for the bushfood industry 1998–2002*. Research paper No. 98/111. Rural Industries Research and Development Corporation, Barton, Australian Capital Territory.

Russell-Smith, J. 1985. Studies in the jungle: People, fire and monsoon forest. Pp. 241–67 in R. Jones (ed) *Archaeological research in Kakadu National Park*. Australian National Parks and Wildlife Service, Canberra.

Ryan, E. 2002. Blown to Witewitekalk: Placenames and cultural landscapes in north-west Victoria. Pp. 157–63 in L. Hercus, F. Hodges & J. Simpson (eds) *The land is a map: Placenames of indigenous origin in Australia*. Pandanus Books, Australian National University, Canberra.

Sackett, L. 1979. The pursuit of prominence: Hunting in an Australian Aboriginal community. *Anthropologica*. Vol. 21, pt 2, pp. 223–46.

Sagona, A. (ed) 1994. *Bruising the red earth: Ochre mining and ritual in Aboriginal Tasmania*. Melbourne University Press, Melbourne.

Satterthwait, D.F. & Satterthwait, L.D. 1983. Plants and Aboriginal life. Pp. 11–2 in B.D. Morley & H.R. Toelken (eds) *Flowering plants in Australia*. Rigby Publishers, Sydney.

Sauer, C.O. 1963. *Plant and animal exchanges between the Old and the New Worlds*. Edited and compiled by R.M. Newcomb. Los Angeles State College, Los Angeles.

Scarlett, N.H., White, N. & Reid, J. 1982. Bush medicines: The pharmacopoeia of the Yolngu of Arnhem Land. Pp. 154–91 in J. Reid (ed) *Body, land and spirit: Health and healing in Aboriginal society*. University of Queensland Press, St Lucia, Queensland.

Schmidt, A. 1993. *The loss of Australia's Aboriginal language heritage*. Aboriginal Studies Press, Canberra.

Schulze, L. 1891. The Aborigines of the upper and middle Finke River: Their habits and customs, with introductory notes on the physical and natural-history features of the country. *Transactions, Proceedings and Report of the Royal Society of South Australia*. Vol. 14, pp. 210–46.

Schürmann, C.W. 1844. *Vocabulary of the Parnkalla language*. Dehane, Adelaide.

Schürmann, C.W. 1846. *The Aboriginal tribes of Port Lincoln in South Australia, their mode of life, manners, customs …* Reprinted in J.D. Woods (ed) 1879. *The Native Tribes of South Australia*. Dehane, Adelaide.

Scott, M.P. 1972. Some Aboriginal food plants of the Ashburton district, Western Australia. *Western Australian Naturalist*. Vol. 12, pt 4, pp. 94–6.

Seddon, G. 1972. *Sense of place: A response to an environment, the Swan coastal plain Western Australia*. University of Western Australia Press, Nedlands, Western Australia.

Semple, S.J. 1998. The antiviral properties of traditional Australian Aboriginal medicines. *Proceedings of the Nutritional Society of Australia*. Vol. 22, pp. 1–6.

Semple, S.J., Reynolds, G.D., O'Leary, M.C. & Flower, R.L.P. 1998. Screening of Australian medicinal plants for antiviral activity. *Journal of Ethnopharmacology*. Vol. 60, pp. 163–72.

Seton, K.A. & Bradley, J.J. 2004. 'When you have no law you are nothing': Cane toads, social consequences and management issues. *Asia Pacific Journal of Anthropology*. Vol. 5, no. 3, pp. 205–25.

Sharp. N. 1993. *Stars of Tagai: The Torres Strait Islanders*. Aboriginal Studies Press, Canberra.

Sharp, N. 2002. *Saltwater people: The waves of memory*. Allen & Unwin, Sydney.

Shepherdson, I.G. (Ella) 1981. *Half a century in Arnhem Land*. Ella and Harold Shepherdson, One Tree Hill, South Australia.

Silberbauer, G.B. 1971. Ecology of the Ernabella Aboriginal community. *Anthropological Forum*. Vol. 3, no. 1, pp. 21–36.

Silberbauer, G.B. 1981. *Hunter and habitat in the Central Kalahari Desert*. Cambridge University Press, Cambridge.

Simek, R. 2003. Germanic and Norse mythology. Pp. 232–49 in J. Parker & J. Stanton (eds) *Mythology: Myths, legends, and fantasies*. Global Book Publishing, Willoughby, New South Wales.

Simpson, J. 1998. Introduction. Pp. 1–13 in J. Simpson & L. Hercus (eds) *Aboriginal portraits of 19th century South Australia*. Aboriginal History Monograph. Australian National University, Canberra.

Sims, M. 1978. Tiwi cosmology. Pp. 164–7 in L.R. Hiatt (ed) *Australian Aboriginal concepts*. Australian Institute of Aboriginal Studies, Canberra.

Singh, G., Kershaw, A.P. & Clark, R. 1981. Quaternary vegetation and fire history in Australia. Pp. 23–54 in A.M. Gill, R.H. Groves & I.R. Noble (eds) *Fire and the Australian biota*. Australian Academy of Science, Canberra.

Smith, C. 1880. *The Booandik tribe of South Australian Aborigines*. South Australian Government Printer, Adelaide.

Smith, H. 1990. *Tiwi: The life and art of Australia's Tiwi people*. Angus & Robertson, Sydney.

Smith, K. & Smith, I. 1999. *Grow your own bushfoods*. New Holland Publishers, Sydney.

Smith, L.R. 1980. *The Aboriginal population of Australia*. Aborigines in Australia Society, no. 14. Academy of the Social Sciences. Australian National University Press, Canberra.

Smith, M. 1982. Late Pleistocene zamia exploitation in southern Western Australia. *Archaeology in Oceania*. Vol. 17, pp. 117–21.

Smith, M. 1996. Revisiting Pleistocene *Macrozamia*. *Australian Archaeology*. Vol. 42, pp. 52–3.

Smith, M. & Kalotas, A.C. 1985. Bardi plants: An annotated list of plants and their use by the Bardi Aborigines of Dampierland, in north-western Australia. *Records of the Western Australian Museum*. Vol. 12, pt 3, pp. 317–59.

Smith, M.A. 1986. The antiquity of seed grinding in Central Australia. *Archaeology in Oceania*. Vol. 21, pp. 29–39.

Smith, M.A. 1988. Central Australian seed grinding implements and Pleistocene grindstones. Pp. 94–108 in B. Meehan and R. Jones (eds) *Archaeology with ethnography: An Australian perspective*. Prehistory Pacific Studies, Australian National University, Canberra.

Smith, N.M. 1991. Ethnographic field notes from the Northern Territory, Australia. *Journal of the Adelaide Botanical Gardens*. Vol. 14, pt 1, pp. 1–65.

Smith, N.M., Wididburu, B., Harrington, R.N. & Wightman, G.M. 1993. *Ngarinyman ethnobotany: Aboriginal plant use from the Victoria River area, northern Australia*. Northern Territory Botanical Bulletin No. 16. Conservation Commission of the Northern Territory, Darwin.

Smith, N.M. & Wightman, G.M. 1990. *Ethnobotanical notes from Belyuen, Northern Territory, Australia*. Northern Territory Botanical Bulletin No. 10. Conservation Commission of the Northern Territory, Darwin.

Smith, P.A. & Smith, R.M. 1999. Diets in transition: Hunter-gatherer to station diet and station diet to the self-select store diet. *Human Ecology*. Vol. 27, pp. 115–33.

Smith, W. Ramsay 1930. *Myths and legends of the Australian Aboriginals*. Harrap, Sydney.

Smyth, D. 1982. Aboriginal occupation of inland Cape York Peninsula: A report on ethnobotanical fieldwork along the Archer River in September 1981. *Australian Institute of Aboriginal Studies Newsletter*. Vol. 17, pp. 8–13.

Smyth, D. 1993. *A voice in all places: Aboriginal and Torres Strait Islander interests in Australia's coastal zone*. Revised edition. Resource Assessment Commission, Canberra.

Smyth, D., Taylor, P., Willis, A. (eds) 1986. *Aboriginal ranger training and employment in Australia: Proceedings of the First National Workshop July 1985*. Australian National Parks and Wildlife Service, Canberra.

Smyth, R. Brough 1878. *The Aborigines of Victoria*. 2 volumes. Victorian Government Printer, Melbourne.

Soong, F.S. 1983. Role of the margidbu (traditional healer) in western Arnhem Land. *Medical Journal of Australia*. Vol. 1, 474–7.

South Australian Department of Education, Training and Employment. 2001. *Ngarrindjeri Dreaming stories*. DETE, Adelaide.

Specht, R.L. 1958. An introduction to the ethnobotany of Arnhem Land. Pp. 479–503 in R.L. Specht & C.P. Mountford (eds) *Records of the American-Australian Scientific Expedition to Arnhem Land*. Volume 3. Melbourne University Press, Melbourne.

Specht, R.L. 1972. *The vegetation of South Australia*. Second edition. South Australian Government Printer, Adelaide.

Spencer, W.B. (ed) 1896. *Report on the work of the Horn Scientific Expedition to Central Australia*. 4 volumes. Melville, Mullen & Slade, Melbourne.

Spencer, W.B. 1918. What is nardoo? *Victorian Naturalist*. Vol. 14, pp. 170–2; Vol. 15, pp. 8–15.

Spencer, W.B. & Gillen, F.J. 1899. *The native tribes of Central Australia*. Macmillan, London.

Spencer, W.B. & Gillen, F.J. 1904. *The northern tribes of Central Australia*. Macmillan, London.

Spencer, W.B. & Gillen, F.J. 1912. *Across Australia*. 2 volumes. Macmillan, London.

Spencer, W.B. & Gillen, F.J. 1927. *The Arunta. A study of a stone age people*. 2 volumes. Macmillan, London.

Stack, E.M. 1989. Aboriginal pharmacopoeia. *Occasional Papers (Northern Territory Library Service)*. Vol. 10, pp. 1–7.

Stanbridge, W.E. 1857. On the astronomy and mythology of the Aborigines of Victoria. *Philosophical Institute of Victoria, Transactions*. Vol2, pp. 137–40.

Stanbridge. W.E. 1861. Some particulars on the general characteristics, astronomy, and mythology of the tribes in the central part of Victoria, southern Australia. *Transactions of the Ethnological Society of London*. Vol. 1, pp. 286–304.

Stanley, T.D. & Ross, E.M. 1983–89. *Flora of south-eastern Queensland*. 3 volumes. Queensland Department of Primary Industries, Brisbane.

Stanner, W.E.H. 1936. Murinbata kinship and totemism. *Oceania*. Vol. 7, pt 2, pp. 186–216.

Stanner, W.E.H. 1953 (1979). The Dreaming. Pp. 23–40 in *White man got no Dreaming*. Australian National University Press, Canberra.

Stapleton, M. & McDonald, P. 1981. *Christmas in the colonies*. David Ell Press & Historic Houses Trust of New South Wales, Sydney.

Steele, J.G. 1984. *Aboriginal pathways in southeast Queensland and the Richmond River*. University of Queensland Press, St Lucia, Queensland.

Stephens, E. 1890. The Aborigines of Australia. *Journal and Proceedings of the Royal Society of New South Wales*. Vol. 23, pp. 476–503.

Stephenson, R.A., Breinl, J.D. & Wissemann, A.F. 1983. *Farm characteristics and management practices in the Australian macadamia industry*. Queensland Department of Primary Industries, Brisbane.

Stern, G. 1984. The native medicine chest. *Nature and Health*. Summer issue. Vol. 5, no. 5, pp. 87–92.

Stewart, K. & Percival, B. 1997. *Bush foods of New South Wales: A botanical record and an Aboriginal oral history*. Royal Botanic Gardens, Sydney.

Stirling, E.C. 1896. Anthropology. Pp. 1–157 in W.B. Spencer (ed) *Report on the work of the Horn Scientific Expedition to Central Australia. Part IV — anthropology*. Melville, Mullen & Slade, Melbourne.

Stocker, G.C. 1966. Effects of fires on vegetation in the Northern Territory. *Australian Forestry*. Vol. 30, no. 3, pp. 223–30.

Stocker, G.C. 1971. The age of charcoal from old jungle fowl nests and vegetation change on Melville Island. *Search*. Vol. 2, pp. 28–30.

Stocker, G.C. & Mott, J.J. 1981. Fire in the tropical forests and woodlands of northern Australia. Pp. 425–39 in A.M. Gill, R.H. Groves & I.R. Noble (eds) *Fire and the Australian biota*. Australian Academy of Science, Canberra.

Stone, A.C. 1911. Aborigines of Lake Boga. *Proceedings of the Royal Society of Victoria*. Vol. 23, pp. 433–68.

Strehlow, T.G.H. 1965. Culture, social structure, and environment in Aboriginal Central Australia. Pp. 121–45 in R.M. Berndt & C.H. Berndt (eds) *Aboriginal man in Australia: Essays in honour of Emeritus Professor A.P. Elkin*. Angus & Robertson, Sydney.

Strehlow, T.G.H. 1968. *Aranda traditions*. Melbourne University Press, Melbourne.

Strehlow, T.G.H. 1970. Geography and the totemic landscape in Central Australia: A functional study. Pp. 92–140 in R.M. Berndt (ed) *Australian Aboriginal anthropology*. Australian Institute of Aboriginal Studies and University of Western Australia, Perth.

Sturt, C. 1849. *An account of the sea coast and interior of South Australia, with observations on various subjects connected with its interests*. Republished as a facsimile in *Journal of the Central Australian Expedition*, 1984, pp. 115–264. Edited and introduced by J. Waterhouse. Caliban Books, London.

Sutton, P. (ed) 1988a. *Dreamings: The art of Aboriginal Australia*. Penguin Books, Melbourne.

Sutton, P. 1988b. Dreamings. Pp. 13–32 in P. Sutton (ed) 1988. *Dreamings: The art of Aboriginal Australia*. Penguin Books, Melbourne.

Sutton, P. 1988c. Responding to Aboriginal art. Pp. 33–58 in P. Sutton (ed) 1988. *Dreamings: The art of Aboriginal Australia*. Penguin Books, Melbourne.

Sutton, P. 1994. Material culture traditions of the Wik people, Cape York Peninsula. *Records of the South Australian Museum*. Vol. 27, pt 1, pp. 31–52.

Sutton, P. 1995. *Wik-Ngathan dictionary*. Caitlin Press, Adelaide.

Sutton, P. 2003. *Native title in Australia: An ethnographic perspective*. Cambridge University Press, Cambridge.

Sutton, P. & Rigsby, B. 1986. People with 'politicks': Management of land and personnel on Australia's Cape York Peninsula. Pp. 155–71 in N.M. Williams & E.S. Hunn (eds) *Resource managers: North American and Australian hunter-gatherers*. Australian Institute of Aboriginal Studies, Canberra.

Sutton, T.M. 1889. The Adjahdurah tribe of Aborigines on Yorke's Peninsula: Some of their early customs and traditions. *Proceedings of the Royal Geographical Society of Australasia. South Australian Branch*. Vol. 2, pp. 17–9.

Sveiby, K. & Skuthorpe, T. 2006. *Treading lightly: The hidden wisdom of the world's oldest people*. Allen & Unwin, Sydney.

Swadling, P. & Hope, G. 1992. Environmental change in New Guinea since human settlement. Pp. 13–42 in J. Dodson (ed) *The naive lands: Prehistory and environmental change in Australia and the south-west Pacific*. Longman Cheshire, Melbourne.

Sweeney, G. 1947. Food supplies of a desert tribe. *Oceania*. Vol. 7, no. 4, pp. 289–99.

Sykes, B. 2001. *The seven daughters of Eve*. Corgi Books, London.

Symon, D.E. 1979. Fruit diversity and dispersal in *Solanum* in Australia. *Journal of the Adelaide Botanic Gardens*. Vol. 1, no. 6, pp. 321–31.

Symon, D.E. 2005. Native tobaccos (Solanaceae: *Nicotiana* spp.) in Australia and their use by Aboriginal peoples. *The Beagle: Records of the Museums and Art Galleries of the Northern Territory*. Vol. 21, pp. 1–10.

Symons, P. & Symons, S. 1994. *Bush heritage: An introduction to the history of plant and animal use by Aboriginal people and colonists in the Brisbane and Sunshine Coast areas*. The authors, Nambour, Queensland.

Taplin, G. 1859–79. Journals. Typescript. Mortlock Library, Adelaide.

Taplin, G. 1874. *The Narrinyeri*. Reprinted as pp. 1–156 in J.D. Woods (ed) 1879. *The native tribes of South Australia*. E.S. Wiggs, Adelaide.

Taplin, G. (ed) 1879. *Folklore, manners, customs and languages of the South Australian Aborigines*. South Australian Government Printer, Adelaide.

Tasman, A. 1898. *Abel Janszoon Tasman's journal of his discovery of Van Diemen's Land and New Zealand*. Edited by J.E. Heeres. Amsterdam. Republished pp. 23–6 in T. Flannery (ed) 1998. *The Explorers*. Text Publishing, Melbourne.

Tate, R. (ed) 1882. Miscellaneous contributions to the natural history of South Australia. *Transactions and Proceedings and Report of the Royal Society of South Australia*. Vol. 4, pp. 135–8.

Tattersall, I. & Schwartz, J.H. 2000. *Extinct humans*. Westview Press, Boulder, Colorado.

Taylor, L. 1996. *Seeing the inside: Bark painting in western Arnhem Land*. Oxford University Press, Oxford.

Teichelmann, C.G. 1841. *Aborigines of South Australia*. Committee of the South Australian Wesleyan Methodist Auxiliary Society, Adelaide.

Teichelmann, C.G. & Schürmann, C.W. 1840. *Outlines of a grammar ... of the Aboriginal language of South Australia*. 2 parts. Thomas & Co., Adelaide.

Telban, B. 1988. The role of medical ethnobotany in ethnomedicine: A New Guinea example. *Journal of Ethnobiology*. Vol. 8, pt 2, pp. 149–69.

Tench, W. 1788–92. *A narrative of the expedition to Botany Bay & a complete account of the settlement at Port Jackson*. Edited by T. Flannery. 1996. Text Publishing, Melbourne.

Testart, A. 1982. The significance of food storage among hunter-gatherers: Residence patterns, population densities, and social inequalities. *Current Anthropology*. Vol. 23, pt 5, pp. 523–37.

Therik, T. 2004. *Wehali: The female land: Traditions of a Timorese ritual centre*. Pandanus Books and Australian National University, Canberra.

Thieberger, N. & McGregor, W. (eds) 1994. *Macquarie Aboriginal words*. Macquarie Library, Macquarie University, New South Wales.

Thieret, J.W. 1958. Economic botany of the cycads. *Economic Botany*. Vol. 12, pp. 3–41.

Thomas, G. 1997. Wattle we eat. *The Australian Gardener*. April issue, pp. 92–3.

Thomas, K. 1983. *Man and the natural world: Changing attitudes in England, 1500–1800*. Allen Lane, London.

Thomas, N.W. 1906. *The natives of Australia*. Archibald Constable & Co., London.

Thomas, W.J. 1943. *Some myths and legends of the Australian Aborigines*. Whitcombe & Tombs, Melbourne.

Thomson, D.F. 1932. Ceremonial presentation of fire in North Queensland: A preliminary note on the place of fire in primitive ritual. *Man*. Vol. 32, no. 198, pp. 162–6.

Thomson, D.F. 1939a. The seasonal factor in human culture: Illustrated from the life of a contemporary nomadic group. *Prehistorical Society Proceedings*. Vol. 5, No. 2, pp. 209–21.

Thomson, D.F. 1939b. Notes on the smoking-pipes of North Queensland and the Northern Territory of Australia. *Man*. Vol. 39, pp. 81–91.

Thomson, D.F. 1949. *Economic structure and the ceremonial exchange cycle in Arnhem Land*. Macmillan, Melbourne.

Thomson, D.F. 1950. The Australian Aboriginal as hunter and food gatherer. *Walkabout*. Vol. 16, pp. 29–31.

Thomson, D.F. 1955. The Australian Aborigine as hunter and food gatherer. *The Melbourne Age Literacy Supplement*, 23 July 1955.

Thomson, D.F. 1961. A narcotic from *Nicotiana ingulba*, used by the desert Bindibu: Chewing a true tobacco in Central Australia. *Man*. Vol. 61, pp. 5–8.

Thomson, D.F. 1962. The Bindibu expedition: Exploration among the desert Aborigines of Western Australia. *The Geographical Journal*. Vol. 78, pt 1, pp. 1–14; pt 2, pp. 143–57; pt 3, pp. 262–78.

Thomson, D.F. 1964. Some wood and stone implements of the Bindibu tribe of central Western Australia. *Prehistorical Society Proceedings*. Vol. 30, no. 17, pp. 400–22.

Thomson, D.F. 1975. *Bindibu country*. Nelson, Melbourne.

Thomson, D.F. 1983. *Children of the wilderness*. Currey O'Neil Ross, Melbourne.

Thomson, D.F. 1985. *Donald Thomson's mammals and fishes of northern Australia*. Edited and annotated by J.M. Dixon & L. Huxley. Thomas Nelson Australia, Melbourne.

Thomson, D.F. 1987. *Aboriginal artefacts in the Donald Thomson Collection: A microfiche catalogue*. Compiled by E.G. Ramsay. University of Melbourne and Museum of Victoria, Melbourne.

Thomson, N. & Merrifield, P. 1988. *Aboriginal health: An annotated bibliography*. Australian Institute of Aboriginal Studies, Canberra.

Thorne, A. & Raymond, R. 1989. *Man on the rim: The peopling of the Pacific*. Angus & Robertson, Sydney.

Thozet, A. 1866. *Notes on some of the roots, tubers, bulbs, and fruits used as vegetable food by the Aboriginals of Northern Queensland*. W.H. Buzacott, Bulletin, Rockhampton.

Tietkens, W.H. 1880. Letter to the president of the Linnean Society. *Proceedings of the Linnean Society of New South Wales*. Vol. 5, pp. 280–2.

Tietkens, W.H. 1891. *Journal of Mr. W.H. Tietkens' Central Australian exploring expedition*. South Australian Government Printer, Adelaide.

Tilbrook, L. 1983. *Nyungar tradition: Glimpses of Aborigines of south-western Australia 1829–1914*. University of Western Australia Press, Perth.

Tindale, N.B. 1925. Natives of Groote Eylandt and of the west coast of the Gulf of Carpentaria. Part 2. *Records of the South Australian Museum*. Vol. 3, no. 1, pp. 103–34.

Tindale, N.B. 1926–27. *Journal of a museum trip to Cape York Peninsula, North Queensland*. Unpublished manuscript. South Australian Museum Archives, Adelaide.

Tindale, N.B. 1933. *Journal of an anthropological expedition to the Mann and Musgrave Ranges, north west of South Australia, May–July 1933, and a personal record of the anthropological expedition to Ernabella, Aug. 1933*. Unpublished manuscript. South Australian Museum Archives, Adelaide.

Tindale, N.B. 1936. Notes on the natives of the southern portion of Yorke Peninsula, South Australia. *Transactions of the Royal Society of South Australia*. Vol. 60, pp. 55–70.

Tindale, N.B. 1938. Prupe and Koromarange: A legend of the Tanganekald, Coorong, South Australia. *Transactions of the Royal Society of South Australia*. Vol. 62, pp. 18–23.

Tindale, N.B. 1938–39. *Harvard and Adelaide Universities Anthropological Expedition, Australia, 1938–1939, journal and notes*. 2 volumes. Unpublished manuscript. South Australian Museum Archives, Adelaide.

Tindale, N.B. 1939. Notes on the Ngaiawung tribe, Murray River, South Australia. *South Australian Naturalist*. Vol. 20, pt 1, pp. 10–2.

Tindale, N.B. 1941. A list of plants collected in the Musgrave Range and Mann Ranges, South Australia, 1933. *The South Australian Naturalist*. Vol. 21, no. 1, pp. 8–12.

Tindale, N.B. 1952. Some Australian Cossidae including witjiti (witchetty) grub. *Transactions of the Royal Society of South Australia*. Vol. 76, pp. 56–65.

Tindale, N.B. 1957. Journal of visit to the north west of South Australia and adjacent parts of Western Australia by Norman B. Tindale. April–May 1957. Unpublished manuscript. South Australian Museum Archives, Adelaide.

Tindale, N.B. 1959. Totemic beliefs in the Western Desert of Australia — part 1: Women who became the Pleiades. *Records of the South Australia Museum*. Vol. 13, pt 3, pp. 305–32.

Tindale, N.B. 1966. Insects as food for the Australian Aborigines. *Australian Natural History*. Vol. 15, pp. 179–83.

Tindale, N.B. 1972. The Pitjandjara. Pp. 217–68 in M.G. Bicchieri (ed) *Hunters and gatherers today: A socioeconomic study of eleven such cultures in the twentieth century*. Holt, Rinehart & Winston, New York.

Tindale, N.B. 1974. *Aboriginal tribes of Australia: Their terrain, environmental controls, distribution, limits, and proper names*. 4 maps enclosed. Australian National University Press, Canberra.

Tindale, N.B. 1976. Some ecological bases for Australian tribal boundaries. Pp. 12–29 in N. Peterson (ed) *Tribes and boundaries in Australia*. Australian Institute of Aboriginal Studies, Canberra.

Tindale, N.B. 1977. Adaptive significance of the Panara or grass seed culture of

Australia. Pp. 345–9 in R.V.S. Wright (ed) *Stone tools as cultural markers*. Australian Institute of Aboriginal Studies, Canberra.

Tindale, N.B. 1978. Notes on a few Australian Aboriginal concepts. Pp. 156–63 in L.R. Hiatt (ed) *Australian Aboriginal concepts*. Australian Institute of Aboriginal Studies, Canberra.

Tindale, N.B. 1981. Desert Aborigines and the southern coastal peoples: Some comparisons. Pp. 1855–84 in A. Keast (ed) *Ecological biogeography of Australia*. Junk, The Hague.

Tolcher, H.M. 2003. *Seed of the coolibah: A history of the Yandruwandha and Yawarrawarrka people*. The author, Adelaide.

Tonkinson, M. 1994. Healers. Pp. 454–6 in D. Horton (ed) *The encyclopaedia of Aboriginal Australia*. 2 volumes. Aboriginal Studies Press for the Australian Institute of Aboriginal and Torres Strait Islander Studies, Canberra.

Tonkinson, R. 1978. *The Mardudjara Aborigines: Living the dream in Australia's desert*. Holt, Rinehart & Winston, New York.

Tonkinson, R. 1982. The *Mabarn* and the hospital: The selection of treatment in a remote Aboriginal community. Pp. 225–41 in J. Reid (ed) *Body, land and spirit: Health and healing in Aboriginal society*. University of Queensland Press, St Lucia, Queensland.

Trigger, D. 2003. Introduction. Pp. 1–27 in D. Trigger & G. Griffiths (eds) *Disputed territories: Land, culture and identity in settler societies*. Hong Kong University Press, Hong Kong.

Troy, J. 1994. The Sydney language. Pp. 61–78 in N. Thieberger & W. McGregor (eds) *Macquarie Aboriginal words*. Macquarie Library, Macquarie University, New South Wales.

Tunbridge, D. 1985a. Language as heritage: Vityurna (dried meat) and other stored food among the Adnyamathanha. *Journal of the Anthropological Society of South Australia*. Vol. 23, pt 7, pp. 10–5.

Tunbridge, D. 1985b. Language as heritage: Flora in place names: A record of survival in the Gammon Ranges. *Journal of the Anthropological Society of South Australia*. Vol. 23, pt 8, pp. 3–15.

Tunbridge, D. 1987. Aboriginal place names. *Australian Aboriginal Studies*. No. 2, pp. 2–13.

Tunbridge, D. 1988. *Flinders Ranges Dreaming*. Aboriginal Studies Press, Canberra.

Tunbridge, D. 1991. *The story of the Flinders Ranges mammals*. Kangaroo Press, Sydney.

Turner, G.W. 1972. *The English language in Australia and New Zealand*. Second edition. Longmans, London.

Turner, M. 1994. *Arrernte foods: Food from Central Australia*. Institute for Aboriginal Development Press, Alice Springs.

Tynan, B.J. 1979. *Medical systems in conflict: A study of power*. Northern Territory Government Printer, Darwin.

Urban, A. 1993. *Wildflowers and plants of inland Australia*. Portside Editions, Fishermen Bend, Victoria.

Urry, J. 1985. 'Savage sportsmen'. Pp. 51–67 in I. Donaldson & T. Donaldson (eds) *Seeing the First Australians*. Allen & Unwin, Sydney.

Urry, J. & Walsh, M. 1981. The lost 'Macassar language' of northern Australia. *Aboriginal History*. Vol. 5, pt 2, pp. 90–108.

Van Oosterzee, P. 1995. *A field guide to Central Australia: A natural history companion for the traveller*. Reed Books, Sydney.

Veitch, A.S. 1981. *Roses and boronia: A mid-Victorian romance*. Australian Broadcasting Commission, Sydney.

Veth, P.M. & Walsh, F.J. 1988. The concept of 'staple' plant foods in the Western Desert region of Western Australia. *Australian Aboriginal Studies*. No. 2, pp. 19–25.

Vickers-Rich, P., Rich, T., Rich, S.L. & Rich, T. 1997. *Diprotodon and its relatives*. Kangaroo Press, Roseville.

Von Brandenstein, C.G. 1988. *Nyungar anew: Phonology, text samples and etymological and historical 1500-word vocabulary of an artificially re-created Aboriginal language in the south-west of Australia*. Pacific Linguistics Series C — No. 99. Department of Linguistics, Research School of Pacific Studies, Australian National University, Canberra.

Von Mueller, F. 1881. *Select extra-tropical plants, readily eligible for industrial culture or naturalisation, with indications of their native countries and some of their uses*. T. Richards, Government Printer, Sydney.

Waddy, J.A. 1979. Ethnobiology of Groote Eylandt: A progress report. *Australian Institute of Aboriginal Studies Newsletter*. Vol. 11, pp. 46–50.

Waddy, J.A. 1982. Biological classification from a Groote Eylandt Aborigine's point of view. *Journal of Ethnobiology*. Vol. 2, pt 1, pp. 63–77.

Waddy, J.A. 1988. *Classification of plants and animals from a Groote Eylandt Aboriginal point of view*. 2 volumes. Australian National University, North Australia Research Unit, Darwin.

Walker, A. & Zorc, R.D. 1981. Austronesian loanwords in Yolngu-matha of northeast Arnhem Land. *Aboriginal History*. Vol. 5, pt 2, pp. 109–34.

Walker, J.B. 1888–99. Notes on the Aborigines of Tasmania, extracted from the manuscript journals of George Washington Walker, with an introduction by James B. Walker, F.R.G.S. Pp. 238–87 in *Early Tasmania: Papers read before the Royal Society of Tasmania during the years 1888 to 1899 by James*

Backhouse Walker. M.C. Reed, Government Printer, Tasmania.

Wallace, A.R. 1890. *The Malay Archipelago, the land of the orang-utan and the bird of paradise: A narrative of travel with studies of man and nature*. Tenth edition. Macmillan, London.

Wallace, P. 1983. Black civilisation: Women of the Western Desert. *This Australia*. Vol. 2, no. 2, pp. 60–63.

Wallace, P. & Wallace, N. 1968. *Children of the desert*. Thomas Nelson, Melbourne.

Walsh, F. 1990. An ecological study of traditional Aboriginal use of 'country': Martu in the Great and Little Sandy Deserts. Pp. 23–37 in D.A. Saunders, A.J. Hopkins & R.A. How (eds) *Australian ecosystems: 200 years of utilization, degradation and reconstruction*. Surrey Beatty & Sons, Sydney.

Walsh, F. 1995. Interactions between land management agencies and Australian Aboriginal people: Rationale, problems and some lessons. Pp. 88–106 in J.L. Craig & E.M. Mattiske (eds) *Nature conservation 4: The role of networks*. Surrey Beatty & Sons, Sydney.

Walsh, M. 1993. Classifying the world in an Aboriginal language. Pp. 107–22 in M. Walsh & C. Yallop (eds) *Language and culture in Aboriginal Australia*. Aboriginal Studies Press, Canberra.

Warlukurlangu Artists 1992. *Kuruwarri: Yuendumu doors*. Aboriginal Studies Press, Canberra.

Warner, W.L. 1958. *A black civilization: A study of an Australian tribe*. Revised edition. Harper & Row, New York.

Watson, P. 1983. *This precious foliage: A study of the Aboriginal psycho-active drug pituri*. Oceania Monograph no. 26. University of Sydney, Sydney.

Watson, P. 1994. Bush medicine. Pp. 170–1 in D. Horton (ed) *The encyclopaedia of Aboriginal Australia*. 2 volumes. Aboriginal Studies Press for the Australian Institute of Aboriginal and Torres Strait Islander Studies, Canberra.

Webb, L.J. 1948. *Guide to the medicinal and poisonous plants of Queensland*. Council for Scientific and Industrial Research, Melbourne. Bulletin No. 232.

Webb, L.J. 1960. Some new records of medicinal plants used by the Aborigines of tropical Queensland and New Guinea. *Proceedings of the Royal Society of Queensland*. Vol. 71, pt 6, pp. 103–10.

Webb, L.J. 1969a. Australian plants and chemical research. Pp. 82–90 in L.J. Webb, D. Whitelock & J. Le Gay Brereton (eds) *The last of lands*. Jacaranda Press, Milton, Queensland.

Webb, L.J. 1969b. The use of plant medicines and poisons by Australian Aborigines. *Mankind*. Vol. 7, no. 2, pp. 137–46.

Webb, L.J. 1973. 'Eat, die, and learn' — the botany of the Australian Aborigines. *Australian Natural History*. March 17, Vol. 9, pp. 290–5.

Wearne, G. & White, N. 1998. *Supporting natural and cultural resource management in the Arafura wetlands and catchment: A community based approach*. Centre for Indigenous Natural and Cultural Resource Management, Northern Territory University, Darwin.

Wesson, S. 2001. *Aboriginal flora and fauna names of Victoria: As extracted from early surveyors' reports*. Victorian Aboriginal Corporation fro Languages, Melbourne.

West, A.L. 1999. *Aboriginal string bags, nets and cordage*. Occasional Papers, Anthropology and History No. 2. Museum Victoria, Melbourne.

Wharton, G. 2005. *Northern sandalwood (*Santalum lanceolatum*) on Cape York Peninsula: A report on historical sources for the Indigenous Economic Support Unit, Queensland Department of State Development and Innovation*. Infotracker Historical and Information Research Services, Holland Park, Queensland.

Wheeler, J.R. (ed) 1992. *Flora of the Kimberley region*. Western Australian Herbarium, Department of Conservation and Land Management, Como, Western Australia.

Whelan, R. 2003. Indigenous knowledge: Can it improve fire management in the Sydney region? Pp. 211–8 in G. Cary, D. Lindenmayer & S. Dovers (eds) *Australia burning: Fire ecology, policy and management issues*. CSIRO Publishing, Collingwood, Victoria.

White, H.F. & Hicks, C. Stanton 1953. *Life from the soil*. Longmans Green, London.

White, I. 1983. Children of the wilderness. Pp. 1–5 in D.F. Thomson *Children of the wilderness*. Currey O'Neil Ross, Melbourne.

White, M.E. 1994. *After the greening: The browning of Australia*. Kangaroo Press, Sydney.

White, N.G. 2003. Meaning and metaphor in Yolngu landscapes, Arnhem Land, northern Australia. Pp. 187–205 in D. Trigger & G. Griffiths (eds) *Disputed territories: Land, culture and identity in settler societies*. Hong Kong University Press, Hong Kong.

White, N.G. & Meehan, B. 1993. Traditional ecological knowledge: A lens on time. Pp. 51–65 in N.M. Williams & G. Baines (eds) *Traditional ecological knowledge: Wisdom for sustainable development*. Centre for Resource and Environmental Studies, Australian National University, Canberra.

White, P. & Flannery, T.F. 1992. The impact of people on the Pacific world. Pp. 1–8 in J. Dodson (ed) *The naive lands: Prehistory and environmental change in Australia and the south-west Pacific*. Longman Cheshire, Melbourne.

Whiting, M.G. 1963. Toxicity of cycads. *Economic Botany*. Vol. 17, pp. 271–301.

Whittle, T. 1970. *The plant hunters*. Heinemann, London.

Wightman, G.M. & Andrews, M. 1991. *Bush tucker identikit: Common native food plants of Australia's Top End*. Conservation Commission of the Northern Territory, Darwin.

Wightman, G.M., Astuti, I.P. & Munawaroh, E. (eds) 1994. *Sundanese ethnobotany: Traditional plant knowledge from Ciamis and Tasikmalaya, West Java, Indonesia*. Northern Territory Botanical Bulletin No. 19. Conservation Commission of the Northern Territory, Darwin.

Wightman, G.M., Dixon, D., Williams, L.L.V & Injimadi Dalywaters. 1992. *Mudburra ethnobotany: Aboriginal plant use from Kulumindini (Elliot), northern Australia*. Northern Territory Botanical Bulletin No. 14. Conservation Commission of the Northern Territory, Darwin.

Wightman, G.M., Gurindji elders, Frith, R.N.D. & Holt, S. 1994. *Gurindji ethnobotany: Aboriginal plant use from Daguragu, northern Australia*. Northern Territory Botanical Bulletin No. 18. Conservation Commission of the Northern Territory, Darwin.

Wightman, G.M., Jackson, D.M. & Williams, L.L.V. 1991. *Alawa ethnobotany: Aboriginal plant use from Minyerri, northern Australia*. Northern Territory Botanical Bulletin No. 11. Conservation Commission of the Northern Territory, Darwin.

Wightman, G.M. & Mills, L. 1991. *Bush medicine identikit: Common medicinal plants of Australia's Top End*. Conservation Commission of the Northern Territory, Darwin.

Wightman, G.M., Roberts, J.G. & Williams, L.L.V. 1992. *Mangarrayi ethnobotany: Aboriginal plant use from the Elsey area, northern Australia*. Northern Territory Botanical Bulletin No. 15. Conservation Commission of the Northern Territory, Darwin.

Wightman, G.M. & Smith, N.M. 1989. *Ethnobotany, vegetation and floristics of Milingimbi, northern Australia*. Northern Territory Botanical Bulletin No. 6. Conservation Commission of the Northern Territory, Darwin.

Wilhelmi, J.F.C. 1861. Manners and customs of the Australian natives in particular of the Port Lincoln district. *Transactions of the Royal Society of Victoria*. Vol. 5, pp. 164–203.

Wilkinson, G.B. 1848. *South Australia — its advantages and resources — being a description of that colony and a manual of information for emigrants*. John Murray, London.

Williams, N.M. 1986. A boundary is to cross: Observations on Yolngu boundaries and permissions. Pp. 131–53 in N.M. Williams & E.S. Hunn (eds) *Resource managers: North American and Australian hunter-gatherers*. Australian Institute of Aboriginal Studies, Canberra.

Williams, N.M. 1998. *Intellectual property and Aboriginal environmental knowledge*. CINCRM Discussion Paper No. 1. Centre for Indigenous Natural and Cultural Resource Management (CINCRM), Northern Territory University, Darwin.

Williams, N.M. & Baines, G. (eds) 1993. *Traditional ecological knowledge: Wisdom for sustainable development*. Centre for Resource and Environmental Studies, Australian National University, Canberra.

Williams, N.M. & Hunn, E.S. (eds) 1986. *Resource managers: North American and Australian hunter-gatherers*. Australian Institute of Aboriginal Studies, Canberra.

Williams, W. 1839. *A vocabulary of the language of the Aborigines of the Adelaide district...* MacDougall, Adelaide. Reprinted in T.A. Parkhouse (ed) 1926. *Reprints and papers relating to the autochthones of Australia*. The author, Woodville.

Willsteed, T., Smith, K. & Bourke, A. 2006. *Eora: Mapping Aboriginal Sydney, 1770–1850*. State Library of New South Wales, Sydney.

Wilson, G., McNee, A. & Platts, P. 1992. *Wild animal resources: Their use by Aboriginal communities*. AGPS, Canberra.

Wiminydji & Peile, A.R. 1978. A desert Aborigine's view of health and nutrition. *Journal of Anthropological Research*. Vol. 34, pt 4, pp. 497–523.

Woods, J.D. (ed) 1879. Introduction. Pp. vii–xxxviii in J.D. Woods (ed) *The native tribes of South Australia*. E.S. Wigg & Son, Adelaide.

Worsnop, T. 1897. *The prehistoric arts, manufactures, works, weapons, etc., of the Aborigines of Australia*. C.E. Bastow, Government Printer, Adelaide.

Wreck Bay Community & Renwick, C. 2000. *Geebungs and snake whistles: Koori people and plants of Wreck Bay*. Aboriginal Studies Press, Canberra.

Wright, R.V.S. (ed) 1977. *Stone tools as cultural markers: Change, evolution and complexity*. Australian Institute of Aboriginal Studies, Canberra and Humanities Press, Atlantic Highlands, New Jersey.

Wyatt, W. 1879. Some account of the manners and customs of the Adelaide and Encounter Bay tribes ... Pp. 157–68 in J.D. Woods (ed) *The native tribes of South Australia*. E.S. Wigg & son, Adelaide.

Yallop, C. 1982. *Australian Aboriginal languages*. Andre Deutsch, London.

Yen, D.E. 1977. Hoabinhion horticulture? The evidence and the questions from northwest Thailand. Pp. 567–99 in J. Allen, J. Golson & R. Jones (eds) *Sunda and Sahul*. Academic Press, London.

Yen, D.E. 1995. The development of Sahul agriculture with Australia as bystander. *Antiquity*. Vol. 69 (Special no. 265), pp. 831–47.

Young, E. 1981. *The Aboriginal component in the Australian economy: Tribal communities in rural areas*. Development Studies Centre, The Australian National University, Canberra.

Young, E. 1992. Hunter-gatherer concepts of land and its ownership in remote Australia and North America. Pp. 255–72 in K.J. Anderson & F. Gale (eds) *Inventing places: Studies in cultural geography*. Longman Cheshire, Melbourne.

Young, E., Ross, H., Johnson, J. & Kesteven, J. (eds) 1991. *Caring for country: Aborigines and land management*. Australian National Parks and Wildlife Service, Canberra.

Youngs, M.J. 1985. The English television landscape documentary: A look at Granada. Pp. 144–64 in J. Burgess & J.R. Gold (eds) *Geography, the media and popular culture*. Croom Helm, London.

Yunupingu, B. 1995. *Rirratjinu ethnobotany: Aboriginal plant use from Yirrkala, Arnhem Land, Australia*. Conservation Commission of the Northern Territory, Darwin.

Yunupingu, M. & Williams, N. 1995. Introduction. Pp. v–vii in B. Yunupingu *Rirratjinu ethnobotany: Aboriginal plant use from Yirrkala, Arnhem Land, Australia*. Conservation Commission of the Northern Territory, Darwin.

Zeppel, H. 1999. *Aboriginal tourism in Australia: A research bibliography*. Wildlife Tourism Research Report Series No. 2. Cooperative Research Centre for Sustainable Tourism, Gold Coast, Queensland.

Zohary, M. 1982. *Plants of the Bible*. Cambridge University Press, Cambridge.

Zola, N. & Gott, B. 1992. *Koorie plants, Koorie people: Traditional Aboriginal food, fibre and healing plants of Victoria*. Koorie Heritage Trust, Melbourne.

Common Plant Names Index

178

Scientific Plant Names Index

General Index

and claypans) 38, 42, 45, 49, 55, 57, 62, *78*, 80–1, *82*, 92, 100, 124–6, 133
 filter 80
 plants *79*, 80–4, *82*, *84*
 sponge 82–3
 straw *50*, 81
 thirst quenchers 81, *83*
watercraft (canoes and rafts) 19, *47*, 52, *59*, 112, *113–5*, 114, 116–7, 128–9, 132
weather, *see* seasons
weeds, *see also* rubbish species 133–6
Weipa 134
Western Australia
 central 24, 62, 80–1, 88, 108, 126, 135
 northern 55, 90, 103, 108–9, 114, 120, 124–6
 southwest 18–9, 25, 27, 39, 48, 55, 57, 65, 67, 73, 78, 80–1, *82*, 87, 89, 105, 124, 133
Western Desert 12, 15, 28, 38, 49–50, 54, 97, 99, 108, 114, 120, 135, 138, 142
whistling tree, *see also* spirits 26–7
White, C. *29*
White, H.F. 6
White, I. 19
White, N. 129

Wild Dog Hill *94*
wilderness, *see also* European views 11, *25*
Wilhelmi, J.F.C. 40, 77
Wills, W. 76, 87, 107
wombats 92
Woods, J.D. 6
Woolls, W. 105
worldview 11–6
Worsnop, T. 123
Wreck Bay 146

Yalata 58
Yirrkala 132
Yodko 18
Yorke Peninsula 17, 24, 55
Young, E. 23
Yucatan 135
Yuendumu *26*

Zygomaturus, *see also* animal extinction; megafauna 63